What is a Sacred Center?

Sometimes known as "vortexes," sacred centers are concentrated points of psychic or soul energy—put there by cosmic and natural forces of earth and sky, or through states of altered human awareness still resonating at the site. Some places belong to ancient civilizations, while others echo the spiritual vibrations of more historical, even contemporary human actions. Still others are pure manifestations of the soul of nature, the immortal gods, the Great Spirit.

We feel drawn to venture into this sometimes dimly familiar Otherworld to partake of its variety of magic. . . to recharge our spiritual batteries. . . to heal Mother Earth and allow Her to heal us. . . to find truths from a higher or deeper reality. . . to affirm our own significance in the grand scheme of eternity. . . to plug into and feel our roots in Nature and the past. . . to trace the fabric of Destiny. As such, visitors to sacred centers are not mere tourists, but pilgrims on a very personal quest for enlightenment and empowerment.

Millions of Americans, jaded by the hollow goals of materialism, feel a growing uncertainty, restlessness and inner yearning for higher meaning and greater significance in their lives. They need to retreat to some special place, some genuine source of spiritual replenishment to revive their thirsty souls. The sacred centers included in this book abundantly fill that need. Our country is uncommonly rich in their numbers and powers. And we shall all be richer for seeking them out in our own quest through life.

D1569203

To Write to the Authors

We cannot guarantee that every letter written to the authors can be answered, but all will be forwarded. Both the authors and the publisher appreciate hearing from readers, learning of your enjoyment and benefit from this book. Llewellyn also publishes a bi-monthly news magazine with news and reviews of practical esoteric studies and articles helpful to the student, and some readers' questions and comments to the authors may be answered through this magazine's columns if permission to do so is included in the original letter. The authors sometimes participate in seminars and workshops, and dates and places are announced in *The Llewellyn New Times*. To write to the authors, or to ask a question, write to:

c/o THE LLEWELLYN NEW TIMES
P.O. Box 64383-348, St. Paul, MN 55164-0383, U.S.A.
Please enclose a self-addressed, stamped envelope for reply, or $1.00 to cover costs.

SACRED SITES

A Guidebook to

SACRED CENTERS & MYSTERIOUS PLACES IN THE UNITED STATES

Edited by Frank Joseph

1992
Llewellyn Publications
St. Paul, Minnesota, U.S.A. 55164-0383

FIRST EDITION

Front cover photograph: "Sedona Speaks" © by L'aura Colan
Cover design: Christopher Wells and Terry Buske
Back cover photographs: Wizard Island by Richard Ely,
    The Great Serpent Mound courtesy of Ohio Historical Society

Library of Congress Cataloging-in-Publication Data

Sacred sites: a guidebook to sacred centers & mysterious places in the United States / Frank Joseph.
        p.   cm.

    Includes bibliographical references.
    ISBN 0-87542-348-5
    1. Sacred space—United States-Guidebooks.   2. United States—Guidebooks.   I. Title.
E158.J87   1992
917.304'928--dc20   92-13184
                                                                          CIP

Llewellyn Publications
A Division of Llewellyn Worldwide, Ltd.
P.O. Box 64383, St. Paul, MN 55164-0383

Dedication

To Shadow Cat, the inspiration for this Guidebook.

Table of Contents

Introduction: What is a Sacred Site?   *ix*

Alabama   1
   Mound State Monument   3
   Russell Cave   13

Alaska   21
   Mt. Denali   23

Arizona   33
   Montezuma's Castle   36
   Sedona and Oak Creek Canyon   38
   Tuzigoot National Monument   40
   Walnut Canyon   41
   Sunset Crater   41
   Wupatki National Monument   42
   Cochise Stronghold   48
   Cave Creek   50

California   55
   Tlamco's Sacred Center/Golden Gate Park   57
   Pinnacles National Monument, Bear Gulch Cave   69

Colorado   79
   Manitou Springs   81

Connecticut   87
   The Sleeping Giant Mountain   89

Florida   95
   Madira Bickel Mound   97
   Leverock's Altar Stone   103
   Crystal River   107

Hawaii   115
    Halema'Uma'U: Pele's Home at Kiluaea   117
    The Wizard Stones of Waikiki (O'ahu)   126
    Haleakala, Island of Maui   131

Illinois   139
    Gold Pyramid House   141
    Cahokia (Monk's Mound)   145
    Gorham Petroglyphs   151

Indiana   157
    Angel Mounds   159
    New Harmony Labyrinth   165
    Great Circle Mound   169

Kentucky   175
    Wickliffe Mounds   177

Louisiana   181
    Poverty Point   183

Missouri   191
    Towosaghy   193
    Fantastic Caverns   199

Montana   203
    Ancient Buffalo Site   205
    Missouri Headwaters   220
    Lewis and Clark Caverns State Park,   221
    The Continental Divide   221
    Butte   222

New Hampshire   219
    Mystery Hill: America's Stonehenge   221

New Jersey   229
    Tripod Rock   231

New Mexico   239
    Chaco Canyon National Monument   241
    Three Rivers Petroglyph   249
    Bandelier National Monument   253

New York   261
    Niagara Falls   263
    Thompson Park Lightlines   273

North Carolina 279
    St. Mary's and Holy Trinity 281
    The Devil's Tramping Ground 289

Ohio 293
    Octagon Earthworks 295
    Great Serpent Mound 301
    Fort Ancient 305

Oklahoma 311
    Spiro Mounds 313
    Heavener Runestone 305

Oregon 327
    Balancing Rocks 329
    Multnomah Falls 333
    Crater Lake 337

Pennsylvania 345
    Indian Echo Caverns 347

Tennessee 353
    The Parthenon 355
    Old Stone Fort 361
    Saul's Mound (Pinson Mounds) 367

Texas 373
    Enchanted Rock 375

Utah 381
    Zion National Park 383
    Hovenweep (Deserted Valley) 389
    Canyonlands, The Needles District 393

Washington 403
    Beacon Rock State Park 405
    Stonehenge 409

Washington D.C. 413
    The Lincoln Memorial 416
    Arlington National Cemetery 420

Wisconsin 425
    Aztalan 427
    Lizard Mounds 433

Symbol Key to Maps

 **Major City**

 SACRED SITE LOCATION

Town
WITH A SACRED SITE

What is a Sacred Site?

The Great Pyramid of Egypt. Britain's Stonehenge. The Acropolis at Athens. These are the places people generally think of when "sacred sites" are mentioned. But it is not necessary to travel overseas or to only the most famous sites for a personal mystical experience at a spiritually charged spot of deep antiquity. Unknown to most Americans, their country has its own prehistoric pyramids, one even larger at its base than its Egyptian counterpart. There are full-scale replicas of Stonehenge and the Parthenon, not in ruins, but as they appeared when new. Beyond these unsuspected parallels with the Old World, the United States abounds with natural and man-made locations of unique and profound spiritual powers. Largely unrecognized, sacred sites occur throughout North America, sometimes in our own backyards. The purpose of this guidebook is to acquaint readers with these domestic sites, to define their numinous qualities and suggest simple rituals for tapping into their special energies.

There are growing numbers of new books about sacred centers on the market. *Sacred Sites* stands out from all the rest in that it covers the spiritual as well as the physical aspects of many magical sites unknown even to adepts on the subject. Our authors tell prospective visitors how to open themselves up psychically and fine-tune their innate sensitivities to the ancient voices and lingering energies of each location. Many guides to mystical sites are written by persons who have never even seen the places they presume to know; their descriptions may be replete with misleading information. Contrary to the remote speculations of these armchair authors, all the contributors to this guide describe sacred centers which are intimately known to them, sites which are often near their homes and with which they have been personally acquainted for many years.

But what exactly is a "sacred site"? It is a place of singular numinous power generated by focused spiritual forces. Sometimes

known as "vortexes," they are concentrated points of psychic or
soul energy put there by cosmic and natural forces of earth and sky;
or caused by the interaction of human awareness and the eternal vi-
talities of nature which still resonate at the site, long after the person
has departed. Some places belong to ancient civilizations, while others echo with the spiritual vibrations of more historical, even contemporary human actions. Still other centers are pure manifestations of the Soul of Nature, the immortal gods, the Great Spirit. We
feel drawn to venture into this sometimes dimly familiar Otherworld to partake of its variety of magic, to re-charge our spiritual
batteries; or to heal the Earth and to allow Mother Earth to heal us; or
to find the answers to questions from an alternative, higher or
deeper reality; to reassure ourselves of our own significance in the
grand scheme of eternity; to feel our roots in Nature and the past; to
trace the fabric of Destiny. As such, visitors to sacred centers are not
mere tourists, but pilgrims on a very personal quest for enlightenment and empowerment.

Few persons who seek out the places described in *Sacred Sites*
will fail to be mightily impressed by their mystery and beauty. Indeed, a sense of wonder is essential to a full-bodied appreciation of
any sacred center. But our higher purpose should be to communicate with it, if not in words, then in emotion. To experience such
places with a detached and analytical attitude may have its rewards,
although a soul-to-soul contact with the resident genii can be more
personally significant. The rituals included in this book have been
designed to assist the visitor in making this sort of psychical connection with the specific site described; thus rites appropriate for a particular sacred center may not be effective for another. But it should
be kept in mind that a truly memorable experience depends not so
much on the accurate performance of any ritual, but on the open and
sympathetic attitude of each visitor. There is no revelation without
correct and willing openness.

The individual pilgrim should come to a sacred center with
humble reverence and a pure heart. Nothing specific should be expected or anticipated, thus leaving ourselves open to whatever the
site wishes to offer us. If we do not always receive what we desire,
we are almost invariably presented with something we need. We
must approach the *genius loci*, the spirit of the place, with veneration
and a sense of giving. Gladly we take whatever the site has to offer,
and are sincerely grateful for the opportunity to visit. Only in such a

respectful mind-set will sacred centers live for us. If we make ourselves worthy of their interest, they will reveal themselves to us miraculously.

It is important, too, to leave something of ourselves behind in holy places. A pinched offering of tobacco or sage, a few drops of blessed or pure water, a seed or flower from your garden, a crystal or attractive stone; gifts such as these are appropriate and powerful. They go on working long after the visit has ended, serving as a physiological link between the pilgrim and the sacred center.

Certainly, the ideal medium for accessing a spiritually charged site is meditation, either before or after, but especially during a visit. Readers unfamiliar with simple meditation techniques are urged to read *Meditation, the Inner Way* by Naomi Humphrey. Humphrey's straightforward explanations and effective methods may be mastered with little time and effort. Meditation clears the mind and opens our inner awareness to the voices, music and visions of a sacred center.

A common form of meditation useful at most sacred centers involves controlled breathing. Sit comfortably in a quiet place, eyes closed. Take a deep breath through the nostrils, hold it for seven counts, then exhale out the mouth as though blowing out a candle flame. Repeat twice more. Then breathe normally, counting each inhalation. At the 42nd breath, count back down to one. For the duration, concentrate only on breathing and counting. Mental disturbances, outside sounds and stray thoughts, are normal and do not invalidate the entire meditation. Ignore them, let them pass and complete the count. Finish by taking three deep breaths as at the beginning. The numbers involved in this method are very old and sacred. Seven is the number signifying the Completion of Cycles, while three is universally associated with Divinity. Forty-two represents six sets of seven, six being the number of Perfection. Over the Ancient Egyptian Otherworld presided the Forty-two Judges, symbolizing the attainment of heaven. The sacred numerals implicit in breath-meditation are part of the mental clarity achieved through a reoriented balance with the inner order of the cosmos.

Pure meditation, in which the conscious mind is focused on the breathing alone, is certainly appropriate for accessing the resident energies of any sacred center. An alternative, although not necessarily superior form is visualization. As one enters deepening levels of meditation, a conscious effort is made to picture in the imagination a

simple appropriate image or symbol. The advantage of visualization lies in the creation of a powerful, direct link with the "spirit of
place." While focusing on a particularly relevant image, the innermost feelings and receptivities of a visitor are often more readily
and strongly activated. During both visualization and breathing
meditation either the *genius loci*'s own symbolic manifestation or
the entity itself may appear in the mind. Such appearances can be
startling, to say the least. But the visitor is reminded that he/she is
in control at all times. The visitor must decide for him/herself
whether to dwell on the intrusive image or voice, or merely relegate
it to part of the meditation. Symbols for some sites are included
under "suggested ritual." But each pilgrim to a sacred center should
have no difficulty selecting the proper image on which to concentrate and hold in the mind while meditating. For example, the spiral,
signifying the soul's journey or evolution, appears on artifacts from
the vanished civilization at Wisconsin's Aztalan. If no such local
symbolism is readily apparent, the universal glyph for the sacred
center, ⊕, should be effective.

That the *genius loci* of sacred sites addresses itself to the receptive visitor, there is no doubt. Anecdotes of genuine mystical encounters at these hallowed places are many and convincing. After
visiting Illinois' Cahokia pyramid, across the Mississippi River
from St. Louis, an Australian tourist experienced the most vivid vision of his life when, in a waking dream, he saw the summit of the
gargantuan earthwork flashing great sheets of blue lightning. The
strong presence of Ohio's Serpent Mound experienced with remarkable similarity by many visitors and the officially documented
visions at Oklahoma's Spiro Mounds over the last one hundred
years are matters of public record. Events such as these comprise the
real magick of a sacred center and are available to everyone with the
proper receptivity.

A valuable aid to highlighting that receptivity and the opening
of our inner awareness is the portable tape player. Preselected music appropriate to the character of a particular site, when played
while visiting a sacred center, can make the location come alive. It
will be found that the music soon becomes something more significant than mere background accompaniment, as it begins to themati-
cally define subtle nuances in the special environment. If the experience has been particularly meaningful, the listener will find that the
music selected for his or her visit will thereafter always evoke that

place and its identifyable feelings. The great variety of atmospheric New Age tapes offers a wide selection from which to choose. Some classical pieces conjure the emotions no less effectively. Climbing Alaska's Mt. Denali to the evocative sound of Alan Hovannes's *Magic Mountain Symphony*, for example, can be a never-to-be-forgotten event. At other sacred centers, such as New Mexico's Chaco Canyon, Native American dances would seem particularly powerful in helping to visualize the inherent imagery of a site. Music, too, is a gift to the *genius loci*, creating an instant, vibrant bond between the visitor and the visited.

It should be remembered, however, that music is an audio aid, and not always necessary or even appropriate. The pilgrim will often do better by listening to the special sounds of a place, particularly its silences, with the unassisted ear. The visitor must decide what should best assist in the appreciation of each sacred center.

A more than useful item in the pilgrim's travel kit is a quartz crystal. The numinous qualities of this mineral are clearly introduced by Phyllis Galde in *Crystal Healing, the Next Step* (Llewellyn Publications, 1988). Readers unfamilar with the mystical properties of crystals are urged to acquaint themselves with her eminently informative investigation. Suffice it to mention here that crystals magnify and store certain forms of energy. They are included in some of *Sacred Sites'* suggested rituals because they simultaneously enhance the visitor's receptivity and his/her projected spiritual powers. When walking through a sacred center, carry a crystal in the left or receiving hand. For some rituals the crystal may be transferred to the right hand. In any case, they are user friendly and easily mastered.

Some of the contributors to *Sacred Sites* were initially reluctant to write publicly of these sacred, often vunerable places. Indeed, a great many spiritual centers in the U.S. are so fragile, that our first impulse was to protect them against disclosure. Moreover, until fairly recently many persons who venerated the places described in this book felt that they themselves had to remain concealed, or else risk persecution and invasion of privacy. But since then we have entered a New Age, whose chief purpose is to make spiritually valid phenomena and information available to the curious and the uninitiated. The sacred centers of the earth were not given exclusively to a secret elite—but rather they belong to everyone, even at the risk of desecretion. We are convinced, however, that this guidebook will do far more good than harm, for the awakening of mankind will not be possible without the personal mystical experiences provided by the hallowed corners of the planet. Moreover, by calling attention to so many hitherto neglected sacred centers, we are lending impetus to their protection under responsible local authorities.

The fundamental responsibility for anyone visiting a sacred center is to preserve it. Karmic justice awaits persons who willfully damage or desecrate consecreted ground, and simple recognition of this higher law should be sufficient to instill the properly awed respect due in the presence of a holy precinct. Our readers are advised to obey the public authorities entrusted with the maintainance of lands on which hallowed places are located for future generations. Most of the sites described here are already protected by official state agencies.

Whatever the means of evocation, the great benefit in visiting a sacred center is the deeply personal mystical experience such a place commands. The mystery religions of the Ancient World flourished for thousands of years because they similarly involved each individual initiate in an intimate communication with divinity. By meeting with such emotionally transfiguring spiritual forces, we are rendered capable of that which the Greeks called "katharsis," a "purging" of the human spirit when touched by the Divine and supercharged with profound emotion. Only at such moments are mortals convinced of the reality of their own souls, because they feel them. It is precisely this cathartic experience, our link with spiritual reality, that is missing from modern civilization.

Millions of Americans, dissatisfied by the ideals promulgated by our consumer society, are feeling a growing uncertainty, restlessness and inner yearning for higher meaning and greater significance in their lives. They need to go to some special place, some genuine source of spiritual replenishment, to revive their thirsty souls. The sacred centers included here abundantly fill that need. Our country is uncommonly rich in their numbers and powers. And we shall all be richer for seeking them out in our own quest through life.

OUR WRITERS

Oz Anderson—A Wiccan priestess, Oz is a frequent guest lecturer on the university circuit, and once performed (by request) a spell for the success of a NASA experiment in the Australian outback. In her own words, she "seeks to help spread the message of the return of the living Goddess to Her former places of power at the heart of the sacred circle."

Kathleen L. Boehme—After graduating from the Oblate School of Theology in San Antonio, she went on to become a certified lay minister in the Catholic Church and today serves as Co-Chairman of the Pastoral Council. Kathleen has taught courses in Raja Yoga for the past fifteen years and is presently an administrator at the University of Texas in San Antonio.

Alice Bryant—Co-author of *The Message of the Crystal Skull* (Llewellyn Publications, 1989), Alice is a Science of Mind practioner, whose research has taken her to the remote areas of Mexico and Yucatan. Her expertise on the Crystal Skull generates lecture engagements across America and she is regarded as the foremost authority on the unique artifact.

Lyn Chamberlain—Former editor of the agricultural magazine *Alabama Farmer*, Lyn designs and teaches classes for the Continuing Education Department at the University of Alabama (Huntsville). She was first place winner of 1984's Alabama Media Women's Communication Contest, and she recently completed her first novel, *Legend of Fire Eye*, a creation allegory.

Sandra Tabatha Cicero and **Chic Cicero**—Sandra is a graduate from the University of Wisconsin (Milwaukee) with a Bachelor's Degree in Fine Arts, a background which she has put to excellent use with her husband, Chic, in creating the *New Golden Dawn Ritual Tarot* (Llewellyn Publications). Chic is a former jazz musician and club owner, who has twenty five years experience as a practicing ceremonial magician.

D. J. Conway—Author of *Norse Magic* and *Celtic Magic* (Llewellyn, 1988), D. J. is presently working on a book detailing ancient magical practices around the world. She was born and reared in the Columbia Gorge area of Oregon, where her affinity for the state's sacred centers is rooted in her childhood origins.

Lynne Dusenberry Crow—She was trained as a child by Montana's Salish Indian elders, who had adopted her father. In 1974, Lynne won first place in Llewellyn Publications's Gnostica Challenge essay competition, and she has subsequently written for the company's *Gnostica News* and *Moon Sign Book*. After completing her master's degree in Linguistic Anthropology she went on to become a nationally recognized teacher of esoterica.

Scott Cunningham—His life-long study of Hawaiian culture makes Scott a true scholar and leading authority on the native islanders' ancient traditions. Personally familiar with Hawaii's sacred centers, his extensive library includes more than three hundred volumes on the subject. His eleven books released by Llewellyn Publications feature the popular *Magical Herbalism* and *The Magic in Food*.

Dea—Founder of the Boreadean Order of Druid and Feryllt for the preservation of Celtic mysticism, she is also director-coordinator for a group of practicing psychics known as "Lionhardt." Dea is presently engaged in an in-depth study of Druidical rites and philosophy as they apply to the modern world.

Ashleen O'Gaea—A frequent visitor to Arizona in her youth, Ash has lived in Tucson for almost 20 years. She shares a barrio home with her husband, Jim, their 11-year old son, three cats and a one-eyed koi called "Eddie the Trout." Ash still experiences the desert's singular power and today celebrates Wiccan sabbats with her family at the sacred centers she describes in her portrayal of numinous Arizona.

Breid Foxsong—Editor and publisher of the award-winning *Sacred Hart* magazine, Breid makes her home in Buffalo, New York. She is a folklore researcher, composer and Traditional Wiccan priestess.

Diccon Frankborn—His years in Japan, South East Asia and Africa won him the attention of the U.S. Foreign Assistance Program, but Diccon's deeper interests have always gone into the research of earth's energy alignments and power spaces. He is the former editor of the Soothsayer's Guild of the Society for Creative Anachronism and he is an adept Wiccan practitioner.

L. Christine Hayes—Born in Venezuela, she established the Star of Isis Foundation, a mystery school designed for the enlightenment of human-planetary consciousness through the alchemy of divine origins. Christine authored *Magii from the Blue Star* (Burning Bush Publications) and the acclaimed *Temple Doors*.

P. Scott Hollander—Winner of the Golden Key Award for poetry three years running and the author of *Stellar Almanac: A History* *and Tour Guide of the Infernal Kingdom of Hades, My First ABC: A Primer for Wiccan Children,* and *Reading Between the Lines: Introduction to Graphology* (Llewellyn Publications). Scott publishes *The Wiccan Advertiser,* a business quarterly, from her home near Hamden, Connecticut.

Frank Joseph—A native Chicagoan, he is a book reviewer for *Fate* magazine who travels widely in search of clues to the sunken city of Atlantis. He has published several feature articles and a book *(The Destruction of Atlantis)* about the lost civilization, together with his investigation of a possible Atlantean artifact in *The Message of the Crystal Skull* (Llewellyn Publications, 1989).

Anodea Judith—Together with her husband, Richard Ely (a consulting geologist whose photographs accompany his wife's writing), Anodea conducts "Science and Mystery Tours" to sacred centers, such as Macho Picchu, in Peru. Author of *Wheels of Life: A User's Guide to the Chakra System* (Llewellyn Publications), she is a practicing therapist and teacher of ancient religious beliefs.

LaVedi R. Lafferty—*The Eternal Dance* (Llewellyn Publications, 1984) was an outgrowth of LaVedi's 20 years teaching experience and her fondation/management of an esoteric center in Alaska. Listed in *Who's Who in the West* and *Foremost Women of the 20th Century,* her expertise extends to meditation techniques, astrology and past-life recall.

Anne Lyddane—Author of *Kaleidoscope: A Study of Multiple Lives* and *Astrological Color Magic and You,* Anne was for 18 years the Staff Astrologer at Llewellyn Publications. She also writes for Llewellyn's *Moon Sign Book* and yearly calendar. A former teacher in Asheville, North Carolina and Charlottesville, Virginia, she today offers private consultations in transformational astrology to clients from around the world.

Florence Wagner McClain—Classical pianist, artist, historian, photographer and archaeologist, her authoritative opinions are regularly sought after for identification of pre-Columbian remains throughout America's Southwest. Florence authored *A Practical Guide to Past-Life Regression* (Llewellyn Publications, 1989), and conducts intensive research into the problem-solving aspects of past-life therapy.

Sandra Rachlis—With degrees in anthropology and sociology, Sandra's insights to Montana's sacred centers are profound. A psychic and visionary since childhood, she works in close cooperation with the natural and human communities through group ritual, art and hands-on procedures.

Louise Riotte—Author of an international best-seller, *Carrots Love Tomatoes*, her numerous books about esoteric gardening are sold from Europe to North America and Australia. Louise is a regular contributor to Llewellyn's annual *Moon Sign Book* and writes a weekly column, "Gardening with Louise," in her hometown newspaper, *The Daily Ardmoreite*.

Edna Ryneveld—A former school teacher and copywriter, Edna today owns and operates a farm in rural Missouri. She is the author of *Transits in Reverse*, and has published numerous magazine articles dealing with the sacred and the mysterious.

Bruce Scofield—He is not only a researcher of New England antiquities, but their champion and preserver as well. Bruce co-authored *Fifty Hikes in New Jersey* (Back-country Publications, 1988) and his "A Possible Summer Solstice Marker in Northern New Jersey" appeared in the Summer/Fall issue of the *New England Antiquities Research Association*, 1983.

Jim Sutton—He is a photojournalist with 30 years experience in television and newspapers throughout Tennessee, Florida, and his native North Carolina. Jim is a frequent contributor to various New Age publications across the country. He owns J & L Enterprises.

Jenine E. Trayer—Native to Harrisburg, Pennsylvania, Jenine is director of a press alliance group and is active in several esoteric organizations in Pennsylvania and Oklahoma. When not illustrating or writing, she spends her time with her husband and four children in their 100-year old home.

ALABAMA

RUSSELL CAVE

Birmingham

Moundville
MOUND STATE MONUMENT

Montgomery

Mound State Monument

Lyn Chamberlain

Farmers and artisans built the huge earthen mounds that lie along the Black Warrior River in West Central Alabama. Once this city of 3000 was the cultural and ceremonial center for an area that stretched from present day Tuscaloosa to Demopolis in South Alabama. Smaller sites with one or more mounds denote outlying villages which were part of the Moundville complex.

Mound State Monument consists of 320 acres and 20 preserved mounds. It provides the finest, if not the largest, example of the Mississippian Culture, which thrived at the from the 9th to the 14th centuries and was named for the river system that roughly marked its spread. Like other societies from the period, the Moundville Indians built huge earthen domiciliary and mortuary mounds. Each mound had an earthen ramp which once provided access to the top, upon which homes, temples and other buildings of wood were constructed.

Many of the motifs and symbolic representations recovered here are similar to those found throughout the Yucatan and Central America. The mounds themselves suggest the pyramidal shape of Mesoamerican structures. While theories of Aztec traders abound, there is no conclusive evidence to support a connection between the two cultures.

The Moundville site faces the river—approximately, but not true, north. Ramps were built on any side of a mound, but some mounds appear to face one direction intentionally. The Temple Mound, which is the largest, has been restored and wooden steps added. Along with two smaller mounds it is the older part of the site, forming a rough triangle pointing away from the river. Directly behind the Temple Mound is another wider, lower mound, part of a great circle of smaller mounds surrounding a courtyard. The entire complex was once surrounded by a palisade of high upright posts.

Mound State Monument.
Photo courtesy of the State Museum of Natural History,
Moundville, AL.

While most of the mounds are domiciliary, upon which people built their homes, some appear to be burial mounds. They hold copper ear plugs, breast plates and other artifacts associated with the elite class among Mississippian tribes. Structures on these mounds were probably charnel houses with burials made in the floor. Domiciliary mounds also contain burials; burying family members in the floor of the home was a common practice for the period.

An excellent museum at Mound State Monument exhibits artifacts recovered from the site. It also provides a panoramic display of the Moundville Indians' lifestyle, explaining methods for making pottery, tools and ceremonial objects.

A small "Indian Village" has been reconstructed based upon structural remains unearthed during archaeological excavation. Daily activities and ceremonies are portrayed here through the use of life-size models.

LIFESTYLE OF THE MOUNDVILLE INDIANS

To the Moundville Indian, there was no separation of the political, economic, religious and social structures. The chief was a powerful figure with jurisdiction in all areas. Like others in his chiefdom, he stood about 5'7" and had strong features, a broad face and a prominent jaw. He was physically robust and well-nourished, with a lifespan of 30 years. Also like his subjects, his skull was deformed through spending the first months of his life on a cradleboard.

At his death, the temple and houses on top of the great mound where he lived were burned. Sometimes retainers and kinsmen committed suicide or were sacrificed on the grave. Then all was covered with a layer of earth and new buildings were constructed.

Elite status in the community afforded the privilege of living on the earthen mounds. At approximately the end of every generation, the buildings on top of the mound were burned and covered, creating a foundation for new lives. Sometimes the ashes were raked out in an even layer across the top; at other times, they were gathered into a pile so that the new mound was not flat. Occasionally, appendages were added to a mound.

The people wore ear plugs, bracelets, arm bands of copper, and beads and pendants of shell. Hides and garments of vegetable fiber woven into fabric made simple garments. Body paint was made from bloodroot. Around the neck, many wore gorgets (ornamental stone disks of sandstone, slate or granite).

Society was organized around family groups with rank determined by the power of whatever ancestors an individual might claim. Ancestors may have been human or supernatural. Most likely each family was represented in the Moundville city, but during most of the year the largest part of the population lived away from the central sites on individual farmsteads where they built a thriving agricultural economy based on corn, squash and beans.

This economy was bolstered by extensive trade. Copper here came from the Great Lakes. Marine shells from the coast were being traded all up and down the country, and some types of flint as well. Greenstone from eastern Alabama and Georgia, galena and quartz were all imported. Sandstone and greenstone were the most common materials for Moundville tools.

Pottery was an important medium for decoration, particularly non-utilitarian pottery. Effigy pots were shaped to look like animals and people. Moundville exported a distinctive black pot that has been found far from home. Moundville Black Pottery was primarily a funerary or ceremonial ware.

In spite of the reliance on agriculture and trade, Moundville Indians lived in a warrior society. Pottery and shells were decorated with skulls and bones. During feast periods, the Indians gathered at the Moundville site for games ceremonies, and rituals that included human sacrifice. They worshiped a Fire-sun deity and they honored the wind and the rain. Their pipes were made of clay or stone, and they smoked a mixture of Chamberlain tobacco, sumac and inner bark of dogwood which they called *kinnikkinnik*. Black drink, a purgative drink made of the dahoon holly, was served in a pottery cup with rounded bottom that could not be set down when filled.

SYMBOLS OF THE SOUTHERN CULT

The Moundville Indians were part of the Southern Cult rooted in the late prehistoric Mississippian stage, and sometimes called the Southern Death Cult because of its trail of long bones and skulls. The cult is thought to be the result of a religious revitalization or complex that swept down the Mississippi Valley and through the deep central South around 1200 A.D. It was significantly associated with a Fire-sun deity and a warrior code, as well as human sacrifice.

Many motifs are classic Mississippian, such as the rattlesnakes, woodpeckers or predatory birds and eagle warriors. Others are Pan-American, such as the long-nosed god masks, reminiscent of Yacatecuhtli, god of Aztec traders. The feathered serpent, a universal symbol of the union of heaven and earth, appears here, along with raptorial birds and rattlesnakes with residual wings. Their eyes are depicted as forked, weeping or winged. The Indians also used the sunburst, the cross and a curious bi-lobed arrow.

A common motif is a human male with face always in profile. Arms and legs take a variety of postures that are impossible unless the man is flying. Feathers hang from or are attached to the arms, and he usually has a tail and a birdlike headdress with bands on his wrists, ankles, calves and upper arms. This is not a god, but a representation of the shaman become a supernatural being.

Temple Mound.
Photo courtesy of the State Museum of Natural History,
Moundville, AL.

The rattlesnake disk, thought to have been used for religious and war ceremonies, was discovered here. It is the most famous of the Mississippian artifacts, and is on display at the museum. The 12.5 inch circular stone disk is notched at regular intervals and carved with an eye on an open hand. The hand and eye are elements of the human anatomy that bring creation into being through action. Therefore the symbol might represent creative force, or as is often the case in both Egyptian and pre-Columbian America, clairvoyant action. It is surrounded by two knotted rattlesnakes, one facing the same direction as the fingers, the other facing the direction of the wrist.

The disk is displayed with the fingers pointing up, and it is often assumed that the eye is etched on the left palm. However, both the bracelet on the inside of the wrist and the nails are displayed, and so the eye could just as easily be on the back of the right hand and could have been used pointing downward. Or up in one situation and down in another, perhaps suggesting the idea of completeness.

For reasons as mysterious as their origins, the mound builders abandoned their elevated lifestyle and their strict class structure around 1500 A.D. But they carried their cosmology and their ideologies with them as they moved into recorded history as Alabama's "Civilized Tribes"—the Cherokee, Choctaw, Creek and Chickasaw.

MYSTICAL SIGNIFICANCE
(Frank Joseph)

The predominant spiritual experience for the pre-Columbian inhabitants of Moundville occurred in what archaeologists call the "Southern Death Cult." It is an unfortunate term, because it conjures in the minds of many people ghastly images of human sacrifice and bloody appeals to the Dark Side. Actually, it only refers to funerary artifacts discovered in the mortuary mounds, with no implication of ritual murder. The so-called "Death Cult," while finding one of its leading centers at Moundville, was by no means confined to that prominent site. Followers practiced its elaborate ceremonies throughout the Mississippi Valley and the Deep South until the early 14th century. Only an idea of a fundamental power could have spread it as far as it did and cause it to endure for several hundred years.

Keys to unlock their sacred mysteries are the symbols its practitioners designed in copper sheets, on clay pottery and stone pipes and tablets. Chief among these was the spiral. It not only appeared on ritual materials, but the people themselves formed religious processions in a communal spiral, including large numbers of dancers stepping away from a central fire. "An interesting sidelight of these dances," writes Galloway, "is that the participants warmed their hands near the fire and then rubbed their eyes to give them the power to see snakes." This gesture perhaps explains the Southern Cult's enigmatic symbol of an open eye in the palm of a hand. The ancient Alabamans believed that the life force turned in a spiral, so that movement in such a pattern would put them in accord with the active powers of the cosmos. As Galloway affirms, the spiral "appears to be a generalized or universal force."

As mentioned, the spiral was also identified with the snake who glides between this world and the next, the Underworld. The creature is, therefore, a special medium linking the dimensions. He sheds his skin and is the living symbol of regeneration, fertility of the soil, for animals and human beings. In imitation of the rattlesnake, Southern Cult shamans used gourds as rattles to call upon sympathetic serpent magic for healing, a theme still alive in the caduceus, a twin snake entwined around a staff—the world-wide emblem of medical science.

The weeping eye motif displayed throughout the Moundville complex stood for rain from God's omnispective eye, but it simultaneously implied the essential compassion and redeeming beneficence of the cosmos. Victory in struggle was signified by the peregrine falcon, "a swift, aggressive bird whose attack culminates in a war-like blow, instantly killing its victim." The bird-man theme is also a warrior symbol, but he likewise impersonated the spirit of decisiveness in life's vital problems, personal transformation and spiritual transcendence beyond the human-all-too-human. The warrior aspects of both the falcon and the bird-man were not limited to the prehistoric battlefields of the American plains, but characterized the internal victories each individual must overcome to transcend his mortality through union with our loftier nature.

During rituals, they partook of a consciousness-altering drug, *Datura stramonium*. Combined with the music and the pageantry of their ceremonies, the hallucinogenic affects of jimsonweed undoubtedly made the flashing copper images take on an existence all their own. And particular use was made of extraordinary crystals in these shamanistic frenzies. Most outstanding was the Ulunsuti, a large, clear specimen with a trace of red hematite suspended within it. The hematite was interpreted to be blood. This super-crystal was said to have come from the forehead of an Underworld serpent, an apparent parallel with the well-known Third Eye of psychic vision. The red-flecked mineral encased within the crystal provided whoever possessed it with the power of clairvoyance, prophecy, levitation and astral projection, but it could turn on its mortal owner if not regularly propitiated, or "fed," with fresh sacrifices. No legendary item, several Ulunsuti have been recovered from the graves of suspected shamans.

Generations of Southern Death Cult practitioners have impacted the earthworks and ceremonial precincts of Moundville with lingering spiritual energy. Modern visitors still tap into these psychic storage areas by visualizing any of the native symbols associated with the sacred center, which may be powerfully enhanced by holding a favorite crystal in the left (receptive) hand during meditation.

For example, concentrating on the image of the bird-man will assist in astral projection capabilities or spiritual transcendence of any kind, just as envisioning the peregrine falcon will activate our innate warrior powers to conquer an obstacle. The centuries-old human energies still resonating at Moundville are there for us to realize and utilize our higher, truer nature, and to access the fundamental powers of a living sacred center bequeathed to us by our spiritual forebears.

RITUAL

Standing atop the highest mound, the stir and activity of feast and ceremony remains. Beneath it lies the solid peace of a place where people have came to terms with the cycle of life and death, destruction and regeneration. The energy of this place is one of communion with the earth, of strength and regeneration.

This is a spot for meditation. An excellent way to do this is to stand quietly on top of the temple mound, away from others, perhaps at the edge of the mound gazing across the site, or at the opposite side, facing the woods.

Begin a slow, rhythmic pattern of breathing, inhaling through the nose and exhaling through the mouth. Hold both the inhaled breath and the exhaled breath for the same length of time as the breathing. Counting is a good way to do this, and five, the number of fingers on the hand, is a good number to use. The count should be even and the pattern as slow as possible without causing strain—inhale, 1-2-3-4-5; hold, 1-2-3-4-5; exhale, 1-2-3-4-5; hold, 1-2-3-4-5.

Visualize a beam of light coming down through your head and moving downward through the center of your body, brought in by your inhaled breath. As you exhale, the light moves outward through the cells of your body, absorbing first sky, then earth, and finally the aura of this place. As it is absorbed, it is brought back to you by the force of the inhaled light. Allow the beam of light to move down through you and on out through your feet, penetrating and absorbing the layers of life and death recorded in the mound. Continue until you feel that flow inside yourself. Give thanks for your experience and release it to enjoy the rest of your visit. It is now yours to reclaim at anytime you desire in the privacy and quiet of your own meditation place.

FOR MORE INFORMATION

Directions
From Tuscaloosa, take SR 69 south 13 miles to Moundville. Mound State Monument is clearly marked.

Facilities
The park is open from 7:45 a.m. to 9 p.m. daily. Museum hours are 9 a.m. to 5 p.m. seven days per week, except major winter holidays. Camping facilities are located in an area well removed from the daily activity of the park and museum. All 30 spaces are equipped with water and electric hookup, tent pads, and grills. Six sites have full hookups with disposal units; four sites are pull-through; and two sites have 220 volt hookups. A dumping station is located adjacent to the sites, and a centrally situated bath house provides modern shower facilities. For security purposes, the gates are locked from 9 p.m. to 7:45 a.m. daily. Nature trails run through the park, and information on primitive camping areas is available at the museum.

A conference center is available for rent at daytime and evening rates. Picnic tables are located in a shaded area along the river.

Further Information
For more rates and other information, contact Mound State Monument, P.O. Box 66, Moundville, AL 35474 or telephone (205) 371-2572.

For Further Reading/Bibliography
Cirlot, J. E. *A Dictionary of Symbols.* New York: Philosophical Library, 1962.

Hudson, Charles. *The Southeastern Indians,* University of Tennessee Press, 1976.

The Southern Ceremonial Complex: Artifacts and Analysis. The Cottonlands Conference. Edited by Patricia Galloway, Lincoln: University of Nebraska Press, 1978.

Russell Cave

Lyn Chamberlain

Just south of the Tennessee border in eastern Alabama, nestled high on the wooded east side of Montague Mountain overlooking Doran's Cove, lies a cave where archaeologists have uncovered an unbroken record of human habitation extending back over 10,000 years. Russell Cave is the site of the longest continuous use by man on the North American continent and holds remains of the oldest campfires in the Southeast. Layers of earth reveal a detailed history reaching back through the Mississippian, the Eastern Woodland and the Archaic Periods and even into the Paleo-Indian Period.

The record shows the advent of such technological innovations as the development of pottery and the use of the atlatl, a throwing stick which gave a spear more power and distance. Cultural advances appeared with bear's teeth necklaces, most likely worn as a sign of prestige by those who had killed a bear. The necklaces were followed by the wearing of gorgets, ornamental necklaces made first of stone and later of shell or clay carved with symbolic and religious motifs.

Burial customs advanced from the practice of throwing a body over a cliff or into a corner to fairly elaborate burials. Men learned to polish stone, make vessels of hide and lamps of hollowed bones stuffed with bear fat.

As debris in the cave built up, these early housekeepers solved the problem by carrying in enough earth to cover it and make a new floor. That practice continued in a limestone cave, which by nature slows disintegration, and which has provided us with one of the best records available of mankind's past.

Historical ownership began in 1817 when Captain John Wood, a Cherokee Indian, was given the land in payment for war service. But the treasure inside was not discovered until 1953 when four amateur archaeologists from the Chattanooga Chapter of the Tennessee Archaeological Society explored it.

Entrance to Russell Cave.
Photo courtesy of National Park Service.

They dug only a few feet when they realized the importance of their discovery and contacted the Smithsonian Institute. The Institute and the National Geographic Society conducted three seasons of archaeological exploration, digging to the depth of 43 feet and uncovering the story of life in Russell Cave expanding over a period of 8,000 years.

To preserve the site for scientific study, the Society purchased the 310-acre site, made liberal grants for research, and finally presented the grounds to the National Park Service, who maintains it. The entire living area has not been excavated. Knowing that archaeological methods and procedures constantly improve, the Society and the Park Service have reserved large portions for future study.

Russell Cave is a gaping cavern system that extends 270 feet into Montague Mountain. The opening on the east side is 107 feet wide. Whether by accident or design, early man rose to face the sun.

A sister cave to the north is connected by sloping tunnels in the rock wall. At the bottom of this cave runs Dry Creek. The creek, coupled with the tunnels, provided air conditioning in the summer and a ready supply of fresh water during the winter.

Both caves are part of a cavern system that extends at least 7 miles into the hill. Temperature remains a constant 58 degrees.

A burial mound near the cave holds twelve skeletons, though no artifacts were found. The burials are dated at approximately 400 A.D., but current data gives no further information. Were these people interred singly or in a group? Were they members of the same family or victims of a common calamity?

Around 30,000 people visit the monument each year, some of them spelunkers wanting to explore the uncharted sections of the cave. The annual Indian Day Festival has become a popular event on this day, special programs and demonstrations illustrate early man's lifestyle. Visitors both hear and see how man lived, how he chipped flint, made and decorated pottery, designed weapons and brained-tanned skins.

THE RECORD UNCOVERED

The Russell Cave story begins 10,000 years ago when a portion of the limestone ceiling fell, pushing the creek aside and raising the floor of the cave well above the water level. Then a small band of nomadic Indian hunter-gatherers found the cave a warm and safe place to spend the winter. The band was small, probably no more than 15 or 20, and may well have been a family group. Most likely they were searching for food when winter caught them.

Their tools were simple and portable, reflecting their lifestyle—chipped stone scrapers and knives, bones fashioned into fishhooks. Weapons were points of flint or quartz fastened to a stick to create a spear. Bone awls and needles suggest that they worked hides into items of clothing. Their diet consisted of nuts and game— deer, turkey, squirrel, raccoon, rabbit, gray fox, skunk and bobcat; turtles, fish and shellfish.

They wasted little of their game. Flesh was roasted or stewed in containers of bark or skin. Hot rocks dropped into containers heated the water. Hides became clothing, and bones were made into tools.

For thousands of years their lives changed little, though near the middle of the Archaic Period they became more sedentary as they improved the exploitation of local food resources. Postholes suggest they erected canopies, probably of hides, to protect themselves from the constant dripping that occurs inside a limestone cave. Impressions of clay matting in one layer suggest they used baskets and vessels of perishable material. Storage pits, later used to catch rubbish, begin at this period.

For the most part, their tools became more varied and sophisticated, often made with polished stone. One notable exception is the
spear point. Early points were finely detailed, often evenly fluted.
Later points appear less skillfully made. The change was not the result of less skill, but better technology. Improved methods of notch-
ing the base and fastening the point to the shaft allowed the point to
bury itself deeper in its target. The fine sharp point was no longer
needed.

At this period, the Indians buried family members in shallow
pits scraped out of the cave floor. Bodies were sprinkled with red
ochre made from hematite.

Some artifacts found in the cave from the Archaic Period are
more often associated with peoples in other places—bearleg lamps
were more common in the north. To make the lamp, the Indian hollowed out the foreleg bone of a bear and stuffed it with fat. No other
evidence of trade this early exists. Did Archaic Man already have
trade routes? Or did he simply adapt a tool from his neighbor on one
side and pass it along to the neighbor on the other?

By the end of the Archaic Period, bear teeth necklaces had
given way to rings, ear plugs and gorgets of stone, shell and bone.
Many objects from this period were purely for decoration, pleasure
or ritual.

The common date for the beginning of the Woodland Period is
1,000 B.C. The period is marked by the beginning of settled village
life and the growing importance of trade and individuals with ranks
of chief, priest, and chief warrior. At this time the cave was used
mainly as a winter shelter. Large amounts of stored foods are found
from this period.

Both pottery and the bow and arrow, a further technological
advance on the spear, appear in Russell Cave. Tools show considerable refinement in their construction and an obviously wider range
of use. Changes came, too, in the methods of burial. Mounds were
built sometimes over bones and sometimes over substantial log
tombs. The mound might contain one body or several. Where early
pottery has surfaces decorated with fabric impressions, later pottery
were made by wooden paddles carved into a variety of designs.

During the Mississippian Period, only occasional bands of
hunters traveling from their cities in the rich river bottoms found
shelter in the cave. The Cherokees who followed seldom used the
cave, nor did the white man.

MEDITATION

For many people, it's difficult to do an active meditation in a public place, and the rough, pockmarked surface of the area makes it unwise to step too far off the trail. However, it's worth looking for a quiet spot along the trail, or to visualize as much of it as possible. Even though some of the images will put you inside the cave, a physical location on the hiking trail above is better.

Remember that visualization includes not only visual images, but all sense information. The more thoroughly you can construct all sense images, the more meaning the meditation will have for you. If you are the type of person who can soak up the aura of a place and reconstruct it later in the privacy of your own meditation room, so much the better.

Begin by relaxing yourself with slow, regular breathing. Allow the pressures and events of your present life to drop away from you. See yourself changing form from your present appearance to that of a short dark-skinned hunter gatherer who originally moved into the cave to find shelter from the winter.

In your mind's eye, walk into the cave and crouch beside the fire. As you visualize this, allow your body to drop to a squatting position, supporting your weight with your hands on the ground. Hold this position and continue the slow, regular breathing as you visualize the warmth of the fire and the sound of the cold wind outside.

Near you, a deer skin draped inside a circle of rocks holds water and chunks of meat. As you scoop rocks from the fire and drop them into the soup, you are thankful this method of cooking is available in the cave. On the hunt, food must be cooked directly over the fire and is difficult to chew.

As you allow the images to slip away, raise yourself to a crouching position, still supporting yourself with the fingertips of one hand. In the other hand you hold a spear. The end of it is cradled in a hollowed deer antler tied to a stick. It is a weapon which your brother saw used by another band. The weapon is good; it gives your spear's power more distance.

Your stomach growls, and you hope the rabbit feeding in front of you cannot hear from this distance. If he does, your own hunger will have to wait. You have gone hungry too many times because an animal caught your scent as you crept up to kill him.

As you crouch, continue the slow, rhythmic breathing. Do your best to bring the feelings of the scene inside yourself. Experience the hunger. Experience also the discomfort of holding yourself poised, alert and quiet as you prepare to kill the rabbit.

When you have gone as far as possible with this image, bring yourself to a semi-upright position. You are standing, but your back is bent. Your arms hang loosely at your sides. The cave is your permanent home. Like others in your family, you have specific tasks to perform for the entire group. Yours is to plant seeds. It is spring and you are scratching the ground with a forked stick to make holes for the seeds which you had collected and saved in a basket last year. Tomorrow you will need to spend your day watching that birds do not scratch or wild animals do not dig to steal the seed from the loosened soil.

Now stand upright with your arms hanging loosely at your sides. Stand straight and tall, for you are about to become an adult. You understand that your grandparents once lived in the cave, but your parents were wise enough to build a hut of wood and thatch nearby.

Today there will be a great ceremony in honor of yourself and others your age. You will stand before the priest chieftain and he will hang a beautiful shell ornament around your neck. It is engraved with a symbol which represents the four directions of the wind and another symbol which signifies your own place within the tribe.

Feel inside yourself the pride and joy you experienced at that moment. As you release the image, raise your arm slowly, bringing them straight out in front and then high overhead. Lift your gaze to the tree line at the top of the mountain. In your mind's eye, return gently to your present self. Now see the sky light coming down through your hands, through your body and out your feet into the earth. As it sinks deep into the earth it turns, flowing back up through you and returning to the sky.

Experience within yourself, not only the flow of light, but the flow of humanity, the flow of time cycling ever upward. Feel yourself as part of that flow before you release the visualization to continue with your visit.

FOR MORE INFORMATION

Directions

From Chattanooga or Huntsville, take US 72 to Bridgeport. Follow Jackson County 91 west to Jackson County 75. Russell Cave is about 8 miles west of Bridgeport and is well marked.

Lodging and Facilities

Russell Cave National Monument is open from 8 a.m. to 5 p.m. daily except for Christmas Day. It is free of charge.

A visitor center museum provides exhibits and audio-visual programs. The cave shelter exhibit also has a slide program. Other parts of the cave are closed to the public except by permission of the park service. Upon request, park rangers will demonstrate Archaic Man's tools, weapons, and methods of cooking. Prearranged group tours are available.

In season, the park has an Indian garden. There is a self-guided, 1/2-mile ethnobotanical trail with interpretive signs and a mile-long hiking trail along the side of the mountain.

Thus picnic facilities are limited to prepared meals, and there is no lodging on the grounds. Cooking and fires are not allowed. Food is available in Bridgeport, Stevenson (13 miles) or in South Pittsburgh, TN (16 miles).

A number of state, county and commercial campgrounds lie within 10 miles of the monument. Other lodging is available in Stevenson, Scottsboro (30 miles), Kimball, TN (16 miles), Monteagle, TN (30 miles) or Chattanooga (45 miles).

Wild cave exploration requires permission from the superintendent. Conditions in the cave are greatly affected by weather conditions, so cavers are asked to call ahead to make arrangements and to obtain the list of minimum equipment needed.

The annual Indian Day Festival is held on the third Saturday of April. Special demonstrations and programs relating to the lifeways and cultures of the people living in the region and Russell Cave are presented at that time.

Further Information

For further information, please call the monument at (205) 495-2672.

ALASKA

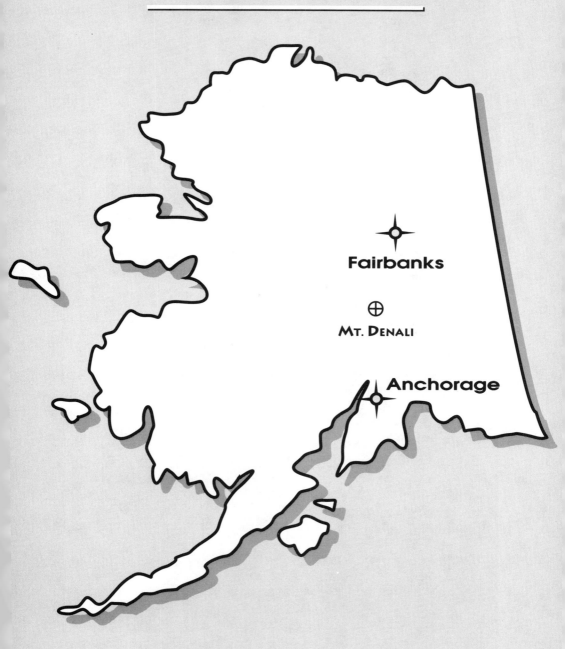

Fairbanks

⊕
MT. DENALI

Anchorage

Mt. Denali

LaVedi R. Lafferty

Mt. McKinley, towering above the impressive snow-capped 600-mile arc of the Alaska Range at 20,320 feet, is the highest mountain in North America. Measured from the 2,000-foot lowlands near Wonder Lake to its summit, its vertical relief of 18,000 feet (greater than that of Mt. Everest) makes it the tallest mountain in the world. Frequently hidden in clouds, the mountain makes its own weather, with permanent snowfields covering over half of its slopes. Ice on the mountain is hundreds of feet thick in places and winter temperatures can plunge to below -95°F.

Mt. McKinley National Park was established through the efforts of naturalist Charles Sheldon in 1917, who wanted to protect the area's large animal population of moose, caribou, bears, ball sheep and other wildlife. He had wanted the park to be named Denali after the Athabascan native name for the mountain, meaning the "High One"; however, his suggestion was not enacted until 1980. At that time the park boundaries were greatly expanded to include the entire Mt. McKinley massif, which more than tripled the size of the park.

The park is now known as Denali National Park and Preserve, though the name of the mountain was not officially changed. Due to the area's significance as a subarctic ecosystem, it is also designated as an International Biosphere Reserve. The park now encompasses 6 million acres. The mountain itself is part of the Alaska Range, which divides the interior plateau from south-central Alaska. This range began its formation some 65 million years ago, resulting from the Denali fault, producing North America's largest crystal break. Two tectonic plates move against each for 1,300 miles, from the Yukon border to the Aleutian peninsula. Volcanic eruptions are common on the peninsula and earthquake tremors frequently occur in the environs of the park.[1]

The mountain, visible for hundreds of miles in many directions, sits like a crown upon Alaska, "The Great Land" (an appropriate title derived from the native name for the country). For untold centuries nomadic people hunted upon Denali's northern reaches, fished the rivers for salmon and gathered edible plants and berries. The summer's harvest was mostly dried in preparation for wintering in warmer areas. Denali remains a largely unspoiled wilderness of wildlife, tundra carpeted with miniaturized plants and flowers, wide valleys with wandering rivers, visible creeping glaciers and panoramic, sweeping vistas.

Mt. McKinley (Mt.Denali).
Photo courtesy of Alaska Division of Tourism.

MYSTICAL SIGNIFICANCE

Among the Athabascan natives, also known as the "Tena," ancient tales of creation and magic were transmitted orally, handed down from generation to generation. Since the Tena share a common ancestry with the southern tribes of Navajo and Apache, whose language comes from the same lingual roots, parallels may be expected in their shamanistic traditions. The Alaskan Tena have historically been a peaceful people, following the example of Yako, the ancient shamanistic Adam of their forefathers.

The narrative of Mt. Denali's creation was recorded in 1903 by circuit court judge, the Hon. James Wickersham, who had received the story from Koonah, the blind sage and chief of a Tena band. At his seasonal encampment in Kantishna, facing south toward the great mountain, Koonah tells of the divinities and demons associated with Denali.[2]

Softly, Koonah speaks of the time long ago, before Denali, the High One, existed. Consistent with other Native traditions, he tells of "the world before," the one that existed before the world as we know it today. He speaks of the battle between good and evil that resulted in the manifestation of our physical world, the creation of a spiritual pantheon and of human procreation.

The old chief continues the tale, describing the magician Yako as straight and tall as a spruce tree, as gentle as a young caribou, as strong as a bull moose and as wise as a beaver. He lives alone, because there are no women in the land, no villages or other people. A mighty shaman, Yako is characterized as having the ability to move with the silence of a shadow and the power to change the form of animals, land and sea; but he desires a wife and has none.

Yako is told by Ses, the great brown bear, that far to the west in the village of Totson, the Raven war chief, there are beautiful women of Yako's race. Totson, however, is a mighty hunter of both bear and walrus, and he is a killer of men. This greatly disturbs Yako, until Ses tells him that the women of Totson's village are distressed by bloodshed and death. Yako decides that he will travel to Yunana, the distant sunset land far to the west, to seek a wife from Totson's village.

In the spring, after the winter snows melt, he builds a canoe from spruce and birch wood, covering it with sheets of birch bark sewn with spruce roots and caulked with spruce gum. He launches it upon the mighty Yukon River and drifts upon the current, until he reaches the salt water of the ocean. Yako paddles his canoe across the open waters to the land of Totson.

Upon arriving at the seashore of the village, he sings a beautiful song to the Raven chief, describing the land he comes from and his mission. He begs Totson to grant him a wife, so children may be born in the land to the east. Totson, however, is jealous of Yako's song, his many attributes and his magical powers. He refuses to welcome Yako to his village. Instead he disappears into his underground dwelling to ready his throwing stick, arrows and magic war spear so that he can kill the friendly Yako.

The women of the village, having heard Yako's song, are pleased but frightened. The wife of the second chief of the village offers Yako her daughter, the child Tsukala, and warns him of his danger. The women of the village then become jealous and try to prevent Tsukala's mother from giving her daughter to the handsome and mighty youth. Yako extends his magic paddle to the beach and has her mother place Tsukala upon it. He draws it back and places Tsukala upon a bed of sheep's wool inside the canoe. As the village women raise their clubs to strike Tsukala's mother, Yako creates a magic wave that casts her to safety and overwhelms the threatening women.

Totson, rushing out, casts spears and arrows after the fleeing Yako. Then he raises a storm, hoping to destroy Yako's light canoe with wind and waves. This failing, he pursues Yako in his skin war boat with his war bow, arrows, spears and throwing stick, riding the wild sea waves. Using his powerful magic, Totson increases the size and strength of the waves in a greater attempt to destroy Yako's canoe.

Yako, however, is a more powerful magician and he carries a wave-quelling stone, which he sends skipping ahead. Where the stone passes the waters are stilled, opening a path of quiet water for Yako's canoe to pass through, while Totson must labor through stormy seas in pursuit. Even so, the Raven chief follows rapidly and gains upon Yako. Guided by Yako's streaming black hair, Totson shoots all of his arrows and throws all of his spears to no avail. Finally he attempts to kill Yako with his great war spear, which never fails. He throws his spear directly at Yako's exposed back. Yako, seeing the shining spear flying through the air, calls upon his most powerful magic. He changes a great wave that is approaching Totson into a mountain of stone. The war spear strikes its crest and glances upward with the crash of breaking rock. The mighty spear flies higher, impelled by the strength of Totson's throw, sailing over the quiet waters until it reaches the crest of a still greater wave. Yako immediately turns this wave into a greater mountain of stone. The spear is again deflected and flies high into the southern sky to land among the stars.

Totson, the mighty warrior of blood-stained hands, then meets disaster. His war boat crashes into the mountain of stone and he is thrown onto the rocks. There he is instantly changed into a Raven. Dripping from the sea waters and without weapons, the transformed Totson flies to the top of the new, magically formed, mountain.

Exhausted from his exertions, Yako falls into a deep sleep. When he wakes, he finds himself at his home camp in a spruce forest. Tsukala has grown into a woman and she has prepared food for him. Yako gazes around him and sees the great mountains he created from the waves of the sea. The greater one, which had sent Totson's spear into the stars, came to be called Denali, the High One. The lesser mountain, first struck by Totson's war spear, is traditionally known by the native people "Totson-to-kadatlkoitan." The path of water quieted by the skipping stone became the valleys of the Yukon and Tanana Rivers, the home of the descendants of Yako and Tsukala. Their children, taught the skills by their parents to live in peace, justice and plenty, would, in their generations, migrate far to the east and south.

Another chief, from the Porcupine region, tells of a period following this time of early creation. He speaks of the time when Naradkaka, great-horned bison and mammoths wandered the land and a great lake named Mun-na filled part of the Yukon Valley. It was a time of plenty when Kaath, the king salmon and his cousin, Whokadza, spawned in the shallows of the lake, while Dinnaji, the bull moose, fed on the tubers of water lilies along its shores and summer nests surrounding the lake held Toba, the swan, Tunsa, the snipe, Dilkuu, the robin, and Delthowa, the warbler.

Then came the day when Dzadukaka, the dread northern spirit of cold, looked upon this happy land. His heart was filled with envy and he caused his flame-bearer, Yoyekoi, the aurora borealis, to report the source of the people's happiness. Upon learning that it came from the warmth of Mun-na and the great forests, he caused the north wind to blow fiercely, snow to form deep glaciers and ice to form in Mun-na. The giant animals all froze to death, leaving their bones where they are found today when annual floods wash away river banks.

In the south, Roletkaka, the spirit of heat, whose flame-bearer is Sa, the sun, saw this and determined he would restore the frozen land. These powerful shamans caused warm winds to blow and sent warm floods to melt the snow and ice, for Sa has greater power than Yoyekoi of the northern lights. Mun-na, the great lake, was, however, destroyed forever. The mighty rivers in assisting Rolet-kaka filled the deeps of the lake with silt and sand. Forests grew upon the alluvial plane and plenty was restored to the people of the land.

The crest of Denali is considered to be the throne of Sa, the solar shaman and Master of Life. Annually he conquers Dzadu of the north, the demon of snow, and renews life with warming rains, green growth, spawning fish, migrating waterfowl, roaming caribou, sheep, moose and animals awakened from their winter's sleep.

In modern esoterics, though not commonly known, this great mountain is considered to be a major global power point. In the tradition of the Great White Brotherhood, it acts as a reception, anchoring and transmittal center of cosmic energies related to spiritual evolution on earth.

SUGGESTED RITUAL

The choice periods to visit Denali for ritual work are during the Summer Solstice, when Sa makes his annual appearance as the Midnight Sun or during the first two weeks of September. The latter is after the peak of the tourist season and is also after the summer rainy season. The mountain is more likely to be visible in the fall and the park displays itself in a glorious show of breath-taking colors preceding the snows of Dzadu which herald the arrival of winter.

The mountain is best approached from the Kantishna (area of Koonah the story teller) and Wonder Lake, located in the middle of the park and accessible by road. From the campground at Wonder Lake a trail leads westward to a natural power point, a knoll, which rises and faces directly south toward the mountain. On the top of this knoll is a natural circular clearing, where ritual may usually be performed without disturbance. The best time for this is at noon or midnight during the Summer Solstice; or at sunrise or sunset in the autumn.

It is suggested that the walk to the knoll be done with a reverent and meditative attitude, allowing absorption of the expansiveness and magnificence of the area. The ritual that follows is designed to receive and share the unique energies of this site with all life on our planet.

Upon arrival at the knoll a brief meditation is suggested for further attunement to the site. If in a group, join hands in the middle of the clearing. A focalizer should be selected to end the attunement when connection with the site is felt. A simple way to do this is by a squeeze of hands, sent around the circle from person to person.

Then, proceeding to the outer perimeter of the clearing, take three deep breaths, hold each one a few seconds and exhale with a slight vibration through the throat. Following this, begin to circumambulate the clearing to your right (in a clockwise direction) three times, visualizing an increasingly glowing ring of brilliant, scintillating, silvery-white light surrounding it. Upon completion spiral again into the middle of the clearing and turn individually to face the east.

Raise your hands overhead, reaching for the sun, with palms cupped inward, as if to form a receiving chalice overhead. Visualize shafts of light extending from the sun to your hands, with solar light pouring in, forming a golden, whirling disk a few inches above your head. When you feel or sense the vibrating presence of this disk, visualize a shaft of light extending from it through your body to a point below your feet, linking you with the telluric forces of our planet. When you sense the vibrating reality of this disk, visualize the energies of these two disks merging into a third one at your heart center.

The following brief invocation of synthesis, designed to unite the soul and personality in communion with universal purpose, may then be intoned with the right arm and hand extended forward and the left hand placed over the heart center:

The sons of men are One and I am One with them.[3]
I am the soul,
I am the Light Divine,
I am Love,
I am THAT I AM.[4]
Peace and plenty to all beings,
East (upon intoning, turn to the south),
South (next turn to the west),
West (turn to the north),
North (return to the east and extend arms upward),
Above (extend arms downward),
And below (visualize release of the collected energies).
Let the Greater Will be done,
Let the Plan of Light and Love work out.[5]

Close by intoning the OM three times and quietly leaving the site, returning in silence to Wonder Lake. It is suggested that experiences not be shared until this return is made, as this increases anchoring and assimilation of the process.

FOR MORE INFORMATION

Location

Denali National Park is located 120 miles south of Fairbanks and 240 miles north of Anchorage. It is accessible by air, rail, bus or highway.

To arrange air transportation contact ERA Aviation/Alaska Airlines by calling (800)426-0333 or Continental USA and Hawaii at (907) 243-3300 in Anchorage.

For a scenic trip by rail, write or call the Alaska Railroad Corporation, Passenger Service, P.O. Box 107500, Anchorage, AK 99510-7500 or call (907) 265-2494 (Anchorage), (907) 456-4155 (Fairbanks) or (800) 544-0552 (Continental USA and Hawaii).

Bus service to the park is provided by several companies. Travel arrangements may be made by calling Denali Express at (800) 327-7651 or (907) 274-8539 Anchorage; Alaska Sightseeing Tours at (907) 276-1305 Anchorage or (907) 452-8518 Fairbanks; or Grey Line of Alaska/Westours at (907) 277-5581 Anchorage or (907) 456-7741 Fairbanks.

You may also drive to the park. Private vehicles are not usually permitted past the Savage River Campground, 15 miles inside of the park. Shuttle buses are provided on a daily schedule, leaving frequently from the Visitor Access Center near park headquarters and traveling to Eielson Visitor Center and Wonder Lake. The buses make scheduled stops, as well as to view wildlife. You may get off the bus enroute, except in closed areas, and may change buses as desired. During the peak season of July and August buses may be crowded. After the close of the season, usually following Labor Day, bus service may not be offered. A private vehicle may be needed to access the interior of the park at this time (they are allowed when public transportation is not available). Gasoline is not available on inner park roads.

The trip by bus one-way to Wonder Lake takes about 5-1/2 hours and food service is not available, so take along food and drink. Weather during the summer can be wet, windy and cool, with temperatures ranging from 35°F to 75°F. Warm clothing and rain gear are necessary. Good footwear and insect repellant are advisable, though by September the rainy season is normally past and insects are usually greatly reduced. Unpredictable weather in May, early June and mid-September may delay or hasten the opening and closing dates of park roads and facilities. Recorded information regarding conditions is available by calling (907) 683-2686.

For the hearty, backcountry permits may be available from park headquarters during the winter. Dog sled passenger trips are offered by Denali Dog Tours, P.O. Box 670, Denali National Park, AK 99755.

Local Assistance

Upon arrival at the park, information and literature is available from the Visitor Access Center located near the entrance to the park. The admission fee is $3 per person, with those under 17 or over 62 and the disabled admitted free of charge.

Free backcountry permits for overnight camping must be obtained from this center. Information regarding areas of the park that are closed for hiking, due to activities by bears or other wildlife, is provided by the Visitor Access Center.

Information by mail is available by writing to the Superintendent, Denali National Park and Preserve, P.O. Box 9, Denali Park, AK 99755. A free list of maps and other publications is available from the Alaska Natural History Association, P.O. Box 838, Denali Park, AK 99755.

General information plus interesting displays and films are provided by Alaska Public Lands Information Centers. These are at 250 Cushman St., Fairbanks, AK 99707, (907) 451-7352 or, for deaf access, (907) 451-7439; and at 605 West 4th Ave., Anchorage, AK 99501, (907) 271-2737, or for deaf access, (907) 271-2738.

Accommodations and Services

From late spring until early autumn, park concessions near the park entrance offer full-service hotel accommodations, youth hostel facilities, food service, groceries, gasoline and automotive services, camping supplies (including propane), showers and a narrated wildlife tour by bus. No other services are available within the park. For information you may write to: Outdoor World Limited, P.O.Box 87, Denali National Park, AK 99755, or call (907) 683-2215 during the summer or (907) 276-7234 during the winter.

Private campgrounds and hotel accommodations are also outside the park, near both the north and south boundaries. Permits to
camp within the park must be applied for in person at the Visitor
Access Center. During peak months there could be a delay getting a
campsite at Wonder Lake, which only has 28 tent spaces, with none
for trailers or large campers. It is usually possible to get a space at
Riley Creek Campground near the park entrance, which has 102
spaces for tents, trailers or campers. It is possible to camp at Riley
Creek and enjoy the nearby trails and activities, while waiting for a
space at the Wonder Lake campground, located 85 miles from the
park entrance.

Pets must be leashed at all times and are not permitted on the
buses or the backcountry trails. Campfires are only allowed in certain campgrounds, with firewood available at the store near the
park entrance. No open fires are allowed in the backcountry and all
garbage and trash must be packed out or deposited in garbage bar-
rels provided at the campgrounds. Both the Riley Creek and Wonder Lake campgrounds provide flush toilets and tap water. Opera-
tive firearms are not allowed inside the park, though bear repellant
spray may be carried. Care should be taken not to leave any food exposed or in a tent where you are sleeping that might be attractive to
a bear. Grizzly bears are seen throughout the park and should not be
approached for any reason.

Notes

1. Denali, National Park Service, U.S. Department of the Interior,
   GPO: 1990-262-100/20031 Reprint 1990.

2. Wickersham, Hon. James. *Old Yukon*, Washington D.C.: Washington Law Book Co., 1938, p. 243.

3. Bailey, Alice. *The Externalization of the Hierarchy*, Lucis Publishing
   Co., 1972, p. 142.

4. Bailey, Alice. *Discipleship in the New Age*, Lucis Publishing Co.,
   1972, p. 123.

5. Ibid, p. 158.

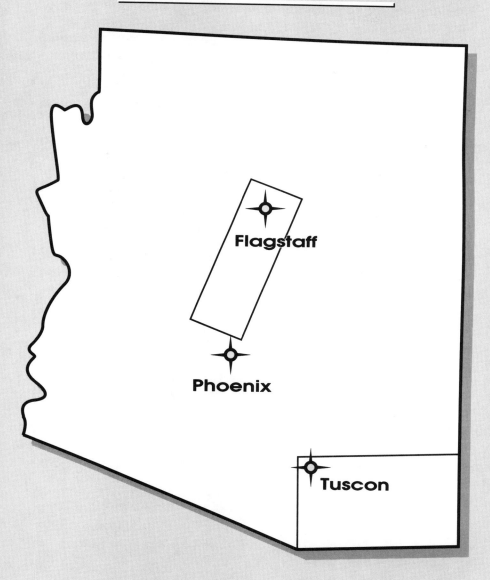

ARIZONA

Flagstaff

Phoenix

Tuscon

Various Sites in
Central and
Southeastern Arizona

Arizona

Ashleen O'Gaea

Arizona. The Wild West, rattlesnakes, cactus. Mines. The Grand
Canyon. All sacred in American folk history; but Arizona's roman-
tic movie mystique is nothing compared with the reality. The reality
is desert, pine forest, rocky peaks, rushing rivers, caves, fertile valleys—an extraordinary power that can overwhelm you if you let it.

Wherever you are in Arizona, stop and stand still for a moment. Notice how big the sky is and pay your respects to the directions, saluting them far away on the horizons.

> *Hail, Old Ones of the East, Guardians of the wide skies. You
> whose home is in the sunrise, you whose strong wings open
> across the desert, I greet you and ask your blessings. Hail, Old
> Ones of the South, Guardians of the blazing heat. You whose
> home is in the highest noon, you whose fiery heart burns across
> the desert, I greet you and ask your blessings. Hail, Old Ones of
> the West, Guardians of the precious liquid of life. You whose
> home is in the whispering dusk, you whose secret seas[1] are hid-
> den across the desert, I greet you and ask your blessings. Hail,
> Old Ones of the North, Guardians of the mountains and dwell-
> ers in the Earth. You whose home is in the stillness of midnight,
> you whose vast rocky embrace holds us all, I greet you and ask
> your blessings.*

Then take time, if you can, to open each chakra. Stay long
enough and you'll see an Arizona day open its own chakras, from
the violet morning sky that releases the sunrise to the scarlet evening sky that welcomes the setting Sun back to Earth.

This land is old, old and wise; wise and energetic and inspiring.
This land speaks in many voices to many peoples. Arizona's
Navajo, Hopi, Apache and other Native cultures are all distinct,
their stories and rituals different in many ways. And yet they are

alike in their uncompromising view of life—and land—as interconnected. As widely as the gods and spirits wander this land of red
rock and big skies, the narrowness of the stereotypical tourist's focus will not suffice. Out of respect to the nature of this magnificent
land, then, we do not look at a single site, but at a shire-sized portion
of the larger mystical landscape.

Central Arizona Sites

Between the site of Montezuma's Well, on I-17 just north of Camp
Verde, and the Wupatki National Monument, on AZ 89 north of
Flagstaff, is an approximately 80- by 40-mile corridor along 89, and
AZ 179. Passing through desert environments ranging from lush to
lava, this enchanted corridor is an adventurous track. Along it lie ruins still pulsing with energetic memories of Native tribes whose
mysterious departure is still not fully understood. Along these meandering asphalt trails, too, lie spectacular natural features that
make it very clear why Natives have called these lands sacred for
thousands of years.

MONTEZUMA'S CASTLE AND MONTEZUMA'S WELL

Follow I-17 north from Phoenix, keeping to the freeway past
Cordes Junction [say, "cor-dess"] and beyond Camp Verde, you
come to Montezuma's Castle, now a National Monument. Here, in a
wide, shallow cave, are five stories of maze-like adobe apartments
built into the high canyon walls, taking advantage of the elements.
A few miles upstream on Beaver Creek is Montezuma's Well, an
enormous spring-fed sinkhole. Literature and displays describe the
cultural and geologic significance of the cliff-dwelling and sinkhole,
but you have to experience the mystic strengths of the place for
yourself.

The castle never sheltered Montezuma, but housed a community of Sinaguans ["see-naw-guons"], natives who peopled the area
until the 15th century. The Spanish explorers named them the people "without water"; the abundant spring water in the well was just
one secret this holy land kept from the European invaders. There is
still much magic here, and most of it is still hidden from visitors.

When you visit the castle—the trail is wheelchair and stroller accessible—lay your hands on the ancient rock foundations of the pueblo. Take deep breaths, and be aware of the desert scents the air will bring you. Touch a *metate* ["meh-tah-tey"], the set of grinding rocks that serve even today as mortar and pestle for preparing corn meal. Kneel before it, on the ground or in your imagination, and visualize the corn-grinders of long ago, blessed by the Corn Maiden herself.

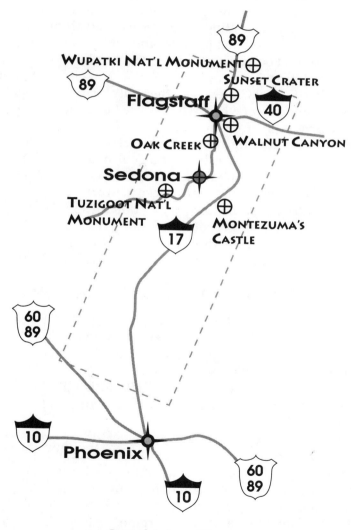

Central Arizona Sites

Let the pueblo's memories transport you for a moment to an earlier understanding of the world that did not separate the holy from the humble. Touching the old tools and the venerable adobe, you can "let your fingers do the walking" along the Good Red Road. Wander the grounds here, find a private place, and just sit for a few minutes. Sit and breathe deeply, and try to remember what it was like to live here centuries ago.

At Montezuma's Well (McGuireville Exit off I-17) there is a wonderful old sycamore. Spend some time leaning against it, breathing deeply and letting the magical desert air fill your lungs. If you are not too distracted by other tourists, you may hear the ancient drums, still beating out the Mother's pulse.

The Natives who occupied this large area—from Montezuma's Well north to Sunset Crater—call the well a *sipapu* ["see-pah-poo"], a place of emergence, where The People (as most tribes call themselves) came forth from the underworlds. Here one of the first, Kamalapukwia, magically survived a terrible flood, and with her grandson Sakaraka'amche, became a guardian of the Native people and the source of their medicine power. The Great Mother is said to live, old and stooped, among the rocks in nearby Boynton Canyon.[2]

The Hub Cafe at the Cordes Junction turnoff has a reputation for great road food, and of course off-ramp restaurants dot the freeway. For camping information, contact the Coconino National Forest at 2323 East Greenlaw Lane, Flagstaff, Arizona, 86001.

SEDONA AND OAK CREEK CANYON

Farther north on AZ 179 (there's a signed exit from I-17) is Sedona. Nestled at the mouth of Oak Creek among spectacular red rock formations in the high desert of central Arizona, Sedona is a world-renowned vortex. Near the intersection of several ley lines, Sedona is a pleasant town of about 7,000, although the population soared in August of 1987 as people gathered for the Harmonic Convergence.

Built up through tourism, Sedona attracts campers, casual travelers and elegant resort vacationers. Restaurants, galleries and charming shops offer plenty to do for those who are not inclined to hike or ride. Complete information about food, lodging, seasonal temperatures and tourist activities is available from the Sedona-Oak Creek Canyon Chamber of Commerce, Box 478, Sedona, Arizona, 85336; (602) 282-7722.

Sedna, goddess of harmony and balance, is said by ancient legend to dwell "in the red rock castle that bears Her name," and a host of other ancient gods and spirits have left their marks on the landscape here. Though Sedona is a sophisticated settlement, it is easy to reach wilder areas where the mysterious power of the land is still palpable.

It is appropriate anywhere in this area—really a gateway to vast holy lands farther north—to pay respect to the age and wisdom of the land. Part of the great Permian Basin, the red Coconino sandstone is some 215,000,000 years old!

Sedona.
Photo © 1991 by Ashleen O'Gaea.

Medicine wheels are still made by Natives and tourists; some are old enough to be three or four feet high by now. Build a small one aligned to the directions, or add rocks or leave an offering of corn or

aligned to the directions, or add rocks or leave an offering of corn or feathers at one you find, while you open yourself to the memories and confidence of the land. Raise your hands to the Sun, breathe deeply—and walk barefoot if you can, even for a little way.

If you are camping at a developed site or off the road in Oak Creek Canyon (especially beautiful in the spring and fall), you'll be able to do a cleansing ritual in the energetic Oak Creek—even while you're enjoying yourself on Slide Rock!

TUZIGOOT NATIONAL MONUMENT

West from ALT AZ 87, southwest of Sedona, is the Tuzigoot National Monument, protecting pre-Columbian ruins from about 1300 c.e. (Between Tuzigoot and Sunset Crater, about 70 miles north on ALT 89 intersecting with AZ 89 in Flagstaff, there are several ruins, many of them protected.) Built almost 700 years ago, Tuzigoot was abandoned sometime in the 15th century. The walls are of the reddish Coconino sandstone, shaped and laid without mortar. The clusters of a few small rooms facing and surrounding fields and work patios are typical of what you will see throughout the area.

These ruins are not often crowded, and there is usually an opportunity to be alone in a room, with the rocky foundations of the dwelling walls, or with a rock or a tree or a vista that attracts you.

To honor the lives that created the numerous settlements in Oak Creek Canyon and northward, the spirits that guided them, and the plant and animal life that still goes on here, offerings of feathers, corn, stones or even flowers you find while you're walking are appropriate. Your solitude may last long enough for you to raise your palms overhead to the Sun, or chant softly for a moment. You will probably want to take your shoes off and the feel the Mother's heartbeat more directly.

Journeying slowly north from Sedona on scenic AZ 179 you will find your own mysterious and sacred places. This land is ancient and its power is great. Interlaced with ley lines, majestic sandstone cliffs and sculptures, and replete with the magical lore of several tribes, the land itself, and the religious philosophy of interconnectedness shared by all the tribes who've ever lived here, make it difficult to separate individual sites from one another. Here in this calm and ancient landscape, Nature Herself urges us to see differently, to see wholly and understand that these canyons and mesas do not stand alone, but draw their power from their integration.

WALNUT CANYON

Where AZ 179 intersects I-40, turn east to Exit 204. Walnut Canyon is easy to reach from Flagstaff, where plenty of motels and restaurants (as well as Northern Arizona University and the Museum of Northern Arizona) welcome travelers. At Walnut Canyon, the cliff-dwellings are quite intimately accessible, though the stairs and pathways are steep.

The canyons and stunning formations here are as rich with Native lore as they are with color and natural sculpture. It is not hard to find yourself cut off from the sight and sound of other people, alone with the reverence the Sinaguan people left behind when they moved on. Breezes through pueblo adobe-work carry the voices of the ancient spirits that have taught and guided all who've lived here.

If you find yourself alone for a moment, lay both palms against the rock or adobe walls of a room and breathe deeply, asking that the gods and spirits of the place make your path a smooth one and keep your soul alert to the divine beauty of the Earth and the power of Her sacred places.

As you walk, chant under your breath: "Earth is our Mother, we all live on Her," or use other words that will connect you with the Native love for Mother Earth. Make a discreet offering of corn or feathers; you may find just the feather you need on your walk. Without obstructing any paths, you might even find enough small, flat stones and a place against the canyon's towering rock walls to build a mini-pueblo and leave it as an offering.

SUNSET CRATER

Up north in the San Francisco Peaks facing Sunset Crater (AZ 89 about 21 miles north of Flagstaff), the Earth's breathing holes inhale and exhale on six-hour cycles guided by the Moon. (These mountains were named in 1629 after St. Francis of Assisi, who had a close relationship with animal spirits.) Even as far south as Sedona, the breath of the Earth can be heard, though not every sighing hole has been mapped.

Sunset Crater is part of the Sunset Crater National Monument, which is equipped for everything from the simplest car and tent camping to the most elaborate RV-ing. In the summer, the Sunset Crater campground features ranger programs—narrated slide shows—on subjects ranging from wildlife through star-lore and Native tales to geologic history and the formation of the surrounding lava flows and volcanic cones.

Sunset Crater was too damaged by hikers[2] to allow any more people on its slopes, but there are nearby cinder cones that you can climb. On the easy-to-walk, self-guided (there's a brochure) nature trail around Sunset Crater, there are many turn-outs and vistas. It is not hard to find a small, private place to leave an offering (pine nuts are nice, and so are juniper berries, and both are abundant in this part of the world), and spend a moment alone with the land.

One of the most exciting sites on the nature trail at the base of Sunset Crater (so named because the cinders at the top of the cone are sunset red and orange) is an ice cave! Though the cave was closed in 1984 due to a collapse, you can step just into the entrance and a few feet back; don't go any farther. This is a rare[3] co-mingling of fire and ice, and a meditation on that duality would be appropriate. If you spend a few moments alone in the ice cave, turned away from the entrance's light, you'll probably not be interrupted.

The spectacular lava fields—plains of cinders and maze-like jutting cliffs riddled with tunnels and collapsed caverns—extend beyond the Monument boundaries. Not far from the well-developed campground, graded side roads will lead you up into the "lava woods."

A Full Moon here, on a cinder "beach" in front of the sharp black cliffs, is a treat. Young aspens grow here, their willowy branches and whispering green leaves a life-affirming contrast to the ancient lava formations. After dark, privacy is virtually assured, and the wildest beast we have ever seen here is a skunk. (There are bears, but they don't come down from the San Franciscos often.)

WUPATKI NATIONAL MONUMENT

Here, in the San Francisco Peaks west of Sunset, live the *kachinas* ["kah-chée-nahs"]. They are not gods. They are anthropomorphic representations of spirits—plant, animal, place. Their appearance is symbolic. Most stories hold that when The People first emerged, the kachinas stayed with them, guiding and teaching their rituals before The People's disrespect annoyed the kachinas so greatly that they moved away.

When Sunset erupted in the winter of 1064, the Sinaguans moved away, leaving their pit houses to be buried under lava and ash. They did not return to build again until the next century. Then the "house builders" lived in the Wupatki Basin till the mid-13th century. And while more than 100 rooms have been revealed at Wupatki (*Wupatki* means "Tall House" in Hopi; *Wukoki* means Big House; *Lomaki* means "Beautiful House") the Citadel has been left unexcavated—a way of sharing the past with the future. Meanwhile, there is plenty to evoke the medieval life of this place for today's visitors.

Wupatki.
The pine roofs are gone now, leaving sun roofs here at Wupatki, but the Sinaguans who lived here led lives totally exposed to the elements anyway, in physical and emotional harmony with the spirits that rule here still.
Photo © 1991 by Ashleen O'Gaea.

The Visitor's Center at the Wupatki National Monument, on the northwest curve of Sunset Crater's 35-mile scenic loop drive, sells audio cassettes of Carlos Nakai's flute music. He composed it and arranged traditional songs here especially for the magnificent

Wupatki.
Aligned to the rocks that support them and to nearby
encastled hills and outcroppings, these hand-built walls
at Wupatki, tall and straight, still salute the sun.
Photo © 1991 by Ashleen O'Gaea.

San Francisco Peaks, where the kachinas live. If you can buy one of these tapes and play it while you're making the leisurely (take a picnic!) 35 mile drive, you'll feel the energies of this land even in the car. In Native lore, this is a landscape of great adventure, well recounted in the books for sale at the Monument's Visitor's Centers.

Stop at each ruin and tour it. (There are brochures available at the sites.) You may be alone—and even when there are other tourists, a few minutes' patience will usually suffice to have the place to yourself. Nor are the hand-built dwellings and ceremonial centers the only attractions here. Beside Wukoki's ruins, for instance, are the wind's pueblos. These are delicate mini-caves eroded into the red sandstone hillocks, making delightful patterns; anywhere around one of these charming formations is a good place for ritual.

With a stone, a feather, a cone of incense and a small shell, you can make an offering of a tiny altar to the four directions. Take a handful of cornmeal with you and throw it to the winds for good luck! (If you don't have any cornmeal handy, use a scrap of bread or cookie, or a dram of water or soda—the important thing is to return some sustenance to the land that has given us life.)

The outline of a huge, southwest flying bird figure can be traced over the mystical landscape of north-central Arizona; the ley lines and imposing natural features suggest a pentagram and a hexagram as well. (The pentagram's two lower points are at Courthouse Rock and Lee Mountain, in the lower wing of the bird.)

Bird symbols are not uncommon to the cultures that peopled this area. There were corresponding settlements in old Mexico, where parrot feathers and other brilliant feathers were used in ritual. Trading blocks of precious salt for parrots and sea shells, Arizona's Native tribes learned to cherish exotic feathers too, in addition to those of the hawks and eagles that live in the high deserts and mountains and share their ritual power with respectful Natives.

We were fortunate on one visit to the Citadel ruin to find a long, bright iridescent blue and gold feather, inexplicable except as a gift from the gods. Another time, somewhere along the 35-mile loop, we watched a pair of eagles playing, diving and circling and swooping over the tall rocks that must have been their home. Magic has not gone underground in this place.

North and west of Sunset Crater and Wupatki is the Grand Canyon. North and east is the Four Corners area and El Malpais, New Mexico's Badlands. The Painted Desert and the Petrified Forest are there, too, and well worth seeing. But nothing can match the area between Montezuma's Well and Wupatki for dazzling desert power!

FOR MORE INFORMATION

Suggested Reading

Bahti, Tom. *Southwestern Indian Tribes*. Flagstaff, AZ: KC Publications, 1968.

_____. *Southwestern Indian Ceremonial*. Flagstaff, AZ: KC Publications, 1970.

Feher-Elston, Catherine. *Children of Sacred Ground: America's Last Indian War*. Flagstaff, AZ: Northland Publishing, 1988.

Mann, Nicholas R. *Sedona: Sacred Earth. A Guide to Geomantic Applications in the Red Rock Country*. Prescott, AZ: Zivah Publishers, 1989.

Notes

1. This refers not only to the underground springs, pools and rivers that gurgle wonderfully to the surface where you least expect them, and not only to the treasured pools of rainwater that collect in even the tiniest crevices. This refers as well to the fact that millions of years ago, what we call Arizona was a sea bed! It is possible in many places to find fossils of sea creatures, plant and animal, and to find fossilized wave patterns as well!

2. It was also damaged in 1928 when a Hollywood movie company dynamited it to simulate an eruption. This flagrant commercial blasphemy inspired Sunset's protection as a National Monument.

3. Ice doesn't often form in large caves where there's enough space for air circulation, because circulating air keeps the temperature up. This cave is too small to entertain air currents, so there's ice in it almost year-round.

Southeastern Arizona

Another bewitched area is the southeast corner of Arizona. Tucson is at its northwest corner; its boundaries are I-19, I-10 and the Mexican and New Mexico borders. Like the corridor between Montezuma's Well and Wupatki, this corner of Arizona holds much mystical power and many sacred sites, and it is difficult to discuss or experience them in isolation from one another.

At the area's heart, Tombstone, with its historic buildings and OK Corral, is a charming place to wander along the sheltered wooden sidewalks. Bisbee, an old mining town (you can tour the Lavender Pit Mine and Dine—and you can stay—at the Copper Queen Hotel; write to the Bisbee Chamber of Commerce for more information) is the southern center of the rectangle, at the intersection of AZ 90 and 92. In Benson, Willcox and Douglas, all small towns that bustled 100 years ago, more of Arizona's history is preserved, as it is in Sierra Vista and Patagonia, due south of Tucson.

And throughout this desert land, among the several "sky islands"[1] that dot the landscape, the old magic is still very strong. Through corridors like I-10's Texas Canyon and in the San Pedro Valley's riparian riverside near Benson, the power of the land makes itself felt even through several lanes of asphalt and commercial industry. In the barely inhabited spaces east of Douglas and Willcox, it is almost impossible *not* to commune with Nature.

It was in this relatively small area (roughly 120 miles by 60 miles) that the large drama we call the Old West was enacted, over a period of about 20 years. In the 19th century, the Anglo urge to dominate the territory by white settlers was almost as strong as the Native love of the land and its spirits.

The Civil War got as far west in Arizona as Yuma, but the real action didn't start until the war was over and the untamed Southwest was opened by sheep and cattle ranchers and entrepreneurs who appreciated how casually the law was applied in these parts. Arizona is mindful of its history and its reputation—and the deserts, meadows and mountains in the southeast still reflect the energy raised in the days of "cowboys and Indians."

The "vibes" that have made this land holy for thousands of

years still shimmer in the air, still echo in the hawks' cries, still haunt our souls. There are one or two sites, though, that merit particular attention, keeping in mind that their power is fed and supported by the great sacred desert in which they exist.

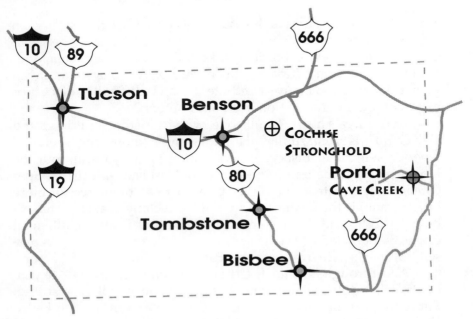

Southeastern Arizona Sites

COCHISE STRONGHOLD

The Cochise Stronghold, west of AZ 666 just north of Sunsites, was just that—Cochise's stronghold. (Farther north on AZ 666 is the settlement of Cochise; nearby is the 8100 foot, mile-long Cochise Head, a reclining profile of the chief.) The emotional intensity of the events this area has witnessed still charges the atmosphere.

This land was part of the Apache homestead, and a last shelter; but its power was great already when the Apaches came. You cannot ignore the energy, so it is fortunate that the Native reverence did and does prevail. It is hard to resist the urge to get out and walk—or dance or run or fly!—for the magic here is canyon magic, swift and nimble like the waters and winds that race between the steep walls.

There are room-sized boulders here, huge rounds and thrusts of porphyry, a granite that erodes like sandstone. There are deep empty pools, tunnels, cavelets, oak glens, and, if there's been enough rain, wild streams. There's camping here, courtesy of the U.S. Forest Service, which means there's a couple of water faucets for cooking and tooth-brushing, a "one-holer" for a toilet, and a small per-night fee. The nearest motels are in Willcox (back to I-10 and east) and Benson (back to I-10 and west); there are tiny restaurants scattered through some of the smaller settlements.

Cairn at Cave Creek.
When there aren't many flat rocks available, you can build an elf-light
with what you can find. The cairn in Cave Creek is made of conglomerate
rocks and some limestone; it's capped with a hand-sized granite chip.
At night, a votive candle will flicker inside.
Photo © 1991 by Ashleen O'Gaea.

Whether or not you have time or inclination to camp here, try making an elf-light as you "talk to" the spirits that live here. Building an elf-light—a ritual created some years ago by Tucson artist (and Witch) Faerie Moon—is easy. Collect flat rocks, and on a base ring of stones surrounding a large hearthstone, stack the next rounds so that a votive candle's light will shine from its glass container through the chinks. Once this tower is a bit taller than the candle, cap the elf-light with another wide, flat stone. Keep the candle burning in its glass container while you're there and when you leave, remove your candle without disturbing the cairn. Even when birds and small animals knock the rocks out of symmetry, the ruin of your elf-light is still an offering to the land and its spirits.

CAVE CREEK

Very near Arizona's southeastern border with New Mexico is Cave Creek (not to be confused with the Cave Creek east of Phoenix). Recently threatened by corporate gold miners, and still in need of our support[2], southeastern Arizona's Cave Creek is a world-famous birding area. But this delicate environment conceals more than rarely-seen songbirds. One of only three quartz crystal caves in the United States is hidden here, too, its entrance guarded by a locked Forest Service gate.

For a returnable deposit, the key can be obtained from the District Ranger's office in Douglas, Arizona. Write to the District Ranger at Rural Route 1, Box 228-R, Douglas, Arizona, 85607; or call (602) 364-3468. The Gadsden Hotel, a survivor of Arizona's gunslinging past, is a Douglas landmark and an evocative place to stay. (Write to the Douglas Chamber of Commerce for more information about the Gadsden.) Lodging and restaurants northeast of Douglas are few and far between, so take a picnic cooler and water even if you're not camping.

After you've picked up the key to Crystal Cave in Douglas, take AZ 80 north, through Rodeo, New Mexico, and back into Arizona toward Portal. About eight miles north of Portal, the road forks. Bear to the left. (If you've forgotten something, a few supplies are available at the Portal Store, a charming stone building under the pale orange walls of rock.) As you drive into the Canyon, 8400 foot cliffs rise on your left and the volcanic Silver Peak climbs 7,975 feet on your right. Even if you're not going to explore the cave, take your time through this canyon. Its beauty is always refreshing.

The Cave Creek Ranger Station is about a mile and a half from Portal, and just beyond it is the first campground. Keep going on the paved road, past the Southwestern Research Station's swimming pool. Bear left again at the next fork in the road—Crystal Wash is about half a mile further, on your right.

Though the graded road through Cave Creek and its many campgrounds is not difficult, Crystal Wash is not passengercar friendly. If you have a four-wheel drive vehicle, you can make it part way up, but whether you park along the side of the road at the mouth of the Wash or a few hundred yards upstream, you'll walk the last half-mile or so to the cave entrance.

The walk is not terribly hard, but you will need sturdy hiking boots and sunscreen, and *as always* anywhere in the desert, water; and if you plan to explore the cave, of course, you'll need light. Experts recommend three sources—one on your helmet, one in your hand, and one on your belt. (The first time we visited Crystal Cave, we were wearing ordinary tennis shoes, no helmets, and carrying only one flashlight each. It can be done like that, but now that we have good shoes, helmets, and more light, we wouldn't recommend it.)

Don't be discouraged by inexperience, though. The first time we visited, it was with a five year-old child, who did just fine. You don't need ropes for Crystal Cave; besides good shoes, gloves if you have them, and lots of light and water, take your camera! You should take out with you whatever you take in, and you *shouldn't* take out anything you *didn't* bring in.

Crystal Cave *is* dangerous, but so are the Interstates! Unlike the Interstates, however, Crystal Cave is a magical place. In the small rooms on the way through the entrance tunnel or in the large mezzanine room, or in any of the crystal-encrusted chambers throughout the cave, you feel the Earth's cool, soothing embrace. And you have all the privacy you need for a reverent moment or a full-blown ritual. (The acoustics are pretty good, by the way. Chants and songs sound great almost anywhere inside.)

RITUAL

What we now call the Ceremony of the Crystal Cave was originally bilingual, in Anglo-Saxon as well as modern English. We found it *very* powerful; here are the words in modern English.

Standing in one of the small rooms just below the entrance hall where the iron gate swings into the cave (and where you can safely leave anything you don't need *in* the cave), cast a Circle if you like—but do it without candles or incense to protect the cave's delicate eco-balance. These words can be spoken before you begin your exploration or when you are ready to leave the cave. They can be spoken by one person, spoken by one and affirmatively repeated by another or others, or spoken in unison by two or more people. Pause between each sentence.

The light within us shall illuminate the many darknesses around us. In this finite cosm, we embrace the several infinities that surround us. Our primal humanity rises from the neglected stones beneath our feet, through us and from us, to clarify the vision of our hearts and minds. We are here to claim the strength of darkness, the strength of peace and silence, and we will have it with us now and when we go from this place. In the name of the Earth, we go in peace.

If you cannot or would rather not explore the cave, spend some time in the Wash anyway. You'll find beautiful rocks here, many with clear or delicately colored quartz crystals shining from them. Build an altar with the ones that speak to you, and conduct your ritual in full sun, or in the shade of an overhang.

It is unusual, but you can recharge your crystals here, even under the Sun, because this is a mother-land for crystals, and it renews them to be among their own kind again no matter where they used to live.

Cave Creek (and its South Fork) slides and rushes by most of the campgrounds in the Canyon. Even when the campsites are full, if you wander by the stream you may find a living rock or a twig or branch of livewood.[3] Sometimes the sight of one of these stones or sticks, or the feel of it in your hand, lets you know that it is spirited, alive with age and wisdom and an awareness that is no less real for being different than ours.

You will know livewood or livestone when you find it by the whisper of adventure it calls from within you. Pay attention to that whisper when you hear it, and if there are words to say for the stone or the wood you've found, they will be on your tongue. Whisper them back, and the ritual, that began in the subtle guest of a walk by the stream, will be complete.

You may well spot wildlife. Antelope and deer live here; so do skunks and javelina and the ubiquitous coyote. The "hero" of many stories, the coyote is the trickster and a teacher. You may also spot roadrunners, quail, turkey vultures and hummingbirds!

Take these delightful sightings for blessings.

If you are here for more than a few hours, and you see any animal three times or more, perhaps it is one of your totems. You may feel inspired to dance for this animal, starting slowly and letting the spirit move you as it will. Maybe you will even find a bone or a feather to keep as a talisman or return as an offering.

Cave Creek.
Imposing cliffs rise thousands of feet above pine, oak, juniper
and sycamore trees. Hundreds of caves are hidden in
Cave Creek Canyon's lichen-covered granite escarpments.
Photo © 1991 by Ashleen O'Gaea.

(You are not likely to encounter anything dangerous. There are snakes, but most are harmless, and none of them are looking for trouble. It's a good idea to turn rocks over with your toe before you pick them up, though, just in case there's a scorpion underneath. Most people make enough noise to warn snakes and other creatures away from their path. If you plan on doing any hiking away from the trails, wear sturdy shoes, long pants and sleeves, a hat, and carry water.)

In a way, every inch of Arizona is magical country. Simply be-

cause so much of it seems barren to the inattentive eye, the discovery that there is life *everywhere* from the hottest sands to the coldest
lava fields, from the lowest desert to the highest mountain.

Because the deserts here, and the plants and the animals, are so
unlike what most visitors know, they are thrilling to see. It's that little "ooh," the little shudder of delight that passes through most people when they first see a blooming cactus or a wild pig, a desert
storm or an oak grove, is what tells you that magic is afoot. History
and culture would be enough, but in Arizona there is much more.

FOR MORE INFORMATION

Bisbee Chamber of Commerce, Post Office Box BA, Bisbee, AZ,
85603.

Bloomer, Howard. *Short Excursions in Arizona.* The Franklin Press,
Phoenix, AZ, 1974.

Cave Creek Ranger Station, Portal, AZ, 85632; (602) 558-2221.

Douglas Chamber of Commerce, 1125 Pan American Avenue,
Douglas, AZ, 85607.

Tombstone Chamber of Commerce, Post Office Box 339, Tombstone, AZ, 85603.

Notes

1. Sky islands are mountainous oases jutting up from the desert
   floor. The rise in elevation is swift, the change in vegetation drastic. Spring- and rain-fed streams, some of which run year-round,
   support a wide variety of plant and animal life that belies the
   myth that the desert is barren.

2. For more information and to add your voice to the chorus de-
   manding federal protection for this unique area, write to the U.S.
   Forest Service, care of the Douglas Ranger Station, and/or to your
   Congresspeople.

3. Livewood is what we call twigs or branches or boles that have
   fallen or been taken with permission from a tree in which a
   Dryad, a tree spirit, lives, and in which a bit of the parent Dryad
   still lives. A livestone is similar: it is a rock of any size in which a
   tiny clone of the original mountain, cliff or cave spirit still dwells.
   When you hold livewood or livestone in your hand, you feel as
   though you are meeting someone, not just holding a stick or a
   rock.

CALIFORNIA

San Francisco
TLAMCO

⊕ PINNACLES
NATIONAL MONUMENT

Los Angeles

Golden Gate Park

LaVedi R. Lafferty

In the heart of San Francisco, the city's rush and roar is muted by the lush green growth of Golden Gate Park, the Presidio of San Francisco and scattered, smaller parks. The peaceful, soothing atmosphere of these sites is striking in contrast to their urban setting. This area, according to esoteric tradition, was once the center of an Atlantean city, known as Tlamco.[1]

TO GOLDEN GATE PARK

Where once the Wisdom-City's temples rose
    Within her "Gates of Gold," our latter day
This noble pleasure ground but loves, and knows,
    Nor guesses where the fanes of Tlamco lay;
Yet who shall say what spell that vanished race
Bequeathed forever to this mystic place?

For through this realm enchanted, wanderers stroll—
    Or from the Seven Seas, or dwellers near—
And cares forget, while from each weary soul
    Life's heavy burden slips—till peace reigns here
Where blue sky arches over flower and palm,
    And west winds whispering, breathe a healing balm.

Here creep the old and sad, so long denied
    The welcoming smile these sunny spaces hold;
Fond lovers weave their golden dreams beside
    Gay, laughing children counting poppy gold;
To all the Park brings rest, and sweet relief
    From work or pain, or haunting wraiths of grief.
Ella M. Sexton[2]

Tlamco's Sacred Center.
Photo by LaVedi R. Lafferty.

Tlamco was a temple city of seven hills which marked the orbits and diameters of the planets, while also forming a map of the Pleiades. The evidence of these ancient temple sites remains today for those with the ears to hear and the eyes to see. In the center of the city was the Temple of the Sun, located at the present intersection of Haight and Shrader Streets, near the area chosen by the flower children of the 60s to start their peace and consciousness movement. Haight Street remains an active center of the counter culture.

To the north of the city center stood the Temple of Jupiter, a celestial observatory, located on Lone Mountain. The Lone Mountain Campus of the University of San Francisco now occupies the top of this hill. In the time of Tlamco, the diameters of the planets were calculated from the observatory to a scale of one-hundred millionths. The Temple of Venus was located to the southeast of the observatory, in the vicinity of the present Alamo Park, a peaceful and beautiful site overlooking the city of San Franciso and some much photographed turn-of-the-century period homes. The Temple of Mars was located to the southwest of Lone Mountain, on a site no longer preserved. The Temple of Saturn was situated on the south side of what is now Buena Vista Park, facing Corona Heights. The latter overlooks the city and has a museum placed beneath its craggy crown.

Northwest of Lone Mountain, on the edge of the San Francisco Presidio, was the Temple of Uranus, located on the upper end of Mountain Lake. This area is now a park with numerous waterfowl and a pair of swans on the lake and huge eucalyptus trees growing along its northeastern shore. In the heart of the ancient city and in the center of modern Golden Gate Park, stood the Temple of Neptune on the top of what is now known as Strawberry Hill. Surrounded by Stow Lake, bridges lead to the foot of the hill, a man-made waterfall tumbles out of the hillside and a serpentine path circles the hill to its top, where a fanciful stone circle has been created that brings heartfelt visions of sunken Atlantis to mind.

The earthen remains of these ancient temple sites show the planets placed in their respective relative positions, while also corresponding to a star map of the Seven Sisters of the Pleiades. Respectively, the planetary to star correspondences were as follows: Uranus to Alcyone, Neptune to Merope, Saturn to Celaeno, Jupiter to Asterope, Venus to Tayeta, Mars to Maia and Mercury to Electra (the Temple of Mercury having been located near to the Temple of the Sun).

Overlooking the Golden Gate from the Presidio are three hills understood to symbolize an end of the Bridge of Kinvat; the etheric bridge extending from the star Sirius to earth. To the south of Corona Heights rise the Twin Peaks, now topped by a radio station and its large red and white tower. It is said that a circle drawn to intersect the peaks, the North Dome in Yosemite and an ancient stone arrowhead in the San Bernardino Mountains equals one fifth the diameter of the moon. To the west of the peaks lies Laguna Honda, a lake believed to have been the original source of water supplying Tlamco via aqueducts which flowed around the Temple of Neptune and emptied into a nearby lake.

MYSTICAL SIGNIFICANCE

The ancient site of the city of Tlamco, while seldom recognized, has great significance, as witnessed by the innovative lifestyles and the force of movements begun in San Francisco. Ancient and modern residents have responded to the potency of the energy radiating from this large-scale natural power point. The Atlantean temples were constructed to harmonize with earthly, planetary and stellar energies, up to the time of the final submergence of Atlantis. At that time mighty earthquakes rocked the globe, leveling Tlamco as well. From the Mayan calendar this is calculated to have occurred in 8498 B.C., and was possibly the result of a comet or an asteroid striking the planet on the east coast of North America.[3]

The three hills overlooking the Golden Gate symbolizes the earthly end of the Bridge of Kirtvat (Chinvat Peretu) and represents a Buddhic connection with the Great White Lodge of the Dog-Star, Sirius. Kinvat is called the bridge of the gatherer or judge, leading to the higher mental plane from lower Dusakh Abyss (astral plane).[4] "The Dog Sirius (Sura) is another watchman of the heavens; but he is fixed in place, at the bridge of Kinvat, keeping guard over the Abyss Dusakh out of which Ahrilian (desire-mental principle) comes."[5] The bridge is crossed by fixing the hills in concentration, by steadying the mind until desire is stilled and fixity of purpose is gained through the power, tenacity and will seated in the causal body. When the feather of the personality (desire) balances perfectly with the heart of the soul (love), the bridge may be crossed. This etheric column is said to be held fast to earth by the pressure of a vortex. At the time of the submergence this column is said to have closed in upon itself at the upper end.

The city of Tlamco is believed to have been laid out in a circular pattern with the Temple of the Sun at its center. No physical evidence remains of this site except an atmosphere that is perceptible where it once stood. The ancient religions generally agree that the visible sun was the reflector of, rather than the source of power, reflecting the light of the spiritual sun. As Paracelsus wrote, "There is an earthly sun, which is the cause of all heat. There is an Eternal Sun, which is the source of all wisdom, and those whose spiritual senses have awakened to life will see that sun and be conscious of His existence; but those who have not attained spiritual consciousness may yet feel His power by an inner faculty which is called Intuition."[6]

From the heart of the city of Tlamco streets are said to have radiated out to the other temples in a circular design similar to the great city in Atlantis described by Plato in *Critias*. The sites of the temples of Mercury and Mars are obliterated, but the Temple of Venus would have been located in the vicinity of Alamo Square, four blocks of green knolls overlooking Steiner Street with its row of ornate, often photographed, pastel-colored houses, typifying Venus which rules all things beautiful and artful.

Venus was known as a feminine planet and its temples were overseen by the priestesses. Venus is considered to be the daughter of the Moon and symbolic of the many forms of her Great Mother. In Greek and Hindu legends of the birth of Venus she emerges from the sea, symbol of the source of all life. She was thought to be the goddess of protection, acting through the love of divinity and inspiring humanity towards the bounties of life, its refinements and higher sentiments, as well as its pleasures. Mars, on the other hand, is opposite in polarity to Venus and the temples dedicated to Mars were masculine, housed warriors and were related to defense and aggression acting through the manifestation of power and destroying energies.

The vanished Temple of Mercury would have been related to use of mind, communication and development of conscious intuitive perception. The Temple of Jupiter, related to higher consciousness, was at the top of Lone Mountain where Hotara Observatory now stands. Jupiter is a planet of expansion and preservation, representing the triumph of the soul over earthly experience and attainment of universal awareness. It rules both universal wisdom and higher education. The Jupiterian energies appear to still be manifest on this site, as demonstrated by the Lone Mountain Campus of the University of San Francisco placed here.

The Temple of Saturn, located on Park Hill in what is now Buena Vista Park, dealt with the mysteries of death. Saturn represents another aspect of Venus, but instead of birth into material life, it brings physical death and rebirth into the life of the soul. Through Saturn's disciplines we are taught how to live selflessly in the world of matter and be directed toward karmic fulfillment and spiritual values. This is a slow process that often involves the acceptance of responsibilities and gradual elimination of illusions, leading toward liberation by depersonalization of the self.

The Temple of Uranus, which stood on the northern shore of Mountain Lake, also dealt with affairs of the dead and is said to have housed the Hall of Judgement. The cemetery of Tlamco is supposed to have been located south of the lake on hills which form a natural division between Golden Gate Park and Sutro Heights.

Uranus, or Ouranos, was the eldest of the gods and his name means "heaven." He wed Ge, the earth goddess, who bore Saturn (Kronos). Unable to bear the light of the electrifying life-force, the human children of the gods were buried in form and darkness, under the dominion of Saturn and time. As humanity learns to reach beyond the limits of earth and to utilize the power of the outer planets, Uranus, Neptune and Pluto, higher intuitive faculties are awakened and cosmic insight begins to manifest. The Temple of Uranus was connected with the realization of life beyond form, higher guidance and directed cosmic energies.

The site best preserved is where the Temple of Neptune once stood on the top of Strawberry Hill. As a higher octave of Venus, Neptune inspires the creative imagination, mystical experience and clairvoyance made manifest through a selfless emotional nature, one that loves without expectation of return. The temples dedicated to Neptune were schools where those chosen for their psychic ability learned to use and direct their aptitude. A monastery stood at the top of Strawberry Hill.

Perhaps of greatest significance of all is the placement of the temples to form the map of the Pleiades. Traditionally considered as the center of the Milky Way Galaxy the Pleiades, located in the constellation of Taurus, frequently had temples oriented in relationship to them. In Mexico it was held that a destruction of the world had occurred at their midnight culmination. From the center of a particular star in the Pleiades issues a ray of divine spirit that merges with life on earth. The energies of this ray can be gathered and united via the will until the necklace of the Pleiades loosens the belt of Orion, the latter considered to be the band of causation and limitation. In anatomical terms, the belt circles the body at the dividing point between higher and lower energies, while a necklace, circling the throat represents insight gained through the higher head centers and shared as truth.

SUGGESTED RITUAL

Two sites are eminently appropriate for ritual: Strawberry Hill (Temple of Neptune) and Mountain Lake (Temple of Uranus). On the top of Strawberry Hill a stone circle has been set and the atmosphere is decidedly mystical, though it is least likely to afford full privacy, unless approached at sunrise. The latter site, St Mountain Lake, offers a natural circle formed by the eucalyptus trees and reasonable seclusion, though it also would be most private at sunrise. This site feels the closest to nature energies, being essentially undisturbed.

At the Mountain Lake site a ceremony invoking the influence of the Pleiades and the Cosmic Virgin is suggested. Choose one of the natural circles formed by the towering trees and stand in the middle. Center yourself by taking a few deep breaths and focusing your awareness inwardly. Then facing the east, extend your right hand with the index and middle fingers pointing outward. Take a deep breath and visualize energy gathering in your hand. Visualize this energy flowing outward as blue flame, and turning to your right draw a full circle of blue flame around yourself, following the outer perimeter of the natural clearing you have chosen. Know that you stand on hallowed ground.

Think of yourself as working consciously as a soul, a channel for the energies you seek to invoke and share with your environment through yourself. Facing eastward, open and continue with the following adaptations of Atlantean invocations:[7]

May the energy of the Divine Self inspire and the light of the Soul direct; may I be led from darkness to light, from the unreal to the real, from death to immortality.

Proceed with the following, still facing the east and with arms extended forward, palms upward, in a receptive pose:

O Thou who in thine incomparable beauty risest from the deep!
Thou who dwellest in all form, and givest life to all emanations!
Thou who ridest on the whirlwind!
Gird Thy children with the armor of Light.

Turn to the south, raising your arms overhead, still in a receptive posture:

Thou who at thy rising doth manifest the splendor of truth,
And at Thy meridian causest the fruit of the earth to ripen in its season,
Give, at thy setting, peace to all thy children.

Turning to the west, extend your arms outward, palms outward in cosmic communion:

Thou who dwellest in the manifest and the invisible,
And makest one the astral deep and the mountain of substance,
Grant union to the souls of thy people.

Finally, turning to the north, cross your right arm over your left over your heart and in, an anchoring mode:

Thou whose sandals crush the head of malice and discord
And who dost establish on the rock of eternity thy seal of power,
Make on thy right hand a dwelling for thy children of mortality.

Contemplate the meaning, as in Milton's description of creation in relation to the sun:[8]

...the gray
Dawn and the Pleiades before him danc'd,
Shedding sweet influence...

Bearing in mind the influence at your throat of the necklace or rosary of the Pleiades, sound the OM three times with deep feeling. Then in closing touch your hands behind you and before you, at the same time visualizing the release of the energies of the magical circle you have created.

On Strawberry Hill, where the stone circle brings to mind watery visions of lost Atlantis, a different type of ritual invocation is suggested, designed to dispel Neptunian fog. Standing in the center of the stone circle create a ring of fire around you as previously described and focus yourself in light. Then begin with the following dedication:[9]

I plunge myself into the pool of wisdom. From thence I come,
bearing a knowledge of its mysteries to share with all life.

Feel the presence of your soul, aligning your soul and brain via mind. Sound the OM, then, if in the morning, visualize a deep rose-colored lotus with a stream of rose-colored light pouring forth and engulfing you and any associates. (If at noon visualize a golden lotus or if at sunset change the color to electric blue with a golden sun at the center.)

Withdraw your awareness from the physical to the astral body and be conscious of your feelings. Then visualizing your mental body, recognize yourself as a whole, harmonious and integrated personality—physical, emotional and mental. At you do this visualize threads of golden light connecting these bodies, passing from the heart to the head and connecting you, the personality, with your soul.

Pause and know that you are now standing before the Angel of the Presence, your fully integrated Self, without duality or separation, a manifestation of God in Light.

Turning to the south, voice the following modified portions of ancient Atlantean chants, arms extended if you wish:[10]

> *I stand between the Heavens and Earth! Hark to my joyous chant; the work is done. My ear is deaf to the calls of earth, except to the small voice of souls hidden within form, for they are myself; with them I am at-one.*

Turning westward, continue:

> *One voice rings clear, and in its many tones the little voices of form dim and fade out. I dwell in the world of unity. I know all souls are one.*

> *Swept am I by the Universal Life—I see all lesser energies die out. I am the One. I am the form in which all forms are merged. I am the soul in which all souls are fused. I am the one Life, and in that Life, all little lives remain.*

Turn to the north:

> *Having entered this world of the Self, I remain greater; my daily life is overshadowed.*

> *I the manifesting Self, through the magical power of my nature, revitalize and redeem the self dwelling in form.*

Finally, returning to the east, conclude by visualizing the life and light of the Angel of the Presence in your body and *know* it is there, illuminating mind, rendering your emotional body positive and quiescent, while invigorating the physical. Will that it is so. Then visualize the light pouring through you and share it with all who are close to you and all peoples, while sounding the OM three times. Finish by releasing the energies of your magical circle.

If privacy should be lacking, you may certainly proceed with the above rituals silently and with visualized motions. Your concentration is most important and you should seek to avoid distraction or self-consciousness due to the presence or interruption by others, since these are public parks. The efficacy of these potent formulas depends upon the focused will and visualization.

FOR MORE INFORMATION

Location
The sites described are either within or in the near vicinity of Golden Gate Park in San Francisco. A detailed map of the city is helpful, if you wish to make a full tour of the various locations mentioned. An excellent overview of the city can be gained from Twin Peaks, said to show the eccentricities of the earth's orbit to one fifty-millionth's of its full size. The peaks are reached by going south on 7th Avenue until it becomes Laguna Honda (named after the ancient source of water) then Woodside Avenue which turns into Portola Drive. Turn north as it becomes Portola onto Twin Peaks Boulevard. The streets are short and twisty and it is easy to get lost, but you will arrive if you keep going uphill.

Descending from Twin Peaks if you follow Twin Peaks Boulevard down going northward, with a left on Remberton and another on Clayton, you will arrive at Market. Turning north off Market onto Castro street and west on 15th Street will lead you up toward Corona Heights (known in Atlantean times as Mt. Olympus), where a natural stone formation creates a golden crown at the crest. This site was said to represent one of the rings of Saturn. At present the Randall Museum for children is located on Museum Way, which winds around the stone formation.

Descending eastward from Corona Heights to Divisadero Street, you can proceed north until you reach Hayes Street, then turn east to Stiener Street and you will have reached Alamo Square (vicinity of the Temple of Venus).

Circling the square to Fulton Street and proceeding west will take you to Masonic Avenue. Turning north on Masonic and then west on Turk Street will lead you to Lone Mountain, site of the Temple of Jupiter and stellar reflecting pools of the observatory.

Proceeding west two blocks from the campus to Stanyan Street, then south to Haight Street and east one block to Shrader Street will bring you to the area where the Temple of the Sun stood in the ancient city of Tlamco.

To reach Golden Gate Park go south one block from Haight to Waller Street and turn west. Waller will become Kezar Drive, then Lincoln Way which follows the lower edge of the park. Turn north on 19th Avenue into the park, turn east onto South Drive then north onto Stow Lake Drive, a one-way street encircling the lake and Strawberry Hill (site of the Temple of Neptune). Continue on Stow Lake Drive past the boathouse, keep to the right and park near the bridge that crosses the lake to Strawberry Hill. A stairway leads directly to the top of the hill, passing the waterfall, or you may prefer to take the spiral path leading magnificently to the stone circle at the top.

To reach Mountain Lake from the park return to South Drive, turn west to 19th Avenue and then go north. 19th will become Park Presidio Boulevard. Continue north to Lake Street, then turn east, stopping at the upper end of 9th, 10th or 11th Avenues. A path leads to the lake from 9th Avenue. You can walk to the upper shore by turning right toward a stone wall, then keeping to the left as you follow a road that leads by the grove on the northeastern side of the lake.

One last site that is of interest is an ancient cave near the Cliff House—an old retreat of the Great White Brotherhood. Returning south on Park Presidio Boulevard, turn west on Geary Boulevard, which becomes Point Lobos Avenue As you approach the coast you will see a park and just past it a road that leads down to the seaside and a man-made tunnel. Inside the tunnel is a viewsite into the cave. What was apparently the original entrance to the cave, known as Ingharep in the long ago, has been sealed shut. The cave was said to mark the orbit of Uranus from the center of Tlamco.

Local Assistance

Information about Golden Gate Park is available from the information center at the Academy of Sciences inside the park off South Drive. The Recreation and Park Department office for Golden Gate Park is located at Fell and Stanyan Streets. Its phone number is (415) 558-3706. For general information on the Golden Gate National Recreation Area, you may call (415) 556-0560. For information about the San Francisco area the phone number for the San Francisco Junior Chamber of Commerce is (415) 337-2593.

Accommodations

A full range of hotels and motels, plus RV parks, is available in the area. For information on camping you may call California State Parks Reservations at (800) 444-7275. Information on youth hostels is available from (415) 863-9939.

Notes

1. Colburn, Frona Eunice Wait. *Yermah the Dorado*. New York: The Alice Harriman Co., 1913, p. 2.

2. Ibid, p. i.

3. Muck, Otto. *The Secret of Atlantis*. New York: Wm. Collins Sons & Co. Ltd. and Quadrangle/The New York Times Book Co., Inc., 1978, p. 248.

4. Gaskell, G. A. *Dictionary of all Scriptures and Myths*. New York: Avenel Books, 1960, p. 128.

5. Ibid, p. 694.

6. Hall, op. cit., p. LI.

7. Bailey, Alice A. *Discipleship in the New Age*. Vol. I, New York: Lucis Publishing Co., 1981, p. 547-8.

8. Allen, Richard Hinckley. *Star Names, Their Lore and Meaning*, New York: Dover Publications, Inc., 1963, p. 394.

9. Bailey, op. cit. pp. 357-9.

10. Bailey, Alice A. *A Treatise on White Magic*. New York: Lucis Publishing Co., 1972, pp. 386-7.

Pinnacles National Monument

Richard Ely and Anodea Judith

What makes a particular site on the Earth a sacred site?

In truth the entire Earth is sacred, yet some places seem to have a more powerful presence than others. This may be due to spectacular scenery or unusual features, or it may be something beyond the physical characteristics where an indwelling energy enlivens our beings and expands our consciousness. The identity of this energy remains a mystery. It may be that naturally occurring geomagnetism and telluric electrical energy is particularly concentrated in the sacred place. Some might say that the spirits (devas) of those places are particularly potent and therefore capable of being felt by the average human being. But it is an energy that can be felt tangibly by anyone who enters with an open and reverent state of mind.

The national parks of North America are the natural world's equivalent to the cathedrals and temples of the Old World. This is especially true for people who are involved in Earth-centered religions, for as the tide of environmental destruction rises, parks, wilderness areas and refuges are the main places where one can meet Nature spirits in anything approaching their old power. We have long suspected that those fortunate few places that have been protected had particularly potent devas associated with them, devas that were able to reach enough people to inspire them to undertake the difficult task of ensuring legal protection of their home.

Pinnacles National Monument, located in the California Coast Ranges south of Hollister, is a place of especially potent energy. The park is one of the oldest National Monuments in the National Park system, having been set aside by Theodore Roosevelt in 1908 shortly after passage of the Antiquities Act. What spirit powers do you suppose were active here to arrange such timely protection?

Perhaps it was the spirit of the rocks themselves, for Pinnacles is a place heavily adorned with sculptured rock spires rising out of the earth in a myriad of shapes, colors, and sizes. The rocks, made of

Pinnacles National Monument.
Photo by Richard Ely.

volcanic breccia, have been shaped by wind, rain, and earthquake, have tumbled down hillsides and piled into canyons to create an exciting landscape that changes with every step along the path.

From the hot, dry top of the high peaks, where the light is bright and the view is clear for miles around, to the cool, dark passageways of the two caves where one can crawl through narrow openings in the rocks in pitch darkness, Pinnacles National Monument offers a chance to experience a variety of contrasts. Formed by the combination of volcanic and seismic activity, with a heavy dosage of time and natural weathering, Pinnacles is a place of especially strong earth power.

The major attraction of the park is the Pinnacles Rocks, a 3-mile long, half-mile high ridge of volcanic rock that has been eroded into a fabulous array of cliffs, towers, fissures, ramparts and grottos reminiscent of the Southwestern deserts. The ridge is crossed by two narrow canyons choked by enormous boulders that have rolled and slid from the adjacent heights, as a result of earthquakes on the nearby San Andreas fault. As the boulders rolled into the canyons, they formed what is known as Talvus caves, caves whose floor is the bottom of the canyon and whose ceilings, are the base of the huge boulders unable to fit into the canyon floor. The caves underneath these boulders are accessible by trail, and provide a perfect location for one to have an experience of the chthonic realm of the Underworld in safe and relatively comfortable circumstances.

One can also ascend to the high rocks on a beautiful system of trails, tunnels and stairways cut into the rock by the Civilian Conservation Corps in the 1930s. Here the powers of heaven, light and air are supreme, and you can gaze over miles of wild countryside while swallows swirl and slice the air at 60 mph a few feet from your body.

One of the most fascinating qualities of Pinnacles is the abundance of very large animal shapes that one can see in the rocks. Elephantine shapes are particularly common, in some places forming whole ranks of stone creatures standing a hundred feet high, half emergent from the cliff face. At night in the moonlight it is but a small step to feel the presence of the spirits in these rocks, beings of great antiquity whose spirit may be dwelling there. The method we have found best for perceiving the rock spirits is to look for the eyes in the rocks along with some well defined element of their anatomy. The shock of recognition can be quite startling, giving one the feeling of being watched at all times by silent, unmoving guardian entities. We recommend finding one of these beings who particularly appeals to you, and sitting quietly in your personal meditative posture while in contact with the rocks. Allow your mind to vibrate more and more slowly until you perceive the presence of something very old and very slow. Be silent and listen.

THE UNDERWORLD JOURNEY—BEAR GULCH CAVE

There are few natural places that lend themselves quite so perfectly to a ceremonial Underworld journey as Bear Gulch Cave in Pinnacles National Monument. Formed by huge boulders choking a canyon, the cave extends a quarter of a mile along a cascading seasonal underground stream. Surrounded outside by the towering cliffs of breccia, and located a few miles from one of the most active earthquake faults in the world, the cave is a place of extraordinary natural earth power.

The Underworld has always been a place of miracle and mystery. Legends of death and rebirth, challenge and quest, ruin and renewal, say that the Underworld is a kind of sacred chamber in which the secrets of the universe are kept.

In ancient times, powerful ceremonies were conducted in honor of the Underworld and its mysterious position in the spiral from death to rebirth. Between early August to the Winter Solstice, rituals such as the Eleusinian Mysteries of ancient Greece were held to honor the Great Mother's power to create life amid darkness and death. These rites were often performed in caves, which represented the womb of the Earth Mother, and thus the vaginal pathway to Her inner mysteries and rebirth.

Traditionally, an Underworld journey consists of certain key elements. R. J. Stewart, in his book *The Underworld Initiation*, describes them as follows:

1. The Gate to the Underworld must be sought by the Traveler.
2. He or she finds the Gate, and passes within.
3. The Journey has specific stages, encounters, and beings.
4. At the culmination of a series of transformations, the Traveler is released from the Underworld; at this point the Keys to a new Mystery are received.

At the Gate to the Underworld there are signs warning of the danger within; sometimes the traveler is required to make some sort of sacrifice or offering in order to proceed. Often the Underworld is approached by stages, with several gates one must pass through. At each of these gates, the Traveler may be met by an archetypal energy or entity—e.g., the dog Cerberus, the Furies, Tantalus—who may make demands for offerings and sacrifices; or else present a challenge, an enigma, or a test of courage or will. Orpheus was able to descend into the Underworld unimpeded because of his ability to enchant these entities with his melancholy song—including the King of the Underworld himself, Hades, who is said to have cried tears of iron when Orpheus sang. Hades found a different way of testing Orpheus, the result of which Orpheus lost his beloved Euridice to the Underworld forever.

In the Sumerian myth of the Goddess Ishtar's descent into the Underworld there were seven gates, each of which took away an article of clothing, tokens of her power; thus She entered the last Gate powerless, naked and unadorned, where she was held prisoner by her sister, Allutu, the Queen of the Underworld. She then became lifeless for a metaphorical three days, and at which time all vegetation on earth withered in sympathy for her. Eventually her loved ones above where able to send down the magic Waters of Life to revive her.

In the Eleusinian Mysteries, the journey to the Underworld consisted of a long passage from town to town, with nine days of fasting before entering the sacred precinct of the Telesterion. During the journey there were a series of dramatic events depicting the story of Demeter, the Grain Goddess, in search of her daughter, Persephone, who had been abducted into the Underworld. Travelers entered the emotional state of the grieving Goddess during their nine days of travel; their charge was to find Persephone in the Underworld and convince her to return to her mother. Though a mystery was revealed only to participants in the Underworld chamber, and to this day never revealed to any non-initiates, participants were able to transform this grief into a joyous experience of rebirth. And thus the cycle of death into life was assured for yet another year.

Bear Gulch Cave is a long pathway winding around huge fallen boulders, and is open at both the upper and lower end. If conducting an Underworld journey, it is best to begin at the top of the cave, which allows one to go downhill as they make their descent. This involves traveling the Moses Spring nature trail (about one mile uphill, gently sloping) over the top of the cave as far as a steeply descending path to the cave entrance, which is marked by a metal gate. The gate is open 24 hours a day, except in the case of possible flood or rock instability, in which case it would be closed for safety reasons. (Trail maps are available at the park entrance.)

As the boulders overhead allow occasional shafts of light to penetrate the cave, the passage is most dramatic when traversed at night with a flashlight, candle, or lantern. It is not permissible to park all night in the parking lot below without prior permission from the Park Service, but an evening sojourn into the cave is allowed. Because few people choose to do so one can be relatively assured of quiet and solitude after the last hikers and climbers have gone in at sunset.

The upper portion of the cave passage is far narrower than the lower passage. We have found there to be six natural chambers connected by a sinuous path around the boulders. Some of the passages require crawling on hands and knees, and the floor is often wet. One can fit through with a small backpack on, and the narrow passages are only a few feet long, and well-marked by white arrows painted on the rocks. It is not difficult for anyone in reasonable physical condition to fit through these passages, but someone with claustrophobia may feel a bit panicky.

The six natural chambers around the rocks, divided by narrow passageways, comprise the first six of the seven gates. After six natural gates, one enters a large flat roofed circular chamber with a nearly level floor, about 40 feet in diameter, and with a ceiling height of about 15 feet. The ceiling is formed by a huge single boulder, approximately 100 feet high that slid from the upper mountains in prehistoric time. Here one can meditate in the cave, sing devotional songs, drum or dance. The large chamber is about one-third of the way along the complete passage.

The other side of the large chamber comprises the last gate, and opens northward to a long and beautiful descent downward. The walk is mostly down a winding flight of stairs (about 150) carved into the rock. There are railings at precipitous places, and one can hear the sound of a creek flowing through during the rainy season, and see the beautiful carving and watermarks left on the rocks by the millennia of water flowing through the passage. The descent is a

Pinnacles National Monument.
Photo by Richard Ely.

sacred walk, and we recommend that it be done alone with candle-light, rather than flashlight. One wants to take their time and feel the deep mysteries of the Mother's depths around them.

Eventually, the descent levels out and there are additional side chambers where one can enter into a deep meditation on one's purpose. There is a final metal gate to the outer world where one can exit the cave and return to the parking lot down the hill, or turn around and return up the stairs and go back up to the large chamber.

There is a second cave in Pinnacles National Monument called the Balconies Cave, most accessible from the west side of the park. This is a wonderful cave to explore, but does not lend itself to a vision quest, as it is smaller, and lets in a lot more light. However, the winding and fairly level walk to Balconies Cave along Old Pinnacles Trail passes the base of spectacular rocky spires, is good for bird watching and easy enough for children and inexperienced hikers. Both caves are exciting for children and safe enough for them to explore.

There are many more miles of beautiful trails at Pinnacles which climb to heights and traverse astounding rock formations. Most notably, the High Peaks trail, which is fairly strenuous, leads to a cluster of rock formations that have numerous fissured passageways among them, as well as scenic views of the surrounding countryside. The rocks at the top have a labyrinthine quality reminiscent of ancient mystery sites. Each spire is something to explore, and the rock spirit energy is particularly strong.

Climate
In summer months, Pinnacles Monument is very hot and dry. One must carry water and be prepared for temperature above 100 degrees. Even in the hot, dry summer season, the cave is still cool and damp, with a fairly constant temperature day or night of about 55-60 degrees. In the spring, Pinnacles abounds with wildflowers and the climate is milder. The best time to visit is from March to May when the wildflowers are in bloom and the creeks are flowing. Winter can be surprisingly mild during the daytime, although the nights are cold. The advantages of the winter are that the creeks begin flowing again, the grasses, ferns and mosses become green and lush, visitors are few and campsites are easy to come by.

FOR MORE INFORMATION

Where To Stay

There are two campgrounds at Pinnacles. The privately owned Pinnacles Camping Ground is just outside the eastern boundary of the monument, off Highway 146. It is a lovely wooded campground along a year-round creek with 78 private campsites, 14 large group sites, a swimming pool, showers, and a small store where you can buy firewood and snack food. Chapotral Campground is within the park and located on the west side of the monument at the end of State 146, close to Balconies cave. This campground has 25 walk-in sites that are particularly popular with rock climbers. Most visitors prefer the east side because more trails and facilities are available there, and the larger campground assures a better chance of getting a site. The closest motels to the park are in Hollister, King City and Soledad.

Things To Do

Ranger presentations are given in Pinnacles Campground that give information on the geology and the local flora and fauna within the park, there is also a small visitors center with an excellent geologic display, publications and maps.

Hikes and trails are numerous, with varying levels of difficulty. The short walk to Bear Gulch Caves is relatively easy, though uphill, and the long walk through the valley to Balconies Caves is relatively level. The High Peaks trail is strenuous but worth the climb, and for those who want to rest quietly in the scenery, one can go through the caves to a small reservoir and sit upon its shores. Chalone Peak trail is long and dry with less spectacular rock formations, but a very wide view from the top. For those more adventurous, there is a 7.6 mile North Wilderness trail which goes from the Chaparral Campground to the Old Pinnacles Trail, at a point 1.6 miles from the Chalone Creek picnic area.

Pinnacles is also known for its rock climbing. The challenging cliffs made of the tough volcanic breccia make it ideal for rock climbing—lots of handholds with very sturdy rock There are hundreds of established routes for everyone from beginners to experts. For more information on rock climbing. One can refer to Paul Gagner's book, *A Climber's Guide to Pinnacles National Monument*. The Visitor Center also sells a small guidebook for $2.50 with information on trails, history, geology, and natural history.

How to Get There

From the north, the east side of Pinnacles is about three hours from the San Francisco Bay. To reach the east side one takes US Highway 101 south to Highway 25, which passes through Hollister, as far as State Highway 146, and then go 5 miles west on State 146 to the park. The west side of the park can be reached in about four hours from the Bay Area by following Highway 101 south past Salinas to Soledad where one turns east on State 146, 15 miles to the park (note: State 146 consists of two segments that do not connect across the park).

From the south one can enter the park from the west by taking US Highway 101 to State 146 at Soledad. To enter the park from the east, leave Highway 101 at King City, 18 miles south of Soledad, and take Highway G13 for 15 miles east to State 25, then north 14 miles to State 146 and turn west.

There is a gate fee of $3 to get into the Monument. This fee is good for seven days, and also gives you a trail map.

COLORADO

Denver

Manitou Springs

Manitou Springs

Anne Lyddane

In this era of polluted waters, it is heartening to see the residents and visitors to Manitou Springs filling bottles and jars with the sparkling, effervescent liquid pouring from various springs in the downtown section of this little spa resort town.

Although there are approximately twenty-six of these springs, only around seven are actually active for present use. The Mineral Springs Foundation of Manitou has formed to restore and preserve these natural waters. These springs filter out the limestone and dolomite that lie deep under the mountains and dissolve the minerals and carbon dioxide, providing the distinctive flavor and sparkle.

Strolling around this delightful small city, you walk past several of these springs right on the main street, as well as several roads winding up into the hills. Each of the available springs has its individual taste according to the mineral content. The Manitou Spa in its lobby offers you a taste of their bubbling soda spring, as well as homemade lemonade during the summer months. You may also stop and seat yourself on the corner of the Avenue, helping yourself to the flowing waters in a fountain there. Around that corner and up a winding street is another easily accessible fountain with deliciously foaming waters. Another choice appears at the foot of the attractive stone post office, tiled into the wall and gushing forth clear, clean soda water.

Manitou Springs lies at the foot of Pikes Peak, and was founded around 1872 and called the "Saratoga of the West." Much of its current architecture is Victorian in style, with large, fertile gardens and gazebos to charm you. A creek runs right along the main street, and there are several parks and playgrounds, walks and trails throughout the town.

MYSTICAL SIGNIFICANCE / RITUAL

The word "Manitou" comes from Algonquin and it means "Great Spirit," or a hidden, magic power controlling nature. When the first white men came here, they found that the word "Manitou" was frequently associated in Indian usage with water, springs, creeks or waterfalls, denoting the Indian's reverence for these waters.

When Lt. Pike and his party arrived here, they discovered bubbling springs at the foot of Pikes Peak which were worshipped by the Algonquin, Arapahoe, Kiowas, Ute, Comanche, Shoshone, Cheyenne and Sioux. The springs were called "Medicine Fountains," and gifts such as robes, blankets, knives, beads, etc., were bestowed upon them. At times, whole villages visited the springs to pay homage to these sacred fountains. Several tribes in this region believed that these waters were the home of a spirit who breathed through the springs, causing their motion. They thought this water god had the power to ordain the outcome of war expeditions, and they left gifts to propitiate the Spirit.

All of these Indian nations regarded the springs of Manitou with a sense of holiness and awe. They undoubtedly had rituals fitting their needs and concepts, both of which no longer are available to us. However, Manitou Springs is not a difficult place in which to engage in your personally tailored ritual. Since its inception, it has called to those who are individualistic, lovers of freedom of expression and style, and there is a wonderful sense of non-judgment present. During the months from late May to late September, the town is full of visitors enjoying the clean, fresh air, the lofty mountains, the evergreens and the brilliant sunshine. Draw apart to your chosen spot—whether it be near a spring, fountain, the wooded hills, or one of the parks along the creek.

The Great Spirit Manitou is not always only in the springs and waters, but rides high in the mountains, healing and regeneration pouring from nature forces to you. This region offers you opportunities for releasing pain, guilt, grief, angers and any residue you wish to dissolve. Here is a suggested ritual you may find useful:

Breath is always important, so fill your lungs with the healing spirit, taking the air down deeply into your lungs, and exhaling slowly. Repeat inhale, relax, dismiss tensions and stress—exhale. If you have decided to work at a spring, take your glass or bottle filled with the waters, and sip. Feel the cleansing throughout your being.

Let go and feel poisons leave you forever.

Some of you may be clairaudient, and you will hear music, singing, drums, a chorus of voices in gratitude and blessing. Others may be clairvoyant, and will see some of the tribes and their responses. Emanations from Manitou may also appear flowing toward and then through you. Whatever your reactions, let go of all negativity. If you decide to do this exercise at sunrise, feel the rays of its warmth. If at sunset, enjoy the gorgeous colors vibrating over the mountains. During the day, let the music of the streams and creeks, the sunshine, the fragrance of flowers and plants heal you.

Manitou Springs.
Photo courtesy of Anne Lyddane.

Spend whatever time seems best to you. Then, picture our planet which needs cleansing and healing so badly. Fill it with light. Let the flowing vitality of the Great Manitou Spirit encompass not only You, but All. Refreshing, healing and transforming results contribute joy, love, peace and brotherhood.

If you decide to enjoy your ritual at night, the brilliant, scintillating stars and light of the Moon add further beauty and force. There is a special, effective Light streaming from these skies above Manitou. When you complete your ritual, you will feel integrated, restored to the Higher God Self you truly are.

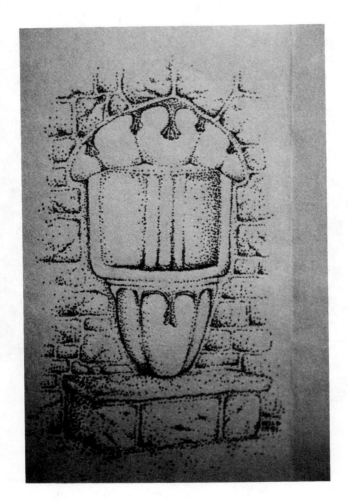

Wheeler Spring.
Original drawing by William Wild.

FOR MORE INFORMATION

Directions

Take Exit 141 on Hwy 24 from I-25. Go west about 4 miles to the Manitou Exit.

Lodging

There are numerous places to stay for all size families, or singles, as well as budgets in Manitou Springs and environs.

Suggested

Manitou Spa Bed and Breakfast Hotel, Manitou Ave. Expensive. Includes use of whirlpool, fountain, breakfast and hor d'oeuvres and beverages.

Gray's Avenue Hotel, a Victorian Bed and Breakfast. Listed in the National Register of Historic Places, built around 1886. Prices range from $45 to $70.

El Colorado Lodge. Pool, patio, barbeque grill, basketball and shuffleboard courts, medium prices.

Garden of the Gods Campground. Near all places you may wish to visit. Every amenity. Tent on Manitou Creek area; adult region, youth hostel.

There are many other opportunities available, with a wide variety of prices and moderate facilities.

Restaurants

Great varieties of food and drink, from continental, expensive restaurants to small bars and family-style eating places. Many health food menus too.

Craftwood Inn—casual, country elegance. Expensive, but so charming.

The Briarhurst Manor—a Tudor mansion, spacious lawns, gardens and views. International cuisine; the Chef has served royalty.

CONNECTICUT

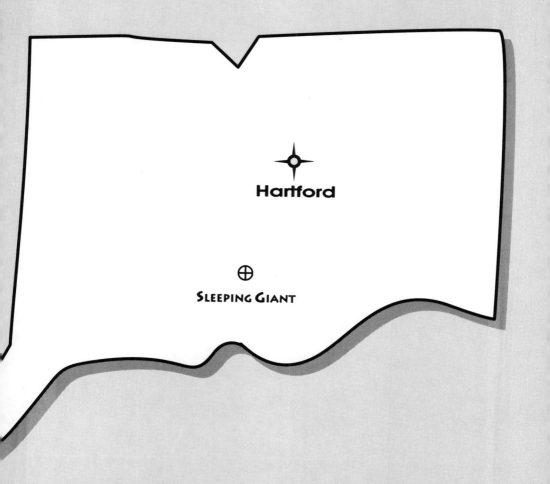

Hartford

SLEEPING GIANT

The Sleeping Giant

P. Scott Hollander

Trap rock, a layered basalt, is common in Connecticut. It's often cut into gravel and used to form a durable roadbed for streets and highways. Trap rock ridges, the result of early volcanic activity, are just as common; there are five such ridges in the small city of Hamden alone. But there is only one, located mostly in northern Hamden about six miles north of New Haven, that runs from east to west. And that one has the unmistakable shape of a supine human form.

Two miles long, covering about 2500 acres, and rising up to 739 feet (at the Chest) above the flatlands surrounding it, the Sleeping Giant lies on his back with his head to the west, his feet to the east, and his square, clearly defined chin raised defiantly to the sky.

A completely natural landmark, the Giant has, from earliest times, inspired fascination and even awe in anyone who has approached him. The original Amerindian inhabitants of the area held him in reverence; and the practical, "god-fearing" and unsuperstitious Yankees who've taken their place have fought miners, developers and vandals to keep the Giant pristine and intact. To anyone who has ever visited the area, and certainly to those who live here, the Giant is a living presence with his own distinct personality. And pages of lyrical descriptions of the Giant all refer to *his* view; *his* parklands; *his* mountain.

To geologists, of course, this is all nonsense. The Blue Ridge Mountains, so called because the native trees impart a distinct bluish haze when seen from a distance, are simply five traprock ridges called First Ridge, Second Ridge, and so on; layered volcanic rock riddled with springs and underground streams. But there are few residents of the area who could tell you which is First Ridge and which is Fifth. Events or places are located on the Head, the Chest, the Right Knee, the Left Foot, and so on. And the underground water you hear when you walk the Giant's trails "prove" he still lives, because the blood still flows through his body.

89

The Sleeping Giant (head is at left).
Photo courtesy of P. Scott Hollander.

It's that very anthropomorphism, in fact, which has saved the Giant intact when other trap rock ridges in the area have been gradually reduced to gravel. After generations of dedicated intervention, more than 1400 acres are currently protected park land (the Sleeping Giant Association hopes to acquire at least 2000 acres by the end of the century). The mountain is crisscrossed with nature trails, and maintained not only by park rangers who keep the trails open and safe, but by hikers and campers who automatically pick up and clean up any rubbish or accidental debris they may find. Lying across the center of busy, thriving, and growing city areas, the Giant alone retains almost all of his natural form, along with most of his original plant life.

THE LEGEND

Amerindian legend names the Giant "Hobbomock," and gives two different accounts for his long sleep. This shorter story, which Indian mothers supposedly told to their children to warn them not to be greedy, says that the Giant was originally the chief of a northern tribe who made regular trips to the seashore for fish. Overfond of oysters, which were plentiful in the bay, the chief once ate so many that he fell into a deep sleep. A wicked spirit passing by decided it would be fun to make the chief's sleep permanent—hence the warning not to overindulge in this tasty delicacy! Another version says that it was Hobbomock himself who overindulged; that one day the greedy god ate too many oysters and fell into a sleep from which he never woke.

But a more complete legend, and probably a more authentic one, explains not only the origin of the Giant, but also of other geological oddities in his vicinity. For example, geologists have determined that the Connecticut River once flowed straight from the center of the state to New Haven Harbor, and that its course changed sometime during the Ice Age. Indian legend agrees. It tells us that the Connecticut Indians, proud of their river, never forgot to give thanks to their own gods for the pleasures and livelihood derived from its waters. But they neglected to placate Hobbomock, the spirit of evil. Enraged at their neglect and jealous of their devotion to the river god, Hobbomock in a fit of temper stamped his foot in the river bed and changed the course of the Long River, diverting it from their valley. (At Middletown, where the Giant's foot came down, the river veers sharply to the east and then back again. The abrupt curve is the exact shape *and size* of the toe of a giant moccassined foot.)

Alarmed, the good spirit Kietan cast a spell on the angry god, to prevent him from causing any more damage. And Hobbomock fell into an enchanted sleep (after a full meal of oysters) forever. The legend adds that Kietan also hid treasure in the Giant's pockets, so that one day the people of the valley would be repaid for the loss of their river. And the Giant does indeed have treasure in his pockets; long after the Indians were gone, geologists found pockets of silver, gold, copper, iron, lead and quartz on the mountain; in small quantities, but more than enough to be counted as treasure for a tribe that sold 130 square miles (including the Giant) for eleven bolts of cloth and a coat.

The story of Hobbomock's punishment also explains the large boulders standing in the hills nearby—some of them weighing ten tons or more, and none of them native rock—and corresponding small lakes and large pot-holes, called "Giant's Kettles" in neighboring towns. We are told that the boulders were pulled from the earth (of Cheshire) and thrown into the (East Haven) hills by the Giant as he struggled against his final sleep.

As long as there were still Indians living in the area, the top of the mountain was a sacred place for Kietan, as well as the home of other tribal spirits. The Indians believed that Kietan lived in a towering pinnacle of rock overlooking a magical lake, and they came often to his sacred place to seek—and receive counsel. To some extent this legend is "confirmed" as the result of a sighting by an early colonial who knew nothing about it until much later. Samuel Payne found the lake for himself on a hunting trip through Sleeping Giant Mountain. He reported that on one moonlit evening just before full dark he was standing at the edge of the lake for the sake of the view. All sounds stilled for a brief moment, and in that moment he saw a ghostly birch-bark canoe emerge from the cliff face and glide silently across the surface of the lake, to disappear into the shadows. Later investigation showed that at the time he was alone (or, at least, the only living human!) on the mountain.

With the passing of his people, Kietan too departed, and the magical lake is now no more than clear mountain spring, with no visions of spirits or deities reported in recent times. But perhaps it's fitting. If Hobbomock was enchanted to sleep because he was jealous of Kietan, it does seem like justice that now Kietan is forgotten, and the love, care, and loyalty of the current inhabitants of the area is given fully and only to the Sleeping Giant.

VISITING THE GIANT

Sleeping Giant Mountain is visible from New Haven Harbor. But the Giant is big enough also to be visible closer to from built-up city streets, especially if you approach from the south along Route 10 (Whitney Avenue). It requires no imagination (or preparation for a sighting by native guides) for any visitor to clearly see the giant profile of a sleeping Indian.

The view from a distance is impressive enough, but from the moment you step on the mountain you know there is a living presence. (And you don't forget to thank him periodically for letting you walk all over him!) There are no recorded or remembered rituals involving Hobbomock per se; but it can be said just visiting the Giant is a ritual in itself, since nearly everyone who comes holds some kind of private converse with the old man.

Beyond that, the Giant's mountain is just a nice place to be. Carefully supervised by a dedicated volunteer organization, Sleeping Giant Park is a perfect place for nature hikes. There are well-marked trails of different lengths, some easy, some difficult. The Park Association offers a free guide book, complete with a map of all open trails; tags on trees, plants and bushes help the hiker identify native growth and natural formations. There are waterfalls and mountain streams; deep wooded areas that feel untouched and old as time; and, from the heights of the mountain, views that stretch for miles. With nearly 30 miles of marked trails, and 1400 acres of protected park land, even at those times of year when most people visit the Giant, it is possible to distance yourself enough that you can feel you're the only living being on the mountain—except for Hobbomock.

If you want to go you do have to walk, though; no motor vehicles of any kind are allowed on any of the trails. The Park Association is very protective of the Giant's property: dogs must be leashed, no fires are allowed except in supervised picnic areas, marking trees or cutting plants or flowers is prohibited, and picking up any litter you may find is encouraged.

Listed like that, it can sound like there are more regulations than view, but no one notices it; with the inevitable exception of those few people who try to hurt everything, the Giant's guests tend to be more than courteous without being told. It's not the rangers who keep visitors to the Sleeping Giant in order; it's Hobbomock.

There have been other Indian legends ignored by white settlers who took over their land, but the Sleeping Giant continues to hold people in thrall. Hobbomock awake was a bogey Indian mothers used to frighten their children into obedience. But asleep, there is no sense of evil or anger anywhere in his influence. And those who walk his trails never come away unchanged.

FOR MORE INFORMATION

Directions

Take I-95 to Exit 38 (connector to Wilber Cross/Merritt Parkways: get on Wilber Cross Parkway north toward Hartford). Take Exit 61 from the Wilber Cross to Whitney Avenue (Route 10); turn right (toward Cheshire) off the ramp. If you drive more than one block without passing the Town Hall, you turned the wrong way off the ramp. Go straight on Whitney for about two miles. Entrance to Sleeping Giant is on the right.

Lodging
    There is no longer any camping at Sleeping Giant. Area motels include:
    Sleeping Giant Motel (across the street from the Park entrance above)—3400 Whitney Ave, Hamden, CT 06518. $40 single; $45 double; special rates for longer stays or for groups.
    Howard Johnson—2260 Whitney Ave., Hamden, CT 06518. $60 Single, $65 double; weekly stay $35/night single or double; flexible rates for groups.

Additional Information
    Mailing address: Sleeping Giant Park Association, P.O. Box 14, Quinnipiac College, Hamden, CT 06518. For Ranger Station on the Mountain: call (203) 789-7498. (Mornings are best; if you get no answer try again, as they are in and out most of the day).
    Additional information and trails map: Trail System Guide, Sleeping Giant State Park, compliments of the Sleeping Giant Park Association, 1989 edition.

Bibliography
Sachse, Nancy Davis. *Born Among the Hills: The Sleeping Giant Story.* Sleeping Giant Park Association. October, 1982.

Hartley, Rachel M. *The History of Hamden, 1786-1936.* 1943.

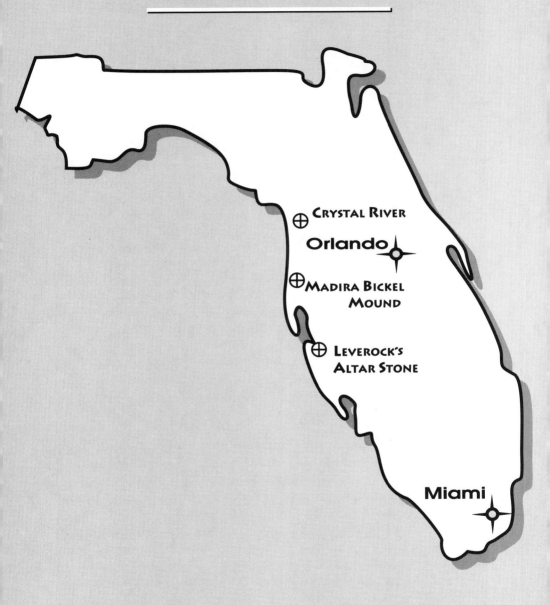

FLORIDA

⊕ CRYSTAL RIVER

Orlando ✧

⊕ MADIRA BICKEL
MOUND

⊕ LEVEROCK'S
ALTAR STONE

Miami ✧

Madira Bickel Mound

Sandra Tabatha and Chic Cicero

Just a few minutes off the Sunshine Skyway, heading south from St. Petersburg, is a wonderfully magic sacred center located on Terra Ceia Island. Madira Bickel was the first ancient structure in Florida to become an archaeological site in the state. Situated on ten wooded acres, it lies off the beaten track, secluded yet accessible. Relatively few people frequent the area, giving it a welcome measure of privacy.

Beyond the parking lot, visitors find a small burial mound immediately to the right. Built from white sand, it is only 18 inches high and 10 feet across, but was in use as a focus for ritual activities for more than a thousand years. Some 100 feet south of the diminutive mound stands a much larger temple structure. Set among arching palms and many other exotic trees dripping with Spanish moss, the flat-topped earthwork is 100 x 170 feet at its base and 20 feet tall, with a level area at the summit 40 x 40 feet. The vicinity of the temple mound is thickly wooded, so much so the ramp leading to its top is virtually all visitors may see of the structure from its base. But the jungle setting lends the whole site an atmosphere of intense power and profound mystery. Most of the trees at the top and sides of the earthwork are too far north of their normal range. Their abnormal location is made possible by the mound's high elevation; together with its proximity to the Gulf waters, the plants are protected from colder temperatures. Moreover, the structure is composed largely of seashells, which provide limestone, ideal material for the growth of exotic trees.

A few houses lie beyond the ten fenced-off acres of the site. The Madira Bickel Mound area allows a greater degree of privacy for ritual activity and meditation than most other public sacred centers.

Madira Bickel Mound; the Greater and Lesser Temple Mounds.
Photo by Tabatha and Chic Cicero.

MYSTICAL SIGNIFICANCE

The Madira Bickel Mound sits on a small portion of an extensive Timucuan community once located on the shores of Miguel
Bay. Historians speculate it was the original site of the village of
Ucita, referred to by DeSoto during his notorious expedition
through Florida. The Timucuans themselves were the prehistoric
natives who underwent a least three distinct cultural phases from
about 200 B.C. to 1500 A.D. During the first period, when the mounds
were raised, life was simple for a relatively small community of
hunter-gatherers. A second period beginning around 900 A.D. represented the Timucuans's most artistic phase, with the production
of decorated pottery and luxury goods. It was a time of dependence
on the sea for food. The third period, starting about 1300 A.D., witnessed the people less indebted to the sea and more reliant upon agriculture. At this time their conceptions of the afterlife changed, too.

They raised new temple mounds of the gods of the sun and the
rain. The Madira Bickel structure contains evidence for all three
phases, so it must have been regarded by many generations of
Timucuans as the most sacred center of their age-old community.
The prodigious mound was built almost entirely of seashells, and
their symbolism was particularly significant to the ancient archi-

tects. One of the esoteric meanings inherent in the seashell defines the prosperity of one generation arising from the death of the preceding generation. It implies the concept of death and rebirth, the natural life cycles, which were comprehended and revered by the ancient Timucuan sun-worshippers.

Because of its jungle-like environment and canopy of gnarled trees, the Madira Bickel Mound has an atmosphere of deeply prehistoric and primal power. It beckons to our subconscious with alluring memories of an almost forgotten, organic past. Here, we may regain parts of ourselves neglected and obscured in the greedy vortex of the modern world's insane scramble for existence and pleasure. An astral journey into the lost Timucuans's realm comprises an ideal setting for valuable meditation. By awakening old, pre-birth memories, we not only learn more about our own identities, but begin to tap into the group subconscious of mankind. A mental projection into the past can be a worthwhile learning experience toward our spiritual evolution. Moreover, the unconscious mind may take an active role in reviving meaningful images from what is commonly termed "the imagination." As every inventor and ceremonial magician will attest, all created things begin in the imagination before manifesting into the physical world.

SUGGESTED RITUAL

Seated in the center of the ceremonial space at the summit of the mound, close your eyes and begin to breathe deeply, slowly. In your mind's eye, envision yourself and the mound in the present. Then gradually picture the scene changing with the seasons, except that for this visualization, spring is followed by winter, fall and then summer. Time is rolling slowly backward into the past. The seasons here are not as dramatically defined as in northern climates, but the changes are noticeable, nevertheless. Feel the warm, sunny days of spring, followed by the brisk days of winter. Fall is cool and comfortable. Summer is intensely hot and humid, with sudden, afternoon thunderstorms. See the seasons alternating, going backwards into time, one after the other. The pace of the change of seasons begins to accelerate faster and faster, becoming a blur. Years, decades, centuries pass. The cycle of change gradually slows, eventually grinding to a stop. Six hundred years have passed since you began your meditation. It is now a warm, perfectly beautiful day in spring, in the year 1392.

The mound on which you sit is no longer over-shadowed by large trees. You are able to see a great distance from your position, out over the palm trees and palmetto scrub. Directly before you stands a tall, wooden, spiked staff set into the top of the mound like a flag-pole. Behind you is a square ceremonial building with a thatched roof. From your vantage-point you can see a sprawling native community. A great cooking fire burns near some of the huts attended by a small group of women with long, straight black hair wearing seashell necklaces and skirts made of Spanish moss. On the ground before the fire lies a carpet of palm leaves covered with an abundance of food: fish, rabbits, turkeys, shellfish, alligators, corn, pumpkins, sweet potatoes and artichokes. The smell of cooking is pungent but appealing. Naked children play around the busy, gossiping women. Nearby, men, young and old, are engaged in easy conversation, but some are arguing over the worthiness of newly made arrows.

Suddenly, there is a great commotion. The shrill hooting of a conch shell horn sounds alarmingly across the village. More men and women in loin cloths, their long hair rolled up to the top of their heads, hurry to an assembly area. From the angular hut at the center of the community emerges a priest-chief, accompanied by two attendants. One carries a burning torch. The bodies of all three men are practically covered with entwining tattoos, but the priest-chief is the most impressive. The rolled braids of his shiny hair are encircled by shell beads and he wears a shark tooth necklace with polished shell bracelets. His fingernails have been cut to make them resemble an animal's or demon's claws.

The hollow call of wooden trumpets announces his appearance. Regarded by his people as a living descendant of the sun-god, they silently, breathlessly observe his every move and gesture. He addresses them in an unknown language, but, in your astral state, you realize he is announcing the start of an all-important ritual in honor of the solar deity to celebrate his vernal equinox.

A procession led by the three priests, together with a trio of tribal elders, begins to climb the long, sloping ramp of the temple mound. Behind the celebrants are two young men, who carry between them the prepared carcass of a deer stuffed with meat, shellfish and vegetables. The sacrifice is adorned with necklaces of symbolic acorns and holy seashells. Crowds of common people gather around the great temple mound on all sides, as the two young servers hoist the deer offering to the top of the wooden pole directly in front of your sitting position. They tie it securely, then turn away to walk back down the processional ramp. One of the elders holds a beautiful conch shell filled with an aromatic brew. With deep respect, he hands it to the priest-chief, who raises it skyward, then takes a long drink. He turns it over to another priest, who repeats the sacred libation. The shell is passed around the circle of six men. After all have drunk the ritual concoction, the trio of elders descend from the summit.

Alone, the priest-chief enters the temple building behind you, as the two lesser priests begin to dance around the building and call upon the son of the sun-god to reappear with the favor of his father. The chief emerges momentarily, resplendent in the majestic antlers and dappled skin of a deer, the recognized attire of the shaman, the spiritual leader and magician, master of transformations and altered states of consciousness. In his claw-like hands, he holds two ceremonial rattles made from painted, incised seashells. He shakes them at the heavens, as he sings an invocation to the sun-god. Calling upon his celestial father with words of praise and power, he petitions him to smile upon the people entrusted to his care. At this most sacred moment, when day and night are poised in the balance of the cosmos, the sun-god will be honored by the entire village for his expected bounty, with a great feast to do him homage.

One of the lesser priests hands the burning torch to the son of the sun. Swinging it rhythmically, he dances around the pole of sacrifice, his steps symbolically recounting the story of the world's birth; how the Sun-god fell in love with the Earth-goddess; how he courted her with golden rays which made the plants blossom with ripening fruit. The priest-chief's graceful movements are delicate, yet powerful. At the climax of his dance, he sets the deer carcass ablaze with his flaming torch. As the sacrifice is consumed, renewed excitement breaks out among the villagers. Now they dance and gesture skyward. Their joy is contagious, and you, too, feel swept up in the communal emotion of their moment. All the priests descend the mound, as the great day of regeneration continues throughout the realm.

Left alone to contemplate the image of solar sacrifice and rebirth, you realize how vital the well-being of the sun has always been to the Earth and all the creatures who live on it. In their own way, the Timucuans gave thanks and respect to the eternal powers of Nature, upon which they, as much as ourselves, depended. They understood the cycle of death and revivification which permeates the world. If these natural cycles of flux and reflux are interfered with or abused, the result is a world of imbalance and disaster. This is but one of the lessons you will take back with you.

At your own time, end the mediation by passing through the change of seasons again, but now go forward in time through Spring, Summer, Fall and Winter. Breathe deeply. Accelerate the cycle until you approach your own time and then stop in the present. Bring your consciousness back to the here and now and ground yourself by placing both hands upon the earth. After leaving the mound, you should further ground yourself by eating a snack or a meal.

FOR MORE INFORMATION

Directions
Take I-275 south from St. Petersburg. This becomes the Sunshine Skyway which crosses Tampa Bay. The first body of you encounter after crossing the Bay is Terr Ceia Island. Take the exit for Highway 19 toward the town of Palmetto. Look immediately for a small road on the right called Terra Ceiga Road. Continue down this road and turn left on Center Rd. Turn right at Bayshore Road and watch for signs. The site is on the left.

Lodging
Sun 'n Fun RV Resort, 2125 Fruitville Rd., Sarasota (1/2 mi E of I-75 on Fruitville Rd. exit), $20 per night. Other suggested accommodations: Best Western, 5218 17th St. E. Ellenton, $44 single; Daystop Inn 644 67th St., Circle E, Brandenton, $29.95 single; Econo Lodge (1-75 at SR 64, Exit 44) 607 67th St., Circle E, Bradenton, $26 single; Scottish Inns, 6511 14th St. W. (US Hwy 41), Bradenton, $35 single.

Additional Information
Madira Bickel Mound State Archaeological Site, c/o Gamble Plantation, 3708 Patten Ave., Ellenton, FL 33532. Telephone: (913) 722-1017.

Leverock's Altar Stone

Sandra Tabatha and Chic Cicero

Sometimes a sacred object will turn up in the most unlikely place. Such is the case of the carved altar stone at the entrance to a popular sea food restaurant located in New Port Richey, Florida. This 8-foot long by 4-foot wide limestone relic was found a few years ago when the restaurant was being built. The owner had the stone placed in front of the building, not far from its original resting place. Since then, state-certified archaeologists have determined that the carvings on the stone in front of Leverock's Restaurant are authentically ancient.

The stone sits in a small garden corner on the left side of a brick sidewalk which leads to the restaurant. Palm trees and trimmed bushes surround the relic. Two human faces can easily be seen carved out on different sides of the stone. A small cavity has been carved out on the stone's upper side.

MYSTICAL SIGNIFICANCE

The stone was carved by prehistoric artisans sometime between 1 A.D. and 400. The unique images of two human faces cut into the rock with primitive tools are very likely effigies of local priest-chiefs who governed the tribe as living descendants of the gods. Possibly, the sun and rain gods were given human faces by the ancient artists who worshiped them. The cavity which was cut into the top of the stone indicates that it was used as an altar in religious ceremonies. It is likely that food and other precious items were placed in the cavity as an offering to those who ruled the elements of the Timucuan world.

Cirlot says that, "Stone is a symbol of being, of cohesion and harmonious reconciliation with self." The durability of stone seems far stronger than that of biological beings who are subject to the forces of decay and death. The stone symbolizes unity and strength. Throughout history, mankind looked upon Rock as the dwelling

place of the Creator. Mystics have long regarded rocks as close to the
source of human life . . . and we are ever striving for the solidity and
integrity that the stone signifies.

Leverock's Altar Stone.
Photo by Tabatha and Chic Cicero.

A religious altar usually represents the manifested universe. A
stone altar with carved images of deities or their descendants is a
powerful center of these sacred ideas brought into form. It is a synthesis of man's striving for reconciliation with the Eternal . . . that
which is Divine and lives forever. By carving a sacred image into a
stone, the idea behind the image lives on, like the sturdy rock, seemingly unchanged by the passage of time. By tapping into the energies of such a stone, we can explore timeless stability and wholeness . . . an energy which is cohesive and durable. Through such objects as the altar stone, we can gee a glimpse of "the Dwelling Place
of the Creator."

Closeup of Leverock's Altar Stone.
Photo by Tabatha and Chic Cicero.

SUGGESTED RITUAL

Since the stone is immediately in front of a popular restaurant, a ritual which explores the stone's sacred properties must be brief and discreet.

Walk up to the stone and place your left hand over your heart. Take a series of deep breaths and imagine a shaft of light coursing through your body, from the top of your head to your feet. This energy is centered in the area around your heart. Fill you whole being with this divine light. With your right hand, touch the altar stone and visualize the light flowing down your arm into the stone, blessing and awakening its Divine inhabitant. Feel the texture of the stone and picture the Eternal Being who dwells within it. See this Being in whatever tradition or mythology suits you most, for He/She is Eternal, existing in many different places and many cultures. As you pull together the image of this Being in your mind, feel the many aspects of yourself (personality, Higher Self, Divine Self) pulling together and solidifying. All fragmentary parts of yourself; the different moods, different faces you show to the world, the Ego, the Spirit, the Soul...all coming together in a cohesive, unified form.

Gathering strength from the rock, you feel your Self coming together as One. Unified, you are able to contact the Eternal Being in the Stone, for you and the Being ARE One. Feel free to ask for guidance or assistance in any matter that troubles you. Offer a blessing or a prayer. See the light which flows through both you and the Stone grow more brilliant. Bask in this light for a moment, then thank the Dweller in the Rock.

FOR MORE INFORMATION

Directions

Take I-75 south to State Road 54. Drive 22 miles and turn right on US Hwy 19. Leverock's Restaurant is located at 2375 US Hwy 19 South.

Lodging

Seven Springs Travel Park, 8039 State Rd. 54, $14 per night; Cypress Point Campgrounds on Lake Tarpon, 4500 US Hwy 19 North, Film Harbor. Tent spaces available, $18 plus tax per night. Other suggested accommodations: Benchley Motel, 7541 US Hwy 19, $22 plus tax, single; Knights Inn, 7631 US Hwy 19, $27 plus tax, single; Holiday Inn, 5015 US Hwy 19 North. $54 single.

Crystal River

Sandra Tabatha and Chic Cicero

The path leads south from the museum, passing two midden mounds, which cover a total area of over 400 feet, implying an extensive period of habitation. The priest-chief's house was once located at the second of these kitchen mounds, while his village of thatched palmetto huts occupied the general area. Further south stands one of Florida's largest temple mounds, rising 30 feet above the marshy swamp and fresh water of Crystal River. Its ancient ramp on the structure's northeast side is presently concealed by trees and a nearby trailer park. Fifty wooden steps now climb up the side to the flat-topped pyramid's summit, long ago adorned by a square temple. The view from the top is awesome, and so are the resident energies of this impressive sacred center.

Northeast of the temple pyramid lie a pair of burial mounds. Just east of the first earthwork stands a 5 foot, 6 inch ceremonial stone. Erected in 440 A.D., the stele was part of a solar calendar arranged in sand, shell and stone. The likeness of a human head has been incised into the western side of the weathered monolith, a probable representation of the sun-god, given the stone's participation in the solar calendar.

Continuing northward beyond the burial mounds, visitors pass an open area known as the Plaza. There, the ancient Floridians gathered to observe colorful ceremonies held on the temple mound. Once a broad precinct, it is presently covered by palm trees. Another ritual pyramid is located at the northernmost end of the site. The somewhat oblong structure is 235 feet long and oriented northwest-southeast, an alignment found throughout Mississippian Culture in North America and down to the Mayas of Yucatan. The orientation apparently refers to the rising of the planet Venus, which was associated with the legendary culture-hero, Feathered Serpent. The earthwork was erected later than its companion piece near the river, and three buildings once stood on the long, level ritual area at the summit. They contained sacred objects and the priests' paraphernalia—quartz crystals, deer antlers, decorated pottery, hallucinogenic herbs, etc. Three large oak trees presently occupy the former positions of the original shrines.

Crystal River; Stairway to Heaven.
Photo by Tabatha and Chic Cicero.

MYSTICAL SIGNIFICANCE

The Crystal River site was an important and powerful ceremonial and cultural center that flourished for 1,600 years. It represents one of the very few locations where incised stele have been found in North America, a discovery that strongly suggests the ancient Floridians were in touch with the Mayas, hundreds of miles to the south. The entire complex—its pyramid temple mounds, burial earthworks and remarkable stele—is actually typical of a lowland Maya city. Investigators believe Crystal River was probably a way-station in the northward spread of ideas, if not of the Mayas themselves, from Yucatan. Moreover, some trade items recovered at the site indicate contact with people of the Hopewell Culture, hundreds of miles away to the north. Clearly, the early residents of Crystal River maintained far-flung commercial and cultural ties.

One of the Ancient Stelle.
Photo by Tabatha and Chic Cicero.

Their most prominent material remains consist of the solar calendar described above. Designed with rock and shell, it proves that worship of the sun was an important cult practice in prehistoric Florida. The Mound Builders used their rudimentary observatory to

predict spring and fall equinoxes, and the summer and winter solstices. Through its arrangement of earth and stone, the priest-chief
could determine the four important solar dates within an accuracy
of a few days.

The Crystal River calendar operated as follows: On each side of
a burial mound stands a monolith. The horizontal dimension of
each erect stone is at right angles to a line leading from the stele to a
temple mound. The ramp of each temple pointed slightly east of the
monolith. The carved image on Stele I fronted sunrise at the summer
solstice. An observer facing the stone would look over into the sunset. If he stood on a large rock beside the stone, he would have been
able to align the sun, the top of the stele, and a point on the shell midden.

From Stele II, observers watched the sun go down behind a
shell midden at the winter solstice. At the spring equinox, they saw
sunrise over the center of a burial mound. Turning of solar energy
represented a crucial moment for the Mound Builders. In dread that
the sun might not return, they held elaborate ceremonies to invoke
the favor of their sky-god at twilight on the winter solstices and at
dawn of the summer solstices. The priests observed the sun at its
highest point from the temple mounds and implored the shining
omnipotence never to desert his worshippers. By undertaking the
construction of a solar observatory, the ancient natives of Crystal
River forged a cultural link between religion and science, a link
most mystically inclined persons embrace today.

Sacred numbers play an important role in the esoteric values of
the site. Duality is a recurring motif: two temples, two stele, the twin
middens. It is the number most associated with the concept of the
Holy Father, the archetypal masculine energy. The standing stone is
likewise considered an image of the divine male energy, an interpretation that compliments the solar worship of the resident Mound
Builders' virile sun-god. The two temples, together with their respective monoliths, yield the number four, which alludes to the
physical world divided into quadrants (the four cardinal directions)
and renders the site a perfect place to contemplate the grand design
of the cosmos. The burial mounds are three in number; since three
refers to the Great Mother, the bodies interred there symbolically return to the archetypal womb, the Navel of the World, from which all
life issues forth and must return for rebirth. The Crystal River complex, its informative museum, numinous temple mounds, peaceful

setting and mysterious stele, offers receptive visitors memorable opportunities to personally explore and experience a genuine sacred center of great significance and lasting beauty.

SUGGESTED RITUAL

The ideal moment in which to perform a meaningful ritual at Crystal River would take place during an equinox or solstice, even though trees presently obscure some of the solar alignments. But the sacred center is an amazingly powerful site on any given day of the year. The location also offers some degree of privacy for ritual and meditation. Begin the ritual near the two midden mounds, south of the museum. As you walk toward them, begin what is known as the Four-fold Breath: inhale to the count of four, hold the air in your lungs to the count of four, exhale to the count of four, and keep the lungs empty to the count of four. Visualize the ancient power of the site stirring into life all around you. Seek this energy. It surrounds you. As you pass the middens, pay particular attention to the second smaller mound, where the priest-chief's house once stood. As you walk deeper to the complex, the primal energy gets stronger. Then you reach the first temple mound, pause at its base and stretch forth your arms directly out from the sides of your body forming a cross. (If you are not afforded the privacy necessary for this, keep your arms at your sides with the palms forward to receive energy from the mound.) Walk the 50 steps to the summit. As you do this, feel your heart center fill with Divine white Light. The higher you go, the more the energy fills you.

Visualize yourself climbing from the Earth to the Heavens as though you have left your body at the base of the pyramid, walking now in astral form. Once there, face the river and fold your arms across your heart. As you do so, imagine the sunrise breaking through the last vestiges of night. Feel the sun of your own being rise in your heart, becoming alive and vital with divine power. Visualize a column of golden white brilliance descend and cover both you and the entire mound. (Note: if you have companions with you at the site, let one of them remain at the base of the pyramid while the others space themselves apart on the steps. Once you are filled with the sun's energy, project it from your heart center down your arm, to the heart of the next person down from you. The energy should be passed from person to person until the individual at the base of the mound receives it. He or she then directs the energy to the earth; placing both hands upon the ground. While performing this, think of the Sun's healing warmth caressing Mother Earth.)

After meditating for a while at the first temple, continue on to Stele I and face the figure carved in the stone. A wire cage surrounds the stone so it is not possible to touch it. However, one can still project at the rock and try to visualize its divine inhabitants.

After communing with the Stele, continue on toward the burial mounds. Place your left hand on your heart and extend your right hand at the mound. Project energy out from your heart center, down your arm and into the burial ground. You are highly charged with power from the temple mound, and you use some of this Divine energy to bless those who have passed on at this Sacred center. Do this at all three burial sites.

At the second temple mound, repeat the ritual procedure given for the pyramid mound. (Note: if you are in a group, three people can position themselves on the rectangular mound, while the rest form a straight line leading down the long ramp. The three individuals on the mound should simultaneously project the solar energy to the next person on the ramp, who then passes the energy as before.)

Continue on to Stele II and repeat the ritual performed at the previous standing stone.

If you have a large enough group, you may wish to split up and have each person meditate at a different mound or stele. For a predetermined period, everyone should perform his or her own personal meditation. At the end of that time, the group may reassemble at any location in the site to discuss and compare their meditation experiences.

FOR MORE INFORMATION

Directions
Take I-75 south from Ocala to State Road 44 west. At Crystal River, turn north on US Hwy 19. A few miles north of the town turn left at State Park St. Follow the signs to Crystal River State Archaeological Site.

Lodging
Quail Roost RV Campground, 9835 N. Citrus Ave., Crystal River. Tent spaces available, $10 per night. Lake Rousseau Safari Campground, 10811 N. Coveview Ter., Crystal River, $15 per night.

Other suggested accommodations: Days Inn, US Hwy 19 north of Crystal River, $39 plus tax, single; Econo Lodge, US Hwy 19 north of Crystal River, $25 plus tax, single.

Additional Information

Write or phone Crystal River State Archaeological Site, 3400 Museum Point, Crystal Rivers FL 32629. Telephone: (904) 795-3817.

There is a one dollar fee for use and up-keep of the site. A brochure containing a map of the mound complex is available at the Visitor's Center.

Bibliography

Askew, Walter H. and Charles Benbow. "Mounds Unraveled Lost Tribe's Mysteries." *The St. Petersburg Times*, May 15, 1993.

Cirlot, J. E. *A Dictionary of Symbols*. 2nd ed. New York: Philosophical Library, 1971.

Dill, Glen H. "Suncoast Past." *The Suncoast News*, October 8, 1978.

Neil, Wilfred T. "Indians Made Their Home Here From 10,000 B.C." *The St. Petersburg Times*, March 4, 1975.

Wilfred T. Neil. "1,500 Years Ago." *Pasco Times*. Date Unknown.

HAWAII

Honolulu

THE WIZARD STONES

HALEAKALA

HALEMA 'UMA' U

Hawaii

Scott Cunningham

Before discussing some of the sacred sites of Hawaii, it is imperative to say a few words regarding the performance of rituals at such places by non-Hawaiians.

Many Hawaiians are quite sensitive about their religious ancestry. I've had many friends who were born and raised in Hawaii; one of them knew many of the old ways, but wouldn't speak of them. Once, when I'd again asked him about ancient Hawaiian spirituality, he told me with a friendly smile, "White people have their own gods, their own magic." His message was quite clear.

Such an attitude is understandable. Non-Hawaiians don't share in the rich cultural heritage of the Hawaiians. Though many of the old ways are gone forever, most locals acknowledge their heritage and have heard the old stories. They're aware that a certain mountain is sacred, know that a rock behind Tutu's house was once a human being, and that a goddess once swam in Pearl Harbor. They're aware of the spiritual power that exists within the *aina* (land) which had once been theirs is land now owned by corporations or the United States. Though many adhere to conventional religions (Buddhism, Shinto and Taoism, Christianity), they're still aware of the spiritual dimension of their homeland.

This awareness can make native Hawaiians sensitive to what could be construed to be yet another invasion of *haole* (foreign; Caucasian) influence in their lives—non-Hawaiians visiting Hawaii's sacred sites.

Approaching these special places with the proper attitude is the best way to avoid offense. Try to have the correct mind-frame when performing rites in Hawaii. If you come from a Christian background, forget the tales that you may have heard that the old Hawaiian deities were devils and demons. If you're Pagan, it's best not to worship Diana, Athena or some other *haole* deity while in Hawaii—at least, not at sacred sites.

117

Remember that the land is sacred—from the coral reefs and beaches to the mountain tops; that the *akua* (gods and goddesses; spiritual energies) created the land; that *mana* (spiritual power) is present in all things, and that it can never be destroyed, though it can be transferred. Sacred sites are sacred precisely because they contain vast amounts of *mana*, and because, usually, the *akua* were worshipped there.

Because the *akua* possess great amounts of *mana*, and because *mana* can never be destroyed, they're still present—in the earth itself; in the reefs; in the waters, in the rain, lightning and wind; in the volcanoes and in the plants.

The ancient Hawaiian religion lives on in the hearts of its people, and in the *mana* of their ancestors. Because this is true, do nothing at sacred sites that would be disturbing. Don't climb on ancient walls or terraces. Don't litter. Don't joke or speak loudly when on sacred ground.

Avoid using elements of foreign spirituality while performing rituals at ancient Hawaiian sacred sites. Candles, robes, finger cymbals, incense, Tibetan bells, European herbs, pre-recorded Western Pagan or New Age music, metallic instruments of any kind, the use of the word "Om" and similar tools can be quite useful, but are foreign to old Hawaii. They shouldn't be used if you truly desire to feel the spiritual power of the land. This is the least that we can do to show our appreciation of traditional Hawaiian spirituality.

Traditional Hawaiian spirituality is a fascinating area of study. For more information, consult the books that I've listed in the bibliography at the end of each section.

HALEMA'UMA'U
PELE'S HOME AT KILAUEA

The Big Island of Hawaii is the largest in this chain of volcanic islands. One-half hour from Kilo and some two hours distant from the resort area of Kailua-Kona stands Kilauea, the most active volcano on Earth. Within it lies Halema'uma'u, the legendary home of the goddess Pele.

Kilauea is one of five volcanoes that have created the Big Island. It lies along the southeastern slope of the much larger volcano, Mauna Loa. Kilauea is surmounted by a huge caldera, and within the collapsed top of this volcano rests the now cool lava lake known as Halema'uma'u.

Halema'uma'u is a deep pit within the vastness of Kilauea. A 1/2 mile in width, 280 feet deep, Halema'uma'u seems barrenly serene. Though virtually devoid of vegetation, Pele's home possesses a rich mixture of textures and colors. Yellowish-white streaks mark its cracked, rippled lava floor. The crater's walls arch abruptly upward. Fumes composed largely of water vapor, carbon dioxide and sulfur dioxide rise eerily from parts of the crater. Long-tailed frigate birds soar overhead. All is quiet.

But as recently as April 30, 1982, a small lava lake formed within Halema'uma'u during an eruptive period. On November 5, 1967, spectacular lava fountains billowed from the floor, creating a lake of molten lava some 100 feet deep.

Outpourings of lava at Halema'uma'u are rare today, but this could change at any time. The lava usually appears miles from Halema'uma'u along Kilauea's East Rift. Recent lava flows in this area have devastated the coastal town of Kalapana, destroying over 100 buildings and historical sites. Thirty days after I stepped onto the famous black sand beach of Kaimu in 1990, it was consumed by lava flows.

Though Halema'uma'u may seem cold, we know that Pele still lives there, wrapped in Her cloak of flames.

Pele

For untold centuries, Hawaiians have reverenced Pele. Temples were built beside lava flows and near the edge of Halema'uma'u. Offerings of a particular type of berry were always given to Her before humans enjoyed the tartly sweet fruits. Persons whose families acknowledged Pele as a divine ancestor would offer the bodies of their deceased family members to Pele, but no humans (virgin or otherwise) were ever sacrificed to Pele.

Today, long after the collapse of the traditional Hawaiian religion in 1819, acknowledgement of Pele continues. When lava flows threaten villages and towns on the Big Island, many long-time residents offer sacrifices of fruits and flowers to ask Pele to protect their homes.

To the Hawaiians of old, the *aina* was sacred. Today, when many of the ancient ways have vanished, respect for the land continues. Locals born and raised on the Big Island may have but misty ideas concerning other Hawaiian deities, but nothing can erase the visible presence of Pele. All walk upon Her works.

Offerings left at the rim of Pele's Volcano.
Photo by Scott Cunningham.

There are still priestesses of Pele, who chant the old prayers in honor of Pele and perform timeless ceremonies at the edge of Halema'uma'u and near lava flows. Pele is still worshipped, both openly and in secret. Even locals of Christian background usually acknowledge the presence of Pele, and most scientists who study the volcano are unwilling to deny Her presence.

Pele wasn't originally from Hawaii. Her home was Kahiki. Pele may have left Her ancestral homeland simply because She longed to explore the open seas. Or Her sister, the sea-goddess Na-maka-o-kaha'i, may have driven Her away in anger.

In either case, Pele left Kahiki in Her brother's canoe, taking some of Her family with Her. After many adventures, She arrived at the Hawaiian island of Ni'ihau, seeking a place where She could dig a pit deep enough to safeguard Her sacred fires. This small island adjacent to Kaua'i didn't satisfy her, for seawater rushed in, making it an unsuitable home for the fiery Pele.

So she sailed from island to island but was always thwarted by the water of Her sister, the sea-goddess. Finally, upon arriving on the Big Island of Hawaii, she dug a deep pit that remained dry. Satisfied, Pele placed Her fires there and dwelled within Her house of flames. Pele's spirit lives to this day in Halema'uma'u.

After many adventures, the woman Pele died. She became a true Hawaiian goddess. Her spirit continued to appear in numerous physical forms, testing humans' loyalty to Her. She sent lava flows to create new land and to destroy those who had offended Her. The Hawaiians knew that their deities possessed human qualities, and Pele was no exception.

Pele is real. Her spirit can be seen in the curtains of fire that often attend volcanic eruptions on the Big Island. Her form is also seen in the steam rising from the ground, and Her face appears within moving lava. She is everywhere in this land, in these islands of volcanic origin.

Pele can appear as a beautiful young woman, as an elderly Hawaiian woman, or even as a white dog. She comes to warn of volcanic eruptions, and documented reports of such events have occured. At Halema'uma'u, we can visit Her home.

Though originally Pele was worshipped only by members of certain families that claimed Her as an ancestor, today many Hawaiians and persons of all ethnic origins honor Her.

Before You Go to Halema'uma'u

At an altitude of 4,000 feet, Kilauea is often cool or cold. Mornings can be misty or rainy, and the temperature is usually lower than it is at the beach. Later in the day, however, the temperature can rise. To be prepared for anything, layer your clothing for trips to Halema'uma'u. Sturdy shoes or boots are also recommended.

Before you enter the park itself, find an offering to give to Pele. The feathery red flowers of the *ohia* tree are traditional, as are the red *ohelo* berries. Wrap a *ki* (ti) leaf around your offering, if you wish. Do this outside of the park to preserve the protected vegetation contained within it. (Don't be tempted to eat even one of the *ohelo* berries before making your offering.)

If you can't find *ohia* or *ohelo*, buy or find some flowers, leis or ferns before going to the volcano. Any type is fine, especially those that are native to Hawaii. As an alternative, pluck or cut a few hairs from your head to use as an offering. (Coins, incense and bottles of gin are common offerings here. Though hardly traditional, they're the most modern forms of sacrifice to Pele.) Flowers or ferns of any kind are the best offerings, but pick them *before* entering the park.

Before leaving your hotel, call the Eruption Update line at (808) 967-7977 for a pre-recorded message concerning current eruption information. At times new lava flows cover roads, making them impassable. You may also wish to utilize this information in later trips to actual eruption sites, which are usually several miles away from Halema'uma'u).

Once You're There
Crater Rim Road is circular. Your first stop should probably be at the Visitor's Center for a brief orientation. Next, you may wish to peruse the Thomas A. Jaggar Museum, which stands beside the Hawaiian Volcano Observatory. The observatory isn't open to the public, but the museum is, and a stop there will enrich your coming experience.

As you continue to drive on Crater Rim Road, you'll pass many craters and see evidence of the intense volcanic activity in the area. Eventually you'll come to the Halema'uma'u Overlook. Park in the lot. (If buses are just disgorging dozens of tourists as you arrive, you may wish to wait until they leave. Early mornings are the best time to visit.)

At the start of the trail that leads from the parking lot to the overlook, you'll see warning signs regarding the fumes that rise from the Earth around you. These sulphurous fumes may be harmful for persons with heart or lung disorders. Take the signs seriously—this is a powerful area.

The trail to the overlook is marked with a wire fence. No more than 1/4 mile long, the trail is thankfully unpaved. As you move closer to the overlook, still your mind. Sense the ancient forces present here: the creative and destructive forces that are Pele.

Go with a sense of awe. Walk slowly over this sacred ground. Breathe lightly (deep breathing isn't encouraged due to the fumes). Hold the offering in your hand. You may wish to repeat the Goddess' name over and over in a barely audible whisper:

Pele....Pele....Pele....
(Pronounce it "PEH-leh," not "Pay-lay.")

Don't rush. Walk slowly, with deliberate intent. Feel the power emanating from beneath your feet. Sense Her divine presence.

Approach the overlook. If tourists are clogging it, wait for a moment. Stare down into the enormous, bluish-grey pit that lies before and below you. Stir visions in your mind of fountaining lava, of oozing flows of molten orange rock.

Once the tourists have left (or when you can't wait any longer), enter the overlook (a fenced-off area much nearer the crater's rim, with a wonderous view of Halema'uma'u). Look down into its vastness. Sense the presence of Pele.

Hold your offering in your hand. Say any words that come to mind, or use one of the chants included here:

A general chant:

> O Pele!
> Goddess of the burning stones!
> Life for me. Life for you.
> The flowers of fire wave gently.
> Here is your offering!

When offering ohelo berries:

> O Pele!
> Here are your ohelo berries.
> I offer some to you.
> Some I also eat.

While chanting this, make your offering by either tossing it over the edge of the crater into Halema'uma'u itself, or by placing it on the firepit's rim. Do what seems best. (Some people step over the fence and place their offerings closer to the crater's rim. Though I've done this myself, it can't be reccommended due to the steep crater walls below. Park rangers sometimes turn their heads when seeing persons making offerings in this manner, but it still violates park rules.)

Be solemn as you make your offering. If others are present, joking or speaking in loud voices, ignore them as best as you can. Let yourself be enfolded in the power of the place.

Though I've made many offerings to Pele at Halema'uma'u, I've never been bothered by the onlookers that are so frequently present. Sometimes, they seem to have instinctively attuned to my actions, and have even stood back in silence until I've finished.

Some Hawaiians may dislike these words. Some might say that only those of Hawaiian ancestry should honor Pele. I hesitated to include any type of ritual in this section precisely because I didn't wish to offend Hawaiians.

Still, Pele was born in far-off Kahiki. She, Herself, was an immigrant to Hawaii. Many more immigrants have come to Hawaii after Her—Chinese, Japanese, Filipino, Portugese, Samoan, Korean, Caucasian and others. People of every ethnic background make offerings to Pele; impelled by the power, the *mana* of the land, to honor the goddess of the Volcanoes.

Upon reflection, I can't see what harm can be done by anyone honoring the Creatress of these islands.

FOR MORE INFORMATION

Directions

Take Highway 11 from either Kailua-Kona or Kilo. (This is a long trip from Kona, but is well worth the time involved.) Follow the signs after you've entered the Hawaii Volcanoes National Park (a $5 per car admission fee is currently required) to Crater Rim Road. Take Crater Rim Road to the Halema'uma'u Overlook. Park in the lot and follow the path.

Lodging

The closest lodging is Volcano House, which is situated within Hawaii Volcanoes National Park. As of this writing, rooms are about $50 per night. It's a pleasant, lodge-style hotel, not a luxury resort. Reservations are a good idea. Write to: Volcano House, P. O.

Box 53, Hawaii Volcanoes National Park, HI 96718, or telephone them at (808) 967-7321.

Some Bed and Breakfast spots are also available in the Volcano area. Call Volcano Village at (808) 976-7216 for more information.

Most Big Island visitors stay in the Kailua-Kona area, which is two hours distant from the park, although there are many hotels in Kilo as well. Check with your travel agent.

Information Sources

Hawaii Volcanoes National Park Visitor's Center
P. O. Box 52
Hawaii National Park, HI 96718
(808) 967-7311

Thomas A. Jaggar Museum
P. O. Box 52
Hawaii National Park, HI 96718
(808) 967-7643

Bibliography

Beckwith, Martha, *Hawaiian Mythology*. Honolulu: University of Hawaii Press, 1979.

Handy, E. S. Craighill, and Mary Kawena Pukui. *The Polynesian Family System in Ka'u, Hawaii*. Rutland (Vermont): Tuttle, 1977.

Kane, Herb Kawainui. *Pele: Goddess of Hawai'i's Volcanoes*. Captain Cook (Hawaii): The Kawainui Press, 1987.

Kelly, Marion. *Pele and Hi'iaka*. Honolulu: Bernice P. Bishop Museum,1984.

Macdonald, Gordon A., and Agatin T. Abbott. *Volcanoes in the Sea*. Honolulu: The University Press of Hawaii, 1977.

Pukui, Mary Kawena, E. W. Haertig, and Catherine A. Lee. *Nana I Ke Kumu* (Look to the Source). Honolulu: Queen Lili'uokalani Children's Center, 1972.

Westervelt, William D. *Hawaiian Legends of Volcanoes*. 1916. Reprint. Tokyo: Charles E. Tuttle, 1963.

THE "WIZARD STONES" OF WAIKIKI
(O'AHU)

They sit there quietly now on Kuhio Beach at Waikiki: two upright and two flat-lying stones. During the day, thousands of tourists ignore them as they bake in the sun, splash in the nearby surf, rent boogie boards and roll out their towels.

Yet in the morning, as rainbows dazzle the brilliant skies just after dawn, these lowlying stones, nestled among coconut palms, whisper of long-gone times, when four powerful magicians visited these islands.

A metal plaque affixed to one of the stones briefly describes the reason why the Department of Parks and Recreation of the City and County of Honolulu decided to preserve these stones in 1963. But few read the plaque. Few know why these stones have long been regarded as possessing great mana (spiritual power).

Much of the story of these stones has been lost with the passing of time. What is still known hints at the stones' powers.

Long ago, even before the great chief Kahuihewa ruled O'ahu, four wonderous magicians arrived on this island from Tahiti. They soon toured all the islands, finally arrived back on O'ahu, and made their home on Waikiki not far from where the the famous Moana hotel majestically resides today.

These magicians, named Kapaemahu, Kahaloa, Kapuni and Kinohi, soon grew famous for their gentle manners and magical powers. Many healings were credited to them. They possessed great wisdom and were beloved in Hawaii, much as they had been in Tahiti.

Though no one today knows why, these four wizards finally had to leave O'ahu. Before they left, they asked the Hawaiians to create some sort of monument marking their stay and their works of healing magic.

Four large rocks were chosen to commemorate the four magicians. Thousands of Hawaiians moved the rocks, at night, into place. Two were situated in the magicians' home and two in the sea where they often swam.

Kapaemahu, who seems to have been the four's leader, transferred his powers to one stone. Each wizard, in turn, then imparted their powers to one stone each. After a lunar month of ritual celebrations, the four wizards vanished, never to return.

Possessing great mana, the stones were apparently revered for centuries. At the turn of the century, the two sea stones were moved up onto the beach. In time, their significance was largely forgotten, as was their exact location.

They were found once again in 1958 during the demolition of an old building. The plaque affixed to one of the stones was dedicated in 1963. After being moved several times, the four stones were finally placed in their present site in 1980, far closer to Diamond Head than their original position.

They still sit there, quietly emanating power, steps from Kalakaua Avenue on the beach. And they still possess mana.

Visiting the Stones

Visit the stones early in the morning, well before 8 a.m. if possible (dawn is ideal). At this time, Kuhio Beach (the part of the beach that is visible from Kalakaua) is almost tranquil. You'll probably see people unloading rental surboards, photographers taking advantage of the early morning light, and perhaps a few beach boys catching some waves before the tourist onslaught. Otherwise, the beach should be quiet. Take a fern or flower lei with you, if you wish.

Once you're on Kuhio Beach, you can't miss the stones: they're directly beside the police station, and a sign marked "Kuhio Beach" stands behind them. Once you've met, walk slowly around the stones, looking down at them. They've weathered much abuse in the past, including the indiginity of being broken, but they're sacred pohaku (stones). They still contain the mana of those four "wizards" who, more than 300 years ago, traveled from faraway Tahiti to live on O'ahu.

After you've circled the stones several times, place the lei (if you've brought one) on or beside one of the stones. If you've come to be healed, say a short prayer to Kapaemahu, Kahaloa, Kapuni and Kinohi, if you wish.

Then sit before the stones. Shut out the world. Pinpoint your consciousness toward the stones before you. You may want to hold your hands palms outward toward the stones.

Breathe deeply. Sense. Feel.

Let the present-day world fade away. Connect with the ancient power of Hawaii and of its peoples' ancestral homeland, Kahiki.

Accept the mana of the stones. Open youself to this spiritual energy. Let it wash over you. Immerse yourself.

The Wizard Stones.
Photo by Scott Cunningham.

After a time, rise. You might wish to walk around the stones again. Then, if you feel like it, take a swim in the warm pacific Ocean. As you splash in the gentle surf, think of the stones. Remember their mana. Remember Kapaemahu, Kahaloa, Kapuni and Kinohi.

Afterword
Because the stones are within a few yards of the police station (though not in direct sight), I can't recommend performing any elaborate rituals at the stones. If you feel uneasy about even leaving the lei at the base of the stones, take it with you when you wade into the water for a swim afterward. The waves can wash it from you, sending its mana into the sea in which these wizards (kahuna) swam.

Directions
Walk down Kalakaua Avenue toward Diamond Head until you're across the street from the Hyatt Regency, a huge, two tower hotel that occupies a whole city block. The hotel, at 2424 Kalakaua

Avenue, is directly across the street from the beach. Find the police station on the beach. The stones sit beside it.

FOR MORE INFORMATION

Lodging
See your travel agent about hotel or condominium accomodations on O'ahu.

Bibliography
Most O'ahu guidebooks mention the Wizard Stones of Waikiki. I've only found one book that discusses them in any detail. This is:

Gutmanis, June. *Pohaku: Hawaiian Stones*. Laie (Hawaii): Brigham Young University-Hawaii Campus, ND.

Little published information is available concerning these stones.

Haleakalā

Oz Anderson

There are few places on this earth that one can sit on a rocky perch literally above the clouds and wait for a break in the mists to clear the view, some 10,000 feet downwards to sparkling blue ocean. As if this weren't stunning enough, the view close by is. Across a vast unearthly landscape of red, black, and shades of undulating grey stretching for miles in a crater large enough to hold the island of Manhattan. Often likened to a moonscape, this eerie scenery appears at the peak of one of Hawaii's largest volcanoes. Haleakalā, literally "The House of the Sun," is a "sleeping" volcano rising 36,000 feet from the floor of the Pacific Ocean. You can drive to the very top and, on a clear day, look down to the Pacific Ocean which covers 93 percent of the mass of this enormous mountain. If you think this view is dizzying, try to imagine what it would be like if you could see all the way to the bottom of the sea. From the highest points here on southern Maui you can see the towering volcanic peaks of the island of Hawaii in the distance, or look down upon other islands.

Haleakalā is more famous for the beauty that lies within its rim than its awesome size, however. The summit provides some of the most dramatic and mysterious scenery imaginable, thoroughly impossible to describe. Even the best photographs barely capture the grandeur and immense proportions of this sacred place. Haleakalā merely stuns the casual visitor. Those who have the time and inclination to explore more deeply are amply rewarded.

One legend says that Maui, the trickster God of the Hawaiian people, climbed to the top of Haleakalā to snare the sun. The story goes that his mother complained when she hung her *tapa* (bark cloth) out in the sun and the day was too short for the cloth to dry. Maui wove a net from the wiliwili, climbed to the top of the mountain and cast his net upwards capturing the sun. He anchored the net so that it slowed the sun down in its progress, making the summer days both lengthier and more leisurely. His mother, and all the people, were pleased. Perhaps this is why the hot-season days in Hawaii feel so unhurried.

Haleakalā was formed in a succession of Hawaiian volcanoes, as recorded in both mythology and geological history. Geologists say the islands were created in consecutive order from Kauai in the northwest to Hawaii in the southeast. This was caused by the Pacific plate gradually sliding over a "hot spot" or volcanic vent beneath the ocean floor. Legend says that when Pele the flamboyant Goddess of fire and volcanoes arrived, she began looking for a home in Kauai but kept moving south-eastward. Haleakalā was her last stop before migrating on to her current home on the "Big Island" or Hawaii, where she is actively alive and showing her fires to this day. Indeed, Haleakalā's last eruption was only 200 years ago in 1790. Pele in her travels carried with her a giant "digging stick," which she used to gouge out the craters, looking for a place to house and stoke her fires. She dug a particularly great pit at Haleakalā where today, one of the hill-like cinder cones bears the name "Ka Lu'u O ka 'O'o," the plunge of the digging stick.

Haleakalā.
Photo by Oz Anderson.

The formation that a visitor today sees at Haleakalā is not truly a volcanic crater, but a wind and water eroded depression nearly 4000 feet lower than the peak of the original volcano. The cones and volcanic features within were created by smaller eruptions much later than the massive volcanic activity which first shaped the mountain. Haleakalā is definitely not considered extinct, although no one knows whether or when it may erupt again. Some say that before Mt. St. Helens exploded a few years ago, Pele was actually seen purchasing a ticket to the mainland in the Honolulu airport. We may assume that if she is ever seen booking a flight to Maui, that Haleakalā will be her destination. Many Hawaiians believe that she indeed intends to revisit her former home one day.

Among the treats that await your physical senses at Haleakalā are vibrantly colored rocks, volcanic rubble, and sands from different ages and types of volcanic activity.

You will see a lot of "aa," a gravelly type of lava. Within the crater are cones and pyramids formed from the ashes of volcanic fountain eruptions. Although these look small from a distance, the smallest are higher than 60 story buildings. You may see crystals such as olivine encrusted in the volcanic rock, formed as the lava cooled. Many unique native plants survive here, most notably the Silversword. This dramatic floral creature grows for 4-20 years, bursts once into more than a hundred bright purple and yellow blossoms, and then dies leaving its seed scattered on the rough lava where incredibly it begins to grow again almost immediately. Outside the crater, Hosmer's Grove is a good place to experience more of the various life forms. Look for Hawaiian nene, endangered geese that have adapted to life on barren lava and are under protection at Haleakalā.

There is an extreme *kapu* (taboo) on taking volcanic stone from anywhere in the Hawaiian islands. Hundreds of stories attest to the bad luck that follows those who do not respect this prohibition. All Hawaiian lava is believed to be part of the sacred body of the Goddess Pele, and should never be removed from Her. The kapu extends as well to other sacred relics. One story tells of boy scouts in recent years who found a burial of ancient bones while hiking the slopes of Haleakalā. Some of the boys surreptitiously stole a few pieces of the bone. The tales of the ills that befell them range from horrible to tragic. Finally, in desperation, the boys returned one night and reburied the bones, thus ending their streaks of extremely bad fortune. Such stories are common among those who live in these islands.

The spiritual opportunities at Haleakalā are many, befitting its majestic size and the many factors that comprise its nature. In all cultures and lands, high places are associated with spiritual aspiration. The archetype of the hermit meditating on a peak above the clouds bespeaks some natural recognition within us of a particular feeling inspired by physical loftiness. Haleakalā stands out particularly as a place where this sensation may be felt more vividly than at other mountaintops, due in part to the sudden difference in altitude from the crest to the coast only miles away.

Both ancient Hawaiians and modern physicists associate "The House of the Sun" with solar energies; the place where Maui may have pursued the Sun houses a solar observatory today. Spiritually, the Sun is associated with personal aspirations, the self, and the driving or directing influences in one's life. Your own symbolic Sun may be seen as that force within you driving your ambitions, your ego and your passions. Your astrological Sun is an important component of your spiritual personality. Haleakalā is an excellent place to explore the "Sun" within your own being, to allow this force to come to the fore of your attention and be examined. It may be useful to meditate upon solar energies, your personal sense of identity, or even your direction in life before planning a visit to Haleakalā. This may help determine your purpose for coming to this sacred site. The natural forces of Haleakalā are often experienced as challenging, and such challenge can be a great opportunity for personal growth. A clearly determined purpose allows the challenge to be met head on, and used consciously for self transformation.

In all of Hawaii, the forces of nature are particularly awesome. Perhaps it is because the land itself is so young and actively alive, having so recently come from the interior of the earth. Energies and powers seem more raw and vibrant. Winds blow with incredible urgency, and rains and lightnings carry a forceful potency. At Haleakalā the mixture of these elemental forces and stupendous proportions may evoke a sense of fear or self-insignificance, creating an opportunity to confront fears that lie within you. The challenges that may be encountered demand a particular awareness the inner nature of the self. The fears may stimulate recognition and acknowledgement of aspects of the self of which you may not have been aware until now.

There is also a gentle force of assurance that comes to Haleakalā. The Goddesses of mists and soft rains dwell here as well, serving to assuage and moderate the more extreme forces. These feminine energies balance the masculine nature of the site. At sunrise and sunset, clouds roll in from the sea, pouring in and out of the crater like rolling sea-foam or the boiling steam from dry ice. During the day, mists collect and drift, sometimes obscuring the dramatic view at moments yielding a partial surrealistic perspective. There is a calming spiritual reassurance derived from holding your stance while clouds come to first envelop you then gently release you. It is very easy to just treasure this special magick with-child-like innocence.

SUGGESTIONS FOR CREATING A CEREMONY

Because the experience of Haleakalā is so inherently "Self" oriented on the spiritual plane, any ritual work is best planned and designed by the individual. You may wish to use this guideline to create a productive experience.

1. Carefully choose and plan your own time and activities at Haleakalā, tailoring these to suit the type of experience you seek. If hiking for any distance, do not hike alone. Plan ahead and come prepared.

2. Prepare for and perform a ritual act of honoring, acknowledging the Native energies and natural forces. Include a ritual statement of your intentions.

3. Plan and set aside a particular time for your own actual spiritual work, such as an inner journey or meditative exercise. Take your journal and record both your outer and inner explorations.

4. Be sure to ground the experience ritually, so as to maximize its benefits within your own consciousness.

A trip to Haleakalā begins at the Visitor's Center. Obtain a guide map and necessary current information about trails. Be prepared for the cold, which frequently surprises newcomers. Temperatures at 10,000 ft. can be much lower than at the beach, and may drop to freezing inside the crater. Those with limited time or energy may choose to stick to the crater rim trails, such as at Leleiwi overlook or near the Visitor's Center. At Halemau'u there is an exceptionally pleasant and mostly level one-mile hike to the rim. In a full day you can hike into and back out of the crater, a total 8 to 11 miles. Enter via either Halemau'u Trail or Sliding Sands Trail, explore spectacular areas, and hike out via Halemau'u. Sliding Sands is just that, and difficult to go back up. Thirty-six miles of trails cover the crater interior. Overnight camping within the crater is available at two tent locations and in several difficult to reserve cabins. All overnight campers must contact the Rangers first for requirements and information. Many say that you cannot really know this volcano until you have slept within its depths. However, any place at Haleakalā is suitable for spiritual work. The energies are constant and readily contacted. Certain times of day, especially sunrise and sunset, are visually exceptional and powerfully felt. These are excellent times to begin or end any ritual work.

The non-Hawaiian visitor to Haleakalā needs to bear in mind that this is a place of active worship to the Native peoples. To the Hawaiians, Gods and temples are in the natural places as much if not more than anywhere else. People still come to "The House of the Sun" to worship, to chant, to pule (pray), and to leave offerings. While it would be considered inappropriate for a non-Hawaiian to attempt to perform traditional Native ceremonial practices, it is important to show respect to both the Native ways and the resident energies. You may wish to do this by incorporating some concepts of Hawaiian religious practices into your own ceremony as an act of honoring. Hawaiian rites are begun by asking for forgiveness, forgiveness from the God beings, Goddesses, and all spirits and forces from above as well as forgiveness from and for one another and from within. Forgiveness is asked for not only what has gone before, but for mistakes that may be made during the rite or that which may be inadvertently overlooked.

Humility is inherent to Hawaiian spiritual practices, and in your own rite of personal exploration this is well worth addressing. Offerings are often of seaweed collected at the shore, leaves or flowers. The ti leaf is most sacred, as are others, and such leaves or flowers may be strung in leis or woven in special arrangements. Hawaiians also recognize the essential life force in rocks, which are often included in offerings. Every stone contains mana, the power of spirit and life. It is believed that many rocks contain actual spirits or individual consciousnesses. A rock wrapped in a leaf and left as an offering is a living sacrifice. Your own offering might be of leaves and flowers, which will most beautifully carry your intentions and have the least long-term impact on the landscape. With your offering, address the Native energies and ask permission to do your work here. Include a statement of your own intention, the purpose determined in your prior meditation. Make these statements as part of your own prayers before you begin your journey here. Address your own deity (Goddess /God) or guide at this time as well.

Set aside some time to be alone and utilize the powerful energies of Haleakalā for your own internal work. The nature of this work may be planned ahead, or may be allowed to happen spontaneously at whatever time feels "right." Arrive with an intention, fully meet and receive your experience, and remain open to the powerful sense of dawning that resides within this sacred space. Be prepared to accept whatever is happening within your own being at the time. This may or may not seem profound in the moment but may serve to stimulate the beginnings of a new internal process. Attempt to keep in mind the aspects of fear, aspiration and challenge. As you perform your ritual acts, and as you explore this mysterious place, remain receptive to fresh insights about your internal reality. The opportunity to confront a hidden part of your self may come at an unexpected moment. Allow your inner child to surface and come out to play.

Your planned meditative time may be used to integrate a realization of which you are already aware, or to evoke such a realization. At your chosen time, find a place to sit quietly. Prepare yourself by relaxing thoroughly, slowing the breath, and turning your attention inward. You may wish to spend 15-30 minutes in free meditation, in a completely quiet and receptive mode. Alternately, you may wish to close your eyes and visualize your self as clearly as you are able in your mind's eye. Imagine that you see yourself following a trail within the crater at Haleakalā, and pay close attention to every detail along the way—sights, sounds, scents, and sensations. Be sure to record in your journal whatever you experience in your meditations. The meaning may become clear in the future. Some may choose to just sit and write freely in a personal journal, allowing the words to come spontaneously as in automatic writing.

To ground your experience, be sure to again take a little time alone before you leave Haleakalā. Close your eyes and return to the same visualization you experienced on your inner journey, or an image from your writing. Hold this image and draw it into your self as though you were reducing the picture and pulling it into the place of your heart. Place the palms of both your hands upon the ground. Ask your own Goddess/God or guide to assist you in integrating a new vision of yourself as seen from this clear vantage point. Ask for truth. Give thanks, both to your own deity and to the Native energies that have hosted your experience. As you give thanks, whether aloud or silently, let a sincere sense of gratitude flow out your palms and into the ground. Return some of your own mana to this place, which continues to gift so many with its awesome beauty.

FOR MORE INFORMATION

Haleakalā is about 1-1/2 hours drive from Kahului/ Wailuku, via Hwy 37 south, to Hwy 377 and Hwy 378 which leads into Haleakalā National Park. The way is well marked. No food, services or gasoline are within the Park, but water is available. Tent camping is on a first-come, same-day basis at two inner crater sites and one outside the crater. Cabins within the crater are currently allocated for reservation by a lottery system. Requests must be made in writing at least 3 months prior. For more information, write Haleakalā National Park, P.O. Box 369, Makawao, HI 96768 or call (808) 572-7749. Conditions change rapidly and dramatically at Haleakalā. All hikers are advised to check first with the Park Service for safety and preparedness precautions.

Acknowledgements

"Haleakalā" and various related publications of the National Park Service.

My Hawaiian friends, especially Lehua Lopez and Al Lagunero.

Bibliography

Beckwith, Martha. *Hawaiian Mythology*. University of Hawaii Press, Honolulu, Hawaii.

Fodor's Hawaii. David McKay Company, New York.

ILLINOIS

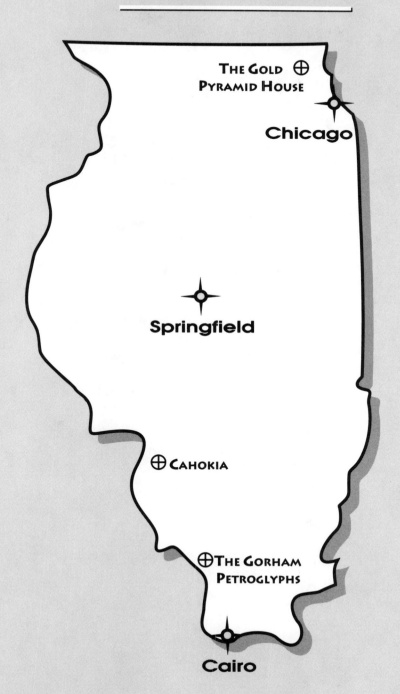

THE GOLD ⊕
PYRAMID HOUSE

Chicago

Springfield

⊕ CAHOKIA

⊕THE GORHAM
PETROGLYPHS

Cairo

The Gold Pyramid House

Frank Joseph

Illinois' newest pyramid is the private home of the James Onan family, who open their untypical domicile to the public each summer (see color plate). Visitors approach the 18-acre estate in which the gleaming pyramid stands surrounded by an 8-foot high wall decorated with hieroglyphic motifs. Commanding immediate attention is the 40-foot tall statue of a pharaoh. South of the 200-ton colossus is a gift shop, where jewelry, clothing, statuettes, plates, prints and numerous other lovely items reflecting Egyptian themes may be purchased.

Leaving through the east exit of the gift shop, visitors skirt a large gravel mound to the left until they arrive at a flight of stone steps leading to a darkened doorway at the top of the mound. The structure is a recreation of the tomb of Tutankhamun, who ruled Egypt 3,350 years ago. A ramp descends gently through a corridor painted with scenes from the Book of the Dead (the Ancient Egyptian guide for the soul's progress to the Otherworld) and opens into an exact copy of the boy-king's burial chamber. The tomb contains a super-abundance of real gold crafted into furniture, a dagger, a large death-mask and statuettes. This brilliant collection is surpassed by far greater treasures in the next chambers, where a full-size, authentic version of the Pharaoh's enormous sarcophagus is reproduced in 14-karat gold. The walls surrounding it are painted with scenes from his funeral and soul's ascension, identical to the Egyptian original. In the adjacent room, gold statues of protective goddesses stand at the four corners of a canopied shrine 7 feet high and 10 feet long, wrought entirely in real gold.

Visitors emerge from these dazzling sights through a south exit and follow the sidewalk to the Pyramid House, about 150 yards to the east. It sits at the center of a surrounding moat, its 12,000 square feet of walls covered with 24-karat gold plate gleaming in the spring-fed waters. Access is across a bridge and walkway flanked on either side by rows of sphinx statues. At 55 feet in height, the Gold Pyramid is a 100th scale replica of Egypt's Great Pyramid, at Giza. Like the original, it is oriented true north. Its interior contains 17,000 square feet of living space, featuring a full-size recreation of Tutankhamun's ceremonial chariot, covered entirely with real gold. The "Chariot Room" also displays some authentic Egyptian artifacts, abundant statuary of gods and goddesses, another solid gold coffin lid with the King's facial features realistically crafted on its surface, and hundreds of marvelous objects to catch the eye and delight the senses.

MYSTICAL SIGNIFICANCE

The Pyramid House is unquestionably an evolving sacred center, one of the latest in North America, although that was not the original intention of its builder and owner. Yet, from its very inception, it has evidenced many numinous qualities typically identified with sacred sites. As an experienced and successful contractor, James Onan knew not to build over an underground water source. Even so, weeks after the foundations of the Pyramid House were laid in 1974, a fresh-water spring inexplicably bubbled up at the very center of the construction. It grew so large that it completely surrounded the structure, making the Pyramid an island. Tests of the spring revealed its excellent purity and high mineral content. Mr. Onan bottled the water, and people from around the world have come to swear by its remarkable curative properties.

Just before the unexpected arrival of the fresh-water spring, a bulldozer broke its steel teeth against a large, immovable outcropping of black rock. Chunks of it were sent to the Colorado Assay Office in Denver for analysis. Meanwhile, the spring continued to rise ever higher, eventually drowning the rock laying just outside the perimeter of the foundation under 20 feet of water. It was then that the Colorado report arrived, informing the astounded Mr. Onan that the sample pieces were gold ore! He is the only person to have found gold in Illinois, and at the very spot of his Gold Pyramid. So far, he has been consistently unsuccessful in retrieving the submerged mass of gold at the bottom of the moat. Clearly, he had been directed to build the Gold Pyramid at this place!

Strange animal occurrences are not unknown at his Pyramid House. For two summers running, in 1986 and the following year, hundreds of jellyfish suddenly appeared in the moat, an "impossible event in the Midwest" according to experts at Chicago's Shedd Aquarium. As suddenly as they arrived, the creatures vanished and have never returned. No similar occurrence has ever been reported in Illinois, if anywhere else in the Midwest. In addition to this, families of vicious birds have taken roost above its eaves outside the northern exit of the "Chariot Room," which as a result is no longer usable because the birds boldly swoop to attack anyone who approaches the glass doors. Coincidentally, the "Chariot Room" contains the faithful replica of Pharaoh Tutankhamun's coffin lid, its golden side panels describing his judgment and apotheosis in the Otherworld. In Ancient Egyptian religion, the King's resting place was guarded at its northern end, the Pathway of the Soul, by Sokar, a bird that attacked anyone who sought entry to the royal burial chamber.

With all this sympathetic magic going on, the Pyramid House complex is becoming a genuine sacred center as opposed to a mysterious place. However, access to its growing numinosity by way of ritual may not be possible due to the crowds of visitors from all over the world who are drawn to the resplendent pyramid each year. Despite the lack of opportunity for meditation or ceremony, however, many experience the site's *genius loci* most often at two spots on the first floor of the Gold Pyramid: at the northern wall, near the middle of the meeting room (which happens to be directly over the center of the spring), and before the sarcophagus lid.

The magic felt in the Pyramid House lingers in the mind and soul long after the visitor leaves it. Experienced practitioners may tap into its resident plenum at a distance. For most, the Gold Pyramid represents a genuine mystic experience to stimulate our sense of wonder, the basis of all elevated feelings.

FOR MORE INFORMATION

Directions

The Gold Pyramid House is located on Dilley's Road, 2-1/2 miles north of Six Flags in Gurnee or about 10 miles south of the Wisconsin border and about 5 miles west of Lake Michigan. From Chicago, take I-94 north to Rt. 132, exit eastbound and turn left on Dilley's Road. Follow the green signs to the Pyramid.

The Gold Pyramid is open Sundays only, beginning the first week end in June through the Labor Day weekend. It opens at 10 a.m., with tours every half hour. The last tour begins at 4:30. Tickets available at the front gate. Adults, $7, children (12 and under), $4. For further information, telephone 1-800-525-3669. Illinois residents call 1-800-847-4864.

Accommodations

Camping: KOA, 8404 South Union Road, Union, IL 60180. April 1 through October 31. Telephone (815) 923-4206. From I-90, exit Marengo Hampshire (Union 76 truck stop), west on Highway 20, 4-1/2 miles to South Union Road. Visa, Master Cards accepted. $14 for two adults with tent site, features firewood, swimming pool, cabins ($22 for two adults).

Highly recommended "theme motels" are the Jailhouse, Hollywood and Sports Inns, 3732 Grand Avenue, Gurnee, IL 60031. Five minutes drive from the Gold Pyramid House. In each room: Nintendo, refrigerator, microwave oven, cable TV with HBO, exercise bike, free local telephone calls. Children under 17 stay free. One person, $34.95 to $45.95; two persons, $39.95 to $51.95. Telephone, (708) 623-7777.

Airport Inn, 3633 North Lewis Avenue, Waukegan, IL 60085. One person, $34.95 to $40.95. Two persons, $39.95 to $45.95. Kitchenette, $35.95 to $49.95. Telephone, (708) 249-7777. Twenty minutes drive from the Gold Pyramid House.

Toll free reservations at Jailhouse, Hollywood, Sports and Airport Inns at 1-800-373-5245.

Cahokia

Frank Joseph

The most spectacular of all the ancient human-engineered sacred centers in North America lies just across the Mississippi River from the modern city of St. Louis. An earthen step-pyramid rises in four gigantic terraces above the Southern Illinois plain. Comprising 22 million cubic feet of soil, its base in excess of 14 acres is larger than that of Egypt's Great Pyramid. Exceeded only by the Mexican pyramids at Teotihinacan and Cholula, it is the largest prehistoric structure north of the Rio Grande. Known as Monk's Mound after the French Trappist monks who briefly occupied it in the early 19th century, the Illinois pyramid is so huge its flat top easily accomodated over 4,000 persons during a Harmonic Convergence meeting in 1987.

During its hey-day, 900 years earlier, the turf-covered colossos may have been entirely encased in clay decorated with fabulous geometric designs painted blue, red and yellow. More certainly, a great, steeply gabled wooden temple then occupied the summit. The building was 48 feet wide and 105 feet long, bringing the original height of the pyramid to over 150 feet. From its lofty vantage-point, the chief priest or regent would have looked out over a 224-acre ceremonial city completely surrounded by a 12-foot high wall more than 2 miles long. Over 80,000 logs arranged in a stockade with regularly spaced watchtowers were plastered with a white limestone cement. The entire metropolitan area covered nearly 6 square miles over a 2,200-acre tract.

Behind the walls, south of Monk's Mound, spread an open-air plaza, where sporting events alternated with religious ceremonies and market activities. Beyond the plaza shimmered an artificial lake reflecting a trio of large pyramidal structures, a conical mound, a ridge-top and a platform, which contained the body of a 45-year old man laid out on a grave of silver mica flecks imported from the

145

Carolinas. Surrounding him were over 20,000 polished marine shell disc beads from the Gulf Coast and 300 sacrificed young girls. More than 120 mounds of various shapes and sizes adorned the area, though only 68 still survive. More than 50 million cubic feet of earth-went into their construction.

Reconstruction of Cahokia around 1000 A.D.
Photo courtesy of Illinois Historical Society, Cahokia, IL.

To the west, the observer atop Monk's Mound would have been able to see a 20-foot high circle of cedar posts painted bright red and arranged in an astronomical position 410 feet in diameter. Known today as Woodhenge, it was an observatory to chart significant celestial events, such as the winter solstice sunrise aligned with the first platform level of the big pyramid itself. Woodhenge also computed the positions of the Pleiades and other constellations of religious and agricultural importance.

An estimated 20,000 people resided within and beyond the walls of Cahokia, although no one knows the real name of the great city. Investigators do know, however, that it did not evolve slowly over the years, but was built suddenly, almost as though transported from some previous location, around 900 A.D. For the next two centuries, it was the dominant capital of the Mississippian Culture. Then, about 1100 A.D., internal violence of some kind occurred, part of the wall was burned, the leaders fled and Cahokia society rapidly deteriorated. By the time Monk's Mound was seen by the first white explorers in the late 17th century, it was over-grown and long abandoned. Who the great civilizers of southern Illinois may have been, where they came from and what became of them are questions archaeologists cannot yet answer with material evidence. Links with Mesoamerica, however, seem obvious; connections made all the more suspicious by Cahokia's own foundation date in the early 10th century, the same period in which the Mayas were evacuating their pyramidal cities in Yucatan. As for the possible post-Cahokian fate of its culture-bearers, see our Wisconsin entry about Aztalan. Visitors to Cahokia are strongly urged to begin their tour of the site at the large, modern museum opened in 1990. From there, anyone can walk through the archaeological park with a portable tape-player rented from the main office. Its recorded guide is the best introduction to everything Cahokia has to offer.

Monk's Mound Today.
Photo by Frank Joseph.

MYSTICAL SIGNIFICANCE

Archaeologists speculatively call ancient Cahokia "the City of the Sun," from Woodhenge's solar orientations. The sun has long been associated with ultimate power, an association implicit in the dominating aspect of Monk's Mound itself. To be sure, that power was once commercial and political, but it was also spiritual, if only in the sense that the enormous effort exerted by thousands of workers and artisans necessary to create the Cahokia megaopolis needed something transcending material and civic motives. Like the builders of Khufu's Pyramid, they were not slaves. They were more likely inspired laborers and craftsmen motivated by a religious ideal whose priestly spokesmen convinced them they were doing God's work in building the City of the Sun.

Comparison with Egypt's Great Pyramid does not end with Monk's Mound's relative size and the motivation of its builders. Both structures are aligned to true north and both are oriented to solar solstices. In fact, the Egyptians referred to Khufu's Pyramid as the Mountain of Ra, their sun-god. While Monk's Mound may be only a little more than a thousand years old, the earliest settlement at Cahokia was been carbon dated to around 3000 B.C., the same era of Egypt's first dynasty. Hesiod and other early Greek historians wrote of an Ecumene, or a world-wide civilization that flourished in a prehistoric Age of Gold. Could that Ecumene have once touched both America and Egypt, where their solar principles, religious, scientific and political, were preserved for thousands of years, generation after generation?

SUGGESTED RITUAL

After visitors complete their recorded tour of the grounds, they should go to the south end of Monk's Mound and stand in front of its broad flight of wooden steps leading up and across the face of this colossal work. Pause there a moment to let the mind take in the grand scale of the structure rearing up before you. Ascend the stairway, admire the massive flanks of the structure on both sides, but do not turn around, even after the first level has been reached. As the climb continues, it is best to envision the stairs lined on either side with priests and ceremonial women, warriors and attendants, something of an easier task after having just seen costumed examples in the museum.

Only when the very top has been reached should one turn to survey the site far beneath. The effect is dramatic and potent enough to activate the imagination, which is the basis of all visionary ability. See Cahokia in the days of its glory with its glistening lake, mighty walls and throngs of people in the plaza. In the west, Woodhenge casts long shadows examined by teams of astronomers. Explore the vast area of the summit. A great temple or palace once stood, not in the center, which was part of a ceremonial courtyard, but toward the rear. It is easy to find its mid-point, which is the spiritual focus for the whole pyramid and the sacred center of the entire complex. Here one should stand in the huge power vortex linking earth with sun-energies. It may become clear to the receptive visitor at this point that the physical reality of the pyramid's soil construction is the structured accumulation of earth power. Consequently, Monk's Mound is the high meeting ground between Mother Earth and Father Sky, the tremendous conjunction of the two elemental sources of life. Views all around are thrilling. This is the place to banish depression, to purge psychic, emotional, even physical toxins; to gather strength, self-confidence, self-mastery, purity of will and purpose. The sun stands for victory over cold and darkness, a gift presented here to the earth and its worshippers.

Envision a golden chain with a polished golden medallion in its center placed around your neck, with the medallion resting over your sternum. Feel grateful to your destiny for bringing you to this supreme sacred center. Offer the pyramid's *genius loci* a pinch of tobacco or a libation of pure water in each of the four Cardinal Directions, and thank the spirit of the sun for his triumphant radiance. As you descend the broad stairway, think of the golden chain and medallion around your neck and imagine great crowds of celebrating people along the steps and in the plaza below, congratulating you on your honored gift from the summit. Their presence at Cahokia is more real than may be suspected.

FOR MORE INFORMATION

Directions

Off I-55/70 at Black Lane south to Main Street, turn right (west) to Cahokia Mounds State Historical Site, open daily from 8 a.m. to dusk. The Interpretive Center Museum is open from 9 a.m. to 5 p.m.

Both are closed New Year's, Thanksgiving and Christmas. For additional information, write Site Manager, Cahokia Mounds State Historic site, P.O. Box 681, Collinsville, IL 62234. Telephone (618) 346-5160.

Accommodations

Motel 6, 1405 Dunn Road, St. Louis, MO 63138. Telephone (314) 869-9400. From I-270 eastbound take Bellefontaine Road, Exit 32, go left on Bellefontaine Road, then right to Dunn Road and proceed to motel, 25 minute drive to Cahokia Mounds, $25 per night, for single.

Best Western Midway Motor Lodge, I-270 and Dorsett Road, Exit 17. 2434 Old Dorsett Road, Maryland Heights, MO 63043, Telephone, (314) 291-8700. $66 to $70 per person. One hour's drive from Cahokia Mounds.

Camping at KOA's Granite City site, 3157 West Chain of Rock Road, Granite City, IL 62040. Telephone, (618) 931-5160. One block south of junction I-270 and Route 3. Then go east 1/2 mile on West Chain of Rock Road. From St. Louis, 55-40-70 East take 270 north to Route 3S. 55 north, take 70 West to Exit 248A, then 3 North eight miles, Illinois 64 take 255 to 270 West, then 3 South. Illinois 55, take 70 West, 270 West to Route 3 South; Master, Visa Cards accepted. Tent site, two adults, $11. Located at beautiful Horseshoe Lake State Park, 10 minutes from Cahokia Mounds.

Bibliography
Daniel, Glyn. *Encyclopaedia of Archaeology*. New York: Thomas E. Crowell Company, Inc., 1977.

Platt, Colin. *The Atlas of Medieval Man*. New York: St. Martin's Press, 1979.

The Gorham Petroglyphs

Frank Joseph

Driving south on Route 3 into the vast expanse of the Shawnee National Forest, the traveler notices a dominant feature on the horizon: an enormous, imposing bluff. It stands alone and, like many sacred sites of unusual power, its presence is felt even at a distance, intensifying the closer one approaches it. Following a dirt road skirting its colossal base, visitors behold a natural formation more bizarre than they may have expected. The sheer cliff face growing straight up some 200 feet is a fanciful mass of twisted forms and writhing shapes unlike any other bluff, giving it the appearance of

The Gorham Petroglyphs.
Photo by Frank Joseph.

151

having been melted. The impression is correct, because this unique forma-tion is not the result of long-term erosion (like the other outcroppings lining the Mississippi River), but rather the result of the earth itself having been broken open, spewing forth a rapidly rising mass of molten rock that eventually cooled and hardened into spiralling configurations. It is Gorham Bluff's magmatic origins which account for its dramatic appearance.

Going through thick undergrowth at the base of the bluff, we enter a shallow, shady depression. It slopes up through some trees to a clearing at the foot of the formation, where a natural stage is set into the bluff itself. A smooth, flat face, like an outdoor movie screen, spans a rectangle 30 by 50 feet. Running in a line near the bottom, at eye-level and just above, are a series of the finest petroglyphs in the Midwest, and the oldest. They comprise the outlines of hands, circles, birds, crosses and less discernable figures. Formerly numerous up and down the Mississippi Valley, petroglyphs are rarely found today, with most of the survivors lingering on in remote locations.

Precise dating for the Gorham images is not possible. Nor may the exact identity of their creators be established with certainty, although many Native American tribes wandered through the area and used the holy signs for unknown centuries.

MYSTICAL SIGNIFICANCE

It was not by accident that the Gorham Bluff was chosen for the permanent display of the sacred petroglyphs. The gargantuan earth-energies which pushed it in a molten, semi-solid condition out of the planet's bowels are so potent that they radiate from the massive formation. For persons in tune with these signals, the bluff is irresistible. Its theatrical milieu, complete with a natural stage setting, as though crafted by some divine agency, was the *mise en scene* for wonderful spiritual dramas, shamanistic initiations.

Here the tribal adepts gathered to inspire the vision quests of manhood, to conjure and cure and to deliberately alter the consciousness of men and women seeking personal contact with the Great Spirit. The petroglyphs are well-preserved and easily read from left to right, from north (the Spirit Direction for most Native American tribes) to south (the traditional "Direction of Becoming"). They begin at stage-left, as it were, with a cross inside a circle beside a crescent moon and star. The ⊕ is an archetype, a universal human symbol found around the world and signifying the "sacred center." The moon in relation to a "star" (probably the planet Venus) marks the time for the beginning of the ritual.

Closeup of Petroglyphs.
Photo by Frank Joseph.

Human figures incised into the rock face walk toward the main body of the petroglyphs. The images of birds in flight merge with palm prints—some child-sized—implying human striving to attain the divine. In front of them lies a boulder decorated with ⊕ and a figure kneeling before a half-man, half-bird creature. This is the Rock of the Shaman, the bird-man symbol of spiritual transformation, and before whom reverence is shown at his place of power. Back at the cliff wall, the largest ⊕ is faced on either side by a pair of deer, one white, the other black. They define the sacred center mysteries practiced here as a power directing and harmonizing the resident energies, a psychic fulcrum positioned mid-point between day and night, the Sacred Balance, the Special Duality. Deer are additionally symbolic of transformation, because of their ability to stealthily appear and vanish in the woodlands, and of regeneration by way of their rejuvenating antlers.

A single palm print appears beside a bird-man, implying the initiate's growing identification with the shaman spirit. In order for him to properly see the penultimate glyphs, he had to climb to he top of another boulder before the cliff face. There he would behold the mingling of human and bird shapes pictured among the stars, as though the elevated soul were being lifted into the higher realms of consciousness. Back down on ground level, the crescent moon reappears, but the Venus-star is further to the right, indicating the passage of time and the end of the ceremony. Sure enough, the final images belong to a bird flying away from the sacred-center cross, symbolizing the transubstantiation of human mortality into the soul's immortality.

Just beyond the theater of petroglyphs, to the right (south), is a small, circular mound with a depression in the center. It is identical to ancient burial mounds found throughout Wisconsin. In the depression of this donut-like structure the initiate experienced or completed his or her vision quest. The confines of Gorham's sacred precinct suggest only a few individuals at a time were shepherded through their initiation by the shaman. To better appreciate the life-changing effect of their spiritual adventure, it is important to realize that all the participants were part of a culture in which nature-mysticism was accepted as a common fact of their existence. They therefore entered upon their psychic exercises already deeply convinced in the efficacy of what they were about to do. Preparatory to their initiation, they fasted in silence and alone at some remote spot. Their consciousness was further altered by mild narcotics administered by the shaman to achieve the desired receptivity. They doubtless never saw the petroglyphs before the moment of their prepared viewing. As indicated by the drawings themselves, empowerment ceremonies took place at night. Hence, the high drama of the scenes—staged under torch light to the Otherworldly music of pipes and drums, together with a ferociously attired shaman chanting in a spirit-voice—must have been impressive, to say the least. For those who long ago experienced such initiation, they undoubtedly felt that they had touched the face of God.

SUGGESTED RITUAL

The Gorham petroglyphs are part of a sanctified place super-charged with centuries of human and telluric energies. Walking through the woods to the sacred precinct at the base of the bluff, the visitor is made to feel abundantly aware of its lingering spiritual potency. It feels like a special place. Prolonged fasts and narcotics are not necessary before coming to the center, nor are the dramatic services of the shaman required.

For modern initiates, the petroglyphs have the effect of a man-dala—a set of subconsciously evocative images used in meditation to achieve altered states of consciousness and spiritual awareness. Thus accepted, something of their ancient magic can still be enjoyed. Their symbolism, as we have seen, is really not so arcane as to have been lost forever in esoteric shamanistic tradition. Approaching them as universal human symbols we begin to tap into their essen-tial meanings which are better accessed through the subconscious than via the so-called "rational" mind.

Begin with the encircled cross and crescent moon at the far left (north) and follow along the rest of the petroglyphs on the cliff face. Go slowly, taking time to notice the story of transformation they tell, appreciating their deep antiquity, the hand, long since turned to dust, that wrought them, and the strong presence of the *genius loci*, who has never quit his charge here at the bluff. Who knows how many of their ghosts still haunt its surrounding woods? Perhaps they have long ago returned in the gigantic eagles that often soar in great numbers just above the tree tops.

But the precinct is friendly, for all its awesome atmosphere. Af-ter the individual visitors come to the end of the petroglyphs, they should proceed to the small, adjacent mound and either sit or stand in its center for meditation. Obviously, any one or several of the in-cised images spread out on the cliff face are ideal symbols to hold in the mind, thereby establishing spiritual contact with the ancient guardian. Leaving the mound, a thank-offering of tobacco, mineral water or an attractive stone is in order.

The petroglyphs are valuable and fragile, unprotected by the presence of any official agency. Some benighted individuals have carved their initials on the cliff face near them, but the holy symbols themselves remain intact. But the Gorham site is not without its pro-tectors. The surrounding Shawnee National Forest is the source of legends, Native American and contemporary, of phantom panthers and even an Illinois version of Big Foot, called the Whangdoodle. Encounters with these creatures go back to pioneer days and long before, but modern sitings still occur. The ghostly panthers and monstrous Whangdoodle are regarded by Indians in the area as ancient shamans who have returned in the forms of guardian spirits.

But there are more familiar guardians at the site. Visitors are advised to mind the snakes. Spiders too bedeck the precinct with their broad webs, living symbols of the sacred center left in their keeping.

FOR MORE INFORMATION

Directions

Exit I-57 west on 13. Stay on 13 after it becomes 149. At Grimsby, turn south (left) on 3 to Gorham. Go west (right) on the first road past the bridge before the bluff. Turn left (south) at the first road west of the bluff. Stay on this unmarked road leading to the last house (white) before a large field, 500 feet past the house. Park the car and enter through the high weeds. Continue straight east, to the bluff. If you have not found the large movie screen-like setting for the petroglyphs, walk a few paces along the base of the bluff in either direction.

Accommodations

Best Western Cheekwood Inn, 40 minutes from Gorham, Exit 18 off I-57. P.O. Box 280, Ullin, IL 62992. Telephone (618) 845-3773. $28 to $38 for single.

Camping may be enjoyed at KOA's Benton site, 1-1/4 hours drive south to Gorham. Address: R. R. 1 North Duquoin Street, Benton, IL 62812. Telephone (618) 439-4860. Master, Visa Card Accepted. $12 for the tent site, two adults.

Bibliography

Brandon, Jim. *Weird America*. New York: E. P. Dutton, 1978, pp 81-82.

Grant, Campbell. *Rock Art of the American Indian*. New York, 1967.

Three Rivers Petroglyphs, New Mexico.
Photo by Diana Person.

Wizard Island, Crater Lake in Oregon. View from the west.
Photo by Richard Ely.

Russell Cave, Alabama.
Photo by Mark Smith Studio.

Oak Creek Canyon, Arizona.
Photo by Ashleen O'Gaea.

Jefferson River, Montana.
Photo courtesy of the State Board of Tourism.

Hovenweep Castle, Utah.
Photo by Florence W. McClain.

Oracle Chamber at America's Stonehenge, Mystery Hill, New Hampshire.
Photo by Brian Sullivan.

Chaco Canyon, New Mexico.
Photo © by L'Aura Colan.

Enchanted Rock, north side of dome, Texas.
Photo by Kathleen Boehme.

New Harmony Labyrinth, Indiana.
Photo courtesy of New Harmony.

Chaco Kiva, Chaco Canyon, Utah.
Photo © by L'Aura Colan.

Mt. Delani/Mt. Everest, Alaska.
Photo courtesy of the Alaska Division of Tourism.

Great Temple Mound, Florida.
Photo courtesy of Chic and Tabatha Cicero.

Great Serpent Mound, Ohio.
Photo courtesy of the Ohio Historical Society.

Fantastic Caverns, Springfield, Missouri.
Photo courtesy of the Convention and Visitors Bureau.

Aztalan, Wisconsin.
Photo by Frank Joseph.

Bandelier National Monument, Tyuonyi Ruin.
Photo courtesy of the National Park Service.

New Harmony Labyrinth, Indiana.
Photo courtesy of New Harmony.

Chaco Kiva, Chaco Canyon, Utah.
Photo © by L'Aura Colan.

Mt. Delani/Mt. Everest, Alaska.
Photo courtesy of the Alaska Division of Tourism.

Great Temple Mound, Florida.
Photo courtesy of Chic and Tabatha Cicero.

Glacier Park, Montana.
Courtesy of the Montana State Board of Tourism.

The Gold Pyramid House, Illinois.
Photo by Frank Joseph.

East-West Chambers at America's Stonehenge.
Photo by Brian Sullivan.

"The Third Eye High," Zion National Park, Utah.
Photo © by L'Aura Colan.

Tripod Rock, New Jersey.
Photo by Bruce Scofield.

Tripod Rock. Solstice Boulders at sunset at the Summer Solstice.
Photo by Bruce Scofield.

Angel Mounds, Indiana.
Photo by Darryl Jones.

"Moon Room," Bandelier National Monument, New Mexico.
Photo © by L'Aura Colan.

"Sedona Speaks," Sedona, Arizona.
Photo © by L'Aura Colan.

INDIANA

GREAT CIRCLE
MOUND

Indianapolis

NEW HARMONY

ANGEL MOUNDS

Angel Mounds

Frank Joseph

Angel Mounds was founded at roughly the same time Cahokia began to decline, around 1100 A.D., although the Indiana center was substantially smaller. Some believe that Angel Mounds was built by migrants fleeing social dislocation at Cahokia. An important cultural link with Cahokia is a common solar alignment. The doorway of Angel Mounds chief temple was oriented to sunrise of the summer solstice, the same fix occurring at Monk's Mound. Cahokia is, in fact, physically linked to Angel Mounds by the Mississippi and Ohio Rivers.

About 4,000 residents inhabited the 103-acre settlement, which included 11 earthen platform mounds surmounted by temples and palaces made of wooden posts and dried grass daubed over with white adobe. The mounds were interspersed by 200 secular dwellings, some for winter, others for summer. Their walls were decorated with geometric themes colored red, yellow and blue, lending the site a cheerful aspect. Nearby were numerous gardens of corn, beans, pumpkin, gourds and sunflowers. Pecans were gathered in a lovely grove beside a step-pyramid 44 feet high and 4 acres in area. There was an unusual plaza sunk like a great bowl into the ground. Within this broad depression ceremonial, athletic and market activities took place.

Originally, the site was almost entirely surrounded by a river channel, practically rendering Angel Mounds an island. Whether or not this river channel was made by the ancient inhabitants is still a matter of professional debate. In any case, Angel Mounds was inexplicably abandoned by its leaders and most of its population about 1310. Why they left and where they went remain mysteries still bedeviling scholars' best efforts to understand America's prehistory. The inhabitants left behind no signs of disease, war, social upheaval, crop failures, overfishing or hunting, earthquakes or severe weather. For the next 140 years, the site was occupied off and on by

159

diverse, small numbers of primitive wanderers who knew little or nothing of Angel Mounds' former glories. By 1450, the place was deserted and unoccupied.

Reconstruction of Angel Mounds.
Photo by Frank Joseph.

Among the unusual items recovered by archaeologists is a mastodon's tooth from a shaman's grave, and burial urns—circular pots containing the bones of infants covered over with pebbles. The most outstanding feature at Angel Mounds is a faithful reconstruction of the large temple building.

MYSTICAL SIGNIFICANCE

The resident energies at Angel Mounds are similar to those found at Cahokia. Both sites, as mentioned above, shared an identical solar orientation. But the Indiana center has a markedly different ambiance, not only because it is smaller than its parent city near the banks of the Mississippi River, but also because, unlike Cahokia, little or no human sacrifice took place, and there were no large-scale acts of social violence. As a result, the godhood here may be less dramatic.

The sacred aspect of Angel Mounds is underscored by its island-like configuration, either natural or man-made. Its origins are relatively unimportant, because the inhabitants of this place either chose the location for its peculiar features, or they purposely altered it (terra-formed it) to conform to their requirements. In many ancient cultures, water was perceived to be a boundary between this world and the next. Consequently passing over the water from mundane existence outside the walls into the other world of pyramid mounds constitutes an important ritual act in and of itself.

The Reconstructed Wall.
Photo by Frank Joseph.

That the inhabitants of Angel Mounds regarded their city as something more than a commercial or political enterprise may also be surmised from the fragments of broken pottery decorated with cultic emblems. Among these are symbols delineating the sacred center: ⊕ 卍 + ╬ etc. In every recovered example, the signs appear mid-point in representations of the sun.

Angel Mounds was the leading sacred center of ancient America's solar cult after the fall of its former capital at Cahokia.

SUGGESTED RITUAL

The public entrance to Angel Mounds is at the same location as the original main gate used by the ancient inhabitants more than seven centuries ago. Pass over the bridge spanning a small stream beneath to enter the prehistoric city, just as its own people did during the days of its florescence. In front of the visitor, to the right (west), stands a group of trees obscuring a step pyramid. Although the trees make this interesting feature difficult to discern, they are maintained as natural prevention against erosion. Beyond it, on the right, spreads the dim outline of the sunken plaza, and further to the west is another line of trees. Pass through this verdant veil and you will enter a distinct energy zone, an open area featuring a large platform mound. A broad wooden stairway leads up its northern side to an impressive, detailed, modern reconstruction of the solar temple that once stood there.

The mound with its new temple projects a gold-green aura that sometimes switches to grayish blue, a color shift observed by receptive visitors over the years. Pause at the edge of the tree line for a moment to pick up on the temple mound's radiance. Two centuries of ritual activity at this site have stamped the ground irrevocably, sanctified it forever. The ancient inhabitants are gone, but they left the spirit-lamps burning. Walk to the structure and climb its broad stairs to the top. A wall defining the holy precinct surrounds it, with a space open for visitors to enter. The interior is bare, but its center is the energy focus for the entire complex.

Originally, the temple contained a splendorous arrangement of ritual items. Two lines of larger than life wooden statues stood guard near the entrance, while the ceiling was hung with polished seashells, lengthy strands of imported pearls and brilliant feathers. Cedar chests decorated with human images stood against the walls interspersed with round and oblong shields. Toward the rear of the hall, more chests stocked to resemble a step pyramid contained more than a million fine pearls. Animal skins and many colorfully dyed mantels hung on the walls.

Outside, make a complete circuit at a normal pace at the top of the mound to the right, followed by another complete circuit to the

left. Descend the stairs with the feeling that you are leaving something behind in the temple. Such feelings establish a psychological
bond with the *genius loci* that will continue to link the visitor to it
long after he or she leaves, all the better to tap into its sympathetic
powers at a distance. Walk to the edge of the clearing for a good
view of the platform mound. Here the setting is peaceful enough
and properly suited for meditation, visualization or contemplation.
An offering of water, stone or tobacco to the generous spirits of the
place may be accepted here.

FOR MORE INFORMATION

Directions

Off 64 at 164, south, off at South Green River Road. North on
South Green River Road to Pollack Avenue. Right (east) on Pollack
Avenue to Angel Mounds State Memorial Park. The site is open
daily, except Monday, from 9:00 a.m. to 5:00 p.m., except Christmas,
Easter, Memorial Day and Labor Day. Admission free. Open 1:00
p.m. to 5:00 p.m. on Tuesdays and Sundays. For more information,
write: Director, Angel Mounds State Memorial Park, 8215 Pollack
Avenue, Evansville, IN 47715. Telephone: (812) 853-3956, or (317)
232-1637.

Accommodations

Best Western Williamsburg Inn, 100 South Green River Road,
Evansville, IN 47715. Telephone: (812) 473-0171. North or south, US
41, Lloyd Expressway, 2 miles east of Green River Road from the
Lloyd Expressway. $45 to $55 single, per person. Five minutes from
Angel Mounds.

Camping at KOA Weather Rock, Rt. 2, Box 150A, Haubstadt,
IN 47639. Telephone, (812) 867-3401. From the junction of I-64 and
US 41, go 1,000 feet north on US 41 to Warrenton Road, go east 1-1/2
miles to KOA entrance. Less than 30 minutes north of Angel
Mounds, Master/Visa Cards accepted. $11 for tent site, two adults.
Open April 1 through November 30.

Bibliography

Black, Glen. *Angel Mounds*, in two volumes. Indianapolis: University of Indiana, 1964.

The New Harmony Labyrinth

Frank Joseph

In 1814, visionary George Rapp led a thousand of his followers from Germany and Pennsylvania to a site near the Wabash River formerly occupied, unknown to Rapp at the time, by the ancient Mound Builders. There they built a unique community dedicated entirely to esoteric spiritual principles. Calling themselves "Harmonists" after their syncretic cult, their religious commune soon rose to prosperity and notoriety. After only 11 years of existence, Rapp was forced to sell his little utopia due to the unremitting hostility of neighboring townspeople, who regarded unconventional ideas as the certain earmarks of Satan.

However, the town was purchased by Robert Owen who only expanded Harmonist concepts. Re-naming the settlement "New Harmony," he built upon Rapp's syncretism, establishing a welfare cooperative of free education, shared wealth and common responsibility in lieu of civic authority. Within two years, his social experiment disintegrated into anarchy and bankruptcy. But the town was saved by Owen's three sons, who, retaining Rapp's Harmonist principles, shifted emphasis from socialism to culture, thus attracting scientists, teachers, artists and researchers from around the country. By the advent of the Civil War, New Harmony was the leading cultural center in North America. The first U.S. geologist, David Dale Owen (no relation to Robert), built a laboratory at New Harmony that later became the first headquarters of the U.S. Geological Survey.

Intellectual freedom proved a better success than political unorthodoxy, and New Harmony drew nationally known figures and built new public facilities right up to WWI. The economic implications of the war, however, were too much for New Harmony, and the community entered a long decline that was halted only in 1965, when it was saved as a national historic monument. Since then, most of the old structures have been restored and new additions made,

most notably, the Roofless Church, an outdoor religious park constructed according to the Harmonist belief that only one roof, the
sky, should embrace all worshiping humanity. Paralleling its earliest population, only a thousand residents live permanently in New
Harmony today. Horse-drawn carriage tours of the town are still
available and highly recommended.

The New Harmony Labyrinth.
Photo by Frank Joseph.

MYSTICAL SIGNIFICANCE

But the mystical center, along with the Roofless Church, is the
singular feature of this unique place. Set a block in from the south
end entrance of New Harmony, on Main Street fronting Tavern
Street, lies the Labyrinth, a landscaped maze of bright green hedges
with a small, one-room wooden building at the very center. The date
of its creation is unknown, although historians assume it was made
by Frederick, George Rapp's adopted son, after the Harmonists first
arrived in Indiana. The original New Harmony labyrinth was com-

posed of shrubs, mostly currant and hazel bushes, together with dogwood trees and flowering plants. At its center stood a curious, circular log house featuring a single door and window. The rough, primitive, vine-covered building was contrasted by its meticulously clean and well-organized interior, After decades of neglect, it fell into ruin. In 1939, the State of Indiana recreated the original structure on a lot adjacent to its former location; this is the labyrinth seen by visitors today.

The labyrinth epitomized the central precepts of the Harmonists' cosmic harmony through the balance of forces. Julie Rutherford, Historic New Harmony's Promotion Coordinator writes that the New Harmony labyrinth "symbolized the difficulties of attaining true harmony and the choices one faces in life trying to reach that goal." The labrys, or Double Axe of Ancient Crete, from which "labyrinth" derives, represented the Earth Mother, her two life-giving breasts, themselves signifying the Sacred Duality of the universe. Passage through the labyrinth was a quest to that ultimate source of life, the eternal womb, from which all emerged reborn in the conscious recognition that there is no death, only eternal renewal. Thus aware of its essential, higher meaning, the modern initiate may also enter upon that journey to re-birth.

SUGGESTED RITUAL

Begin at the peaceful Roofless Church, the perfect place for a preparatory meditation. It is a short stroll to the nearby labyrinth. As you walk through it, realize it is also your spirit-path, not only for those who have used it before, but for other beings attuned to the purified human energy. Think of its mystical significance, so that the eventual appearance of its mid-point structure will have the properly dramatic effect. Reaching that sacred center, the visitor will find the vibrations appropriately harmonious and sympathetic. The gentle focal-point here has a motherly quality and is ideal for contemplation. The site is also suitable for problem solving of all kinds, particularly deep personal problems, because walking through its uncertain pathways is like a jaunt into one's own head. The labyrinthine design is similar to the convolutions of the human mind. Trying to find one's way through the maze of the hedge rows, the initiate identifies with a single thought struggling for resolution and expression by finding the center.

Examine some problem troubling you as you enter the New

Harmony labyrinth. Visitors will feel comfortable bringing along a favorite crystal that fits nicely in the hand, and the magic mineral is good to turn over in the right hand as one turns over a thought in one's mind. When you get to the center, ask the *genius loci* for a blessing. Sometimes initiates are suddenly, deeply overwhelmed emotionally at this point, a perfectly natural, purging reaction, and a wonderful sign that the visitor has been touched by the hand of Divinity.

Remain at the sacred center as long as you wish. Walking one's way out of the maze, the visitor should at least feel the potential for a solution welling up in himself. Minimally, the mind will be better prepared to resolve problems, Often, employing the open-souled attitude, the visitor senses a solution is at hand. Sometimes the answer appears like a gift out of nowhere. For anyone without a specific problem, the New Harmony labyrinth is the place to "get centered" and to re-charge one's spiritual batteries in a dramatic and fulfilling environment.

FOR MORE INFORMATION

Directions

From the east, exit I-64 at 165, south to 66. Right on 66 to New Harmony. From the west, exit I-64 at Griffin south to New Harmony. For additional information, write Julie Rutherford, Historic New Harmony's Promotion Coordinator, P.O. Box 579, New Harmony, IN 47631. Telephone: (812) 682-4488.

Accommodations

Ideally, a stay in New Harmony itself should be part of one's visit to the labyrinth. Guests may spend a night or more at the New Harmony Inn, P.O. Box 579, New Harmony, IN 47631. Telephone: (812) 682-4491. Reservations required. $40 to $59 per person, single.

Camping is available at KOA Weather Rock, Rt. 2, Box 150A, Haubstadt, IN 47631. Telephone: (812) 867-3401. From the junction of I-64 and US 41, go 1,000 feet north on US 41 to Warrenton Road, go east 1-1/2 miles to KOA entrance. About 40-minute drive to New Harmony. Master/Visa Cards accepted. $11 for tent site, two adults. Open April 1 to November 30.

The Great Circle Mound

Frank Joseph

The prehistoric site northwest of Indianapolis is separated from the state's other ancient sacred center, Angel Mounds, by 200 miles and 700 years. The two places are unrelated, totally unlike each other and created by different peoples. Whereas Angel Mounds was inhabited by thousands of permanent residents, no one lived among the eleven strange earth-works above the White River. At a location where the ground was and is too sacred for human habitation, the superbly crafted structures comprise a ceremonial arena for the most important rituals and mass-meetings of a vanished people.

Sheltered for 20 centuries in a deep oak forest are weird features shaped like fiddles, figure-eights and horseshoes; rectangles, ovals and cones. Outstanding among them is the Great Circle Mound, a perfectly surveyed ditch with embankment encompassing a rounded platform structure opening at the south end on a broad ramp. In circumference, it was 1,200 feet, 384 feet across and 9 feet high; it was formed of 66,900 cubic feet of soil. The wonderful precision and perfect proportions of its overall design, to say nothing of its grand concept, bespeak the surveying technology and sophisticated organizational skills of its builders, who disappeared around 400 A.D. Archaeologists classify them as members of the Adena or Hopewell Cultures. Half a dozen of their skeletal remains were excavated in the Great Circle Mound fronting the ramp, or "Gateway," although the 259-acre site was never a necropolis. The bodies were surrounded by flint arrow heads, potsherds, copper spear points and a stone pipe fashioned in the image of a frog. This effigy pipe is of special interest, because tobacco was regarded by the inhabitants as a medium of communication between men and gods. Prayers rose to heaven on its smoke and mild narcotics helped in the vision quest for glimpses of the supernatural. Underscoring its connection with the Otherworld, to which the young men had probably been ritually sacrificed and laid to rest at the ceremonial entrance to the Great Circle Mound, was the frog itself, an archetype known in dozens of cultures around the world as the symbol of the soul's purification, transmigration and regeneration.

Model reconstruction of the Great Circle Mound as it appeared after 1 A.D.
Photo courtesy of Bronnenberg Nature Center Museum,
Indian Mounds, IN.

The 10-foot deep ditch surrounding the Great Circle Mound may once have been filled with water, rendering the central mound an island joined to the "shore" by its gateway ramp. Another large earth-work, similar in size and configuration, although more of a rounded rectangle and less well preserved, lies exactly one mile north east of the Great Circle Mound. Until 16 centuries ago, thousands of people assembled along the ridge of its embankment to watch costumed processions pass through the gateway into the sacred central precinct. For restricted rituals, the same embankment served as a concealing wall for more esoteric ceremonies.

MYSTICAL SIGNIFICANCE

The amorphous nature of Indian Mounds makes them difficult to interpret. But the apparently inscrutable character of the site also contributes mightily to our sense of wonder, which is the essential animus of the spiritual power belonging to all significant sacred centers.

The Great Circle Mound as it appears today.
Photo by Frank Joseph.

The meaning of the fiddle-back and horseshoe mounds in the vicinity of the Great Circle Mound is elusive, no less so their relationships to one another. And there is meaning in those relationships. For example, the distance from the Great Circle Mound's mid-point to that of its companion structure, as mentioned above, is precisely one mile. While it seems ludicrous to suggest the prehistoric Mound Builders used our present system of measurement, the precision of that distance between the two leading features of the area is intriguing. And there are other provocative comparisons. The only structures similar to the large mounds in Indiana occur 150 miles away, in Ohio and 5,300 miles further eastward across the

Atlantic Ocean, in Britain. The Ohio counterpart is among the most
stupendous structures ever raised by the hand of man (see Newark
Mounds, Ohio), and is ten times larger than Indiana's Great Circle
Mound.

Indiana's Great Circle Mound does not appear to have any celestial alignments, but the gateway of its northern companion is oriented with the spring solstice sunrise, which may have occasioned
either the beginning or the conclusion of a ritual that linked both
structures.

SUGGESTED RITUAL

Visitors enter through the gatehouse off Mounds Road and
park in a lot near the pavilion. The little museum on the first floor of
the nearby Bronnenberg Nature Center contains beautifully crafted
copper artifacts, breastplates and headdress ornaments, and a
model of the Great Circle Mound depicting its appearance in the ancient past. The trail outside leads to a forest of lofty oaks, bubbling
streams and colorful song-birds. This is where the vision quest
starts. Here one should be receptive to the concept that each individual human being is no less a part of Nature than the deer or flowers.
Then the visitor may begin to feel that with every breath of air he or
she is clearing the mind and body simultaneously. Our thoughts
and our respiration are purified, redeemed from the industrial
world of inhaled poisons. We breathe again the strangely familiar
old freedom of our arboreal origins. We are woodland spirits no less
than all the other creatures. In our inherent rootedness to Nature
there is something of the oak tree in us. The hawk looks out at us
through our own eye. We create out of ourselves, as the spider does.

It was through deep forest trails such as this one that the Ancient Ones made their way to the Great Circle Mound. At first sight,
it appears as only a short, uniform hill. Going around its eastern
flank, its prodigious size and circular configuration become more
obvious. But only when the visitor stands before its gateway ramp
on the south end is the earth-work fully recognizable in its entirety.
Follow the ramp into the embankment over the ditch to the fence,
which restricts access to the fragile sacred precinct. It is just as off-
limits to us as it was to most of its own celebrants, 1,600 years ago.
The psychic radiation of its center, however, is easily and powerfully discernible here. On either side runs the encircling wall of perfectly sculpted earth, its ridge once crowded with brightly cos-

tumed people, their ceremonial finery reflecting in the ring of water below. In front, the priests, musicians and initiates performed their rites of passage and empowerment in the presence of human and woodland spirits.

Creative visualization here will most effectively tap into the site's Otherworldly resonance. Walk once completely around the Great Circle Mound. Back at the gateway, visit the nearby fiddle-back structure and let the mystery of its meaning filter into your subconscious mind. Do not try to grasp everything with the rational side of your being. Let the living symbolism of the place speak wordlessly to something deeper, more instinctively sensitive. From the fiddle-back mound, follow the trail northward back into the depths of the forest along the high banks of the White River, whose clear waters once brought boat-loads of tribal families to this hallowed place. Soon, the Great Circle Mound's counterpart is reached. Its center is not restricted, and it makes for a perfectly peaceful meditation spot. The vibrations are sympathetic, unexpectedly low-key, but constant. Images to hold in the mind during meditation include the spiral, concentric circles and a frog (remember the stone effigy pipe!). One's spine acts almost as an antenna during meditation at the mound's sacred center, opening our spirit to the energy of the *genius loci*.

A pinch of tobacco, some sprinkled purified water or an attractive stone make suitable offerings and symbolize something of oneself left behind, thereby perpetually connected to the site.

Exiting the mound over the ramp to the east, the receptive visitor feels the transcendent barriers through which he or she passes, like the color ribbons of the rainbow. So it must have seemed to an unknown people, who left their spiritual orientations behind in monumental earth-works, still marking the solstices each year, like cosmic clocks loyally keeping time in the long absence of their makers.

FOR MORE INFORMATION

Directions
I-69 off at Exit 28, north on 9, Scatterfield Road, to 232. Right (east) to Mounds Road. For more information, write Mounds State Park, Anderson, IN 46013. Telephone (317) 642-6627. Open year-round. $2 admission fee. Hours, 10 a.m. to dusk.

Accommodations

Ideally, camping overnight in Mounds State Park is the best way to enjoy its sacred center. Shower/restroom facilities, electrical hook-ups. $11 per tent site, for two adults. For further information, contact Mounds State Park, Anderson, IN, 46013. Telephone (317) 642-6627.

Motel-6, 5810 Scatterfield Road, Anderson, IN 46013. Telephone (317) 642-9023. Ten-minute drive from Indian Mounds. From I-69 (north or southbound) take the Indiana 109-Anderson Exit, #26. Proceed north on Indiana 109 (Scatterfield Road) to motel. $24 per single.

Bibliography

Brown, Joe Epps. *The Sacred Pipe*. University of Oklahoma Press, Oklahoma, 1989.

Harner, M. *The Way of the Shaman*. New York: Harper Row, 1980

Mitchell, John. *The Earth Spirit*. London: Thames & Hudson, 1975.

KENTUCKY

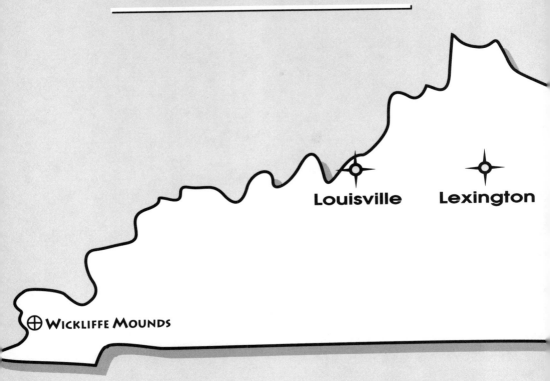

Louisville   Lexington

⊕ WICKLIFFE MOUNDS

Wickliffe Mounds

Frank Joseph

On a strategic rise overlooking the Mississippi and Ohio Rivers, a truncated pyramid boldly dominated the heavily forested region. At its broad base, a moderately sized village of wood and adobe houses was inhabited by a people skilled in the uses of copper and social organization. They buried their dead in family groups, often joining husband, wife and children in a common interment, and orienting their bodies to the southeast—perhaps in alignment with the rising of the "Morning Star," the planet Venus. At any rate, the ancient planners at Wickliffe erected their impressive pyramidal mound of soil and clay in six stages, beginning sometime after 900 A.D. Over the next 400 years, they rose in prosperity and regional influence as part of the Mississippi Culture that spread from Florida to Wisconsin. Then, as suddenly as they had come, they vanished for reasons still sought after by archaeologists.

Today, the facility is surrounded by buildings displaying hundreds of skeletons laid out on elevated platforms. They are the remains of the people who built the Wickliffe settlement more than a thousand years ago. But the leading feature of the site is its dramatic mound. It stood proudly among the collection of sturdy houses on a steeply sloping ridge that gave the structure the noble facade of a river citadel. Upon its flat top perched a high-gabled ceremonial temple of wood and dried grass covered with white lime. From this elevated position, the leaders of Wickliffe society surveyed the abundantly fruitful land for many miles around.

Their stately temple is gone and the vicinity is somewhat overgrown, but the massive earthen pyramid remains almost as impressive as it must have appeared in its hey-day. Immediately behind the large mound sprawled a spacious plaza, where markets, public ceremonies and sporting events were held. The most popular game was Chunkey, a cross between shuffleboard and bowling with a resemblance to Scottish hurling. Other mounds—low, elongated

structures—fronted the plaza. But these features disappeared during scientific excavations in the 1930s. Infant burials at Wickliffe are
common finds, although they appear to be the results of a relatively
high early mortality rate rather than evidence for ritual sacrifice.

Reconstruction of the sacred center as it appeared around 1000 A.D.
Photo courtesy of Wickliffe Museum, KY.

Retrieved artifacts stored in the Lifeways Building, which occupies the former site of the plaza, include beautifully crafted copper items, particularly fish hooks, decorated pottery with geometric
patterns and less identifiable ceremonial items. The pyramid is accompanied by another platform mound, which, while not as prodigious, sets off the larger structure in a wonderful perspective.

MYSTICAL SIGNIFICANCE

Although the pyramidal mound at Wickliffe is not the most
spectacular structure created by prehistoric Americans, it does possess its own magic. No burials were included in its construction, nor
was it aligned to any celestial orientation. Some researchers, however, speculate the long vanished temple building at its summit
may have featured some correspondence with the setting sun.

There is no indication of war or human sacrifice, social upheaval or epidemic. The orderliness of the excavated graves in apparent family groups suggests a peaceful passage through life. It is this ancient tranquility that still resonates at Wickliffe.

Naturally, the site's sacred center is the pyramid itself, especially its summit. From its flat top, views to the north and east of the modern museum buildings are interesting but not particularly moving. So, too, the overlook facing the modern town on the south is uninspiring. But toward the west, the ground slopes dramatically away from the sturdy pyramid and down toward the Mississippi River among vast forests of oak, pine and cedar. Here the mind's eye may catch a glimpse of former times, while the inner-ear fastens on the floating echoes of flute and drum. The receptive visitor may experience the tingle of the primeval earth-energy that first attracted the pyramid's builders so long ago.

The Great Mound as it appears today.
Photo by Frank Joseph.

The Wickliffe mound and its natural environment are useful in the reduction of stress, emotional confusion and anxiety. If we are out of sync with ourselves and/or others, the site offers a restorative pacification of the mind and soul, even if we do not suffer from any particular problem. However, the place is worth visiting as a kind of mystical tonic to keep up our spiritual strengths. And for the new-comer to personal mysticism, it provides an easy, effective introduction to the Otherworld that lies within and around us.

SUGGESTED RITUAL

Visualization, meditation or past-life regression are ideal rituals for the top of the great mound. First, orient yourself to the site at the Lifeways Museum and the surrounding archaeological buildings. Then, following a marked path from the Cemetery Building, visitors reach a park area behind the Museum facing the squarish pyramid. Before approaching it, clear your mind, take three deep breaths, place your left hand over your heart with the palm of your right hand extended in the direction of the earth-work. Envision pure, white light emanating from your heart, streaming down your right arm and out the palm of your hand. The ray of light covers the pyramid, penetrates to its innermost core, leaving it shimmering from base to top. Approach it from the north, the spirit direction; climb its flank to the summit, stand at its centerpoint and turn to face north. Throw a pinch of tobacco and thank the *genius loci* for allowing you to visit the sacred center. Perform the same little offering to the east, south and west, consecutively. Visualize those images appearing as decoration on the pottery displayed in the Lifeways Museum. They are the symbolic keys to unlocking the mystery of Wickliffe Mounds, because they at once tap into the psychic energies of the site.

Following a session atop the Wickliffe pyramid, descend its western flank and walk back around to the park exit.

FOR MORE INFORMATION

Directions

Take I-57 south to Route 3 Exit. East to Route 51. South through Cairo, Illinois, to the stoplight at 60/62. Left over the bridge into Kentucky ten minutes to Wickliffe Mounds. Admission, adults $3; senior citizens $2.75; children six to eleven, $2; under six years, free. Open daily from March to November, 9:00 a.m. to 4:30 p.m. For further information, contact Wickliffe Mounds Research Center, P.O. Box 155, Wickliffe, KY 42087. Telephone: (502) 335-3681.

LOUISIANA

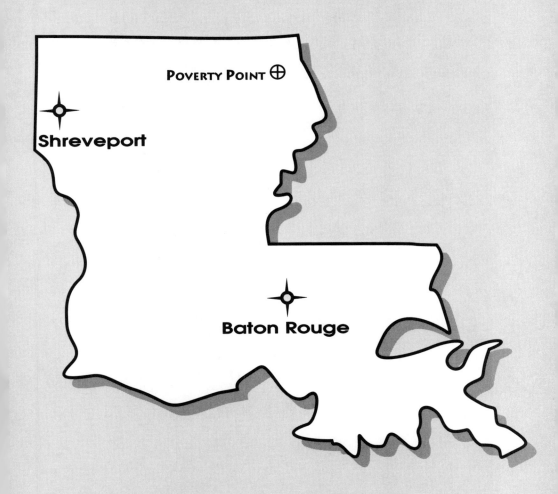

POVERTY POINT ⊕

Shreveport

Baton Rouge

Poverty Point

Frank Joseph

If we were to travel back over the centuries and through the Mississippi Valley from the Gulf of Mexico, we would pass among a vast, pristine wilderness of hardwood forests flourishing with animal life. But soon after entering the Bayou Macon River and following it up into what is now the northeast corner of the state of Louisiana, a huge and unusual city teeming with human activity would suddenly come into view. Ships bearing cargoes of raw copper from the upper Great Lakes, soapstone from the Appalachias, and quartz crystal from Oklahoma and Arkansas crowd the river banks, from which a broad avenue leads to the heart of the metropolis. At its perfect center stands a large, conical mound. Just beyond it lies a curious circle of standing, red-painted posts. On either side of the mound and wooden circle, two broad boulevards spread from the edge of the river. Together, all these peculiar features form an astronomical observatory for charting solstices, eclipses, the positions of the sun and stars.

The area comprising the observatory forms a great plaza for sporting events, markets and public ceremonies. This central section is encompassed by six enormous embankments, the outermost one being more than three quarters of a mile across. About 5 million hours of labor went into the construction of the earth-works, which comprise one million cubic yards of earth formed from 40 million 50-pound baskets of soil. Fine wooden homes belonging to the 2,000 privileged inhabitants perched atop the 10-foot high ramparts, which alternate with five interconnected water canals. Clustered around the concentric rings, an additional 4,000 farmers and workers lived in similar, though smaller, homes on the surrounding plain. They were skilled not only in large-scale construction techniques, but in the manufacture of common household goods. Millennia before convection ovens were re-invented, the ancient residents of the ringed city used them on a regular basis.

Aerial photograph of the ancient city's remains.
Photo courtesy of Louisiana State Archaeological Society,
Poverty Point Museum, LA.

North of the metropolis stands a tall, cone-shaped mound. At
its volcano-like summit, intensely hot cane fires consumed and
purified the bodies of the deceased. There are no burials at this vast,
prehistoric site, because cremation was part of the ancient funeral
procedures observed by the original inhabitants. Closer to the outermost embankment, abutting its eastern side, a much larger effigy
mound, configured to resemble a bird in flight, rises over 70 feet.
A broad ramp, a grand processional gateway, slopes up its western
flank to the top. Its chief rituals and the most lavish ceremonies
took place amid profuse color and spectacle. But all this was long
ago.

The Mississippi River flood plain and the rest of the continent
was once an untouched natural paradise. Here these ancient people
created America's first city, and nothing like it was ever seen again.
For 800 years they prospered, extending their commercial ties over
thousands of miles. Then, as abruptly as they came, they inexplicably deserted their capital, stripping it almost completely bare.
Where they went and what became of them are unknown. Their vast

embankments and prodigious mounds slowly eroded. The once busy water canals dried up, and the overgrown site languished in isolation until 1843, when settlers established a plantation in the area which they called "Poverty Point" after the not particularly productive soil there. But another hundred years passed before archaeologists discovered the sacred center. They were astounded by its profound antiquity: The 400-acre city-state was built 1,200 years before Christ. It flourished at the same time Pharaoh Ramses III sat on the Egyptian throne—which makes Poverty Point the oldest civilization in North America.

Today, the site features a visitor's building, museum, look-out tower, archaeological workshops and picnic grounds. The most precious finds on display include several small sculpted owl figures carved from quartz crystal. A scale model of the earth-works is located in front of the museum.

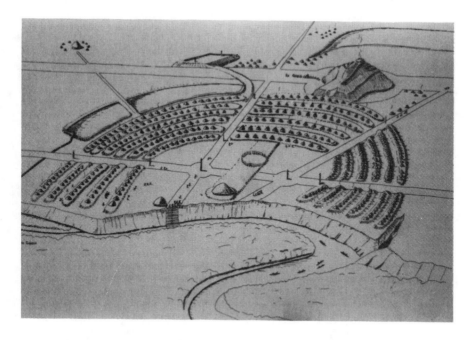

Artist's reconstruction of Poverty Point as it appeared after 1200 B.C.,
minus the completion of the land rings, which were only recently
discovered by infra-red high altitude photography.
Louisiana State Archaeological Society, Poverty Point Museum, LA.

MYSTICAL SIGNIFICANCE

It is impossible to describe the unique metropolis that once reigned at Poverty Point in a guidebook of this kind without calling attention to its remarkable resemblance to the sunken capital of lost Atlantis. Indeed, points of comparison between both dead cities are numerous and compelling.

The most complete ancient source to describe Atlantis is found in Plato's *Timaeus* and *Critias*. He writes of a great city located on a large and fruitful island in the Atlantic Ocean not far beyond the Straits of Gibraltar. The capital of a sea-borne empire, it accumulated terrible military power and cultural magnificence, dominating the entire ancient world. The Atlantians' final bid for conquest, including Greece and all of Egypt, failed, however, the debacle coinciding with a natural catastrophe that obliterated the island. Subsequent investigators expanded upon Plato's account, describing the lost city as the very fountainhead of civilization and the homeland of occult powers.

Amazingly, some of the best physical evidence for the former existence of Atlantis may be found at the abundant site in Louisiana. Plato portrayed the sunken city's unusual lay-out as composed of concentric rings of alternating land and water connected by canals, the same arrangement constructed by the ancient builders of Poverty Point. Atlantis lay south of Mt. Atlas, a volcanic mountain, and a conical mound made to resemble a volcano, even to the cane fires ignited in its crater, was positioned north of the American site. The Atlanteans' sacred numbers were five and six. These recur throughout Poverty Point, most notably in its six land ridges and five canals. The inhabitants of both Atlantis and prehistoric Louisiana were imperialists, whose capitals stood at the hubs of trading empires joined by water routes.

The city at Poverty Point did not develop slowly over many years. Instead, it appeared full-blown on the banks of the Bayou Macon River. Its builders were outsiders, culture bearers from some other land where the arts of high civilization had already been evolved. Underscoring all these comparisons is the common date that connects the two cities. Carbon-14 tests date the construction of Poverty Point to 1200 B.C. According to Egyptian records at West Thebes and the lunar date provided by Plato, the final destruction of Atlantis occurred in 1198 B.C. It seems plausible that survivors from the Atlantean catastrophe sailed into the Gulf of Mexico and up the

Mississippi River Valley to reconstruct a new city in the image of their drowned capital.

The mystical significance of this American relationship with Atlantis involves nothing less than rediscovering our soul-roots according to the life-readings of Edgar Cayce, the 20th century's most renowned psychic. He and subsequent psychics insisted that Atlantean souls are reincarnating in North America. The chief reason seems obvious: As our world nears a major ecological crisis, the souls of Atlantis who experienced the trauma of their world coming to an end are drawn to our like time period. Their presence in our epoch is to resolve the catastrophe for which they were responsible 3,200 years ago; some to prevent that catastrophe from happening again, others to reproduce it once more on a planet-wide scale.

Many visitors who stroll through the trails of Poverty Point may find that they simultaneously walk the trails of their own past lives. It is thrilling to actually see the numerous parallels at the site and to think that the refugees of lost Atlantis might have come to this corner of America so long ago from the across a disastrous sea. The sacred center is extremely powerful, igniting past-life regressions for persons of all backgrounds—but especially for reincarnated Atlanteans.

SUGGESTED RITUAL

Our American pilgrimage to Atlantis begins with the model of Poverty Point at the Visitor's Center. It enables us to appreciate the site's real configuration, which is sometimes lost to the eye at ground level due to the enormity of its dimensions. The museum and regular audio-visual presentations at the theater further contribute to the newcomer's orientation. The museum provides maps offering walking tours with explanations of the points visited.

Trails skirt the banks of Bayou Macon River, then turn toward the concentric rings of the abandoned city. These rings were steeper and more clearly defined in ancient times, but enough of their contours remain to make them clearly discernable. Depressions separating the earth embankments once ran with water carrying boats via interconnected canals throughout the populous capital, and the alternation of land and water energies here generates the correct stimulus for the psychic appreciation of the site. Flash-backs of lives sometimes occur as receptive visitors cross over the fifth and sixth rings (representing the sacred numbers of Atlantis for male and female energies, respectively). The trail leads to a 70-foot high mound shaped to resemble a flying bird, the only feature at Poverty Point different from Plato's description.

The grand scale of the effigy mound and the broad ramp sloping up to its summit define the structures as the ceremonial center of the site. Climbing the modern wooden stairway is the emotional highlight of anyone's visit, not only for the marvelous perspective afforded by its view, but because it is the chief spiritual focal point of the New Atlantis. At the top stands a magnificent oak tree, as though planted by Fate itself, because the oak was a manifestation of Atlas, whose arms upheld the sphere of the heavens. It is the Tree of Life at the Atlantean sacred center of the world, the living axis mundi, replanted by the gods at its most perfect spot. Powerful meditation and/or past life regression are wonderfully facilitated beneath its numinous branches.

Before commencing meditation, a short ritual may be in order. Face the east near the base of the tree, pour out a small libation of purified water, and thank the *genius loci* for allowing the visit to take place. Repeat the libation and thanks, turning to the south, west and north. After descending the bird mound, follow the trail north to Mound B, which may well be a man-made recreation of the sunken Mt. Atlas. The 20-foot high, volcano-like earth-work with its crater mouth is another power point suitable for the vision quest. Its resonance is similar to that afforded by the bird effigy, although not as strong. Even so, something indefinable links the two mounds, almost in a positive-negative charge.

Visitors return to the museum from Mound B, cutting back across the concentric rings to the third sacred center at the hub of the city, where once the movements of the sun were followed. Today, the precinct is not as focused as it undoubtedly was in ancient times, although it still radiates a "centered" feeling perfectly suited to the conclusion of Poverty Point.

FOR MORE INFORMATION

Directions

From I-10, exit north on 17. At the town of Epps, right (east) on 134 to Poverty Point State Commemorative Area, located in West Carroll Parish, east of Monroe on LA 577. For further information, contact Poverty Point State Commemorative Area, HC60, Box 208

A, Epps, LA 71237. Telephone (318) 926-5492. The park is open year round, 9 a.m. to 5 p.m., daily.

Accommodations
Red Roof, 102 Constitution Road, P.O. Box 1803, West Monroe, LA 71291. Telephone: (318) 388-2420. I-20 at Thomas Road Exit 114. Forty-minute drive to Poverty Point, $26.95 per single.

Motel 6, 1501 US 165 Bypass, Monroe, LA 71202. Telephone: (318) 322-5430. From I-20, exit #118A. Proceed south on US 165. Turn left on East Street, then left on Frontage Road to motel. Forty-minute drive from Poverty Point. $24.95 per person.

Best Western Delhi Inn, Route 3, Box 80, Delhi, LA 71232. Telephone: (318) 878-5126. Twenty-minute drive to Poverty Point. Going east on I-20, exit 153; turn right; go one block on Frontage Road to motel. $32 to $36 per person.

Camping at KOA, 4407, I-20 Frontage Road, Vicksburg, MS 39180. Telephone: (601) 636-2025. Exit 4B, first right on Frontage Road, two blocks from Super 8 Motel. Forty-five minutes drive to Poverty Point. $10 for tent site, two adults.

Bibliography
Ford, James A. *The Puzzle of Poverty Point*. Natural History 64(9): 466-472. Washington, D.C. 1955.

Gibson, Jon L. *Poverty Point, the First American Chiefdom*. Archaeology, 27(2) : 96-105, Washington, D.C. 1974.

MISSOURI

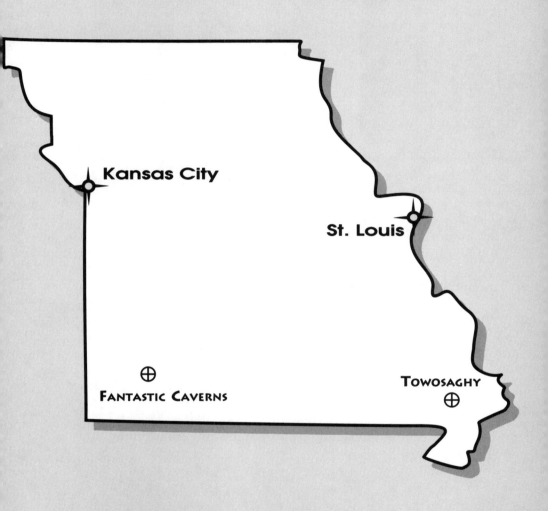

Kansas City

St. Louis

⊕
Fantastic Caverns

Towosaghy
⊕

The Lost City of Towosaghy

Frank Joseph

Standing alone and virtually deserted in the midst of open prairie and surrounding farmlands are the quiet, ghostly remains of a once lively ceremonial center. While Europe groped through the Dark Ages, a city of light and the open air thrived near the banks of the Mississippi River. Unlike most of the other prehistoric sites throughout the United States, Towosaghy appears today just as it did to the first white settlers in the mid-18th century. It has not been "improved" by park officials, nor transformed into a clinical, dispassionate dig by archaeologists. And while the site does not have a museum to explain the past for curious tourists, the relatively pristine character of the ruins speaks clearly and directly to the appreciative visitor. Moreover, the somewhat rough, unmanicured appearance of the mounds lends them an atmosphere of authenticity not always found at better preserved locations.

While there are no explanatory sign posts or interpretive centers to distract from the structures, the site misses the mobs of tourists which sometimes spoil a visit to other sacred centers. Here, undisturbed meditation is always possible without the risk of interference, and visitors have the opportunity to peacefully contemplate or commune with the *genius loci*. The site has been abandoned for at least 600 years, so it naturally bears only a suggestive resemblance to the ceremonial metropolis it once was around 1000 A.D. But despite centuries of erosion and decay, enough may still be seen to stir the imagination to conjure ancient entities.

Originally, Towosaghy was among the most strongly fortified cities in pre-Columbian North America. Three lofty, stockaded walls, thickly coated with white lime, surrounded the 52-acre complex. Massive guard towers abutted the walls every 90 feet, while a 35-foot wide trench entirely encircled the site. This was defense-in-depth, the very existence of which presupposes the presence of formidable enemies in the immediate vicinity. But all information

about the military and political events of those days has been lost.
The heroes who bled and the fate of the vanquished; the achieve-
ments of diplomacy and the success of far-flung commerce; those
who labored and those who loved—no memory of them survives at
Towosaghy, unless it be in the psychic imprint of human history left
behind in the hallowed earth, the sacred center.

Artist's rendition of Towosaghy as it appeared around 900 A.D.
Courtesy of the Missouri State Board of Tourism.

All that lives on is the name, an Osage Indian word for "Old
Town." The Osage did not belong to the nameless, mysterious aristocrats who prospered behind their walled city, but their own ancestors may have served them as members of the working class. The
Old Town sprang into existence during the early part of the 10th
century, and immediately became the hub for many smaller settlements beyond its fortifications. While the majority population
dwelt in related villages in the surrounding area, the socially privileged leaders lived amid comparative luxury in the sacred center,
where maize, beans, persimmon, plums, acorns, pecans, black wal-
nuts and hickory nuts were grown. Deer meat, hides and other exclusive items had to be brought in from outside.

The city itself comprised sturdy houses of post and adobe, featuring sunken floors. There was an expansive plaza surrounded by half a dozen earthen mounds. The largest structure, a ridge-top pyramid, is some 250 feet long, 180 feet wide at its base and 16 feet high. At its summit, the leading ceremonies at Towosaghy undoubtedly took place. Agriculturally rich, regionally influential and militarily superior, the ancient aristocrats flourished for four hundred years. Their sudden abandonment of the entire area in the early 14th century was no less unaccountable than their abrupt arrival. They were part of the Mississippi Tradition, the mass-migrations of which are not properly understood.

Path leading to the conical mound at Towosaghy .
Photo by Frank Joseph.

Today, visitors approach the site from an obscure gravel road. They ascend a low rise that was once the main portion of habitation at the north end of the city. It is an open space occasionally mowed by the resident archaeological workers as the only welcome concession to "improvement." The two surviving earth-works are near the south end of the complex, and paths lead directly through the prairie-grass to both. Near what used to be the western wall stands a

conical pyramid with a depression at its summit, lending it a decidedly volcanic appearance. The structure is 15 feet tall and 30 feet
across at its base. About 50 yards away lies the larger ridge-top
mound. Darkly brooding now, a thousand years ago it was surmounted by two temple buildings and its configuration was more
sharply defined, perhaps sheathed in bright red and yellow clay
painted with cryptic geometric designs in black pigment. There is
no evidence of burial in either earth-work, although some scholars
believe the depression at the top of the cone-shaped mound was
used as a fire-pit stoked by dried cane for cremations.

The bleakness of the setting from late autumn to early spring,
or its verdant tranquillity in summer make Towosaghy an atmospheric place, where the spirit of the past is perhaps more in evidence
than at any other ghost town.

MYSTICAL SIGNIFICANCE

There is much to stimulate the mind and soul at Towosaghy.
We may puzzle over the conjectured causes for its drastic fortifications or try to envision the large ridge-top mound in its originally
colorful splendor. But the place has its own voices in the silence of a
calm afternoon or amid the wind singing through the prairie-grass.
The relatively untouched environment conjures a purity found at
few other archaeological sites.

Because of its isolation, meditation is easier to practice here. Indeed, the place seems to call out for contemplation of some kind.
Many thousands of empowering ceremonies have no doubt im-
pregnated the very soil of the site with reverberating psychic forces,
like the unfading echoes of a vanished race. The entire premises
may be regarded as a sacred center, although the chief focal points
of resident energy are certainly concentrated in its two main physical features, the conical pyramid and the ridge-top mound. The latter structure supported two temple buildings, one of which was set
afire and has since collapsed.

The large mound is oriented east-west, so it would appear
its original dedication was to the rising and setting of the sun, an
orientation common throughout Mississippian Culture. Implicit
here are the eternal birth-death-rebirth cycles revered by the Mound
Builders. Their sun-god was the great life-giver. No doubt, great
gatherings were addressed by the regent or chief shaman from the
mound top in what must have been impressive displays of ritual-

ized splendor on a par with the architectural magnificence of the ceremonial city.

SUGGESTED RITUAL

Although the Towosaghy mound site is not open to the general public, individual visitors are allowed to walk the grounds in daylight hours after obtaining permission (see under Directions). The gravel road leading up to the south end of the precinct with its ridge-top mound skirts its west side along a wooden fence. Entry may be made most usually by climbing over the gate, which is padlocked in the absence of the archaeologists. Proceed north to the single, tall oak standing about mid-point in the site. Directly ahead, in the near distance, lies the ragged but nonetheless impressive ridge-top mound. To the southwest stands the earthen representation of a sacred volcano, the conical mound. Follow the path leading straight to it. The approach is dramatic and the receptive visitor experiences an intensification of feeling the closer he or she comes. Climb its steep slope and either stand or sit in its crater-like depression at the summit. It is the place for meditation, visualization or prayers.

Imagine the depression filling with bright, pure light from deep inside the mound. Visualize the light rising to the lip of the crater and streaming down over the slopes like incandescent lava.

See even to the secret interior of the conical pyramid alive with white light. Then face north, thank the *genius loci* as your spiritual host and sprinkle a pinch of tobacco to the ground. Complete the gesture of thanks three times more, turning to the east, south and west. Look to the ridge-top structure not far away. Imagine white lava flowing from the cone-shaped pyramid across the ground where the plaza used to be, all the way to the foot of the elongated earth-work; rising up its sides, enveloping its summit, penetrating its innermost sanctuary. Visualize it shimmering and connected to the conical mound.

Descend its slope and walk to the larger structure. Atop it, the full extent of Towosaghy spreads out to the north. Envision the golden cycles of the sun arching overhead across the dome of the sky from eastern to western horizons. Know that the powers of self-renewal are boundless and omnipotent. They lie within every individual, sometimes like dragons asleep deep inside subconscious caves, where they have been banished by our reluctance to call upon them. But they could arise to serve our empowerment after they have been awakened by the earth-spirit at Towosaghy.

FOR MORE INFORMATION

Directions
Take I-55 (south or north) to 80. East past East Prairie to FF. South past AA. Left turn (east) at first opportunity. Unmarked road. Right turn (southeast) at first opportunity on another unmarked, gravel road to Towosaghy State Historic Site. For further information and permission to visit the area, contact Ruben Templeton, Park Superintendent, Missouri Department of Natural Resources, Division of Parks, Recreation and Historic Preservation, Big Oak Tree State Park, Route 2, Box 343, East Prairie, MO 63845. Telephone: (314) 649-3149.

Accommodations
Best Western Cheekwood Inn, Exit 181-57, P.O. Box 280, Ullin, IL 62992. Telephone: (618) 845-3773. Exit 181-57 adjoining interstate highway. To Towosaghy, 57 to 55 Interstates. One hour's drive to site.

Camping at KOA, Route 2, Box 272, Portageville, MO 63873. Telephone: (314) 359-1580. Northbound Exit 19, Hayti. Right 500 feet. Left outer road 6 miles. Southbound Exit 27 Nardell. Left turn to East Outer Road 3 miles. Twenty minutes from Towosaghy. $12.95 per tent site, two adults.

Bibliography

Foster, Steven. *Vision Quest*. New York: Prentice Hall, 1988.

Kopper, Philip. *North American Indians Before the Coming of the Europeans*. Washington, D.C.: Smithsonian Institution Publication, 1986.

Hultkrans, Ake. *The Religion of the American Indians*. Berkeley: University of California Press, 1979.

Mitchell, John. *The Earth Spirit*. London: Thames and Hudson, 1979.

Fantastic Caverns

Edna Ryneveld

Beneath rolling Ozark Mountain scenery, just north of Springfield, Missouri, lies a cavern like no other in North America: it is long and level enough to ride through in jeep-drawn wagons. Fantastic Caverns, discovered by a landowner's dog in 1862, and explored for the first time in 1867 by twelve intrepid women with candles, is also extremely beautiful (see color plate). Strategically-placed lights illuminate a wide variety of formations which have developed over millions of years through the action of dripping water. You'll see stalactites, stalagmites, wavy curtain designs, delicate soda straws, and huge columns forming intricate and colorful designs. Though you won't be able to see them, the cave also houses endangered blind cave fish, salamanders, and crayfish, as well as a few Pipistrel bats.

In moments of quiet, when the propane-powered jeep is turned off, you hear a profound and comforting silence, punctuated by the dripping of water. A day or two after a big rain, you may hear rushing water as it funnels through a lower level of the cave to emerge somewhere "outside." Fantastic Caverns is large, with a free flow of air throughout. Despite its turbulent history as a speakeasy and one-time meeting place for the KKK, a feeling of spaciousness and security now prevails. In recent years, its huge Auditorium Room has served occasionally as a theater for the regional opera company. The temperature remains a constant 60 degrees winter and summer.

The cave was never inhabited by Indians, probably due to the extremely small-sized and well-hidden original opening. However, many arrowheads and possibly one Indian skeleton have been found near the Little Sac River and Indian Spring, just a short walk from the Visitor Center and Fantastic Caverns' entrance.

Take this easy walk, called Canyon Trail, down to the river and then upstream for about 50 yards. Oak and other hardwoods keep you company in this park-like setting, and you can feel their silent strength as you walk among them. Depending on the season and the human noise level, birds and other wildlife may be seen and listened to as well.

Once you turn upstream, the river will be on your left and a steep bank of trees and undergrowth on your right. This soon becomes a limestone bluff, and, then, there it is: Indian Spring, trickling over moss-covered rocks down from the high bluff to the river. (In wet weather, it's more like a cascade—it drains the lower River Sanctuary passage of Fantastic Caverns.)

To the left of the spring head, at the base of a high and slightly over-hanging bluff is a large, flat area overlooking the river. It is a perfect place to camp, right by the spring, sheltered somewhat from the strong summer sun. This area is too small for an entire tribe to camp, but one can easily imagine a seasonal tribal encampment down along the river, in the park-like area you have just walked through, with the bluff site reserved for, say, special ceremonies or council meetings or perhaps for the chief or medicine man. It feels safe, protected, calm, quietly happy.

MYSTICAL SIGNIFICANCE

The feeling of this entire area is one of safety and calmness and protection. There is, of course, a feeling of connectedness with Mother Earth, especially within the womb-like cave; but it is more like a taken-for-granted, gently-sustaining "given" than a mind-blowing energy vortex. This is just the sort of calming, reaffirming place one needs as an antidote to the frantic, scattered, and fragmented lives of most modern Americans.

SUGGESTED RITUAL

At the river, center yourself, then find a small twig or leaf that offers itself to you and place it upon the water. As you release it, say to yourself or out loud, "I rejoice upon the Eternal River of Life and willingly rededicate myself to the service of The Universe." (Or Great Spirit, or God, or Goddess, or Mother Earth, or whatever is right for you.) Arise and smile.

In the caverns, also center yourself, then taking a drop of water in your hand (it's always damp, there, and you may even be dripped upon several times), lift it to your third eye. Recall that your words and intentions have power. Say silently, "I bless and am grateful to Mother Earth, who protects and nurtures me. I am cleansed, and open to new vision, from this day forward." Smile and be calmed. Hereafter, make a conscious effort to recall this experience.

FOR MORE INFORMATION

Location

At Springfield, Missouri, from Interstate 44, take Missouri 13 North about a mile to Caverns Road and turn west, or left. There are signs on Highway 13. If coming from Kansas City, you'll be on Hwy 13 South and will turn right onto Caverns Road. Follow this scenic country route, and you'll shortly find yourself at Fantastic Caverns.

Local Assistance

Call or write: Fantastic Caverns, Rt. 20, Box 1935, Springfield, MO 65803. (417) 833-2010.

Fantastic Caverns is open year-round and has an excellent Visitor Center. The restaurant in the Visitor Center is open May through October. Special group tours are available. General adult admission is $10.

Accommodations

Only minutes away in Springfield, you'll find motels and hotels of every class available. There are several choices along Hwy 44. If you continue on 44 East, beyond Hwy 13 North, then take the Glenstone exit (Exit H, south, toward Springfield) you'll find many more to choose from.

MONTANA

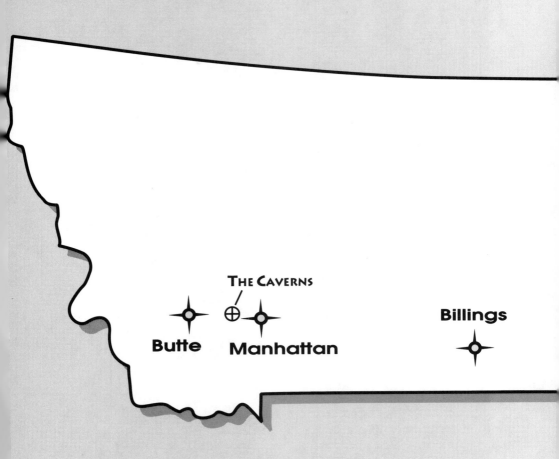

THE CAVERNS

Billings

Butte   Manhattan

Various Sites
Throughout Montana

Montana

Lynn Crowe and Sandra Rachlis

Land itself is holy here, still the domain of massive beings living relatively undisturbed. In eastern Montana, rolling plains lead up to small mountain clusters—forerunners of the main body of the Rockies. Western Montana is filled with range after range of the Rocky Mountains. The truly awesome spaces of our state are alive with personalities and primal energy. In Montana you can absorb holiness, and magically affirm your role in All-That-Is. Montana is an excellent place to speak prayers and intentions, to do at-one-ment rituals, and perform ceremonies with the intent of increasing our planetary atunement with Universal Harmony.

In this article, our approach is to help you participate with the abundant Spirits of Place in Montana. We'll teach you to find your own sacred places, and our perspective will assist in keying minds and hearts to Montana's powerful healing Presences. Taught by the energies themselves, we're sharing a Way of interacting with the sacredness of these lands.

Out of the Great Basin prairies, the high plains sweep toward the shining mountains. Surely these spaces are a living symbol of the ancient Medicine Wheel teachings. Here, you stand at the center of the horizon; 360 degrees of immense landscape meeting the sky. You are at the center; where earth and sky meet is the perimeter of the Wheel. This way of Seeing the circle is always possible, a mountain valley or a forest grove. Magically recognizing and receiving the Wheel is an excellent way to introduce yourself to Spirits of Place.

The four elements are dramatically alive in the land spaces of Montana. We have chosen to emphasize water because the headwaters of the Missouri are here, sacred center of a main life-giving aspect of our continent and the seas. Imbue the high mountain waters with your magical intentions and they will flow with the water throughout the continent and ultimately into the Mother Ocean.

The numinous vista of Cutbank Creek Valley.
Photo courtesy of the Montana State Board of Tourism.

Montana is dry and even arid in parts, and so water in these lands is sacred in several ways. Precipitation is light; what little falls gives life to wild plants and animals, as well as to crops and herds. On a wider scale, the mountain near the Continental Divide stores snow that feeds the Columbia River and the Missouri-Mississippi drainage basin until the first rains of summer. The water table in the Rockies is the indicator of the health of continental water reserves. The lingering snows, and the mountains that conserve them, need our spiritual recognition as the life-givers that they are.

A REGIONAL EXAMPLE OF SACRED MONTANA BETWEEN MANHATTAN & BUTTE

This detailed description of a segment of Montana covers the stretch of country between Manhattan (Montana) and Butte. We're describing it east to west; it works just fine from the opposite direction. For this entire area, stay on the frontage road, old US 10.

This is a pilgrimage between Manhattan and Butte, among the headwaters of the Missouri and some of the waters that feed it. At Three Forks, the Gallatin, Jefferson, and Madison Rivers come together and form the headwaters of the Missouri. Along this route, you can see a small herd of buffalo, Madison Buffalo Jump State Monument, the Missouri Headwaters State Park, Jefferson River Canyon, Lewis and Clark Caverns, the Continental Divide, Homestake Rock Shop at the top of the Divide, and at the western end, Butte—where you might pray for cleansing of the poisoned waters of the earth and for the mountain which is there no more.

Start by getting off I-90 at Manhattan and head west on the old highway. To the north and west are the Horseshoe Hills, where fossil hunters have found trilobite fossils and other remnants of ancient life forms. As you proceed toward Three Forks, watch to the left of the road for a small buffalo herd. This is a good opportunity to stop and make an offering to the buffalo, who once gave life to the humans of this part of North America. At the village of Logan, 5 miles west of Manhattan, turn off to the buffalo jump. Go south under the freeway and follow signs along the graded road.

ANCIENT BUFFALO SITE

Before the coming of the horse, indigenous North American hunters used natural cliff formations to kill a winter's meat supply by carefully guiding and stampeding the huge animals toward and over the brink. Other members of the group waited below to skin and butcher the harvest. This site is at least 500 years old, and was likely used much earlier.

The buffalo was holy to people of ancient times. The process of feeding and clothing the People, preparing meat and leather, was known to be a sacred work. Here is a good place to make an offering, and assure the buffalo of your respect for their lives, and for the on-going life force on the planet and continent. In this place, a good offering would be bits of fresh food, left out in a sheltered spot for the spirits to share.

THE MISSOURI

From Logan, travel 5 or 6 miles to the turn for Missouri Head-waters State Park. This is where the three rivers merge. Here at the source of the Missouri, it is time to turn 360 degrees, recognize the six directions, and invoke a blessing for this waterway and all the waters of the Earth. One water blessing that works for us, is to kneel at the edge of the wild water. Scoop a handful of water and touch it to your forehead; take a second handful and touch it to your heart. Repeat the process. As you do these actions, speak out loud, thanking the waters for their generosity and for the gift of life—yours, and on behalf of all beings. Be sure to include in your ceremony a mention of your intention that all of Earth's waters be beautiful and cleansed. Meditate for a while on the shore, feeling the birth of the great Being that is the Missouri River.

At the Headwaters you are touching United States heritage; here the explorers Lewis and Clark reached a part of their expeditionary goals. Alter you finish acknowledging the Power of the Waters, make a tobacco offering; verbally recognize how that expedition invited exploitation into these far mountains. The words should include a mention of how earth-awareness has shifted among Lewis and Clark's people. Declare that you are working toward a balanced relationship among the Sacred Circle of life forms.

THE CAVERNS

The old highway takes you west through the small town of Three Forks. About 3 miles past the town you come to a junction. Go left on Highway 2. This highway winds through the spectacular canyon of the Jefferson River. Approximately fifteen miles the junction is Lewis and Clark Caverns State Park. These beautiful caverns are named after explorers who never saw them, but who did travel along the Jefferson River far below.

The Caverns are open to the public. To gain access, you'll have to join the small hourly guided tour groups. Thus your presence there will not be private, and your magical work in the Caverns will necessarily be on the Inner Planes. Before going to the Visitor's Center, do a grounding and centering meditation. Then shape your magical purpose, possibly an intention to experience the living rock and give to the minerals who have shaped our lands and our bodies. Because of the ecological delicacy of the Caverns' interior, we recommend that you make any offerings outside of the caves, perhaps before joining the tour.

Once inside, remember to continue your Inner work. This is a chance to worship the pure creative beauty of the Mother. Here is a place where the Mother simply feels like making beauty. In the dark, whether anyone sees it or not, Her inexorable will carves the intricate shapes and delicate formations; her tools are water and time. Deep inside the presence of this great living being, still creating itself drop by drop, we can appreciate that the imprint of the personal style expresses and lived by each one of us in our physical bodies is just as fully an expression of the will of the Great Mystery.

The human species remembers at the cellular level our kinship with the mineral, and also remembers finding shelter and security within protective cave homes. Here is an opportunity to acknowledge our unknown ancestors, who, over thousands of generations, passed the gift of life to their children, and hence to us.

THE CONTINENTAL DIVIDE

The Continental Divide is not just a conceptual line, like the Mexican border, or the Equator, or the 45th Parallel. It is an actual physical divider of the North American continent—the literal top of this land mass, where the waters flow east to the Atlantic Ocean or west to the Pacific. Facing North on this "backbone of the continent," rain falling on your right side will feed the Gulf Stream, while drops on your left will hurtle toward the western ocean down the mighty gorge of the Columbia River.

As you stand on a chosen print along the Continental Divide and send out your prayers, you can feel the lines of power radiating along this ridge to the north and south, and down its slopes and drainages to the two oceans bordering us on the east and west. An offering made on the Divide travels down both waterways; recognize that your circle is bounded by the oceans.

The Continental Divide ridge above Butte is graced by an enormous statue of the All-Mother, known locally as Our Lady of the Rockies. Designed and constructed by citizens of Butte, she shines white and protective over our lands (she does bear a striking resemblance to the Virgin Mary, but Butte lore says that the original intent was to honor all women).

BUTTE

As you drop down from the Divide on the old highway into Butte, you will notice two things: the small city in the valley, and the mining scar to the north of the city. Butte, once known as the home of the Copper Kings, generated wealth for investors in the 1800s when copper was discovered beneath the mountain where the original settlement stood. Millions were made from the "Richest Kill on Earth"—a "hill" (actually a mountainside) which is no longer there, having been literally removed. The first mines were underground, honeycombed beneath the streets and homes of residents. Sometimes parts of Butte still cave in, when segments of the 10,000 miles of subterranean antic mining tunnels give way.

Even before you reach the city of Butte, driving in from any direction, you can note the nearby mountains that are bare of trees. These were cut down to provide structural timbers to shore up the early mine tunnels and to be burned to provide energy for mining and smelting. It is ironic that the mountain named Timber Butte—now relatively barren—was one of the prime sources of such trees. So vast were the effects of mining here that even the weather changed. Because the trees were gone, the ground could no longer hold as much moisture from the yearly rains, and the region turned more arid. Because of the aridity, new seedling trees that might have replaced the cut ones have a poorer chance of survival.

Economic shifts during the 1960s led to pit mining for getting at the rich ores under the mountain. It didn't take long for open pit mining to become the main process. By the late 70s, most of the city on the mountain and the mountain itself were gone. Stores, homes, hotels, and historic areas of the city were evacuated and swallowed by the expanding Berkeley Pit. The Pit ate deeper and wider into the mountain, until it was a mile deep and at least as wide. The city of Butte moved itself down into the valley, and continues to expand there. An auxiliary pit destroyed another landmark to the east of the original hole. The elegant Columbia Gardens with its sculptured flower beds and lawns, antique carousel, and roller coaster was removed. The lovely Victorian amusement park disappeared along with the hillside it had formerly occupied.

Although the Berkeley Pit had been closed for several years, a new ecological threat has developed. The Berkeley Pit, now a mile deep, is filling rapidly with highly toxic water—at the rate of millions of gallons daily. This poisoned water is beginning to seep into the groundwater tables. Other old mining and abandoned industrial sites contribute additional noxious residues to surface waters with each spring's fresh runoff.

This situation is not being ignored. Butte and nearby Anaconda constitute the largest allocation of Superfund monies set aside by the United States Government to clean up the life-threatening aftermath of massive environmental destruction caused by industry. Your prayers and ceremonies can assist your tax money here!

Go to the Berkeley Pit viewing stand in the northeastern part of the city. In this location you have an opportunity for ceremonial healing—not only for the devastated mountainside in Butte, but for all the wounded landscapes planet-wide that have been unawarely brutalized by industrial society. The site of Butte, Montana is not only a symbol for unmindful environmental exploitation, but also a symbol for humans disregarding one another. The destruction of old Butte eliminated culturally rich Italian and Finnish neighborhoods. Regard Butte as a symbol of thoughtless development and charge the symbol with your healing intent. Butte is a place to effectively work for the health of the planet and for human awareness.

As you recognize and consider the Wheel from Butte, your ceremonial purpose could be that what you observe here is the last of such a trend on our planet. Pray for reclamation of this and the many other such sites, and also for an awakening in the human spirit a vision that will forever ensure a harmonious relationship between technological needs and the life force.

Our advice for approaching the above locations can serve as an example for anywhere you go.

FINDING THE RIGHT DIRT ROAD
AND YOUR OWN SACRED PLACES

There you are driving along the freeway and would like to have a little adventure, but don't know exactly where to go and how to get there.

If you have the time, it's a wonderful way to be able to get intimate with some area that strikes the right chord in your heart. Go on secondary roads so you can stop right away when you feel the impulse, or can turn around quickly instead of having to go thirty miles before getting to the next freeway exit.

There is the physical fact that when you move slower, you see more, and thus you get more sense of the neighborhood you're traveling through. You can also see in more detail the plants, trees, birds, animals, the little (and big) effects of water and its habits, and how the weather affects these living communities.

Stop and take out your map of Montana. Look for some indications from the symbols (see map legend) of national or state parks and campgrounds. These areas are designated because they are usually beautiful and powerful—so much so that someone thought it worthwhile to protect them from being logged or paved or subdivided. Sometimes these places are also just too wild to be accessible for economic development and they have kept their integrity, which you can feel as you travel near or through them. Usually, there are highway signs indicating turnoffs to national or state parks and public forest lands.

Once you're on a secondary road on the way to a chosen site, you may see brown forest service signs indicate places of local interest. These are often worth investigating. Example: You're on a paved or graded road and there are many small dirt roads leading off it with these brown signs that might have several places listed, such as:

> "Rainbow Lake - 2 miles"
> "Ranger Station - 12 miles"
> "Perry's Meadows - 3.5 miles"

This is a pretty good indication that if you follow that road there will be some places of scenic beauty with public access.

So take the time to look, think about where you are and consider how this spot relates to all within your field of vision. Frequently check on your inner awareness. Try to let yourself become merged with the sense of where you are. Stop the car if you need to and breathe, meditate, pray—whatever works for you. Get out of the car and listen for a while. If you find yourself moving into non-ordinary levels of consciousness, follow yourself into them. You might find yourself going at a ridge, imagining you are a hawk flying along it; your body may feel an actual physical pull in that direction. Go towards the ridge. Or maybe you'll have a driving curiosity to know where some game trail goes that you notice on a hillside.

When these pulls or feelings happen, there is usually no distinction between person, thought and action. The next logical step, if the place is safe and you feel right, is to lace up your shoes and leave the car behind. Some people feel self-conscious out-of-doors, and have reservations about moving around freely. If you feel strongly drawn to some area, why shouldn't you go there if it's physically and legally feasible (i.e. not fenced private land)?

You could walk up onto the mountain; a one-hour walk could lead you through juniper and cedar groves, pines, little gullies delicate and fragile. You could be in an area frequented by owls, deer, eagles, bears . . . walk with great respect because plants and make homes there.

Stay on paths or game trails lest you damage friable soil structure. Off trail, there are spaces through which no one has walked for decades. The webs of strength and living interaction are palpable, and energy may be drawn from these spaces. Again, respect! One would not want to disturb these spaces without permission of the beings/entities who comprise the unity of the forest.

Visualize and link yourself with the drainage system. Feel the seepage of waters from the high peaks, through the canyons, valleys, and meadows. Remember that all the small waterways flow to the sea.

Let your fantasies develop and let your feet follow them—acknowledge these impulses and give them play. A range of mountains or a river or a forest within your visual field is an entity who might actually be glad for your presence when you come in good spirit. You might even be welcomed when you come with love.

When you are blessed with guidance, you are likely called to a place of individuated beauty and personality. You've been brought by the Beings there to be the human actor in the ritual already in process. Have your offering ready. Open your heart and mind; ceremonial particulars can and often do reveal themselves.

As you walk back down the trail to your car, notice that the entire forest is aware of you in a new way. News of your offering, friendship, and ceremonial participation is radiating throughout the region.

The Sacred Center at Bighorn Canyon.
Courtesy of the Montana State Board of Tourism.

CEREMONY FOR RECEIVING
AND RECOGNIZING THE WHEEL

This meditative process is a way of interacting with areas of land space. It is an approach to using the powerful circle that is already there, different from casting a magical circle—although you should not hesitate to use the placement of a circle around you if that is your usual mode. Perform this wherever your heart draws you to interact with the Beauty and Life around you.

As you stand on the land, turn slowly and let your eyes follow the place where earth meets sky. This is the living Medicine Wheel, defined by the horizon. Try to do this in a place where buildings or wires are not part of the junction of earth and sky. First, acknowledge the directions above and below (earth and sky) by greeting each out loud. Then face the four directions, verbally greeting each. As you speak, open your arms to embrace them. Notice that each quarter of the circle radiates from you at center. Try to absorb the awareness of the entire direction. Notice the Beings there at this moment—clouds, plants, rocks; larger ones like mountains or rivers. Be alert for the moment when you no longer assume that a cardinal direction is a straight line in front of you, but a hint "way over there." Meditate within the awareness of your place at the center of the Wheel, or speak aloud your good wishes for the strength of the life force there.

An offering is a way of giving back, of recognizing the wondrousness of the created order. Whenever you pick an herb or berry for the first time in a season, when you take a stone or seashell, or come to a place you want to honor, give something away. Make sure it is something you like or can use, rather than something you don't want. Various traditions have differing viewpoints on what to use; some Native American teachers recommend against using your hair. To avoid getting caught in a holy place without something to give, it is wise to make a habit of carrying potential offering-items when you venture forth.

Some people carry tobacco, in twist form, or in a pipe mixture. Many Native American traditions suggest using tobacco as an offering because it the property of opening channels of communication between different lands of Beings.

To make the offering, take out a handful of tobacco, or coins, beads, food, matches—whatever you have. Hold it in your hand and talk out loud, "Ho, you life force (or stones, berries, herb, flower, sea shell, lake, river—whatever Being you wish to honor) of this place. I honor your strength and persistence (or beauty or . . .). Receive this tobacco and know yourself recognized."

Continue with a statement of your blessing or intent: that all the brothers and sisters of the waterway, or plant or whatever, will be blessed and encouraged by your action—for instance, have enough moisture, healthy food for the animals there, clean air—for a balance of nature to continue for all the beings of this place and the itself. Place your offering in a spot where it will not be noticed by other humans.

Coming into Montana via I-90 from the east, don't miss the chance to make a tobacco offering at the national monument where George Armstrong Custer met defeat during the Battle of the Little Bighorn. Representatives of North America's indigenous peoples savored a bittersweet victory here—their freedom ended here, despite the victory in battle. It is a good place to think about the changes wrought by the new come North Americans, and to speak your intent regarding the future of earth-based ways upon our lands.

We shared with you the mountain details, because we have more knowledge of Montana's western regions. In the vast eastern reaches of Montana, the plains fall away from the mountains. They have their own awesome secrets, with their sometimes stark, lonely spaces, and glorious skies. There is a powerful beauty on the plains; if you are attracted into these regions to identity places for ceremony, use care, for the human places are often many miles away.

We look forward to sensing the vibrational result of your magical visit to Montana. May your experiences here provide tools for interacting with Spirits of Place wherever you may find yourself.

OTHER AREAS

We have taken you on a short tour of one small region of Montana. We've suggested ways for you to acknowledge Spirits of Place in areas of major significance. You may use the specific actions at those special places, or you may take the concepts and apply them in other regions. You have keys for finding your own special places in the wildlands.

Here are other areas of significance, where the Beings would be glad to see you recognize the circle and make offerings.

Coming into Montana from the West on I-90, a wonderful detour is to leave the Interstate at St. Regis, taking State Route 135 (don't miss a stop at Quinn's Hot Springs). At Paradise, go east on state route (the old Indian route over the western ranges of the Rockies). Near Dixon you can take a short drive through the National Bison Range, where a herd of about 400 buffalo live among elk and mountain sheep. At the Ravalli junction, head north on Highway 93, through the magnificent Mission Valley, along Flathead Lake, and northwest into Glacier Park. While in Glacier, be sure to cross the Divide by taking the exciting Going-to-the-Sun highway (only open in summer), the highest altitude highway in the contiguous States. Pull over several times and recognize the Circle; make an offering.

At the top of this spear Divide crossing, you stand among huge areas of designated wilderness. Nearby are areas not yet secure from exploitation, such as the Badger-Two Medicine Blackfeet Indian sacred lands just south of the National Park. All through here you are in Blackfeet Country.

Leave Glacier Park and head for Browning. Follow Highway 89 south to Choteau. From Choteau, take Highway 287 through Augusta to Wolf Creek and Interstate 15. On this segment, you'll pass through wild, timeless High Prairie country. There are many good places to discover along here, but be alert for rattlesnakes.

NEW HAMPSHIRE

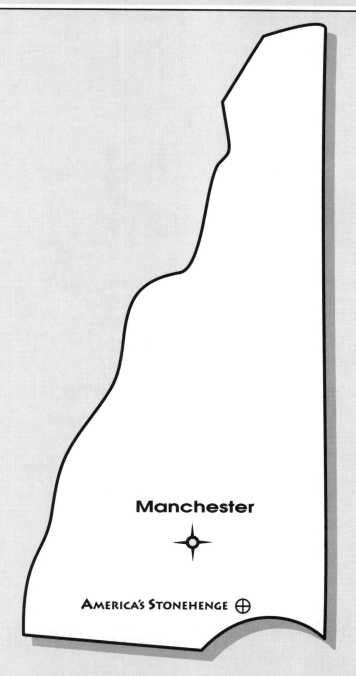

Manchester

AMERICA'S STONEHENGE

Mystery Hill:
America's Stonehenge

Bruce Scofield

New England has had a far more mysterious past than most suspect. Throughout the region are a number of enigmatic stone structures that many believe were built by Europeans thousands of years ago. These intriguing stone works, resembling the megalithic constructions found on the British Isles, have been ignored by many archaeologists who do not have a place for such things in their beliefs about the region's history. Local inhabitants generally pay no attention to them simply because they've always been there. Standing stones with solar alignments, slab-roofed chambers, stone mounds, and even what some insist are Celtic and Phoenician inscriptions, have survived intensive colonial farming, suburban sprawl and highway construction. The fact that a few major sites of this sort still exist is remarkable.

Few people are aware that throughout New England there exists a large number of mysterious sites that consist of several stone chambers and peculiarly arranged boulders, or standing stones. Many are on hills with access to a river; some lie in valleys with views to significant features of the horizon. Most have large boulders or standing stones that align with important sunrise or sunset dates such as the solstices or the equinoxes. The chambers, made of rock walls with huge flat rocks for a roof, usually face the direction of the winter solstice. Some inscriptions have been interpreted to reinforce the calendrical use of the sight.

There has never been a consensus on who built the these ruins or when they were built and today the matter is still one big mystery. Many of these sites were on land that was farmed and many of the chambers were used as root cellars by farmers. But colonial farmers were not known to have worked with massive slabs of rock and there is no mention of colonists constructing stone chambers in the old family histories. The Indians that lived in New England at the dawn of the Colonial Period were not known to have worked with stone.

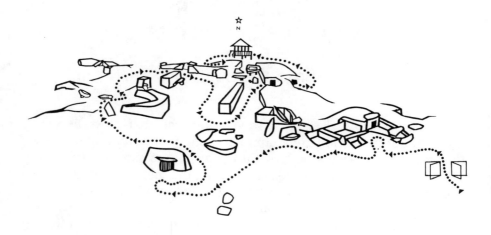

Mystery Hill layout with trails.
Courtesy of Robert E. Stone, President, America's Stonehenge.

We are fortunate to have found one of these sites, the largest of them all, in a reasonably good state of preservation. In southern New Hampshire, on a low pine-covered hill not too far from the Merrimack River, is a group of chambers, underground passages, alignments and inscriptions presently called "America's Stonehenge." The prominence of this site and its post-Colonial history has kept it at the center of the New England megalithic controversy. In the 19th century it was owned by a Jonathan Pattee, a local farmer who built his house among the ruins. He used the chambers for storage and for boarding the town's poor. The site was also a stop along the underground railroad where runaway slaves were sheltered. For many years Pattee's caves, as they were known, were visited by local youth and pilfered for pavement slabs. Nothing of what is known about Pattee suggests that he built the chambers himself.

In the 1930s, William Goodwin became interested in the mystery of the stone ruins and purchased the site. Goodwin, a wealthy insurance executive, was deeply interested in archaeology and he proceeded to clean up the site (it was covered with refuse) and reconstruct it. Eventually, Goodwin became convinced that the ruins were originally built by Irish monks who sailed to New England in the 10th century. He found support for this idea in a Nordic legend that tells of Irish monks fleeing from the Vikings and sailing across the western seas to a new land. To him, the site was the remains of a monastery and the similarity of the constructions to those in Ireland proved the case. Goodwin's ideas, which he published, were rejected by the archaeological establishment. Unfortunately, his excavation methods were crude and imprecise and some of his restoration of the site is questionable.

Goodwin died in the 1950s and the site was eventually acquired by a local engineer, Robert Stone, who renamed the site "Mystery Hill." Since 1958, Stone had dedicated much of his time to the further restoration and proper archaeological investigation of the site. In order to pay the taxes on the property and support the research, he opened the site to the public, charging a small fee. Over the years, a number of investigations have been conducted on the site, some yielding radiocarbon dates as far back as 2000 B.C. Some ancient inscriptions were found that were deciphered by Dr. Barry Fell as being Celtic-Iberian. In 1970, Stone began an investigation of calendar alignments and has determined the site to be at the center of an elaborate series of stone sun and moon markers. This discovery inspired the new name for the site, America's Stonehenge. Today the site, safe from suburban sprawl, is still open to the public. The stone chambers and tunnels, located in an enchanting natural setting, continue to draw visitors and raise controversy.

VISITING THE SITE

America's Stonehenge has a number of walkways that make a tour of the ruins a simple matter. The visitor's lodge, which has a display of artifacts found on the site, allows access to a path that leads past the numbered features of the main part of the site. A tour guide and map are provided so that the ruins can be viewed at your own pace. The site is actually much larger than the central hilltop section where the stone chambers are located. There are over 150 acres of land containing stone walls, sculpted stones, standing stones and a quarry from which the slabs were excavated. It has been noted that the quarrying method employed was an ancient one, utilizing heat and wedging, not one that a colonial farmer with oxen and iron tools would use.

There are several features among the ruins that are particularly interesting. Near the central part of the site, and close to the top of the hill, is a large, 4.5-ton rectangular slab of rock with a long groove cut along its perimeter and out on one corner. It was called the Sacrificial Table by Goodwin and the name has stuck. It certainly does look like it was used for that purpose and its central location makes one wonder. Further, underneath it is an even more amazing feature, a small stone-lined tunnel that connects with a nearby structure called an Oracle Chamber. Within this chamber it is possible for a person to crawl into a niche and speak through a "speaking tube"—the effect being like a voice from under the Sacrificial Table.

Sacrificial Table.
Photo by Brian Sullivan.

The stonework construction of the chambers is interesting and dramatic in and of itself. However, the smaller, less visible features are of some interest. There are several stone-lined drains at the site that still work! One drain was cut out of bedrock, something that required an incredible amount of labor. A well existed that has proven to be a source of quartz crystals. There is a vertical fault in the rock about 22 feet down from which crystals were mined.

The archaeo-astronomical features are what changed Mystery Hill to America's Stonehenge and these are visible from a central viewing platform near the northern end of the site. The platform was constructed in 1975 when it was determined to be the one point from which all the major alignments were accurate. There may have been two stone ruins in this exact location but they were destroyed by Goodwin in his search for the original source of the Sacrificial Table. Encircling the site are strangely shaped stone walls with some large standing stones in few places. From the viewing platform several of these standing stones, a good distance from the main site, are visible through cuts in the forest. To the north is a massive stone aligned with stars that were near north in the distant past. A recent dig in this area yielded a radiocarbon date of 700 A.D. To the east is a fallen equinox stone and a large stone marking summer solstice sunrise. To the west are markers for the summer solstice sunset and a massive marker for the winter solstice sunset. There are other alignments that mark the sun's position against the background hills on February 1st, May 1st and November 1st, days of great importance to the Celtic calendar.

The ruins and alignments of America's Stonehenge are well worth a visit. The peaceful, pine topped hill is inspiring and one could spend an entire day exploring stoneworks and walking along the path to the different calendar markers. In spite of its controversy and contamination, it remains an important ancient site in New England. It's secure existence continues to make the statement that the past in this part of the country is far more complex than is officially acknowledged. These hilltop ruins are intriguing and one can easily imagine it to be an ancient culture's ceremonial center.

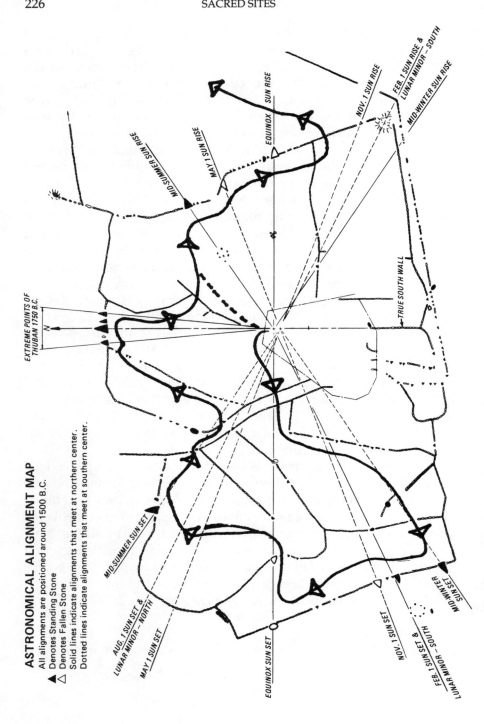

ASTRONOMICAL ALIGNMENT MAP

All alignments are positioned around 1500 B.C.

▲ Denotes Standing Stone
△ Denotes Fallen Stone

Solid lines indicate alignments that meet at northern center.
Dotted lines indicate alignments that meet at southern center.

EXTREME POINTS OF
THUBAN 1750 B.C.

MID-SUMMER SUN RISE

MAY 1 SUN RISE

EQUINOX SUN RISE

NOV. 1 SUN RISE

FEB. 1 SUN RISE &
LUNAR MINOR — SOUTH

MID-WINTER SUN RISE

TRUE SOUTH WALL

MID-SUMMER SUN SET

AUG. 1 SUN SET &
LUNAR MINOR — NORTH

MAY 1 SUN SET

EQUINOX SUN SET

NOV. 1 SUN SET

FEB. 1 SUN SET &
LUNAR MINOR — SOUTH

MID-WINTER
SUN SET

Mystery Hill's Pattee Chamber.
Photo by Brian Sullivan.

FOR MORE INFORMATION

Directions

America's Stonehenge is easily accessible from the Boston region. It is located in southern New Hampshire just north of North Salem, NH. From Boston, follow I-93 north into New Hampshire and take exit 3 onto Route 111, heading east. Drive 5 miles, then turn right onto Island Pond road. Signs will direct you to the entrance which is 1 mile ahead on the right.

The site is open daily from May 1st to October 31st and weekends during April and November. The hours are 10 a.m. to 4 p.m. in spring and fall, and 9:30 a.m. to 5 p.m. in summer. Admission is currently $6.00 for adults. Lodging can be found along nearby Route 28.

Additional information may be obtained by calling (603) 893-8300 or by writing to America's Stonehenge, North Salem, NH 03073.

Further Reading

Feldman, Mark. *The Mystery Hill Story*. Salem, NH: Mystery Hill Press, 1977.

Fell, Barry. *America B.C.* Pocket Books, 1976.

Goodwin, W. *The Ruins of Greater Ireland in New England*. Boston: Meador Press, 1946.

Mavor, James W., and Byron E. Dix. *Manitou: Inner Traditions*. Rochester, VT: International, 1990.

Trento, Salvadore. *The Search for Lost America*. Penguin Books, 1977.

Turtle, Little. "Stone Boy and the Chambers of New England." In *New England Antiquities Research Association Journal*. Vol. XVIII, #3, Winter 1984.

A new book on America's Stonehenge by archaeologist W. E. Hinton is forthcoming. Publication is expected in 1992.

NEW JERSEY

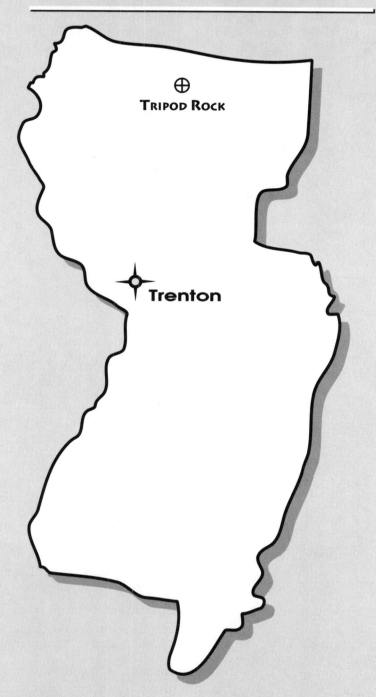

⊕
Tripod Rock

✦ Trenton

Tripod Rock

Bruce Scofield

On a northern New Jersey mountain ridge an unusual configuration
of glacial erratics sits near the edge of a cliff. From a bedrock outcropping, a sighting between two prominent boulders over a third
directs one's eye to the position of the summer solstice sunset. Forty
feet to the southeast is one of the most extraordinary glacial erratics
in the entire Northeast, the approximately 130-ton Tripod Rock,
perched on three stones between 1.5 and 3 feet in diameter. This remarkable assemblage of megaliths, New Jersey's own Stonehenge,
is located in the Pyramid Mountain Natural and Historical area, administered by the Morris County Park Commission.

Tripod Rock has been known for many years by hikers and
naturalists who utilize an extensive trail network in the area. Its current preservation is in part due to its isolation from the main roads.
One must hike the mountain to see the rock. Only in the 1980s, when
developers began to encroach on the site, did Tripod Rock become
known to the general public. Its current status as public land is due
to the efforts of a grassroots committee composed of naturalists and
hikers who put pressure on politicians and state agencies, and some
creative shuffling of land parcels by the New Jersey Conservation
Foundation and the Mennen Company. In recent years, Pyramid
Mountain has become known to many as a place of power and small
crowds gather each June 21st to watch the summer solstice sunset
from between the two markers. But the main attraction is the glacial
erratic Tripod Rock.

Glacial erratics are large boulders deposited by the glacial ice
sheets of previous ice ages. Those erratics that are raised off the
ground and supported by smaller stones are often referred to as
"perched boulders." Many persons have noted similarities between
perched boulders and dolmens, the stone tombs made of upright
stones supporting a capstone, that are found in the British Isles. Geologists have long maintained that the glacial ice sheet, which cov-

ered all of New England, New York State and northern New Jersey, was the sole creator of such bizarre phenomena. The glacier carried with it stones, large and small, scraped from the surface of the land. When the glacial ice sheet became stationary, prior to melt and retreat, its cargo was deposited in place. If a very large stone happened to be carried over smaller stones, it was deposited over them. Differential erosion eliminated silt, sand and smaller stones leaving, in many cases, a large boulder balanced on several smaller stones. This is the official position of the geological establishment in regard to such phenomena.

Tripod Rock—perhaps the largest perched boulder in the Northeast.
It weighs about 160 tons and is supported by three smaller stones.
Photo by Bruce Scofield.

While most perched boulders are simply the extremes on a curve of possible variations in the glacial melt-and-drop process, a few are quite enigmatic and suggest human modifications. In Northern Salem, New York, not far from the junction of I-84 and I-684, and only a few feet from the main road, is found an approximately 90-ton boulder that stands well off the ground on five support stones. This boulder does not lie on a ridge-top but stands in a valley. Around it is much soil, the support stones having been shown to extend about four feet into the ground. There appears to be some pictographic remains on its surface. This stone, which has been known and reported on for over 150 years, is easily accessible by car and has been preserved by the local historical society. It is labeled as a product of the last glacier and no connection with prehistoric man is officially made, a conclusion that some find incredible.

Located on what has come to be know as Pyramid Mountain, Tripod Rock is not near a road and one must hike a mile or more to see it. The boulder itself is larger than the North Salem stone and it is located on a mountain ridge, supported by three stones in turn standing on exposed bedrock. The rock type is a granite-like pre-Cambrian gneiss, the bedrock of the Jersey Highlands geological province in which it is located. Its dimensions are roughly 19' by 10' by 7' and it stands an average of 1.5' off the bedrock. Its weight is approximately 140 tons.

The unusual characteristics of Tripod Rock and its neighboring stones prompted a survey with transit in the spring of 1982. The resulting survey map suggested that a path of sight through two large perched stones about 40 feet from Tripod Rock was in the direction of the summer solstice sunset. Visual confirmation of this event was obtained that year on June 21, facilitated by extensive gypsy month defoliation. Confirmation of the event has also been made in succeeding years and it currently attracts interested persons every June 21. The original survey suggested a possible winter solstice alignment also, but this was not confirmed visually.

From the position of the observer, the summer solstice sunset occurs approximately 15-20 minutes before the true horizon sunset at that time of year. During the period around the summer solstice, a few days before and after June 21, the sun is observed to set over the next ridge to the west, Stony Brook Mountain, at approximately 8:20 p.m. EDT. The exact setting time is questionable, plus or minus several minutes, as foliage prevents an exact sighting of this event. But the effect is still quite striking and worth viewing.

The solstice alignment today is not exceptionally accurate but it could have been used with greater precision. Investigations of the Stony Brook Mountain ridge over which the sunset occurs revealed a slight rise, or bump, at the solstice sunset position. During the investigation, which preceded some later residential development, a

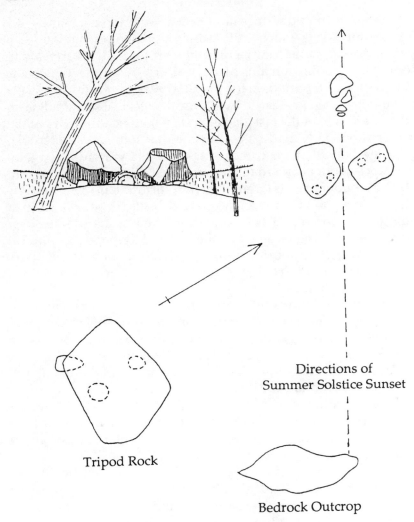

Directions of
Summer Solstice Sunset

Tripod Rock

Bedrock Outcrop

Placement of Tripod Rock.

large, approximately 10′ diameter, boulder was located on this
height, it now having been displaced by the construction. Hypo-
thetically, a small clearing on the top of Stony Brook Mountain,
made by the removal of some trees, would allow for an extremely
clear view of the setting sun. A large stone positioned there could
have been used for precise timing of the solstice. An observer would
simply count the number of days that the sun set behind the rock

and half this amount. The result would be the exact date of the solstice. However, all of this is speculative, and even without it the solstice alignment is reasonably accurate and compares favorably with other better documented calendar sites in North America.

There is nothing definite or conclusive at the Tripod Rock site that indicates it was used for calendrical or astronomical purposes. It is in the entire setting and configuration, and above all its proximity to the odd glacial erratic Tripod Rock that such speculation is at all possible. It is not known for certain if the indigenous inhabitants of the area constructed and utilized astronomical or calendrical devices. However, it is common knowledge that Native Americans had, and have, a great respect for rocks and stones, often singling out those worthy of special veneration. A few interesting facts do suggest that the site may have been known to the early inhabitants of the area. First, just below the ridge is a large, isolated rock shelter, called Bear Rock, that has yielded a number of prehistoric artifacts. Most likely, it was a temporary shelter used by hunting parties. Also, Tripod Rock is located within 5 miles of an area that supported a very dense native population in prehistoric times. It would seem that Tripod Rock must certainly have been known to them.

METAPHYSICAL SPECULATIONS

Preservation of the land containing Tripod Rock and the solstice stones was of prime concern during the 1980s. Because of frequent meetings and correspondence with public officials, official investigations of the area were confined to precision surveying and conservative archaeological speculations. It must be said again that, in the final analysis, there are no factual indications that the site was used by man for sacred or astronomical purposes. The rocks do form an alignment with the solstice sunset, and the site could therefore be used as a calendar device—but there is no hard evidence that it was. However, the strangeness of the site stimulated two other experiments, the results of which have never been published.

On a beautiful fall afternoon in the early 1980s, I brought psychic and channeler Pat Hayes to the site. I told her nothing about it and just let her say and do whatever she felt. As we approached the site, she fell into a deep trance and began speaking in an unknown language. Arriving there she sat down, still in a deep trance, spoke briefly, and answered some questions that my friend and I had. She said that the site was used for hundreds of years by the Indians and was known to be a source of power. According to her, this area is the source of the most powerful earth energies in the region and Tripod Rock acts like a capacitor, storing and focusing the energies that emerge from the earth at this point. She also said that it would be preserved for the future and one day its true name would become known. About 100 yards to the north of the site are some other interesting boulders, one of which is perched. According to Pat, this was a woman's site, a place where women would come when they lost a child or husband.

Tripod Rock.
Photo by Bruce Scofield.

Intrigued by the information revealed by Pat, I brought Dan Travers, alchemist and dowser, to the site. He was quite impressed by the size of the stone, but soon became more interested in the strong lines of force that seemed to converge on it. It appeared to him that several sheets of earth energy crossed directly under the stone. Having learned to dowse from Dan, I followed up on his initial findings and located three major lines of force, noting their compass directions and the approximate distance from the rock that they extended. After several visits to the rock with dowsing rods, I noticed that these lines appeared to shift a bit, and also varied in distance from the rock. It is probable that such shifts coincide with solar, lunar and possibly planetary alignments, but this has yet to be confirmed at this site.

A number of writers, including Mavor and Dix, Fell and Trento, have suggested that perched boulders like Tripod Rock and the North Salem boulder were created by both nature and man and that they served a ritual function in ancient times. It has also been suggested that such megalithic arrangements may have tremendous antiquity and were built not by the Indians the colonists encountered, but by some other previous race. It is true that the many perched boulders that exist in New England have some similarities to structures found in Great Britain and along the Iberian coast. But this is, at present, speculation.

FOR MORE INFORMATION

Visiting the Site
Visitors to Pyramid Mountain should be dressed for a hike. There are several trails to the site, all of which require some climbing. Two maps are available of the area and carefully described hikes to Tripod rock are found in the two guidebooks listed. Proper footwear is a must and you may wish to bring water, food and rainwear. Insect repellent may be needed in late spring and summer. Plan on spending at least two hours for your visit and possibly more if you decide to hike further afield and see Bear Rock or whale Head, two other huge erratics in the vicinity.

Directions
Pyramid Mountain and Tripod Rock are located in northern New Jersey approximately five miles north of the intersection of I-80 and I-287. Follow route 511 (Boonton Avenue) a few miles north of the town of Boonton to a point 0.8 miles north of Boonton Avenue's junction with Taylortown Road. A powerline crosses the road here and there is parking for a few cars alongside the road. Additional parking is available along the entrance road to Mars Park, an industrial park, located just south of this point. There are plans for a new parking area, just south of the powerlines, that will accommodate

more cars. A directory will be located there to direct you to the site should the present parking arrangements be changed.

Lodging

In the vicinity of Morristown, NJ, located within a short drive to the site, are a large number of hotels including a Hilton, Sheraton and Marriot each offering first class accommodations. Other, less expensive motels can be found along US-46 and NJ-10. Car and tent camping is available at Mahlon Dickerson Reservation, administered by the Morris County Park Commission, near Sparta, about 1/2 hour west of the site. For more information contact the Morris County Park Commission at P.O. Box 1295R, Morristown, NJ 07960.

Maps

A map of the extensive trail system on Pyramid Mountain will make a trip there safer and more interesting. The NY-NJ Trail Conference, GPO Box 2250, New York, NY 10116, publishes a five color map of Pyramid Mountain Trails that is waterproof and tearproof. The price is $3.45 postpaid. The Morris County Park Commission also has a map of the area around Tripod Rock. Write them at P.O. Box 1295R, Morristown, NJ 07960.

Additional Readings

Scofield, Bruce. *Circuit Hikes in Northern New Jersey.* New York-New Jersey Trail Conference, New York: 1984.

Scofield, Green and Zimmerman. *Fifty Hikes in New Jersey.* Woodstock, VT: Backcountry Publications, 1988.

Scofield, Bruce. "A possible Summer Solstice marker in Northern New Jersey." *New England Antiquities Research Association Journal.* Vol. XVIII, 1 & 2, Summer/Fall 1983.

NEW MEXICO

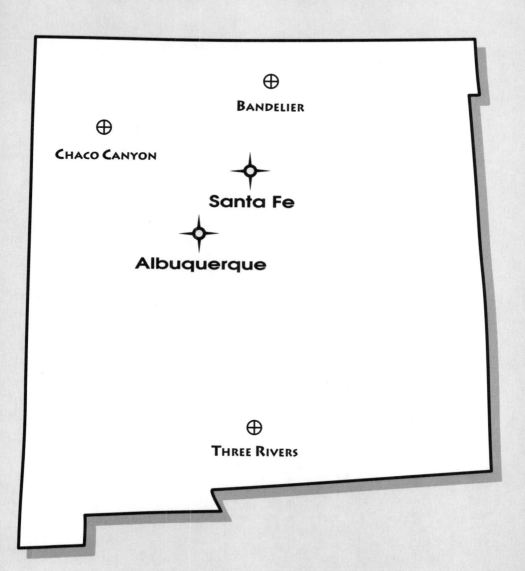

BANDELIER

CHACO CANYON

Santa Fe

Albuquerque

THREE RIVERS

Chaco Canyon National Monument

Alice Bryant

Lying 125 miles northwest of New Mexico's largest city, Albu-querque, the Chaco Canyon ruins were, for hundreds of years, densely populated. Long famous for size and complexity, it has only been in the last quarter century that the sophistication of the inhabitants of these ruins has come to be understood. It is now believed that this was a large trade center for the Anasazi.

Time for the pueblo people had little relation to modern day concepts. No record was kept of the passing of the years; they were not concerned with their chronological age. Life revolved around the seasons and the planting of the crops. For this, it was necessary to have an accurate seasonal record. Quite likely this was the designated task of certain people, most likely a Medicine Man and his apprentices. Preparations for festival dates, the most important of which was the winter solstice, had to be made well in advance, for there would be feasting, ritual clothing, special prayers.

In 1977, atop Fajada Butte, an isolated mesa in Chaco Canyon, one of the most complex solar/lunar calendars in the prehistoric sites of the United States was discovered by the artist, Anna Sofaer. The site is now closed by the National Park Service to prevent damage to the fragile area. However, an excellent video, narrated by Robert Redford, is available in the visitor's center. It gives more information than the visitor who negotiated the difficult and hazardous climb could obtain because it shows the seasonal phases. Huge slabs of rock are delicately balanced in front of a carved spiral, the narrow openings between the slabs allowing the sun to pierce the spiral with a dagger of light. This dagger of light is on both sides of the spiral at the winter solstice, penetrates the very center at the summer solstice and quarters the spiral at each equinox. More incredibly, the rock calendar also pictures phases of the moon.

Ruins of Chaco Canyon.
Photo by Diana Person.

The people of Chaco incorporated other solar orientations into their occupied buildings as well. According to Michael Zeilik, astronomy professor at the University of New Mexico, the unusual corner window in Pueblo Bonito allows a shaft of light to strike the opposite corner of the room at the winter solstice.

At an altitude of between 5,300 and 7,500 feet, the ancient dwellings are situated on the Chaco Plateau where sandstone cliffs rise on the north side some hundred feet above the valleys. The land is bisected by the Chaco Wash, which runs a meandering 150 miles into the San Juan River. Dry in summer, the Wash is subject to huge flash floods during rainstorms. A few small springs dot the canyon walls but on top there are natural water holes cut into the sandstone by runoff water. These occur in sufficient numbers to have supplied the prehistoric peoples with a supplemental water source.

There are some 2,000 archaeological sites in the Chaco Canyon National Park, with 13 large villages called great houses. A system of roads fanned out from the Canyon settlement, like the spokes of a wagon wheel, reaching outlying villages as far as 100 miles away.

Temperatures range widely, even on a daily basis. The summers are hot and the winters cold, current annual rainfall is just above 8" and it is believed that between 300 and 150 it was even less.

With the increase in rainfall after 150, the Anasazi moved into Chaco Canyon and between then and 700, formed one of the most outstanding examples of Anasazi culture in the Southwest.

Evidence indicates that religion was strongly oriented toward the supernatural. Many dwellings contained the *sipapu*. Recognized in Pueblo mythology as the symbolic entrance to the lower world from whence the people came into this world, the *sipapu* is still believed to be occupied by the spirits of the dead. The many ceremonial centers indicate that leadership may have been in the hands of a spiritual elite.

The 8th century saw change in architecture from below ground to above ground. Flatroofed, four posted, open walled shelters were slowly changed to the use of fewer posts and the rock walls were coated with adobe mud. The pit structures were used for storage in the multiroomed houses sheltering extended families.

Between 850 and 920 rooms were built in rectangular blocks with as many as 30 rooms in a line. The kivas became large and somewhat standardized, circular, with a bench built around the entire wall. There would be a ventilator opening with a slab deflecting it. Often there would be a sipapu and always a smoke hole. The log/brush roof would be supported by upright posts. Kivas were individual affairs usually situated in front of a group of dwellings indicating a family type of use.

Between 920 and 1020, this typical Anasazi village saw a change that made it unique. Referred to as the Chaco Phenomenon, the change was the use of planned irrigation diversion. Either the lessening rainfall or the enlarged population, or both, forced the dwellers to resort to artificial watering of crops. The natural basins atop the sandstone cliffs held water long after the run off. The people took steps to harness the flood waters with dams and built an irrigation system to utilize the water on the cliff tops.

Between 1050 and 1150 the now doubled population of some 6,000 people reached its peak of civilization. The heavily populated canyon floor and the outlying smaller units became a trade center reaching into Mexico to the South and North into Colorado. Ceramics and jewelry making reached a peak of excellence that had an impact far and wide among the Anasazi. Possibly influenced from

Mexico, a new style of masonry developed. The strength of the thick walls with centers of unshaped rocks and mud and veneered with shaped stones allowed the construction of multistoried buildings as high as five stories and containing hundreds of rooms. Whether influenced by Mexico or not, this construction was unique to Chaco Canyon. During this phase the great Kivas were situated apart from the dwellings.

The Great Kiva's Sipapu.
Photo by Diana Person.

One of the great mysteries of Chaco Canyon is that, to date, no large burial areas have been found. In the outlying villages burials have been found in the trash heaps but he incredibly low number of burials excavated in the major settlements does not reflect the large population. It is not known at this time how the Anasazi disposed of their dead at Chaco Canyon.

Chaco Canyon peaked around 1100 and a slow dissipation began, when by the late 1200s, the once thriving city became a ruin. Several explanations have been offered: invasion, disease, drought, land depletion. None offer a complete answer though it is known that the San Juan Basin suffered a drought lasting some 60 years between 1130 A.D. and 1190 A.D. This, with the resulting shortage of food, seems to be the most logical explanation. It is known that when the Navajo came many years later, they avoided the abandoned settlement in respect for the dead.

MYSTICAL SIGNIFICANCE

Veritable mystical experiences have been taking place in Chaco Canyon from prehistoric times, and today's receptive visitor should be no less fortunate than the mysterious Anasazi, who flourished there a thousand years ago.

The most frequent paranormal events occur around the sipapu, those ritual entrances to the Otherworld of the Ancient Ones. Even according to those park officials willing to speak frankly, the ghostly vision of a tall, naked man has been observed by both rangers and visitors emerging without a sound from the subterranean sacred center. On at least one occasion, a park employee tried to arrest the apparition, assuming it was an after hours trespasser. But the dignified intruder vanished into thin air as he approached.

Local Indians are not at all surprised by these spectral appearances, and claim the area constitutes a special gap in the heart of Mother Earth, a holy precinct still functioning after unguessed centuries. The naked giant, they explain, is the *genius loci*, eternally replenishing itself from the Mother Earth womb. Interestingly, he has sometimes been glimpsed enveloped in a faint azure luminescence, as his body drips with moisture. Science recognizes the Blue Light Phenomenon as an actual, though so far inexplicable effect, associated with places of focused tectonic energies, e.g., at the interces of earthquake fault lines or in areas of seismic stress. And Chaco Canyon does indeed perch directly over the juncture of two unstable fault lines. The vision's wet appearance is explained by the resident tribal elders as clinging after-birth (or re-birth), as the genius loci renews himself at the sacred center. Merely to see him, they believe, is to be blessed. For it means he has chosen the viewer as a beneficiary, as one who from that moment knows in his or her heart that Chaco Canyon is a holy place of mystic earth power.

SUGGESTED RITUAL

Begin your preparation by gathering earth materials: corn meal and four crystals. If possible enter the Grand Kiva or one of the smaller kivas at dawn or dusk. Walking to the center of the kiva take the cornmeal and honor the four directions of the compass. Begin with the north, place of the earth. go next to the east, place of the wind, then south to the place of water, then the west, place of fire. Hold aloft the right hand, honoring the sun, the moon, the stars above. swing the hand down to point to Mother Earth saying "and the earth below."

If you have four crystals with you place one in each compass direction with the point outward. Be seated in the center of the kiva and center yourself; enter a meditative state.

Petition the ancestors of this Holy Place by mentally going to each of the cardinal points in turn, calling silently or aloud the appropriate place name (earth, wind, water, fire) in the following manner: "I call you forth and I offer my hand." Wait in silence until a response is felt or an appropriate amount of time has passed.

After the four cardinal directions have been addressed direct your energy to the Dog Star, Sirius. Call its energy forth, feeling it blend with yours. Reaching mentally deep into the bowels of the earth call forth the earth energy. Feel it rise and intertwine with your very being until you are cocooned in the loving grasp of the Mother. Holding this presence call forth the Ancient Ones, the Shamans. You have performed the proper rituals and can now enter your private meditation space. Questions and answers are appropriate at this time. Coming out of your meditation feel a deep loving energy within your being.

Feel it radiate out in to the base of all four crystals, letting them amplify this energy. See it shoot out their tips into the direction they are pointing. Feel the energy come out the top of your head at the crown chakra and shoot to the Dog Star, Sirius. Feel it move down your tailbone deep into Mother Earth.

Once again cast a pinch of cornmeal to each of the cardinal directions and above and below, saying each time, "as above, so below," thanking the energy of these elements. After collecting your crystals write down the information you have received from the Ancient Ones. Leave the kiva with a glad heart and a buoyant step, knowing you have affirmed your link with the past and can now stride into the future with confidence and the blessing of the Ancient Ones.

FOR MORE INFORMATION

Bibliography

Lister, Robert H. and Florence C. Lister. *Chaco Canyon*. Albuquerque, NM: University of NM Press, 1981.

Zeilik, Michael. "Sun Watching: Prehistoric Astronomy in New Mexico," *New Mexico Magazine*, March, 1985, pp. 48-55.

Further Information

University of New Mexico Publications in Anthropology.

Facilities

The Visitor's Information Center has indoor bathrooms. A variety of bottled cold drinks are available.

Numerous campsites, each with a fire pit and picnic table, are provided in a special area in Chaco Canyon, with a central bath house offering bathroom facilities. Shower stalls and lavatories with hot and cold running water are provided. There are no motel/hotel facilities available at the site.

Directions

From Albuquerque, North on I-25 to Bernalillo, take the exit to Highway 44. Turn off Highway 44 to Highway 57 at the Blanco Trading Post. It is 16 miles from Blanco Trading Post on Highway 57 to Chaco Canyon. From Farmington, east on Highway 64, 15 miles to Bloomfield, south on Highway 44, to Blanco Trading Post and Highway 57. Highway 57 is not paved but is classified as an all weather gravel surfaced road. Travelers should check with the Highway Patrol during the winter as Highway 44 can be closed during heavy snow storms. In summer, check at Blanco Trading Post as heavy local rains can cause muddy, slippery roads.

Three Rivers Petroglyph Park

Alice Bryant

Late fall is the ideal time of year to visit the Three Rivers Petroglyph Park. Under a cloudless sky of incredible blue the warm golden days are still reflecting the desert heat from the White Sands National Monument to the West. Nestled in the foothills of the Sacramento Mountains under the shadow of Sierra Blanca Peak, stands the Sacred Mountain of the Mescalero Apache. The nights are cool and crisp in the fall and a heavy jacket is a necessity if the visitor plans a late night viewing of the brilliant stars through the crisp mountain air.

The view is panoramic off across the arid valley to the Oscura Mountains in the west. The Sacramento Range with its rugged canyons and forested high peaks towers over the site to the east offering a spectacular view of the 12,000 foot peak of Sierra Blanca.

In ancient rock art, the term "pictographs" refers to drawings, and "petroglyphs" are the designs pecked into the rock surface. Like so many areas in Colorado and Utah that are famous for pictographs and petroglyphs, the formation of Three Rivers Park area contributes to the durability of this ancient rock art. An outcropping some mile and a half long on a low ridge at the edge of the valley, the rocks are covered in an iron oxide patina which is a dark brown, almost black. This shallow coating, when scratched by a sharp object such as another rock or a flintstone, reveals a white inner surface, thus creating a natural canvas for the artist. The low amount of rainfall in the area along with the durability of the patina preserves the rock art for hundreds of years.

The people, the Jornado branch of the Mogollon culture, are believed to have arrived from the West and populated the valley and the foothills around the three small rivers in the area from 900 A.D. to 1300 A.D. Their art resembles the Mimbres style. Water and game were probably the prime considerations for settling in this place, but there may also have been a well-traveled trade route, for the site lies

some 50 miles from the Rio Grande River. Pre-Columbian natives
traveled extensively from what is now Mexico up through Santa Fe,
New Mexico and on into Oklahoma.

The trail winding through the petroglyph area is narrow but
clearly defined. As it meanders along the ridge, footing can be a little
treacherous, so it is recommended that the visitor stop and stand
still while viewing the rock art. There are places where the art is visible in every direction.

Three Rivers Petroglyph.
Photo by Diana Person.

The play of light and shadow at various times of the day brings
to view previously obscured figures. The one dominant theme is a
circle and dots, which may symbolize the sun and the stars. Some of
these are the simple single circles; others are multiple circles within
circles with numerous dots along the parameter.

There are some ten or twelve very distinctive human faces with
minimal stylization; each is unique. There are exquisitely proportioned and detailed figures of lizards and rattlesnakes. Rabbits,
coyotes, mountain lions, bear paws and human hand prints abound.
The mountain sheep are depicted in outline, both in motion and
standing, and in the heavy horned ram's head.

Three Rivers Petroglyph (above, photo by Diana Person).

A mirror handle depicting the ancient Egyptian goddess, Hathor. (Courtesy of Cairo Museum, through Frank Joseph.)

The uniqueness of these petroglyphs lies in the unusual abstract designs that are laced throughout the monument. A dispro-
portionately large amount of the rock art at Three Rivers is abstract
in form. Indian rock art is more commonly stylized: depicting gods,
men, animals.

SUGGESTED RITUAL

The imprint of our spiritual ancestors is heavy on this land. The
visitor can tune into the resonance of this ancient site through meditation techniques. Sitting comfortably and stilling the mind, imagine a laser beam of light coming from above, entering the head, going down through the tailbone, entering deep into the earth, skew-
ering you to the earth.

Breathing deeply and rhythmically, pull the earth energy up
along this laser beam of light running it parallel to the one coming
down form above. Bring it all the way up into and through you, letting it exit the top of the head.

Ask to resonate with this sacred place. The feeling will begin in
the tailbone and run up through you until your whole body vibrates
with the area. Ask for the door to be opened so that you can see and
communicate with the ancient ones, the teachers, of this magical
place.

With the inner eye the visitor may see the ley or energy line that
runs through this site in all its colorful splendor. Gold is the predominant color but there is also some silver streaks. The ley line here
is exceptionally large and deep, being approximately 30 feet wide
and some 50 feet deep. This line runs along the ridge and a long way
to the north where it intersects with other ley lines that are diagonal.
One thick band is shooting up directly toward the Dog Star, Sirius.
This ley line also intersects to the south with other ley lines.

Meditations on this Holy Ground are all, of course, unique to
each individual. Because of the extra large ley line it is a high energy
point. Much can be obtained by the visitor by interaction with this
Holy Ground.

Bandelier National Monument

Oz Anderson

We have not inherited the earth from our parents, we are borrowing it from our children.
—Traditional Native American saying

Imagine a place where everything needed to sustain life is provided in the environment. It might be a canyon full of natural, solar-heated caves where the vegetation is lush, a stream flows clear and constantly, and wild animals are abundant. Here a bountiful life is dependent on a balanced relationship between the environment and the inhabitants, just as everywhere on earth. This microcosmic model exists at Bandelier National Monument.

Bandelier includes 32000 acres of National Park containing thousands of archaeological sites. The main canyon is one in a web extending from the site of what is believed to be the largest volcanic eruption that ever occurred on earth. Over a million years ago, a great mountain exploded in north-central New Mexico with such force that huge boulders landed as far away as the places we today call Oklahoma and Kansas. A tremendous layer of ash, many times deeper than the fallout from Vesuvius or Krakatoa, settled in the surrounding land and over the years formed into a layer of relatively soft pinkish stone. Water erosion cut deep channels into this stone, leaving beautiful sheer-rimmed cliff faces in shades ranging from pastels to a glowing iron-reddish. Today's Jemez mountains bear ravines of striking color and fascinating shapes. Pockets that once held trapped gasses formed swiss-cheese-like patterns and lacy configurations of natural stone, later embellished by erosion and eventually, in some places, by humans.

The people first came 10,000 years ago. By 4000 B.C. they had begun building rock shelters so as to stay through the cold winters. They shaped the holes in the soft stone into chambers large enough for living, and as places for work, learning and worship. At about

253

the same time that the great castles of Wales were being built, 1100-1200 C.E., there was a tremendous tide of immigrants into this area. Some speculate that an emigration from Chaco Canyon to the northwest may have been the cause. Wherever they may have come from, the "Ancient Ones," or Anasazi, had arrived. They brought with them advanced skills in architecture and artistry, culture and probably ceremony.

For 400 years, canyons and highlands all over the wide surrounding plateau teemed with life. The people grew crops upon the high mesas, developed irrigation and water-storage systems. They carved the stone and built great multi-storied cities, with deep ceremonial chambers. They carved symbols into cliff faces and painted the walls of the caves and kivas. They knew the sight and scent of animals and plants, walked along the stream, and sat wondering at the waterfalls. They may have watched the midwinter sun rise through the entry to the plaza in the city they called Tyuonyi. At such an important time, they may have danced and sung in ritual, as do the people of today who claim to be their descendents.

And yet when the Spaniards came no one lived in this place at all. Humans had abandoned the canyon. According to oral histories, the people simply moved closer to the Rio Grande Valley, probably because they had exhausted the resources of the limited ecosystem.

And so, what might be the message for those of us who come to experience this place today?

To understand the sacredness of Bandelier, it is good to try to first connect with the spirits of those who once resided here. From the Visitor's Center, a walk through the ancient structures begins a process of identification and understanding. You first pass a Great Kiva (see "Casa Rinconcada" for more about Great Kivas), and the remains of the city of Tyuonyi. The walk takes you past both created, natural and carved-out quarters used for residence, storage, or as Kivas (ceremonial chambers). In certain places along the way, you may enter some of these spaces. The cave-kivas are wonderful places to sit and meditate. Bizarre and fanciful stone formations interweave a sense of fantasy and imagination with the intriguing structures and odd places, making this seem like an ancient wonderland. As you continue to follow the trail you come to the Long House, a stretch of dwellings that follows the base of the cliff. If you look just above the structures, you will see many petroglyphs, or symbols carved into the cliff faces. To many of today's Pueblo people such symbols carry messages of certain spiritual concepts, much as do the religious symbols and icons of other religions. Oftentimes, if you allow yourself to be receptive, you may find that a particular one of these Petroglyphs "speaks" to you, or stands out in your attention more than the others. Remember the symbol that attracts you, for someday it may have greater meaning.

Other walks and trails lead to beautiful vistas, naturally enchanting spots, and exceptional discoveries. Follow the trail for another mile to a most impressive Ceremonial Cave, but only if you have no fear of heights. The ladders you must climb to get to the cave have been dubbed the Park's best cheap thrill, and well worth it for the experience of the cave-kiva itself. The serious and hardy backpacker may wish to visit one or more of the exceptional sites located further away. Immeasurable opportunities remain in this richly endowed bit of earth.

Tyuonui Ruin, Bandelier National Monument.
Photo courtesy of the National Park Service.

CEREMONY FOR THE SHRINE OF THE STONE CIRCLE

As you drive up and out of the canyon, look for a sign that says "Scenic Pullout, 265 feet," and turn in to the small parking area on your left. It is a short walk to a panoramic overlook of the canyon below. Stop here, and just reflect. Ask the spirits of this place to begin to speak to you, to share their messages. Continuing your drive, just before you reach the highway turn left again into the Juniper Campground area. Follow the road towards the amphitheater and bus parking area. Stop here and prepare for your ritual journey. Take with you a power-piece or item of personal significance, something you wish to charge with blessings and understandings that may come to you. Look for a sign to "Tyuonyi Overlook Trail" towards the amphitheater and to your left. Bear left where the trail forks. The level trail is 1.2 miles long and should take about a leisurely half hour. Your personal rite begins here.

Address the guardians of this canyon, and offer yourself as one who is willing to receive and understand, and to share their message with others. As you walk, it is interesting to consider that until just 50 years ago the only access to this canyon was across this plateau and down the steep canyon side. Imagine what it must have once felt like to be coming from tilling and tending the fields, heading for that lovely green canyon and a comfortable place called home. Be aware of life all around you. You may see deer or birds, or tracks of foxes or mountain lions. Bears, coyotes, ravens, bobcats and bats all call Bandelier home. The wind may blow through the branches of the trees as you take time to absorb the essences of the natural life. Pass another sign. At this second fork, again take the trail to the left. Near the end of the trail on your right, you come to a small stone circle. This shrine is most sacred, and remains in use today. Be here with great care and respect. Walk clockwise slowly around the outer perimeter and build up a sense of what this circle means to you personally, remembering that you have already asked the spirits of this place to "speak" to you. To one side of the stone circle is an entrance. When you are ready, step across and come into the center.

Stand for a moment and look at the mountains and vistas in the distance. You are able to see very far away. Take in the entire view of the horizon all around you. Hold your power object securely in your right hand (or left if you are left-handed). Close your eyes and imagine that your feet are rooted very firmly to the earth in this spot. Let roots grow from the bottoms of your feet and into the ground to a great depth. Imagine that your body begins to expand, growing taller, so that your head grows higher and higher. You are able to look down on the scene that surrounds you, on all the mountain peaks and canyons below. You continue to grow, as your head goes higher than the clouds, into the upper atmosphere and out into space. Your feet are still firmly rooted in the earth. You can look down now at the entire planet, that blue sphere you have seen in photographs of Planet Earth taken from space. Keep the sense of this perspective with you, and open your eyes.

Retain the sense of the ritual clearly in your own consciousness as you carry with you both your rootedness and your elevated perspective, and leave the stone circle. Go to the end of the trail and look down into the canyon. As you look, think of this place and the feelings you have of your own home. Imagine the warmth, safety and comfort this place has held. Inwardly balance this sense and the awareness of your own relationship to the earth that we all call home. Feel the wind coming up the canyon and blowing upon your face. Look for birds riding the currents of air.

Go back to the stone circle and be seated in the center, facing the far mountains. Some call this circle the "Far-Seeing Place." Place your power object on the ground before you. Close your eyes and let that "Far-Seeing" happen inside you; accept whatever images, sensations or realizations that may come to you. On this ceremonial level your consciousness is able to rise above its limited view and "see" further than would usually be possible. Remain rooted to the earth. Reflect on the idea of balance. Repeat quietly to yourself the phrase, "As above, So below."

Think about people who have lived here. Their descendents still come to the very circle in which you are seated to leave offerings, to honor the place of their ancestors. They no longer live here, but other people have come to keep watch over and protect the lands. North of here is Los Alamos, a city created for the express purpose of developing the atomic bomb—a thing whose power has changed the reality of this planet and our race forever. Ironically, some who worked on this project actually lived in the canyon below.

Many forces have moved in this place. A cataclysmic geological event of massive earthly violence was followed by aeons of gentle, quiet, transformation. Eventually, there was a period of fruitful-ness, where our race lived almost as in a miniature garden of Eden. But because the balance was not maintained, the people had to leave.

There is an undocumented "story" about the leaving of the people which says that on a holy day a long time ago, the Sacred Ceremonial Clowns were at ritual play. Clowns are still important characters in the rites and dances of Native Pueblo peoples. These Clowns were tossing an infant back and forth, and accidentally dropped the child to its death. This event was interpreted as an ill omen, and the people left. Ceremonial Clowns are often identified with the overpowering forces of nature, especially such forces as chaos and the unpredictable natures of the elements. Others say that the Clowns may represent parts of our own deep consciousness and sub-conscious selves, like the shadow-parts of individual personalities and the collective unconscious of groups of people. The infant is a symbol common to all cultures, representing the coming age, the newer generations, the promise of continuing life, and the constant rebirth and renewal of plants, animals and human lives.

Continue to meditate on balance, and your own relation to the forces that you sense are at play in Bandelier's dramas, both past and present. When you open your eyes, look first into your own power object and let whatever vision, revelation or understanding you have received travel from your eyes into your personal object. Let this thought-force-energy imbue your object with your new knowledge or insight. Let this message ever remain in this object, so that you need only hold it to be reminded in the future. Now, place both hands over your object and release your visualizations and any remnant feelings of altered consciousness. It is always ritually appropriate to give thanks to the spirits of the place, in this case for giving their messages. It is also true, however, that the spirits of Bandelier are ready to speak and waiting to be heard. Acknowledge this in cooperation, and remember the offering you made of your self in the beginning of your rite.

The walk out is a good time to ground into your consciousness symbols and images which have come to you. Remember the petroglyphs. As you leave the Park, if time permits, you may want to turn left on Hwy 4 and drive into the volcanic crater 15 miles to the west. Along the way you will see more evidence of the converging and contrasting powers that surround the gentle garden you have left. You can see the destruction from a forest fire started by humans many years ago. As you drive the steep road over the mountains, you cross an eroded rim from the eruption that shaped this land. Prepare for an especially expansive sensation when you arrive at the Valle Grande Caldera.

From here you may turn around and return to Los Alamos or Santa Fe, or continue towards Albuquerque on Hwy 4 through beautiful Jemez Canyon, the very spiritual town of Jemez Springs, and Jemez Pueblo. Hwy 4 runs into Hwy 44; turn south, and on to I-25 near Albuquerque. The modern Pueblos of Santa Clara and San Ildefonso are both easily accessible on the return trip to Santa Fe from Bandelier. Cochiti Pueblo, further south, claims direct ancestry from Bandelier. Traditional ceremonial dances are still enacted for the public at many Pueblos in New Mexico. Dates and locations may be obtained from the Indian Pueblo Cultural Center in Albuquerque, 505-242-4943. Corn, Deer, Buffalo and other dances are performed most often near solstices, equinoxes and cross-quarter days (half-way between solstices and equinoxes). When attending such an event, please bear in mind the sacred and religious observations of these people. Act with respect and observe bans on photography.

FOR MORE INFORMATION

Bandelier Nat'l Monument is about one hour north of Santa Fe. From Hwy 285 towards Taos, turn left on Hwy 502 to Los Alamos, and follow signs on Hwy 4 to the Park entrance, which is well-marked. The somewhat steep road into the canyon is paved. Museum, slide-shows, literature, food, beverages, and gift shop available. First-come campsites with tables, firepits, pit-toilets & water on mesa above the canyon. Small fee. Group camping at separate location for up to 50 people; inquire with Superintendent for reservations. Free back-country permits for over 70 miles of high altitude trails, some strenuous. Always consult rangers before heading into backcountry. Please no dogs, no back-country fires, and NO removing or altering any natural or archaeological features, including potsherds. Open every day except Christmas. Special activities include a midwinter sunrise walk, 8:00 a.m. Winter Solstice; and guided nighttime walks in summer. Due to the popularity of the site, early morning, late afternoon, fall and winter visits are encouraged, as well as usage of backcountry areas. For more information, write: Superintendent, Bandelier National Monument, HCR-1 Box 1 Suite 15, Los Alamos, NM 87544; or call (505) 672-3861.

Acknowledgements
"Pathway to the Past, A Guide to Bandelier National Monument"; *Los Alamos Monitor* Special Publication, Los Alamos, NM.

"Frijoles Canyon"; Southwest Parks and Monuments Association Publication.

A very special thanks to Chris Judson, Park Ranger, Bandelier National Monument.

NEW YORK

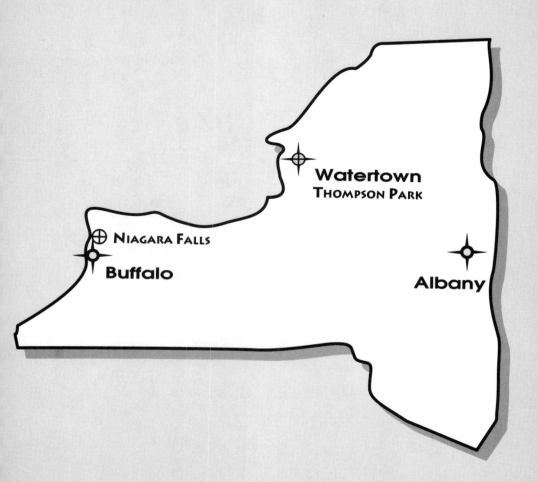

Watertown
THOMPSON PARK

⊕ NIAGARA FALLS

Buffalo

Albany

Niagara Falls

Breid Foxsong

At the eastern end of Lake Erie, the mighty Niagara River begins to pick up speed. Divided by first Grand Island, then rocks and several small islands, it cascades over 150 feet into the Niagara Gorge as the Horseshoe Falls, the Bridal Veil Falls, and the American Falls. There three waterfalls form the famous Niagara Falls. Horseshoe Falls, also referred to as "the Canadian Falls," marks the border between Canada and the United States. It is separated from the others by Goat Island, an ancient Indian burial ground, which got its modern name from the livestock kept there by settlers. Today Goat Island has been converted to Niagara Falls viewing grounds and tourist attractions, but the energy of the Falls still permeates both the island, and the surrounding mainlands.

The Thundering Waters

The area history is fascinating. Obviously, the natives saw Niagara Falls long before any European, but most history books credit a French missionary named Father Louis Hennepin in 1678. He had been told by Iroquois guides of "Thunder Water," the Great Spirit's home. Insisting on hosting a mass there, Father Hennepin was guided to the falls on December 6. Typical of European travelogues of the time, Hennepin described the falls as 5-600 feet high.

Many visitors never realize that the Falls and the islands above them constituted an ancient Iroquois worship site, requiring bravery, strength and courage to attain them by water. Although it is no longer necessary to paddle a frail canoe through the rapids to reach the falls, we can remember and honor the men and women who tested their faith by crossing these waters.

The Iroquois view of the world as being supported on a turtle led the Natives to name the mound of earth separating the waters "Turtle Island." Each island was named according to the type of ritual performed on it, including the Death Island where dances and

263

chants sped the warrior on his way. Turtle Island, or Goat Island as it is now known, was the burial site for warriors whose names have been lost to history. Occasionally a grave is uncovered, and the remains are ceremonially returned to the Iroquois peoples for reburial.

Niagara Falls.
Photo by Breid Foxsong.

There are at least two things anyone interested in the power of the Falls will want to do: Listen to the spirits of the rapids by the Three Sister's Islands, and to stand at the edge of each of the three waterfalls that make up the Niagara Falls. There are two more activities that are certainly worth participating in. If the attractions are open, visit the Cave of the Winds, and ride the Maid of the Mists to the foot of the Falls. These are both (unfortunately) commercial ventures, but well worth the $4-6 they cost.

The Three Sisters are three little islands, at the west edge of Goat Island. Stone arched bridges link the islands to each other and to Goat Island. If you go out to the furthest island, you are less than 300 yards above Horseshoe Falls. The rapids run within 10 feet of the edge of the island, sometimes less than 2 feet away. The shamans of the Iroquois Tribe prayed here, sacrificing food and material goods to the Great Spirit of the Thunder Waters.

Although all the tour guides will tell you of the legend of the sacrificed Indian maiden, the Iroquois "Maid of the Mists" was a young woman who tried to commit suicide over the falls. She was saved by the spirits of the waters and lived under the Falls with them for four years before returning to her tribe. The story of the Indians sacrificing a maiden to the falls was fabricated by a white tourist guide named Burke.

If you stand near the rapids on Three Sisters, close your eyes, and listen, you can hear the spirits of the waves speaking. The Iroquois believed that the spirits of the waters from all over the world came to whisper their tales to the Great Spirit under the Falls. It is said that, if you listen carefully, you can hear news from anywhere in the world, and that, if you ask a question, the spirits will answer. This is difficult to do with other tourists around, however, so try it in the early morning or at dusk, when others are watching the colored spotlights on the falls.

After you have listened to the rapids, go back onto Goat Island and downstream to the Horseshoe Falls. The viewing area, called Terrapin Point, is railed and open to the public from April to November. Terrapin Point consists of the entire northwest tip of the island and extends several feet beyond the cliff. You can get within inches of the water as it begins to fall.

In the winter, this point is buried under layers of frozen mist and snow, sometimes many feet thick. Thus, the point is closed from about November 1 until all danger of ice is gone, usually April 1.

The incredible sight of 675,000 gallons of water a second plunging over the cliff to fall 167 feet onto the rocks below is one that brings awe into anyone's soul. It is unequaled in size, strength and power. This power manifests itself psychically as well. The ion level of the air, and the energy created in the fall, invigorates the body and clears the mind. Water is a universally feminine symbol, but the strength and power of this water balances it to become both male and female, a perfect balance of strength and suppleness. The semicircle of the falls becomes a Grail and the maelstrom below, the Cauldron. Mist from the waters boils up, moving and changing. Visions form, dissolve and reform.

Like a great Mother, the mist sometimes bends over the falls. At other times it seems to stride down the gorge, passing into some other world as it fades from sight. Standing above it, you are suspended in the air between Heaven and Earth. The Creator's decisions seem to make sense from this perspective; it is as if you are peering through a hole in the sky down toward a primal land.

At the northeast edge of Goat Island is Bridal Veil Falls. A narrow falls, it is bridged by a small arch to Luna Island, which separates Bridal Veil Falls from the American Falls. If you are lucky, and there is a full moon out, you may see a lunar rainbow over the falls. Occasionally, the rainbow will be in a full circle. This is rare, but according to the Iroquois Indians, it means that you will lead a blessed life.

On Lunar Island, you can stand at the brink of both the Bridal Veil Falls and the American Falls. Beneath you, at the base of the cliff, is a wooden platform. this is part of the Cave of the Winds Tour. The Cave of the Winds is actually not a cave at all, but a hollow behind the Bridal Veil Falls. Visitors don waterproof slickers and boots, go down an elevator and follow a narrow trail to a series of wooden platforms at the base of the falls. Unfortunately, there is no way to see it unless you pay for the tour, but standing beneath the falls and feeling the mist and the water flowing over you is an absolutely unforgettable experience.

The other tour that is well worth paying for is the boat ride to the base of the Horseshoe Falls. The boats, all named "Maid of the Mists," travel past the outer curve of the horseshoe and actually into the maelstrom in the basin of the waterfall. The effect of the ride is rather like a short trip into the teeth of a hurricane. The overwhelming, raw, natural power of the Thundering Waters is enough to recharge the most deadened spiritual batteries.

MYSTICAL SIGNIFICANCE
(Frank Joseph)

Many genuinely mystical experiences have taken place in the Niagara Falls area. Perhaps a not atypical occurrence befell James Delaney in 1988. Like millions of American honeymooners before him, he and his wife, Ann, went to the Falls after their wedding in 1963. Although childless, their marriage seemed ideally happy and the flame of their mutual love for each other always burned brightly. James became an architect with a New York firm, while Ann kept their beautiful home in the suburbs.

Their life together was the picture of contentment until 1980, when Ann was diagnosed with lung cancer. This disease spread too rapidly for successful treatment, and she died suddenly in 1982, without being able to say goodbye to her husband. Devastated as he was, James tried to reassemble the fragments of his existence, although he never remarried. But every wedding anniversary, he made a special trip to Niagara Falls as a kind of last link with Ann, annual visits which both saddened and fortified him. Nearly six years after her passing, he was still unable to shrug off mourning her, and he began to suffer long bouts of depression. A doctor friend encouraged Jim to take up meditation exercises. He did so reluctantly, expecting nothing, but discovered almost immediately that the present melancholy which otherwise oppressed him began to lift by degrees. The technique he learned did not include mental visualization, but the counting of his breath by sevens from one to forty-two and back down to one. By concentrating only on each breath to the exclusion of all thoughts, his mind cleared and he regained an inner sense of emotional balance.

During his yearly visit to Niagara Falls in 1988, James felt the onset of his recurrent grief as he landed at Goat Island; but he managed to find a secluded boulder near the rocky shore, where he exercised his breathing in private. As before, mental tranquillity gradually dispelled his depression with every breath. But less than halfway into the meditation, he began to experience a wave of enfolding love. The on-rush of feeling was so intense he almost lost count of his breaths. But he maintained his self-discipline until a bright vision formed in his mind. It seemed to come from deep within himself, although it was no self-willed fantasy. His inner-eye focused on the smiling image of Ann, but she appeared peculiarly dressed in buckskins and moccasins. He almost laughed out loud, then tried to concentrate more clearly on the vision, which suddenly vanished.

At the time, the experience seemed real enough, but he was not able to visualize Ann again in subsequent mediations, so he rationalized her strange appearance as merely the result of his on-going grief. In the weeks that followed, however, he experienced a recurring dream of her, as before, in buckskins, but standing near the boulder on Goat Island. Sharing his dream with no one, James returned to Niagara Falls and the scene of his first meditation there. Soon after he began counting his breaths, he drifted into a light trance psychologists refer to as the hypnogogic state, that gray area between wakefulness and sleep. His mind seemed to transform itself into a projection screen, as the movie of his life—or rather of a past life—flashed across his consciousness. He saw Ann and himself as husband and wife in a Native American setting of very long ago. He too was attired with animal skins this time. A story, or more properly, scenes from their life together, unfolded in images he half-remembered. Their union in a distant time was no less happy than it had been in the late 20th century, although just as brief, with his own death at 30. Then his vision of the past ended more abruptly than it began.

James had been unable to induce the same past life regression away from Niagara Falls, but it has recurred there several times, each with variations and additional information during his mediations at Goat Island. With each recollection, his persistent mourning of Ann faded by degrees, until grief was supplanted by assurance in the eternal continuity of the couple's relationship. Less intimidated by death, he became so convinced in the verity of their former existence together, he now feels that they will be reunited in a future life, just as they were in this one. James is equally certain that Niagara Falls is a super-charged sacred sight, resonating with the fundamental life energies implicit in the eternally roaring waters. As such, the Falls generates powerful harmonies conducive to healing the soul through nurturing memories of the past.

RITUALS FOR THE FALLS

For thousands of years waterfalls have been a place of awe and wonder for humankind. Like rushing water everywhere, the sound of the rapids can balm the soul and bring peace and stability into a harried life. Here, the thunder of the water falling is so deep that you can feel the vibrations in your bones, and it becomes a thrumming all around you. No matter where you are in the area, you become more at peace with yourself. In the same manner that the physical power of the Niagara Falls provides electric energy to western New York, its psychic power can regenerate your spiritual and psychic self. There are two rituals that the area particularly lends itself. A re-charging ritual to re-affirm your own strength and powers, and a ritual of release, to let go of tensions, problems and other unbalancing factors.

The ideal time for a regenerating ritual at Niagara Falls is the early morning. Not only is this a time of new beginnings, but the sunrise and the quiet of dawn is ideal for the theme of regeneration. An additional positive factor is that the number of tourists will be minimal and you will be less likely to be disturbed.

Luna Island is the ideal place for this type of ritual. Not only is it surrounded by rushing waters, it is on the eastern side of Goat Island, so it will be bathed in the light of the rising sun. Stand or sit near the railing of the overlook. The closer you are to the edge, the louder the waterfall. Close your eyes and concentrate on the sound of the rushing water and the throbbing sound of the falls on either side of you. Concentrate on one sense at a time. First your hearing, then the feel of the mist on your face and hands. You should be relaxed, and open to the power that you will begin to feel.

Breathe deeply, allowing your diaphragm to expand slowly. Hold your breath for a few seconds and slowly release it. You should take the same amount of time breathing in as you do breathing out. do this for at least 10 cycles, relaxing more and more with each breath.

Visualize yourself on a rock in the center of the rushing water. Remember that you are perfectly safe and cannot fall off the rock. Let the energy stream of the water flow all around you, cleansing your aura, cleansing your life, cleansing your spirit. Feel the strength of the river flowing into you, bringing the life and joy of the water into your soul.

Picture the aura of the water, cleansed by rain, wind and earth, wrapping itself around you, protecting and comforting you. Let the energy within you rise to blend with the water. Become one with the water. Feel its joy as it leaps into the air, creating and renewing. Changing, flowing, leaping off the rocks, then dancing downstream to flow smoothly again.

When you are bursting with energy, begin to flow back into your own body. Slowly separate yourself from the river, but let its depth and power remain within you as you return. Once again, feel the mist on your face. Feel the pounding rhythm in the rocks beneath you. Listen to the voices of each wave, each stone, as they flow past you.

End your ritual as you began it, by breathing slowly, holding the breath, and just as slowly releasing it. You should be renewed and ready to start again. Remember to thank the spirits of the waters and the falls before you leave.

The ritual of release is one that is ideal for any rushing water, and can be easily adapted to a variety of purposes. It does require some preparation, however. Bring an empty envelope along to your next haircut, and ask the hairdresser for your cut hair. Put the cut hair into the envelope and seal it up. You may want to label it so you won't forget what it's for.

Many cultures attach a mystical significance to hair. A common sacrifice among American Indians was to cut a lock of hair and burn it, with the prayers being lifted on the smoke. Modern society has changed, but hair still has a powerful image. The custom of giving a lock of hair to a loved one to carry shows that hair is still considered to be an extension of the person.

In the case of this ritual, you want to use your hair as a symbol of what you want to remove from yourself. Since it is a part of you that you have detached, you can let it go without pain. It is also something that no one but you can sacrifice. It is your hair, only you have power over it.

Take the envelope of hair with you out to the tip of the Three Sisters Islands and stand at the edge closest to the rapids. Opening the envelope, take out a lock of hair. Name it with the emotion or quality that you wish to remove from your life, and cast it our into the water. Watch the waves carry it away from you to be thrown over the falls and carried out to sea. Know in your heart that it can never come back upstream to you and it will never return. Continue to name and remove hair from the envelope until you have cast out everything in your life you do not want.

When you are through naming, if there is anything left in the envelope, cast it out to the water saying, "I remove all negativity from my life." Fold the empty envelope and take it home to burn. You will thereby remove the last traces of the negativity from your life. Remember that no one but you can do this for you. Finish by welcoming new and positive growth into your life. Walk away from the river's edge to meditate on new growth. Let the trees, brush and stones on the islands help you find positive replacements for those things you have thrown away.

FOR MORE INFORMATION

Directions

Take Interstate 90 to I-190 across Grand Island, turn onto the Robert Moses Parkway and follow the sings to Niagara Falls. It is also a major stop on the Seaway Trail, which follows the Lake Erie and Lake Ontario shorelines. Niagara Falls is impossible to miss on any map of western New York.

Lodging

Lodging in the area is easily available. There are over 50 hotels and motels in the Niagara Falls area. Accommodations range from the luxurious to the modest, including trailer parks and campgrounds. Because of the weather in the winter, many of the campgrounds operate in the summer months only, but a few are open year-round. Call ahead to be sure the weather permits camping. The Niagara Falls KOA Campground is located on Grand Island just off I-190, about 15 minutes from Niagara Falls; prices start at $17.95 for two people, with electric and sewer hookups extra. Higher rates apply for more than two.

Other suggested accommodations: Beacon Motel and Campground, 9900 Niagara Falls Blvd., rates vary according to season; Travel Lodge, 200 Rainbow Blvd., $40 single; Buffalo South Motor Inn, I-90 at exit 56, $29 single.

Dining establishments also vary from the Top of the Falls restaurant, overlooking the falls, to more modest restaurants in town. There are also several national chains, and the usual fast food. More information is available from the Niagara Falls Chamber of Commerce at 345 Third Street, Niagara Falls, NY, 14303, or call Niagara County Tourism at (800) 338-7890.

Thompson Park Lightlines

Dea

A municipal park at Watertown features one of the most peculiarly powerful sacred precincts in the United States. It centers in the groves surrounding a hill south east of the city. Much of this rise and the attendant knolls were sculpted out of the earth during the last Ice Age by monstrous floes pushing the land before them, so their origins are geologically dynamic. These telluric forces conjured and concentrated the special earth energies manifesting there today. The same forces molded a natural amphitheater which, at night, provides an impressive vista of the city's lights and skyline, as well as a glimpse of glistening Lake Ontario on the far western horizon.

During the Depression of the 1930s, gangs of unemployed men were put to work in government public works projects at Thompson Park. They built the beautiful stone walls which line the many paths, up the numinous hill and throughout the vicinity, lending the whole area a milieu of inner organization and sense of direction. Doubtless, these walls help channel some of the energies resonating at the location. They lead toward a public swimming pool. Between it and the golf course stand several small groves of various kinds of trees separated by broad, grassy walkways. They shelter an outwardly peaceful, inwardly vibrant spot harboring what has come to be locally known as the "lightlines," and regarded generally as invisible portals into other worlds. Some persons straying near the lightlines have vanished into thin air. The first known occurrence took place in the early 1970s, when an 18-year old man faded away into the vortex before eyewitnesses. The small group of observers saw him ascend the hill around dusk. At the summit, he stood silhouetted against the dying twilight, then grew invisible by degrees. Remarkably, the space into which he vanished was a broad, unobstructed area open and exposed for a city block in all directions. A thorough, if panicky, search of the vicinity, even into the groves surrounding the perimeter of the hill, did not succeed in finding him.

The Thompson Park Lightlines.
Photo by Dea.

Some 20 minutes after the young man's disappearance, he suddenly reappeared about 200 feet from the top of the hill. Badly disoriented, all he could ask was, "Where have you been?" But he had no recollection of his own journey into another dimension. I myself experienced the magic of the Thompson Park lightlines while teaching an outdoor class on a lawn near the grove. In the mood for a break, I went for a brief walk through the normally quiescent area of the vortex. Strolling down a verdant pathway and up another, I took my time admiring the trees and flowers. When I returned to my class, the students all stood wordlessly facing me. I could tell at once from their serious expressions that something unusual had happened during my brief absence. They said that as I walked away along the grove they saw me gradually dissolve in air, only to re-emerge on the other side of the sacred precinct. I experienced no special sensation during my short stroll, but their no-nonsense demeanor convinced me they believed what they reported.

My experience was by no means unique, and unknown numbers of persons have inexplicably vanished and reappeared in a similar manner, mostly near twilight. The lightlines through which they pass appear to comprise a sort of "door" between worlds, which opens at unexpected moments. When opened, it has been known to frighten dogs into howling and to produce anomalous sounds of its own; something like the tramping of horses' hooves and the calling of disembodied voices are occasionally heard in the precinct. Pungent, unusual scents infrequently float through the air around the hill and its dark groves. Most remarkably, a few witnesses reported sightings of amorphous figures sometimes wrapped in thick mists, often on horse-back, which abruptly appear and de-materialize in and out of the lightlines. Interestingly, even these bizarre encounters occur elsewhere, most notably in Britain, in and around Newcastle, near the Scottish border, where ghostly apparitions in Roman uniforms on horse-back are still reported after several centuries of observations. Phenomena identical to the New York lightlines have been known throughout Ireland, where they are still referred to as "stray sod" and are almost invariably associated with the Tuatha da Danann, early, pre-Celtic settlers, whose paranormal powers were usurped by the invading Druids, then banned by the Christians.

MYSTICAL SIGNIFICANCE

Sacred groves and holy hills resonating with strange, numinous powers have been known since the days of the Druids and long before. They are special places set aside by Nature within Nature, as unseen gateways from our own to other worlds of existence, what metaphysical scientists refer to as "dimensions." If fully understood, they could reveal information about the real design of time and space, making travel into the past or future and interplanetary, even inter-galactic, voyages possible. Such places, in which cosmic and telluric powers embrace and intertwine to warp the fabric of timespace, will some day alter our views of existence and open to us undreamt potentials.

SUGGESTED RITUAL

Walk through the groves at the base of the hill, climb to the top and meditate for a predetermined period of time, facing north. As an image to hold in the mind, visualize a single beam of pleasantly white light beaming from heaven and entering through the top of your head, coursing down the spine to light you within. Following meditation, stand still facing north, and say or think, "As a child of my Mother Earth, I thank the spirit of this place for allowing me to visit here! In heartfelt sincerity, I ask, as a friend, to be shown what I need to know."

If you are nimble enough and well-coordinated, say these words (or at least part of them) standing only on the right foot with your right hand over the left eye. The position is not as ludicrous as it seems to modern cynics. It is a posture still used in esoteric Gaelic tradition for developing second sight, the ability to perceive other levels of being. The Druids, who learned their magic from pre-Celtic Atlantean priests of Ireland and Wales, used this same stance for certain conjurings. The ritual position is, as indicated, extremely ancient, representations of it appearing in the predynastic Egyptian god of fertility, Min, and the Hanged Man trump of the Renaissance tarot card deck.

After making the statement, offer a pinch of sage, a few drops of purified water, an attractive stone or whatever feels appropriate. Then follow down into the path that most seems to "beckon," or otherwise appears congenial. A concluding gesture, when leaving the park, includes a kiss of the hand thrown to the Spirit of Place. Do not immediately turn away from the area of transformation, but back off from it for a few steps first as a courtesy showing final respect.

The *genius loci* may engender visions of the future or provide symbolic events personally interpreted as significant omens. Or the experience may lie beyond anything previously encountered. Dreams during the following nights should be particularly revealing and unusually meaningful. In any case, it is necessary that all excursions into the lightlines be undertaken in something more than vain curiosity. The success of a visit to the Thompson Park vortex is in direct proportion to the serious intentions and need of the visitor to solve problems or answer important questions. The *genius loci* is friendly but not to be trifled with. Nightmares are about the least frivolous persons may expect if they abuse the privilege of experiencing the sacred center. Even flippant demeanor is enough to offend the Spirit of Place. Be warned and act accordingly! For most visitors not disposed to clairvoyance, the same ritual described above may apply, save only the petition to the *genius loci* should run something like "Living forces of the grove and hill, help me to know myself! As your friend, open the doors of my mind and soul to your eternal wisdom!"

Despite all the disappearances at the Thompson Park lightlines, none of them are believed to have been permanent nor painful. Such phenomena exist to help, not hurt human beings, to assist them in feeling part of a reality immensely greater and more significant than they know.

FOR MORE INFORMATION

Directions

Watertown lies in the northern half of New York, just east of Lake Ontario. Take I-81 north. Exits 45 through 47.

Accommodations

Best Western Headwaters Motor Lodge, Route 12, Boonville, NY 13309. Telephone (315) 942-4493. $40 to $50 per single. Double occupancy, $55 to $65. One hour's drive southeast of Watertown.

KOA camping, Natural Bridge/Watertown, open all year. Twenty-five miles east of I-81. Exit 48. Go east on 342 to 3 East, turn left. At Deferiet, turn left on 3A and follow to 3 East. Left six miles to KOA. Contact KOA, Box 71A, Natural Bridge, NY 13665. Telephone: (315) 644-4880. $15 per tent site. Twenty-seven miles east of Watertown.

NORTH CAROLINA

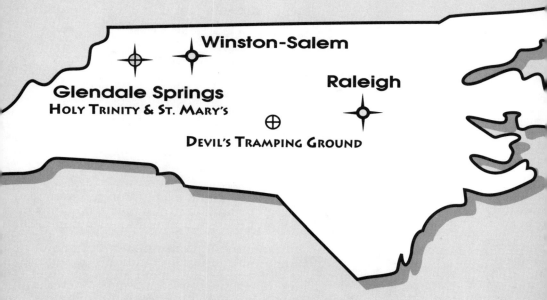

Winston-Salem

Glendale Springs
HOLY TRINITY & ST. MARY'S

Raleigh

DEVIL'S TRAMPING GROUND

St. Mary's and Holy Trinity

Jim Sutton

The Blue Ridge Mountains of North Carolina stand in majestic beauty and are indeed crowned in a blue haze. Earth energies flow freely through every valley and over every hill. It is easy for one to envision fiddlers playing at hoedowns, weddings waiting for circuit riding preachers, and moonshiners tending their stills.

These Earth energies give life to the mountains and instill creativity in the mountain folk. This creativity is seen in the crafts of the mountain people, from musical instrument-making to painting, and others too numerous to mention.

The mountain also abounds with legend and folklore. Every nook and cranny yields some mountain tale. One such tale caught my attention, and its story is fascinating.

Hidden deep in the mountains stand two small churches, which embrace within their walls art of unsurpassed beauty. Beauty rarely seen since Michelangelo painted in the Sistine Chapel during the Renaissance. These churches are St. Mary's in West Jefferson and Holy Trinity in Glendale Springs. A man by the name of Faulton Hodge had been sent to Appalachia to pastor the two mountain churches.

To his dismay, Faulton found Holy Trinity in almost total ruin. It had been abandoned since the 1930s. With its rear wall fallen in, Holy Trinity now served as a haven for weeds and wildlife.

St. Mary's was still a functioning church, but just barely. The congregation numbered only thirteen and the organist knew just three hymns. There was no money to pay for electricity, so candle holders had been fashioned out of coat hangers.

These churches seemed doomed to the same fate as the surrounding communities. The service station only opened for a couple of hours each day. The inn was closed and the lodge rarely opened during the year. The area was poverty stricken and it appeared the churches and communities were soon to become only memories.

Holy Trinity Episcopal Church.
Photo by Johnny Meeks.

One mid-summer night Faulton Hodge attended a party in Blowing Rock, North Carolina. As he mingled with the guests, his mind weighed heavy with the plight of the communities and the churches.

Ben Long, another guest at the party, was a native North Carolinian and an artist. Ben had been in Italy studying fresco art when he had an overwhelming desire to return to North Carolina and paint a fresco in a church.

Even though Ben had very little money, he returned to North Carolina where he traveled from town to town, across the state, begging for the opportunity to paint a church fresco. But no one seemed to care. Finally, utterly discouraged, he told friends at the party America could not keep him any longer. He was bound for Italy again.

The Lord's Supper, a true fresco by Ben Long IV, 1980.
Photo by Tim Barnwell.

While mingling at the party, he heard that one of the guests was an Episcopal priest. He decided to try one last time to get someone interested in his proposed fresco. He spoke to the host of the party, who approached Faulton Hodge on Ben's behalf,

"Do you see that bearded young man over there? He wants to paint a fresco in your church."

Sadly, Faulton shook his head; his impoverished parish could not afford electricity, let alone an artist.

"No, no," said the host, "he wants to give it to you."

"Well, in that case, we'll take it," said Faulton, not entirely sure what a fresco was.

The following day, Faulton Hodge and Ben Long met at St. Mary's. Ben explained that fresco art was the mixing of sand and lime, plastering it on a surface and painting in pigment while the mixture was still wet.

Faulton and Ben stood before the altar facing three walls. They discussed what scene to paint on the left wall. Faulton proposed, "The church is called St. Mary's. Why not paint an expectant Mary?" Ben agreed.

He spent the next few days searching for a model from which to sketch Mary's face. While walking one day he saw a mountain girl approaching him. He knew at once that she was his model.

He asked the girl if she would let him sketch her. She agreed and posed patiently. When the sketch was finished, he thanked her and asked her name. She smiled and replied, "My name is Mary." Then she ambled down the road.

Back in town, Ben could find no one who recognized the girl. The local people knew of no girl in that area called Mary. Somewhat puzzled, Ben began to work on the fresco.

As he worked people would come to peer in windows and doors. Soon the word traveled around the mountain that there was a "real live artist from Italy" painting in St. Mary's. This brought more and more people to watch him work. Sunday attendance also increased. By the time the fresco was finished, the Sunday attendance had sufficiently grown to justify the painting of another fresco.

The fresco of John the Baptist began on the right wall. One night shortly after the fresco was finished, a severe electrical storm hit the mountain. A bolt of lightening struck near the church, sending a thin crack right across the neck of John the Baptist. The decision was made to leave the crack, since, according to Biblical history, John the Baptist had been beheaded.

Soon, people were coming in droves to see this phenomena. The Sunday attendance also continued to grow. Shortly, a third fresco was underway on the rear wall behind the altar. Ben painted a crucifixion scene with Christ, as in a vision, behind it.

After the third fresco was finished, the little church flourished. The service station was busier than ever with so many people arriving to see the frescoes. The town lodge and the inn hummed with activity. New businesses began to spring up. A church and community on the brink of extinction were now teeming with new life.

Ten miles away, on the other mountain, Faulton Hodge stood in the churchyard of Holy Trinity. Ben had once told him that he would love to paint a fresco on its rear wall; but this was impossible as the rear wall had tumbled in.

Faulton was trying to decide whether to have the church bulldozed or not when a big, white car pulled up to the church. An old man got out and hobbled up to Faulton. "This was my mother's childhood church and I wanted to see it," said the old man. Faulton told him that he was afraid the church would have to be torn down as there was no money to fix it.

"Reckon what it'd cost?" asked the old man.

"Around fifteen hundred dollars," stated Faulton.

The old man wrote out a check for the full amount, got into his white Cadillac and drove away, never to be seen again.

The money not only fixed the church, but it also bought pigments for a fresco. Ben began a fresco of the Last Supper on the rear wall, using local people as the models for the disciples. The druggist, a local farmer, Faulton, Ben himself, and even an old mountain dog became enshrined within the painting. Using pigments and the simplicity of the mountain people, Ben created a true masterpiece.

One man with two dying churches, another man with a great gift, crossed paths one mid-summer night. From this chance meeting two lifeless mountains along with their people, sprang forward with a burst of new life and continue in full bloom.

MYSTICAL SIGNIFICANCE
(Frank Joseph)

The mystical significance of St. Mary's and Holy Trinity Churches is too beautifully developed in the telling of their own stories for extensive elaboration. The miraculous elements are obvious and only go to demonstrate that God does not withhold His presence from uncomplicated people living in the remote corners of His world. Both of the little mountain churches are undeniable sacred centers, as manifest in the wonderful synchronicity of the unknown country girl named Mary who posed so perfectly for the Mother of God and the timely arrival of the generous old stranger in the white Cadillac.

While the little church buildings themselves radiate their own special power, the psychic foci at both places are the frescoes. They may be accepted at face value for the splendid artworks they are and the familiar religious symbolism they depict. On another level, however, they are cosmograms, designs which trigger universal, subconscious responses to tap otherwise hidden awareness. They perform the same function as a mandala known to Eastern practitioners, who use spiritually engineered patterns to visualize deeper states of being. The North Carolina frescoes are archetypes, or symbols of inexpressible, profoundly felt meaning common to all human beings. They are particularly useful, because they are keys to our primal identity. We begin to learn who and what we are as individual souls.

St. Mary's Episcopal Church.
Photo by Tim Barnwell.

SUGGESTED RITUAL

The most highly recommended ritual at either St. Mary or Holy Trinity is Vapassana, or breath—meditation. Before visiting either sacred center, find a quiet place and get comfortable. Eyes closed, take a deep breath, hold it for seven seconds, exhale through the mouth gently. Repeat twice more. Then breathe naturally, counting at least 42 inhalations. Count back down to one from the highest number reached. Concentrate only on each breath.

Do not fight intrusive thoughts, but do not dwell on them either. Release them, let them go for this brief session of personal solitude. Conclude by holding the breath for three sets of seven seconds each, as at the beginning. Even a less than perfect Vapassana meditation exercise clears the mind, leaving the consciousness finer tuned and receptive to a spiritually charged environment.

When visiting the little churches, let their frescoes speak to a deeper sensitivity than we usually permit ourselves. To regard them only as attractive art or for their well-known Christian figures would be to miss their intrinsic spiritual worth. Rather, allow their colors and forms to address themselves to the wondering child in every visitor. Do not confront them intellectually, nor even consciously. Approach them instead with an innocent acceptance of their deeper mystical value. The experience can be personally rewarding in the fullest sense and is sure to live in the memory long after leaving.

Dreams during the visitor's first sleep after seeing the frescoes are often meaningful and poignant, because our own most profound subconscious being has been accessed by a pilgrimage to a gentle and unique sacred center.

FOR MORE INFORMATION

Directions

To get to St. Mary's and Holy Trinity from Winston-Salem, North Carolina you travel to North Wilkesboro on Highway 421. At North Wilkesboro, you turn onto Highway 16 and travel north to Glendale Springs. West Jefferson is 10 miles away from Glendale Springs on Highway 221.

From Doone, North Carolina you travel Highway 421 to Deep Gap, North Carolina. At Deep Gap you turn onto Highway 221 which takes you into West Jefferson. From West Jefferson you go

north until you intersect Highway 16, which will take you down to
Glendale Springs.

For more information call: Ashe County Chamber of Commerce (919) 246-9550, Holy Trinity Church (919) 982-3076, St.
Mary's Church (919) 246-3552.

The Devil's Tramping Ground

Jim Sutton

The polar opposite of a sacred center lies in Chatham County, North Carolina. About 36 feet across, it is a circular precinct resembling a wheel.

According to Robert Dowd, Jr., owner of the property on which the circle is located, its existence traces back to the 17th century, if not long before. Its origins could be more deeply prehistoric than most investigators realize, since Indian legends were associated with the circle previous to the earliest white settlement. In any case, it has been a cause for local speculation from at least pioneer days. Today, some UFOlogists theorize it may represent a landing site for alien spacecraft. More down-to-earth speculators believe it is only the result of an old cane grinder pulled round and round over the years by mule teams. Still others would like to think of it as a fairy ring. But persistent traditions recount that it is "the Devil's Tramping Ground," because Ole Scratch, the Devil, still tramps in his circle after sundown, musing on new ways to ensnare mankind.

Over the years, many people have tried to spend an entire night within the strange circle. Most have failed. Only a group of college students supposedly entertained a complete evening at the site. During their sleep, they allegedly underwent some horrific experiences, from which they never fully recovered. Later, a young man tried to sleep in the circle. Around 11:30 that night, he was seen wearing only a blanket, as he headed toward nearby Siler City. Something apparently changed his mind during his brief say at the Devil's Tramping Ground.

The circle appears to manifest certain malefic energies, but only when one or two people try to stay. Whenever attempts are made by fairly large numbers of visitors, nothing happens. Ole Scratch seems to be living up to his reputation as an unsociable sort. Two groups of experimenters did spend a night at the site. But they stayed some 20 feet outside and away from the circle itself. "The

Devil never showed up," was their only comment. Most persons who have slept in or near the circle refuse to discuss their experiences, so little information describing what actually goes on within the precinct is available. However, scientists determined that the area inside the circle is completely sterile. Plant life and trees grow up to its perimeter, but no further. Soil samples taken by researchers from the North Carolina State Department of Agriculture have been unable to trace the cause of its sterility, or to explain the sharp contrast between so much abundant, natural growth surrounding a spot of absolutely dead ground. No doubt, there is something special about the site.

Old timers in the neighborhood are amused by visiting cynics, who flout the legends, then wind up scurrying off during the night of their stay. Some say Ole Scratch left Chatham County long ago, but others disagree. An unfriendly fellow, he refuses to put in an appearance, save at certain times of the year; and then only before one or two people, they claim. They add that the old saying, "There is strength in numbers," applies in this case.

Does the Devil, or something, continue to walk the circle at Chatham County? His "Tramping Ground" is still open to visitors. "So, come on up," says Mr. Dowd, "and see for yourself."

MYSTICAL SIGNIFICANCE

The Devil's Tramping Ground is the inverse of a sacred center, an unholy vortex of spiritual power. While its origins are unknown, it does not represent an entirely unique phenomenon. Other similar locations exist in various parts of the world. A similarly evil *genius loci* pervades Rock Lake and Aztalan (see "Wisconsin"), although it is at least partially balanced by positive counter-energies at that site. Such places are the results of deeply negative human actions interfacing with and/or warping the fabric of Nature (hence, the sterility of the precinct contrasted with its surrounding, verdant environment). Almost invariably, the human behavior that spawns an unsacred center involves violent death and, not uncommonly, ritual murder, creating psychic black holes dangerous for anyone who trifles with them.

Often they are inhabited by the souls of individuals so weighted down by malicious attachment to the material world, that they perversely refuse to go on to the higher realms destined for human life; and they strive to drag others into their dark dimension.

Whatever the real identity of the phenomenon at the Devil's Tramping Ground, it does indeed generate a palpable field of strongly negative energy. Visitors to places of spiritual power must be aware that sites like the Chatham focus exist. Gainsaying their existence is no less ignorant than denying the presence of evil in the world. So too, attempts at destroying or "reconsecrating" them are fruitless and foolhardy.

Experiencing the site may not be altogether pleasant, but it will be educational and assist the intelligent visitor to be aware, if not wary, of the resident energies' true nature at other sites he or she may later encounter. We should never go to any place of spiritual power completely unprepared, nor be so naive as to imagine that every *genius loci* is a beneficent being. The real value of the Devil's Tramping Ground lies in its capacity to let us know how unholy sites feel, so we may recognize them before they can do us harm.

SUGGESTED RITUAL

The authors by no means recommend that everyone should seek out the Devil's Tramping Ground. Not fully mature persons are particularly urged to avoid it. Shallow-minded thrill-seekers and merely curious individuals will gain nothing by their visit. Experiencing the unsacred center should be only in the nature of a learning process for persons already spiritually cognizant and self-responsible. The reader must determine for him-/herself if visiting the Chatham site is proper and worthwhile. Certainly, the best way to reach that decision lies through meditation.

Before a proposed visit to the Devil's Tramping Ground, ask your inner voice, while at the deepest level of the meditation, if you should go to the site. The answer will probably come immediately. If not, give it time. You will be answered. If the inward response is positive, then another meditation session is in order. During that second meditation, visualize the holiest symbol you know. At the close of the meditation, manifest that symbol as your dearest, constant companion for the duration of the visit. Now visualize the brightest, purest white light descending from the heavens, entering through the crown of your head, permeating your entire body and wrapping itself around you like a cloak.

Entering the area of the Devil's Tramping Ground, stand before the circle and recite (only mentally, if preferable) the Shepherd's Psalm, Number 23, from the Book of David in the Old Testament. Place emphasis on the 4th stanza, "Even though I walk through the valley of the shadow of Death, I fear no evil; for thou art with me; thy rod and thy staff, they comfort me." Now envision a ring of fire completely surrounding your body. Whatever comes through its flames will have to be transformed according to your own power.

Walk into the center of the circle, clear your mind and begin to sense the local presence. Then say, "Now let Mother Earth be my witness, with Father Sky above and the falling waters of Styx—the greatest and most solemn oath the blessed gods can take—that I shall never be coerced by the spirit of this place!" Walk out of the circle. Make no offering. Anything left behind will bind visitors to the unwanted *genius loci*.

FOR MORE INFORMATION

Directions
From Siler City, take 421 South for about 9 miles to road 902. Turn right on 902 and travel 6 miles to Harper's Crossroads. Turn right on rural paved road 1100. Go about 2 miles, circle on left in the woods. Or from Siler City take rural paved road 1006 to Harper's Crossroads, a distance of 11 miles. At Harper's Crossroads, turn right on Road 1100, go 2 miles, circle is on left.

Siler City is about 40 miles southwest of Durham, 30 miles southeast of Greensboro.

Accommodations
Red Roof Inn, 5623 Chapel Hill Blvd, Durham, NC 27707. Telephone (919) 489-9421. I-40 and US 15-501. Forty minutes from Siler City. Single, $30.95.

Best Western University Inn, Highway 54 East (Raleigh Road), Chapel Hill, NC 27514. Telephone (919) 942-4132. Two miles west of I-40 and 1/2 mile east of US 15-501 on NC-54. Twenty miles from Siler City. Single, $49 to $59.

KOA Campground, 2300 Montreal Avenue, Greensboro, NC 27406. Telephone (919) 274-4143. Thirty minutes from Siler City. Total facilities. Tent site, $10.

Bibliography
Brandon, Jim. *Weird America*. New York: E. P. Dutton, 1978, pp. 171, 172.

Columbus

Newark
THE GIANT OCTAGON

FORT ANCIENT

THE GREAT
SERPENT MOUND

Cincinnati

The Giant Octagon

Frank Joseph

To explore Ohio's Newark earth-works is to experience one of the grandest miracles of ancient man. The entire vast complex of walls, mounds and apertures is our planet's largest observatory, in addition to being the greatest earth-work in the world. Its titanic scale and precise celestial alignments is on par with Egypt's Great Pyramid or Britain's Stonehenge. The two sacred centers of Newark enfold more than 200 square acres, including a parallel wall running more than 6 miles long. The Great Circle, with its 14-foot high embankment, is 1,200 feet in diameter. But the Octagon enclosure to which it is connected is 11 times bigger. It is joined by a corridor to another circular wall, whose south end features a 170-foot long mound 8 feet higher than the embankment and perfectly oriented to the most northerly rising of the Moon.

The main structure is actually composed of line segments separated by measured gaps. Behind each one stands a uniform mound just off center. The purpose of this peculiar arrangement was to provide accurate fixes for the risings and settings of significant astronomical events: solar and lunar eclipses, solstices, the position of Venus, the appearance of significant constellations, such as the Pleiades, and numerous other sky data—some of which archaeo-astronomers are only just beginning to discover. No one resided behind the far-flung earth-works. Nor did it comprise a cemetery or fort. The vast complex was strictly a ceremonial center, the largest out-door church on earth, where tens of thousands of people gathered for all the mass-rituals of a religion dedicated to the movement of the heavenly bodies.

Archaeologists refer to the prehistoric inhabitants of the Newark area as members of the Hopewell Culture, but little is known of their actual identity. They built the Octagon and related structures around 1200 B.C. Thus, a civilized people with advanced knowledge of astronomy and grand-scale building techniques were flourishing

in the Ohio Valley when Ramses III was erecting his Victory Temple
in Upper Egypt and Homeric Greece ruled the Mediterranean
World. The ancients at Newark outlasted their Old World counter-
parts by several centuries, although their disappearance in the 9th
century B.C. is no less inexplicable than their arrival.

Octagon Mound.
Photo courtesy of the Ohio Historical Society, Columbus, OH.

While the Newark Mounds display many astral alignments, its
chief orientation is lunar. It was a living calendar, in which some 16
generations regulated their existence according to the grand mecha-
nism perpetually moving above them. They were worshippers not
of the earth's satellite, but of time, of all it brought forth and all it destroyed. Things materialized, prospered, declined, expired and returned in various related forms all through the supreme power of
time. By behaving in accordance with the cycles of time, the ancients
probably felt they were living in harmony with the will of the gods.

That same sacred calendar may have originally told them
when to come to Ohio (from where, no one knows) and when to
leave, since long before arriving in Ohio, the people who created the

Octagon colossus some 3,200 years ago already possessed their technology and knowledge of astronomy. Their mysterious evacuation of the site, which involved such great labor to erect, may have occurred also at the behest of their astral clock.

The ancient sacred center has not survived in its entirety. A major square embankment, many mounds and large sections of the parallel walls, were obliterated in the 19th century expansion of the modern town. But the Great Circle and some of its walls are preserved as a state memorial park. The Octagon has likewise been saved from destruction—although under less dignified circumstances—as a golf course. Both sites are open to the public year round, from 10:00 a.m. to dusk.

The Giant Octagon.
Photo by Dennis Graf.

MYSTICAL SIGNIFICANCE

The most splendid rituals at the Newark earth-works were on a level of theater comparable to the grandeur of the site itself. They involved thousands of people at a time, beginning in one of the enclosures, passing through others via miles of ceremonial double walls and climaxing in the Great Circle or the giant Octagon. Thirty-two centuries later, the psychic imprint of millions of celebrants has bequeathed the site with a terrific spiritual resonance—a lingering magic which has not been completely subsumed by the banality of the golf course which stands in its place. Standing in the gateway of the Great Circle, its sprawling 20-acre arena spread out like the stage setting for some titanic outdoor play, the alert visitor has no difficulty picking up on the images of the past. Across this massive ramp of sculpted earth, colorful processions of priests and initiates once passed in great numbers. But the combined psychic energies of so many people made a supersensual impact at Newark still very much alive.

SUGGESTED RITUAL

The modern initiate enters the Great Circle through its gateway ramp, where the awesome proportions of the setting are enough to encourage feelings of respect and strong presence. The mood deepens the closer you approach the heart or, in this instance, the womb of the sacred center. Four small mounds defining the Cardinal Directions form a cross marking the sacred focal point, the axis mundi, the Navel of the World, which lies directly at their center. This is the cynosure of the Great Circle, where the visitor may feel thousands of invisible eyes staring at him or her from the encircling embankment. It represents the proper place and moment to thank the resident spirits with pinched offerings of tobacco in each of the four directions. It is also the spot to undertake the vision quest. Here, as the Native Americans of the southwest would say, one experiences *skalaktitude*, the feeling that magic and living spirituality are everywhere. The mounds offer the prime location for deep meditation. Suggested images to focus on in the privacy of one's own mind include the Morning Star, an aerial view of the Great Circle, a single feather or a cross.

Leaving the mounds and returning to the gateway, the visitor should envision him- or herself as part of a great procession of honored guests. Off to the left (north), just outside the enclosure, steps lead up the side of the embankment to the top cf the ridge. Follow it all the way around to completely appreciate its physical greatness, while maintaining the sense of communion with the Great Circle's spiritual presence. Its inherent preternatural magic will enter the receptive mind, transforming it with a deeper feeling for the unknown, unknowable forces of past and present, of Mother Earth and Father Sky. Returning to the gateway, the visitor nurtures a more profound sense of inner and outer completion symbolized by the circumambulation of the Great Circle. Walking its ridge in the proper frame of mind is to conjure the sympathetic magic of completing the Great Circle of life, fusing past, present and future into a single continuum.

FOR MORE INFORMATION

Directions

From 70, take Exit 132 north to Newark. For further information, contact Mound Builders State Memorial, 99 Cooper Avenue, Newark, OH 43055. Telephone, (614) 3441920.

Accommodations

Motel 6, 5910 Scarborough Boulevard, Columbus, OH 43232. Telephone: (614) 755-2250. 40-minute drive east to the Octagon Mound. From I-70, take Brice Road south, exit 110-A, proceed down Brice Road south. Turn right on motel access road and proceed to the motel. $24 per single.

Red Roof Inn, 2449 Brice Road, Reynoldsburg, OH 43068. Telephone: (614) 864-3683. 40 minute drive east to the Octagon Mound. I-70 at Brice Road Exit 110B. Single, $28.95.

Camping at KOA's Buckeye Lake, April 1st through November 30th. Telephone: (614) 928-0706. P.O. Box 972, Buckeye Lake, OH 43008. On SR 79, 12 miles from I-70. Buckeye Lake Exit 129A. 25 minute drive north to Octagon Mound, $12 for tent site, two adults.

Bibliography

Kopper, Philip. *The Smithsonian Book of North American Indians*, Washington, D.C.: Smithsonian Books, 1986.

Nultkranz, Ake. *The Religion of the American Indians*, Berkeley, CA: The University of California, 1979.

The Great Serpent Mound

Frank Joseph

North America's foremost effigy mound and one of the most powerful sacred centers in the world lies atop a steep hill in the Ohio Valley. Visitors enter the site off the main road via an ascending driveway that ends in a parking lot in front of a small museum. An aerial view of the 1/4-mile long geoglyph is afforded by climbing to the top of a 20-foot observation tower nearby. From this overlook, the snake appears to writhe across the ridge in seven humps, its huge jaws agape before an egg-shaped mound, its tail ending in a spiral. With an average width of 20 feet and 5 feet high, the Serpent's overall length is 1,254 feet, following its coils and humps.

Although the Great Serpent Mound is clearly discernable at ground level and more so from the observation tower, it may be fully appreciated from the vantage point of an airplane at 300 to 500 feet. From any point of view, however, its equipoise proportions testify to the technical and artistic sophistication of its creators. They belonged to the ubiquitous Hopewell Culture, who thoroughly cleaned up after themselves; not a trace of tools, implements or weapons of any kind have ever been excavated in the Mound's vicinity. Construction involved careful planning. Flat stones were selected for size and uniformity and lumps of clay were laid along the ground to form a serpentine pattern. Then basketfuls of soil were piled over the pattern and finally sculpted into shape.

The Great Serpent Mound's location is unique, situated as it is near the western edge of a crater formed by a gigantic meteor that struck the earth about 3,200 years ago (see color plate). It lies in close proximity to other significant sites from the deep past. Among these are Fort Hill, in neighboring Highland County, an enormous stone enclosure above the Ohio Bush River; Mound City, near Chilicothe; and Fort Ancient, described below. The Serpent Mound was never inhabited, serving instead as a ceremonial center attracting worshipers from great distances.

301

MYSTICAL SIGNIFICANCE

In old Europe, the serpent and the egg theme was associated with the deified physician of Ancient Greece, Asclepius. He was regularly portrayed beside a snake with an egg in its mouth coiling around a caduceus staff. This beast was known to the Egyptians as Kneph, the sky-serpent, from whose jaws the Cosmic Egg emerged. As it happens, the Ohio earth-work lies on the crest of a meteorite crater. Did the creators of the Great Serpent Mound witness a meteor's impact and raise the effigy as a visual explanation of the event?

Farther still from the Ohio Valley, at the shores of Lake Nell near the port town of Oban, Scotland, winds a serpent mound less than half the size of its American counterpart—but closely resembling it in virtually every other respect. Even their dates of creation approximate each other, around 1200 B.C. The intriguing correspondences linking the Ohio earth-work with ancient European traditions convinces many observers that it is the handiwork of overseas visitors in prehistoric times, while others reject such parallels as just so much coincidence.

Whatever the original identity of its creators, the Great Serpent Mound embodies the generative impulse of the universe. Out of its jaws emerges the prime symbol of new life, the cosmic egg, the omphalos or sacred stone defining the holy center of all beginnings. The spiral tail is the emblem of the soul and/or the soul's path of evolution developing from a point of infinity into the serpent power of perpetual regeneration to manifest itself in the mundane egg. This interpretation is identical to the Kundalini Serpent of the spine as the body's staff around which the spirit uncoils upward from its spiral base, touching all the chakra points (life-energy centers) in its gradual ascent, to give birth to enlightenment in the conscious mind.

In October 1983, a researcher with neither interest in nor tolerance for the paranormal was examining the Great Serpent Mound for the first time; he was alone after closing time, near sunset, when an uneasy feeling gradually crept over him. He could not shake the sensation that he was being watched, which grew by degrees, until it seemed the woods entirely surrounding the site were filled with people silently and intently staring at him. He noticed, too, that not a breath of wind stirred; no bird sang in the trees. The whole area was absolutely calm and still, as though under a glass dome. "It seemed like the interior of a cathedral," he later said. But the mood was not hostile, and he felt strangely welcome and at peace. The feeling of being watched was so strong, he almost expected to see native faces peering out at him from the leaves. The researcher's unanticipated experience was so powerful and genuine, he thereafter began to reverse his previous antipathy to spiritual possibilities and eventually learned to combine scientific investigation with a more open mind. Years later, he was surprised to read in a Time-Life series, *Mystic Places*, that another visitor to the Great Serpent Mound described a similar encounter, although of a decidedly less amiable character. Indeed, many people have experienced the magic of the Ohio effigy, even without the benefit of formalized ceremonies. It is nonetheless advisable to exercise some introductory form of ritual as a psychological access to this important sacred center.

SUGGESTED RITUAL

The park trail completely encompassing the Great Serpent Mound is the perfect spirit-path to the site. The ancient celebrants reputedly danced around the effigy seven times in some lost ritual. While the modern visitor may not wish to repeat so lengthy an exercise, more than a single circumambulation is necessary to at least approximate the prehistoric ambiance of the place.

When you walk around the Cosmic Egg, thank the *genius loci* with a single pinch of tobacco directed toward the surrounding woodland area, away from the geoglyph. Return along the other side of the figure to the spiral tail. Some persons are able to mediate while walking, concentrating on their own footfalls to the exclusion of all other conscious activity. For those not quite so adept at self-mastery, leaving the trail and sitting in the grass opposite any point in the effigy that feels particularly "right" is advisable. From the correct psychic position, the proper meditation on either the serpent itself or its distinct features (particularly the spiral tail or the egg) should open the mind and soul to all the mystical possibilities still preserved in the Great Serpent Mound.

FOR MORE INFORMATION

Directions

From Cincinnati, take 32 east to 237. Left (north) to Seaman. Right (east) to 770. At the town of Tranquility, north on 770 to 730 Right on 73 to Serpent Mound State Memorial. For further information, contact the Ohio Historical Society, 1982 Velma Avenue, Columbus, OH 43211. Telephone, (614) 466-1500. Open year round. Hours, 10:00 a.m. to 5:00 p.m. daily. Closed Mondays, Christmas, New Year's, Easter.

Accommodations

Motel 6, 5910 Scarborough Boulevard, Columbus, OH 43232. Telephone, (614) 755-2250. One hour's drive south to the Great Serpent Mound. From I-70, take Brice Road south, exit #110-A. Proceed down Brice Road south. Turn right on motel access road and proceed to motel. $24 per single.

Red Roof Inn, 2449 Brice Road, Reynoldsburg, OH 43068. Telephone (614) 864-3683. One hour's drive south to the Great Serpent Mound. I-70 at Brice Road Exit 110-B. Single, $28.95.

Camping at KOA, 29150 Pattor Road, Logan, OH 43138. Telephone, (614) 385-4295. Six miles south of Route 33 on Route 6645. 40 minute drive west to the Great Serpent Mound. $13 per tent site, two adults.

Bibliography

Foster, Stephen. *Vision Quest*, New York: Prentice Hall, 1988.

Harner, M. *The Way of the Shaman*, New York: Harper and Row, 1980.

Mitchell, John. *The Earth Spirit*, London: Thames and Hudson, 1975.

Fort Ancient

Frank Joseph

Sprawling across a bluff 240 feet above the Little Miami River is a colossal network of stone ramparts covered with earth. Running 4 miles in circumference and varying in height from 4 to 28 feet, the walls enclose 100 acres studded with conical mounds and crescent-shaped gateways.

Fort Ancient is part of a state park comprising 764 acres of plant and animal life and featuring 2 miles of trails through enchanting woodlands. The 4 miles of walls left by an obviously gifted people define a gigantic sacred precinct capable of enclosing perhaps 12,000 people at one time. It is not known if such numbers were ever assembled behind the enduring ramparts, but great multitudes certainly gathered there for special occasions. Only a few burials took place within the enclosure, and these apparently contain the remains of dedicated sacrifices made when the site was first opened.

This sacred site comprises two main areas joined by a middle section connecting both with an ancient limestone processional way. Extending for a quarter of a mile from the enclosure are parallel earth-works, which lead to a single, large mound. Across the river, in a clearing, are limestone slabs arranged in the 35-foot long configuration of a snake. A large pole stands at its head to cast a shadow along the length of the effigy on the morning of every summer solstice. An identical serpent image oriented to the winter solstice sunrise lies a short distance from the river bank. (Both effigies are on private property belonging to the Y.M.C.A., but access to them is normally possible through the local museum. Ask the curator there to call the Y.M.C.A. for permission to visit the solar serpents.)

The impressive walls of Fort Ancient do not belong to a "fort," as the first pioneer discoverers assumed, even though its modern name is still in use. The site is a ceremonial sacred center never used for habitation or defense. Its master builders belonged to the

Hopewell Culture that began around 1 A.D. and which came to an end 400 years later for reasons which still elude archaeologists.

There are no known celestial alignments behind the walls, so the crescent-shaped gateways there are all the more intriguing. The precinct contrasts with the solar-oriented serpent effigies outside, across the river. The moon universally signifies inner-quests, psychological states, and subconscious conditions, paralleling the interior of the site. As such, its walls enclosed the internal, deepest spiritual life of its creators. The discovery of a pavement near one of the walls in the narrowing middle section of the site, a feature found nowhere else in pre-Columbian North America, suggests a ritual path perhaps corresponding to the irregular gaps appearing in the enclosure.

Power Mound, Fort Ancient.
Photo by Frank Joseph.

Trees within the precinct were not cleared, so the preserved stands of forest were regarded as sacred groves. There is a kind of plaza or open area near the south overlook, where general assemblies took place. But the groves themselves are set apart by the walls, whose purpose seems to have defined their sacred character. It is this hallowing aspect that was alone responsible for the construction of Fort Ancient, and it is this reverential inter-play of natural and man-made forms which perpetuates its spiritual life. In other words, the groves determined its creation. The ramparts are really like garden walls enclosing naturally sacrosanct ground. It is possible that the shaman, whose bones and a large quartz crystal were found in one of the area's few graves, was the same person who originally determined the site as a sanctum sanctorum. The walls, mounds, gateways and paved pathways are only adjuncts to the sacred grove, the real spiritual focus of the place. The walls would enshrine the center, pay homage to it, define and focus it.

Fort Ancient actually represents one link in a stupendous chain of stone enclosures spanning almost 500 miles from the Mississippi and Ohio Rivers. At least nine similar, though smaller stone structures, all dating to a common era, are known in southern Illinois, and Fort Hill, nearly 50 miles east of Fort Ancient, is practically as large. No one knows how many of these prehistoric ramparts, all located atop high bluffs over-looking rivers in thickly wooded areas, originally stood across the three-state region, although they appear to have been the work of a single race, judging from their uniformity of style and shared dates. Of their surviving number, Fort Ancient is the largest and most easily accessible. The site is professionally maintained and visitors should begin their self-conducted tour at the main entrance, where a small but highly interesting museum displays treasured artifacts excavated from the area.

MYSTICAL SIGNIFICANCE

The spiritual imprint of thousands of celebrants who for at least four centuries conjured and melded their own deepest psyche with the nameless *genius loci* of Fort Ancient remains in this precinct to generate especially potent life-energies which the modern visitor may access by meditation at any spot that seems to have particular personal appeal within the sacred center. The site is extensive enough to include numerous psychic focal points.

At the Path of Transformation, Fort Ancient.
Photo courtesy of the Ohio Historical Society.

SUGGESTED RITUAL

Visitors in search of a vision quest at Fort Ancient should begin at the small park just before the bridge over the Little Miami River. A marked trail at the end of the little parking lot leads into the woods and up the hill. The ascent is steep but not especially strenuous through the deep, dark, numinous forest. Its thick foliage engenders a silence similar to that found inside a cathedral, heavy with some sanctified presence. Only the subdued rush of the river below is usually heard. The purely natural surroundings help to create a proper frame of mind for appreciating the drama of the site. One feels a sense of quest in the upward climb of the trail. Visitors nearing the top may experience the sensation of a subtle transformation, as they approach the flank of a vine-covered wall, the stone perimeter of the precinct. Just beyond it, emerging from the shadows of the forest into the open, they ascend a platform at the north end over-look and are rewarded with an enthralling perspective of the river valley.

On the south sprawls Fort Ancient, its eastern ramparts disappearing into the trees. To the west, the trail resumes along the enclosure bordering the sacred grove. Proceeding down this path, the mighty walls may be seen to good advantage. Here visitors experience the particular resonance of the psychic center. The living vibrations of the place are powerful but kindly, an organic synthesis of nature and civilization, exemplifying the Sacred Duality worshipped throughout ancient times. The gentle exclusion of this godly area, made inviolable by its human engineered walls, suggests the loving balance between mankind and the cosmos. Its grove feels blessed because of the harmonious equilibrium of civilization and nature.

Leaving the sacred grove, visitors pass through an open field, once a plaza or general assembly courtyard, to splendid views from a platform at the south overlook. It is a magic place, where forgotten rituals left their indelible, if vague psychic stamp. Here inexpressible energies rise like invisible, intangible mists from a ghostly fountain. The trail picks up past the picnic tables and leads through two large conical mounds. They are like the positive and negative charged terminals of a telluric storage battery. They flank a spirit path and once defined a point of egress or exit to the sacred center. The path is a gap in the enclosure along which the visitor passes from the mundane to the Otherworld, just as the soul travels from this one to the next and back again. The trail merges into a driveway, through lovely woods to the museum. From here, the main road skirts long ceremonial embankments and leads back down to the parking lot near the river.

FOR MORE INFORMATION

Directions

From Cincinnati, take I-71. Exit at 350, east to Fort Ancient Memorial Park. For further information, contact Fort Ancient Museum, S.R. 350, Warren County, OH. Telephone: (513) 932-4421.

Accommodations

Motel 6, 2000 East Kemper Road, Sharonville, OH 45241. Telephone, (513) 772-5944. Forty minutes drive north to Fort Ancient. From I-75, north or southbound, take I-275 east on Mosteller Road to East Kemper Road. Turn right on East Kemper Road to motel. $25.95

per single.

   Red Roof Inn, 11345 Chester Road, Sharonville, OH 45241. Telephone, (513) 771-5141. Forty minutes drive north to Fort Ancient. I-75 at Sharon Road. Exit 15 west to Chester Road. Single, $32.95.

   Camping at KOA King's Island, Cincinnati, OH 45034. Telephone: (800) 832-1133. Forty minute drive north to Fort Ancient. Exit 25 from I-71 north, or 25A from I-71 south. Base rate, $19.50.

Bibliography
Eliade, Mircea. *Birth and Rebirth*, New York: Harper and Row, 1958.

Foster, Steven. *Vision Quest*. New York: Prentice Hill, 1988.

MacKenzie, Donald A. *The Migration of Symbols and their Relations to Beliefs and Customs*, New York: Knopf, 1926.

OKLAHOMA

Oklahoma City

SPIRO MOUNDS

THE HEAVENER RUNESTONE

Spiro Mounds

Louise Riotte

Shortly before the Arkansas River leaves Le Flore County, Oklahoma, bound for the Mississippi, it meanders through a fertile valley wedged between the Ouachita Mountains to the south and the Ozark foothills to the North. Arkansas' forests give way to Oklahoma's tall grass prairies here, and a profusion of plant life and animal life results from the meeting.

Hundreds of years ago, these abundant natural resources attracted Native Americans to an area of uplands and terraces near a gentle river bend. Now known as the Spiro Mounds site, it is one of the most important archaeological discoveries in North America.

The first frequent visitors came around the birth of Christ. One stop in a seasonal migration between hunting and gathering camps, the Spiro area sheltered deer, opossums, squirrels, rabbits and wild turkeys. Shallow waters in the river's oxbow lakes held easily caught fish. Pecan trees, grapes and berries grew in the rich soil annually deposited by Arkansas.

The people who passed through Spiro at this time hunted with spears tipped with bone or chipped stone points. They wore pendant necklaces of bone, stone or shell, and slender pins ornamented their hair. When group members died, their legs and arms were drawn to their chest, and they were covered with soil.

Sometime before 800 A.D., these people became full-fledged farmers while still maintaining some traditional hunting-gathering practices. Descendents of the hunter-gatherers (perhaps 50-100 at a time) lived at Spiro year round. They chopped down large trees and burned the underbrush to clear the fields. Their four-sided houses were built of vertically placed logs and cane covered with clay; for interior cedar posts supported deeply slanted thatched roots.

By 850 A.D., however, the Spiro Mounds site had taken on a unique character. While continuing the business of raising food, other area villages recognized certain Spiro residents as political

313

and/or religious leaders.

These Spiro chiefs became powerful figures. They controlled trade between the vast reaches of the Plains and the steamy, verdant southeast Woodlands. They directed everyday farmers in the building of mortuary houses where the bodies of the high-ranking dead lay. In addition, they oversaw an activity which changed the site's appearance and distinguished it from neighboring villages—mound building.

Spiro Mounds.
State of Oklahoma, Tourism & Recreation Dept., Oklahoma City, OK.

The mounds (about 15 perhaps at the time of the site's abandonment) were built up from basketfuls of soil. Some mounds supported buildings, some covered burned buildings (possibly old mortuary houses), and others were for burial. Six mounds on the uplands, south of the river, formed a circle around a place in which religious ceremonial could be held.

The religious ritualism at Spiro, as at a group of sites scattered around the Southeast, centered on the care and disposal of the honored dead. Spiro lay at the western limit of this religious practice, now known as the Southern Cult, in which the ruling class depended upon local farmers for food and labor.

By 1450 A.D., the Spiro people had deserted the mound site. Native Americans continued farming in the area, but, for reasons which are not clearly understood, they abandoned the ritual and the pageantry of Southern Cult practices. It is thought that today some of the Wichita are probably the descendents of the Spiro people who had moved west to hunt buffalo.

To the casual visitor, the earthen mounds visible here at the site perhaps offer the most fascination. The site is dominated by two large earthen mounds and a series of several smaller mounds. The excavations of 1981 discovered several small mounds in the plaza. Future excavations are needed to tell of their exact function.

The quantity, variety, and kinds of artifacts found with the burials in the Craig Ward Mounds suggests that the dead were persons of importance, and were disposed with considerable ceremony and ritual. It is interesting to note that the western cluster of mounds appear to have been the scene of ongoing religious and political ceremonies for the living, while the eastern Craig Ward cluster seem to have been exclusively devoted to activities surrounding the dead.

Other artifacts were wooded, stone or copper-covered earspools, T-shaped pipes, effigy pipes in the shape of humans and birds, ceder and shell masks, baskets, fine textiles and blankets, a distinctive type of engraved pottery, arrowheads, spear points, axes, celts (a type of working tool), flint knives almost three feet long, headdress plates made of sheets of copper riveted together and then embossed with bird-like designs, and the conch shell gorgets and bowls whose engraved pictures tell us so much about Spiro beliefs and practices. The engraved shells provide special insight into the ceremonial activities of the Craig peoples. Most of the design motifs that you will see here at the Interpretive Center are taken from these Spiro engraved shells.

The items that found their way into the Spiro mortuaries are related to much more than just mortuary symbolism. Good preservation has provided us with abundant evidence of ritual dress and adornment. One can single out actual ceremonial outfits identifiable on engraved shell objects. Chief among these is the costumery of the falcon-impersonator. The role of the falcon interpreter has been suggested as an important in Spiro social organization. We find the tail element of worked into ornaments in its own right. But the essential element of the falcon is represented by the forked-eye motif, which is one of the more distinctive and widespread motifs in the Late Prehistoric North America. The falcon emerges as a symbol of fierceness and boldness. The symbolism of the falcon and the sun, which has been held to be fundamental to the Southern Cult, finds representation in simple motifs that are repeated innumerably in the most extensive range of artifacts.

At Spiro then, we see in the art forms war-related symbolism in decoration and costumery, intriguingly associated with the prestige and authority of prominent leaders buried here.

MYSTICAL SIGNIFICANCE

There are few ancient sites anywhere on earth which glow with more magical energy than Spiro Mounds. The reason is not immediately apparent to the first-time visitor. Many prehistoric centers are larger, better preserved or located in superior natural settings. This is not to denigrate the impressive, oddly shaped Craig Mound, however, nor to underestimate the undoubtedly magnificent scope of the ceremonial premises. Rather, Spiro casts its spell less from its physical features, as through the very soil of its sacred ground, consecrated and supercharged as it is with the psychic input of 16 generations of shamans. It is a sacred center of immanent power, a fact even the most level-headed archaeologist has difficulty denying.

After its abandonment, beginning in the early 14th century, the site became completely overgrown until around 1800. At that time, Choctaw Indians and their Negro slaves accidentally rediscovered the mounds while clearing the land for timber. Immediately they recognized it as a powerful sacred center, and thus carefully avoided the place as a taboo. Even as late as the first archaeological excavations in 1936, local Blacks hired as diggers by the University of Oklahoma refused to remain on the premises after sundown.

Indeed, no other mound group in North America is associated with more paranormal activity. Most notable is the eerie blue light that has long been connected with Craig Mound, the site's major feature. The aura has been seen numerous times by many eye witnesses over the past hundred years. Even Forrest Clements, commissioned as an archaeological authority to write an official history of Spiro Mounds for the Museum of the American Indian, New York's famed Heye Foundation, reported that the woman who once owned the land on which the sacred center is located was awakened one night by unusual, loud noises emanating from the structure. When she rushed to investigate what she presumed must have been drunken trespassers, she saw the mound "covered by shimmering sheets of blue flame." As she gazed in amazement at the ghostly illumination, a team of huge cats drawing a small, empty wagon appeared at the top of the mound. Without a sound, they drove around the summit several times, then vanished, as the blue haze faded away. Although she could not have known it at the time (circa 1890), the jaguar was the most sacred animal-god in the Mesoamerican pantheon. It was regarded as the shaman-spirit incarnate among the Mayas, the suspected ancestors of the civilizers at Spiro.

Her vision was by no means unique. There were at least dozens of similar sightings throughout the 19th century and down to the present day. Remarkably, Egypt's Great Pyramid at Giza has also been reported to sometimes glow with a blue halo at its peak. Even more common than the blue lights of Craig Mound are the incidents of trauma exhibited by animals brought into its proximity. Seeking to disprove such tales, a skeptic erected a shed for himself and his stock near the foot of the mound at the turn of the 20th century. Not only did he testify later that he witnessed the blue aura on several occasions, but his farm animals "became so prostrated with terror that they were useless the next day." The skeptic abandoned his debunking experiment within the week of his arrival.

When the first excavators broke into Craig Mound, they found a tunnel large enough to stand up in. They followed it through the very center of the structure until they came to a wall made of cedar posts. Cutting through it, they stumbled into an oval vault some 20 feet by 30 feet in dimensions, with a cedar roof arching 15 feet overhead. The whole interior of the chamber was tapestried with fabulous cloth hangings woven of fur, hair and brilliant feathers. On the floor lay the full-length skeleton of a large man decked out in copper armor, polished beads, carved stone ear-spools and engraved conch shells. Near him stood an altar, on which rested a large urn filled with tens of thousands of pearls. In all, over 500 human burials were eventually recovered from the mound.

The cache of copper breastplates and engraved conch shells found in Craig Mound's innermost chamber was the largest pre-Columbian treasure trove discovered to date. Every item appears to have been used strictly for religious purposes. The Spiro site was, in fact, the exclusive domain of the most honored dead, who were accompanied to the Underworld by all the ritual activities of ancestor-worship. No one, except perhaps for a small community of shamans, resided in the holy precinct. The population was scattered in surrounding villages. Spiro Mounds was a place people went to for spiritual empowerment, to communicate with the departed spirits of beloved ones and to experience the telluric greatness of Mother Earth at one of her power-points. The modern visitor should expect no less, if he or she comes with a pure heart.

The ancient people's ritual use of copper signified their devotion to the solar principles of enlightenment, their affirmation of life as an eternal phenomenon. Many of the designs they pressed into copper sheet—intwined serpents, hands with an open eye in the palm, encircled crosses, etc.—underscore the theme of immortality. Their incised seashells imply a link with the ocean, itself representing a universal human archetypes for the subconscious mind. To be sure, numerous shell engravings appear to depict altered states of awareness, either through dreams or in shamanistic ecstasy. It is clear the ancient residents of Spiro Mounds were in tune with the spiritual wave-lengths of Nature in the earth, among the heavens and within themselves. They apparently strove for a cosmic-wide inter-relationship in the cause of universal harmony and of the great personal powers which attend it.

The several, over-sized and splendid crystals found at the site further attest to the psychic sorcery that took place there. As such, Oklahoma's rich sacred center was and is a place of resonate spiritual power still echoing with the eternal drum-beats of potent earth-, sun- and sea-ceremonies if only we have the ear to hear them. Visitors enter the Spiro Mounds Park through the small museum, where some of the copper breastplates and other fascinating discoveries were made over 70 years of archaeological excavations. The marked trail begins just outside the exit door and leads about a 100 meters to a group of trees and a modern shelter. Turning north, the path crosses a little bridge to the elongated, peaked structure known as Craig Mound. Its innermost recesses hid a walled chamber containing the greatest pre-Columbian archaeological treasure found in the United States.

The trail encircles Craig Mound, providing a thorough inspection of its weathered exterior. It is also in keeping with the magic circle, that circular motion the initiate takes, one step at a time, around a spiritual power-point. The Mound is a psychic focus for the entire site, so it was around this particular spot that the ritual activities of the Ancient Ones undoubtedly revolved. Receptive visitors will feel the immanent power of the *genius loci* most strongly, although the purest psychic frequency appears to lay on the west side of the structure, fronting the now vanished plaza, where the dramatic ceremonies were performed.

Standing at the western position on the circular path, face the Mound, point your crystal with your right hand at the earth-work, with you left hand over your heart. Envision pure white light glowing from within you, traveling down your right arm and out your hand to bathe the entire Mound in luminescence, even to its deepest recesses. Then turn to the north and thank the Keeper of the Precinct for allowing you to visit his sacred center. Facing west, the entire site lays before you. Say or think something to the effect, "I greet and honor the holy ones of this place! May my vision quest be worthy of your revelation!" Turning to the south, say, "White Swan, guardian of the path to the Place of Becoming, lead me to my quest!" Bend down to the earth and touch it with the palm of your right hand with these words: "Mother, open the eye of my hand to see the visions of deeper things! Let me walk upon you lightly, as becomes your loving child!" Stand and raise the palm of your left hand to the sky, saying, "Father, open my inner-eye to your will and my higher purpose!" Then resume the path that leads west throughout the remainder of the site.

Park benches along the trail afford opportunities for meditation. The very powerful nature of Spiro Mounds virtually assures a meaningful experience, either while visiting the sacred center or soon after leaving it.

FOR MORE INFORMATION

Directions

From I-40, take the Sallisaw Exit south on Highway 59, 16 miles to the intersection with Highway 9. Then eastward, 8 miles east of the present community of Spiro. The park is situated on the Arkansas River, adjacent to the Corps of Engineers W.D. Mayo Lock and Dam. For further information, contact Oklahoma Tourism and Recreation Department, 500 Will Rogers Building, Oklahoma City, OK 73105. Telephone: (405) 521-2406. The Spiro Mounds Interpretive

Center, Route 2, Box 339AA, Spiro, OK 74959 (Telephone (918) 962-2062) is open May through October, Monday through Saturday 9 a.m. to 5 p.m. Sunday noon to 5 p.m. November through April, Wednesday through Saturday, 9-5 a.m. Sunday noon to 5 p.m.

Accommodations

Motel-6, 6001 Rogers Avenue, Fort Smith, AR 72903. Telephone: (501) 484-0576. From I-40, take I-540 westbound 8 miles to Exit 8A. Right on Rogers Avenue, then right on Barnum Road to motel. Thirty-five minute drive west to Spiro Mounds. $24.95 per single.

Best Western Continental Motor Inn, 2225 East Steve Owens Boulevard, Miami, OK 74354. Telephone, (918) 542-6681. US 44 Turnpike at Miami Exit #313. Twenty minute drive to Spiro Mounds. $38 to $40 per single.

Camping at KOA, P.O. Box 88, Sallisaw, OK 74955. Telephone: (918) 266-2792. One-half mile south of I-40 on US 59, exit 308. Open year round. Ten minute drive east to Spiro Mounds. $10 per tent site, two adults.

Bibliography

Clements, Forrest E. *Historical Sketch of the Spiro Mound.* Museum of the American Indian, Heye Foundation, New York, 1945, Volume XIV.

Johnson, Donald R. Spiro Mounds State Park Interpretive Brochure: *Spiro Mounds, Prehistoric Gateway: Present-Day Enigma; Scenes from Spiro Life, Art Works.* The Oklahoma Humanities Committee, The Oklahoma Archaeological Survey and Emporia State University, 1972.

Philips, Phillip and James A. Brown. *Pre-Columbian Shell Engravings from the Craig Mound at Spiro, Oklahoma.* Peabody Museum Press, Peabody Museum of Archaeology and Ethnology, Harvard University, Cambridge, Massachusetts, in two volumes, 1984.

Underhill, Ruth M. *Red Man's Religion.* University of California Press, 1965.

The Heavener Runestone

Edna Ryneveld

Nestled just north of Ouachita (wah-chee-TAH) National Forest and just south of Poteau in southeastern Oklahoma, along Highway 59, lies Heavener (HEEV-en-er) Runestone State Park, gateway to another time and civilization. The drive to Heavener is through minor hills by the standards of the Rockies or Sierbras, but nevertheless jam-packed with glorious Ozark mountain vistas.

It is deep into one of these vistas that you will find the Heavener Runestone. You arrive at the visitor center on the side of a mountain, overlooking a small valley. Other mountains "blue-out" in the distance. You soon discover you're parked on the rim of a fair-sized ravine. Taking an easy stone and gravel path leading down into this timbered slash into the Earth, you enter another world. There is no traffic noise, no machinery whining, only the sound of a trickling waterfall, a small stream, and perhaps a brief bird cry.

As you wind your way along the trail in this cool, shaded gorge, you find yourself in the strong, silent company of various oaks, hickory, dogwood, elm, and mockernut trees, plus a variety of wildflowers, grasses, and moss. Descending, your eyes are drawn upward toward cliff walls towering above you and to the slabs of stone fallen from them over the years.

Soon, you come to the small wooden building which protects the runestone from weathering, and then, there it is: the huge stone which, itself, fell from the side of the mountain over a millennium ago. Exceedingly hard, fine-grained Savanna sand-stone, it stands 12 feet high, 10 feet wide, and 16 inches thick. Grayish-brown and spotted with lichen, it's shielded by plexiglass to guard against vandalism. But it's the inscription that grabs your attention now.

Eight runic symbols, carved in a straight horizontal line, 6 to 9 inches high and to a depth of 1/4 to 3/16 of an inch, are almost mesmerizing. After brief sorties to take in the whole rock, your eyes come back to the runes like ten-penny nails to a magnet.

The Heavener Runestone at its mystical setting.
Photo by Edna Ryneveld.

A very patient and skillful human hand carved those symbols possibly as early as 600 A.D. or as late as 900 A.D.[1] Dating is tricky for inscriptions. The carbon-14 test isn't much use here, but judging from the hardness of the stone, the weathering, and the runic alphabets used, current opinion places the runes' age at well over 1000 years

---

1.*The Heavener Runestone*, Oklahoma Tourism and Recreation Department Brochure, Oklahoma City, OK 73105, by Gloria Stewart Farley, January, 1990.

old. Oklahoma State University botanists corroborate that statement by confirming that the lichen growing in the inscription had
been there about a 1000 years.

Similar runestones have been found also at Poteau, about 10
miles from the Heavener site, and at Shawnee, Oklahoma, some
miles to the west. Scholars from around the world agree the symbols
are authentic ancient Norse.

The controversial inscription.
Photo by Frank Joseph.

The Heavener symbols, ╳⟨⟨ᛗᛗ╳⟨ᚠ⟨ appeared to have
been written in letters from two Norse alphabets in use at different,
but overlapping, times. They were first transliterated as
GNOMEDAL and variously translated into a modern name, "G.
Nomedal," or "Give Supplication, to God, Man Before Day Has
Set," or "Give Attention to This," or "Sun Dial Valley," or "Monument Valley," Boundary Valley," or "Earth Spirit's Dale."[2] A 1967
transliteration to GAOMEDAT by cryptographer Alf Monge was

2. Pirtle III, Caleb, *Dallas Times Herald,* July 26, 1981.

translated by him to be the date of November 11, 1012 (St. Martin's Day, by Christian accounting) in the form of a complicated cryptopuzzle.

This date fit in nicely with a known Norse settlement on the east coast in 1008. Of the four ships comprising that party, a couple returned to Greenland. It was surmised that at least one ship may have sailed down the coast, traversed the Gulf of Mexico, then made its way to and up the Arkansas River. Which may indeed, have happened, but the "date" translation is not really credible.

In the late 1980s, Dr. Richard Nelson, through meticulous research both in Scandinavia and America, determined that the Oklahoma inscriptions found at Heavener, Poteau, and Shawnee were not in a mixed alphabet, but in the oldest of them, Old Norse, and that the second and eighth Heavener runic symbols were both a form of L. This produced GLOME DAL, meaning, he said, "Valley Owned by Glome," at Heavener and GLOI ALLW (Alu), "Magic or protection to Gloi" for the Poteau Runestone. "Gloi," says Nelson, is a nickname for Glome, a Norseman who apparently owned—and marked—land on Poteau Mountain as early as 600 A.D.

The experts themselves, however, will be the first to admit that their opinions of the rune translations are not "carved in stone." With Old Norse, as with many ancient languages, written and unwritten, much is lost in the mists of time. Even with all our modern technology and techniques, we view the past "as through a glass, darkly."

Frank Joseph postulates an interesting translation. "GAOM," he writes, "is Norse for 'gnome,' a race of small, darkish people in Scandinavian folklore. 'GAOMEDAL' would then translate 'Gnome Valley,' or 'Valley of the Gnomes'. . ." It makes sense for the Vikings to have referred to the place by that name, because they were big, Nordic adventurers, tall, fair-skinned and light-eyed, among a dark, smallish population of Native Americans who may indeed have seemed like gnomes to the visitors.

While this site has never been officially designated a sacred place, a pervading tranquility envelops it. Instinctively you know that this has long been a sacred place in the true sense of the word. As you walk down the path, there is a lone bird call and then complete silence—except for the trickle of water. Even those "not-into-all-this" are likely to find themselves talking in hushed tones, quietly looking about. It is easy to imagine that the inscriber of the runes was probably also thus affected, as you stand before the runestone, listening to the silence and the waterfall, feeling totally at peace and at one with this place.

SUGGESTED RITUAL

The appropriate ritual here might be one of celebrating one's connectedness and oneness with the spirit and wisdom of the Earth and, by implication, Her Creator.

Find an inconspicuous place near water, if possible. (Coming early in the day may make it easier to find some solitude during the tourist season.) If you can't position yourself near water, scoop some up from the stream in your palm and carry it to wherever you feel comfortable. With the fingers of your other hand, flick some water in each of the four directions. Now sit down on stone, facing east, if you can. If you can't sit on stone, hold a small piece in your left hand. Also hold a pinch of earth.

Close your eyes and relax. Imagine a cord, a grounding cord of any size, type, or flexibility, going from your root chakra to the center of the Earth. Align your chakras and mentally surround yourself with white light.

See, in your mind's eye, a few pine needles smoldering on glowing coals, with wisps of fragrant smoke rising up from the interior of the Earth, up through the surrounding trees and beyond, up into the sky, and beyond. Say, in your mind, "With pine's permission, I release its spirit that it may connect me to the Universe, as a cord connects me to the Earth. By using a line, a circle is complete."

Do not call on guides or totems as intermediaries. Tune into the sound of the water. Feel the spirit essence of the stone, the earth, the air, and water yourself, directly. Listen. Feel. You will not even have to try. A connection will be made.

When the time is sufficient, thank the stone arid return it, if you've been holding one. Thank the earth and return it. Thank the mentally-created pine and release it. Go to the water and put your hands into it. Bring them up to touch your face.

Thank the water and release it.

Go in peace, empowered and renewed.

FOR MORE INFORMATION

Location

Heavener is just south of due east of Oklahoma City. near the Oklahoma/Arkansas border and just north of Ouachita National Forest, on Highway 59. Turn off the highway into Heavener and take Morris Creek Road north to the Heavener Runestone State Park sign. Turn east and follow the road up to the Visitor's Center.

In addition to the actual runestone and the trail leading to it, there is a one-mile trail to hike, group shelters, picnic areas, a playground. and comfort stations. Maps are available at the Visitor's Center.

The park is open 8 a.m. to dark daily.

Local Assistance

Heavener Runestone State Park; Rt. 1, Box 1510; Heavener, OK 74937-9998. (918) 653-2241.

Accommodations

Green Country Inn. Hwy 59. Heavener.

Crane Motel, Hwy 59, just north of Heavener.

Numerous other hotels and motels and camping facilities at nearby recreational areas, such as Wister Lake State Park, 1.4 miles west of Heavener, and Ouachita National Forest to the south.

OREGON

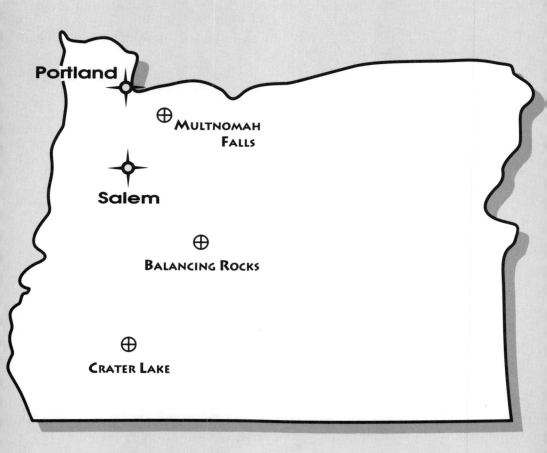

Portland

⊕ Multnomah
  Falls

Salem

⊕ Balancing Rocks

⊕ Crater Lake

Balancing Rocks

D. J. Conway

The Balancing Rocks, which are found in a little canyon in east-central Oregon, look like a scene from another world. It is a barren, exposed hillside gulch formed by a prehistoric lava flow. The bare hardpan slope is covered with conical stone spikes; each one, with a few exceptions, is topped with a flat stone large enough to overhang on the sides. Each balancing rock is unique. The opportunities for photos that will be an item of conversation are immense. This canyon with its unusual formations looks like a forest of giant weirdly-formed stone mushrooms. However, do be on the lookout for scorpions and rattlesnakes!

Around this little pink-toned valley is a backdrop of mountains and flat-topped mesas sprinkled with a few dark green pines. It is very unlikely that you will have to share the canyon with other tourists, as the Balancing Rocks are not publicized nor are they well-known to most Oregonians. We were told that there is a cave in the immediate vicinity containing Indian petroglyphs, but we were unable to locate it.

SUGGESTED RITUAL

Continue to be on the lookout for scorpions and rattlesnakes while you are in this little canyon. Although we saw no snakes, the scorpions were fairly numerous; as far as I was concerned, "four scorpions" are numerous. Earth and Air energies and Nature spirits were quite prevalent.

Although we forgot our pendulums and could do no experiments, it would be very interesting to see how a pendulum would behave in this area. There are strong subterranean currents radiating from the old Newberry Volcano Crater. Natural healing forces from deep within the earth appear to be close to the surface in this little canyon.

Balancing Rocks.
Illustration by William Wild.

To perform a ritual in the American Indian tradition, be prepared to leave a small gift of sage leaves at the base of one of the stone pinnacles. Face each direction, beginning with the North, and turning clockwise during the rite. At each direction chant or say a prayer to the Great Spirit, asking for health, happiness, guidance and prosperity. After each prayer, stand quietly to listen for inner messages.

FOR MORE INFORMATION

Directions
Please call or write for directions at: Fort Rock Ranger District, 1230 N.E. 3rd St., Bend, OR 97701; (503) 388-5664.

Lodging

Bend's 97 Host Motel, 61440 S. Hwy 97, Bend, OR 97701; (503) 382-1951; 17 units, $18–40. Bend Riverside Motel, 1565 N.W. Hill St., Bend, OR 97701; (503) 389-2363; 100 units, $28-44.

Cascade Lodge Motel, 420 S.E. 3rd St., Bend, OR 97701; (503) 382-2612; 29 units, $22–38. Dunes Motel, 1515 N.E. 3rd St., Bend, OR 97701; (503) 382-6811; 30 units, $27–34. Pilot Butte Motor Inn, 1236 N.W. Wall St., Bend, OR 97701; (503) 382-1411; $18–45. Tom Tom Motor Inn, 3600 N. Hwy, Bend, OR 97701; (503) 382-4734; $23–35.

Campgrounds in the general area are not numerous. Deschutes River, off I-84, 17 miles east of The Dalles; 34 primitive campsites, no electric, room for tents; maximum 30 foot RV. LaPine, off US 97, 27 miles southwest of Bend; 95 full hook-ups, 50 electrical, maximum 40 foot RV; handicapped access to restrooms, showers, picnic area, tents. Shelton, OR 19, 10 miles southeast of Fossil; 43 primitive campsites; tents, picnic area; maximum 30 foot RV. Tumalo, off US 20, 5 miles northwest of Bend; 20 full hook-ups, 68 tents; showers, picnic; maximum 35 foot RV.

Additional Information

There are other rock formations in the nearby region that are of interest, especially those called Castle Rocks. These lie to the west of Monty Campgrounds. Fort Rock State Park, 30 miles S.E. of LaPine, Oregon, off Hwy 31, is another interesting feature.

Three other points of interest in the area are the John Day Fossil Beds National Monument with Park Headquarters at Hwy 26, John Day, OR, open Mon.–Fri., 8 a.m.–4:30 p.m. year-round and the Newberry Crater (recently made a National Park), 13 miles east of Hwy 97 between Sunriver and LaPine. Pilot Butte State Park is an old cinder cone which offers unobstructed views of Central Oregon and the Cascade Mountains from its summit.

For more information, contact the Bend Visitor and Convention Bureau, 164 N.W. Hawthorne, Bend, OR 97701, (503) 382-3221.

Bibliography

Drawson, Maynard C. *Treasures of the Oregon Country*. Salem, OR: Dee Publishing Co., 1973.

Hagen, Robert D. *Totally Oregon*. Salem, OR: Oregon Pride Productions, 1989.

Multnomah Falls

D. J. Conway

Multnomah Falls is one of many waterfalls in northern Oregon that empty into the Columbia River. There is possibly the greatest concentration of high waterfalls in North America on the south wall of the Columbia Gorge, the deep chasm through which the mighty Columbia River runs. Eleven falls, over 100 feet high, can be seen from the freeway or the scenic highway.

The Columbia River drains an area nearly as large as Texas, and it carries the second largest volume of water in the United States (after the Mississippi). It is the largest river in the Western Hemisphere to enter the Pacific Ocean; it is also the seventh longest in the United States. From the highway through the Gorge three snow-capped mountains can be seen: Mt. Adams (to the north in Washington), Mt. Hood (to the south in Oregon), and Mt. St. Helens (to the northwest in Washington).

Thirty million years of geological history are visible in the walls of the Columbia Gorge, the result of lava flows, erosion and the uplift that created the Cascade Range. Everywhere can be seen layers of basalt and sandstone.

The most famous of the waterfalls along the Columbia is Multnomah Falls; it is the fourth highest in the US. The main upper portion of the falls drops sheer down 542 feet, while the lower falls drops another 69 feet.

It is possible to climb by a trail to the very top of the falls, but it can be very slick and dangerous because of the mist that rises from the falls and covers the ground. Larch Mt. Trail #441 starts on the left hand side of the lodge at the base of the falls and ascends steeply from the lower falls to the very top. At the one-mile marker, a side trail heads to a viewpoint directly over Multnomah Falls.

Multnomah Falls.
Photo courtesy of the U.S.D.A. Forest Service.

MYSTICAL SIGNIFICANCE

There is an ancient local Indian legend connected with this beautiful waterfall. A very long time ago, the Multnomah Indians lived in the Gorge near a very high cliff along the mighty Columbia River. They were a happy people, living close to the land and in tune with the Great Spirit. There came a time when a terrible sickness fell upon them. Hundreds of Indians died of the epidemic; no one knew of a cure for the sickness. An old medicine man prayed to the Great Spirit for an answer, tenaciously fasting until he had a vision. The solution to the epidemic was a drastic one, but the old man called the people together and related his vision. The only way to stop the sickness, the medicine man told them, was for a pure, innocent maiden to sacrifice herself willingly from the sheer cliff. For a time there were no volunteers; the sickness raged on. But the chief's daughter sorrowed for her people. Finally, she climbed to the top of the huge cliff and, with prayers to the Great Spirit, threw herself onto the rocks below. The sickness left. In memory of her self-sacrifice for the good and life of her people, the Great Spirit caused a silvery falls to drop from the site of her descent.

SUGGESTED RITUAL

Since this a heavily visited tourist stop, even during bad weather, it will not be convenient to perform any obvious ritual. Energy from Water elementals is very strong here and very calming to the nerves and emotions. The best place to absorb this energy in an inconspicuous manner is on the bridge at the bottom of the upper falls. Simply stand in the mist that drifts across the bridge and fill yourself with the gentle but powerful energies whirling around the bridge.

FOR MORE INFORMATION

Directions

Multnomah Falls can be reached either by the US Scenic Highway Route or directly from I-84, the main freeway through the Columbia Gorge. The Scenic Route begins near the Sandy River at Troutdale, just outside and west of Portland, and ends 5 miles west of Bonneville Dam. Sightseers can enter or exit from either end of the Scenic Route.

336 SACRED SITES

Lodging

Nearest motels are in the Portland area. Best Western Fortniter Motel, 4911 N.E. 82nd Ave., Portland, OR; (503) 25-9771. Hallmark Motel, 4810 N.E. Sandy Blvd., Portland, OR; 800-345-5676. Riverside Inn, 50 S.W. Morrison, Portland; (503) 221-0711; 138 units, $45–58. Shilo Inn, 1506 N.E. 2nd Ave., Portland, OR; (503) 231-7665; handicapped facilities. Tigard Inn Motel, 11455 S.W. Pacific Hwy., Tigard, OR; (503) 246-8451. Viscount Motel, 1441 N.E. 2nd Ave., Portland, OR; (503) 233-2401; handicapped facilities; $49–59. Stafford Motor Inn, 8815 S.W. Sun Place, Wilsonville, OR 97070 (1-5 exit 286); (503) 682-3184; handicapped facilities; 80 units, $33–39.

Campgrounds to the east are: Bridge of the Gods Motel & RV Park, 630 Wa-Na-Pa, Cascade Locks, OR 97014; (503) 374-8628. KOA Cascade Locks, Forest Lane, Cascade Locks, OR 97014; (503) 374-8668.

Only one State campground in that area of the Gorge has overnight availability: Ainsworth on US 30, east of Portland; 45 full hook-ups; maximum 60 foot RV; showers and picnic area.

Other State parks with picnic and/or restroom areas are: Bridal Veil Falls, US 30 Scenic Route, 16 miles east of Troutdale; Guy Talbot Park, US 30 Scenic Route, 27 miles east of Portland; Rooster Rock, I-84, 22 miles east of Portland.

US 30 Scenic Route is a 24-mile drive along the old Columbia River Highway; it begins near the Sandy River at Troutdale (off I-84) and ends 5 miles west of Bonneville Dam. Along this route are impressive waterfalls and panoramic views of the Columbia Gorge.

For more information, contact the Greater Portland Convention and Visitors Association, 26 S.W. Salmon, Portland, OR 97204, (503) 222-2223.

Bibliography

Allen, John Eliot. *The Magnificent Gateway*. Forest Grove, OR: Timber Press, 1979.

Hagen, Robert D. comp. *Totally Oregon*. Salem, OR: Oregon Pride Productions, 1989.

Plumb, Gregory Alan. *A Waterfall Lover's Guide to the Pacific Northwest*, Seattle, WA: The Mountaineers, 1989.

Wizard Island—A Journey to Crater Lake

Anodea Judith and Richard Ely

Crater Lake, located in Southwestern Oregon, was created by the collapse of a huge volcano named Mount Mazama 6,850 years ago. The lake sits in a cliff-walled bowl 5–6 miles across, elevated thousands of feet above the surrounding countryside. Crater Lake is the seventh deepest lake in the world, its shores surrounded by steep cliffs that are undeveloped except for a single trail that reaches the lake on the north side. The lake is fed almost entirely by precipitation, receiving only a minor percentage from run off from the surrounding cliffs. As a result, very few dissolved nutrients reach the lake, and it contains perhaps the purest natural water known on earth. Visibility is reported to exceed 130 feet, and algae has been found growing at deeper than 600 feet—greater than anywhere else on Earth. Viewed from the rim its color is bluer than the sky, ranging from royal blue to indigo to turquoise on sunny days, shimmering silver and gold under the clouds. Close to the shore the water is so transparent as to be nearly invisible at shallow depths. But where the submerged cliffs plunge downward, the color is a potent violet blue.

Water in any form is said to be a conduit for the psychic realms. Waters have been associated with healing powers, with emotional fulfillment, with pleasure and with cleansing. Water in the form of lakes has a depth we cannot reach, and yet reflects the Heavens in shining glory. In ancient times, priestesses would skry in water to see visions of the future or of scenes far away. In this aspect, Crater Lake can also be seen as a huge scrying bowl of clarity.

GEOLOGIC HISTORY OF CRATER LAKE

Crater Lake was once the site of a large volcanic mountain named Mount Mazama. This mountain began growing about 400,000 years ago atop a 6000 foot high volcanic plateau built of

337

overlapping low, wide basaltic volcanoes (basalt is a dark, very fluid lava such as makes up the Hawaiian Islands). Mount Mazama was actually a compound landform made up from a series of smaller, overlapping cones of a more viscous lava called *andesite*, each of which was active for a time before the eruptions moved elsewhere. The result was a glaciated peak that towered 12,000 feet above sea level, similar in apace to the other high volcanic peaks of the Cascade Range such as Mount Rainier and Mount Hood.

Approximately 7,000 years ago the magma beneath Mount Mazama was concentrated in a large, relatively shallow chamber about 3 to 6 miles below the base of the mountain. Then a series of huge eruptions of ash and highly viscous *rhyodacitic* lava began that removed two or three cubic miles of magma from the chamber, and produced such features as Llao Rock, a great cliff that overlooks the north end of the lake. Removal of such a large volume of lava from the magma chamber weakened and fractured the overlying rock, allowing the creation of much larger conduits to the surface. What followed was an eruption that dwarfed the recent eruption of Mount St. Helens in 1980, releasing a total of 12 cubic miles of magma, most of which was converted to frothy volcanic ash and pumice.

The climactic eruption, which took place about 6,850 years ago, occurred in two stages: the first stage lasted a few days or weeks, resulting in the removal of about 5 cubic miles of magma from the chamber below the mountain. The second stage of the climactic eruption, which lasted only a few days at most began when Mount Mazama could no longer support itself because of the removal of so much magma from below. A huge circular system of faults formed, and the mountain sank into the partially empty magma chamber like a gigantic piston.

Another 7 cubic miles of magma roared through the ring of faults, mostly in the form of voluminous glowing avalanches of white hot ash that spread up to 35 miles across the surrounding countryside. In the end an area of about 5,000 square miles had been covered with ash to a depth of 6 inches or more, with about 1,000,000 square miles receiving a millimeter or more. The former site of Mount Mazama was now a *caldera*, a steaming circular pit about 4,000 feet deep and 5–6 miles across.

The mountain was quiet now with only the hiss of steam venting from the hot ash to break the silence. Centuries of rainfall cooled the ash fields, and slowly the great pit filled with water to the level where evaporation and leakage through the caldera wall balanced the inflow. Most of the inflow came from rain and snow, although some came as hot springs rising from the slowly cooling magma chamber. This process probably took hundreds of years, because only the excess of inflow over evaporation and leakage was available to raise the water level. Before the water rose to its present maximum depth of 1,932 feet, several minor eruptions occurred that built volcanic cones upon the caldera floor. The most prominent cone is Wizard Island, which rises 760 feet above the lake surface, and a total of 2,250 feet above the caldera floor. Its red and black lava cinders and pointed top beckon mysteriously from each and every view of the lake (see color plate).

LEGENDS OF CRATER LAKE

Not long ago Crater Lake lay within the lands of the Klamath Tribe, a people who had dwelt there for so long that their legends accurately described the eruption and collapse of Mount Mazama. When the Europeans arrived in the area, the Klamath people considered Crater Lake to be a place of such great magical potency that only experienced shamans dared approach it. A number of Klamath Tribe legends about the lake are compiled in *Indian Legends of the Pacific Northwest* by Ella Clark (University of California Press, Berkeley and Los Angeles, 1969).

The myth concerning the origin of the lake recounts the attempt of the Chief of the World Below, who lived inside a great mountain where the lake now lies, to secure a bride from the Klamath people. On one of his visits to the Earth, the Chief saw Loha, the beloved of her tribe. He offered her love, eternal life and freedom from sorrow if she would come and live with him. She rebuffed him in his attempts to win her, and the wise men of the tribe told her to hide herself from him. Then the Chief of the World Below swore to destroy the people with the Curse of Fire, and raged forth from his doorway at the summit of the mountain. The Chief of the World Above saw what was happening and descended to the summit of Mount Shasta to intercede in behalf of the Klamath people.

A great battle ensued, eventually involving all the spirits of earth and air, with oceans of fire and red-hot rocks erupting from the mouth of the Chief of the World Below. The surrounding countryside was consumed in fire, and the tribe fled to find refuge in Klamath Lake. There they held council and their two greatest medicine men told them that the Curse of Fire had been sent as a punishment for the wickedness of the tribe. Only a willing sacrifice would turn away the wrath of the Chief of the World Below. Because there were no other volunteers the two medicine men offered to go, as their years were many. That night they climbed the mountain and jumped into the fiery pit. With that the Chief of the World Below retreated to his home and the mountain fell in upon him. Torrential rains fell and filled the huge hole where the mountain had been, and the Curse of Fire was lifted. From that time on the word was passed from generation to generation of the terrible things that had happened there, and few dared approach that terrible place.

An interesting aspect of this myth is the association of Mount Shasta with the World Above. Today this mountain is considered one of the supreme New Age holy places in North America, attracting numerous seekers of airy astral realms, the White Brotherhood, extraterrestrials and such. Crater Lake is the spiritual compliment to Mount Shasta, providing a superb location for descent into the dark, watery mysteries of the Mother Goddess. In the end both ascent and descent must be experienced by seekers after spiritual wholeness, for those who would walk the path of balance need to be grounded in the sacred earth as well as open to the heavens.

Another legend told of a lake that was bluer than the sky, with a little mountain island that rose from near the center of the lake. The little mountain was the home of the Spirit Chief who ruled over the Land of the Dead. The waters of the lake filled a gigantic cave that led deep into the interior of the earth. Long ago the ancestors of the tribe had emerged here from inside the earth, carried up by the flame and smoke that came from the top of the little mountain. Upon death, the spirits of the Klamath people returned to the lake, with the evil ones being confined to the fire pit at the top of the little mountain. The spirits of those who led good lives were free to roam the lake and the surrounding countryside. The Spirit Chief made a law that, under penalty of death, only the wise elders of the tribe might approach his realm to learn from him and consult the spirits of the ancestors.

GETTING TO WIZARD ISLAND

Assuming that you are a respected elder in your tribe, Wizard Island can be approached by boat during the central ten weeks of the summer season (dates vary from year to year). One can catch a boat hourly at the base of the Cleetwood Trail, located on the north side of the rim, for a cost of $10. The boat ride alone is spectacular, and takes you on a roundabout tour of the special sites one cannot see from the rim, complete with a geological lecture from a park ranger that is quite informative. (Dress warmly—it's windy out there.) Llao Rock, truncated glacial valleys, and a close-up view of the Phantom Ship, a fascinating rock formation rising up out of the lake, are just of few of the sights visible from the boat Wizard Island is a stop on the boat tour—if you catch the earliest boat you can stay on the island the rest of the day before catching the last afternoon pickup. The complete boatride without getting out takes 1-3/4 hours. No overnights are allowed at this time on Wizard Island—heads are counted!

Once on Wizard Island, one can walk on prepared trails across a field of jagged, broken-up lava called "aa" (pronounced ah-ah). Since the island is relatively young, one can witness an early Crater Lake stage in the process of soil formation, with growing plants and trees appearing in the deep crevices in the lava, which helps to hold moisture and break up the lava further.

There are two main trails on Wizard Island, and one is urged to use the graded trails, as traveling across the aa flows is very rough going, and walking across the ash leaves footprints that last for years. One path leads to the western side of the island, where in warm weather, there is a lovely shallow bay suitable for swimming. (The water at any time of year is very cold, however!) There is also a winding trail to the top of Wizard Island, passing through a mature coniferous forest, which leads to the summit crater for which Crater Lake is named—a 300-foot diameter circular depression left by the final eruption of Wizard Island volcano. Wildlife exists on the island, mostly in the form of birds and golden mantled ground squirrels, which were believed to have come across the ice during one of the colder years. (The lake last froze over in 1949.)

From the rim of the crater of Wizard Island, one can see all of Crater Lake. The trail reaches the summit on the west side of the crater. As an entrance to an Underworld gateway, this is an apt location because the sun sets ("dies") in the west, and this direction is mythologically associated with the land of the dead.

The other three cardinal directions are marked by natural features on the crater rim. The eastern side of the crater rim is graced by a large black lava boulder, the most prominent point on the crater

rim and stretching up in altar-like fashion to the Heavens. As the
east is related to the element "air" in western magical systems, this
high rock is a good place to begin the formation of a magic circle
around the crater, if one chooses to do-ritual there. The eastern side
offers the best view of the lake, as the Island is off-center to the western side.

The north side of the crater rim is marked by a pile of lava boulders that form a natural northern altar if you choose to establish one.
A large stand of ghostly dead pine trees, bleached pure white by the
elements, occupies the northern part of the crater, further enhancing
the lower-world qualities of the place. The highest point on the crater rim is located on the south side, forming a natural site for the invocation of the element "fire," as south usually is associated with
this element.

The center of the crater is marked by a large flat surface of black
lava where a small group could gather, with a great flat-topped lava
rock at one side which would serve nicely as an altar. The lowest
point of the crater is not at the center, however, but slightly west of
center. Numerous loose boulders choke the bottom of the pit, concealing the heart of the old volcanic vent and providing secure cran-
nies to leave small, unobtrusive offerings.

RITUALS AND THINGS TO DO

One should choose to spend a number of days at Crater Lake if
at all possible. There are numerous trails to hike such as the short
trail to Garfield Peak (a very lovely afternoon hike, especially recommended for sunset) or the longer hike to Mount Scott, a towering
peak that lets you see the surrounding countryside to the east. These
hikes can be accompanied by rituals of honoring the Earth Mother,
enjoying the wildlife, or enacting personal cleansing that can come
from vigorous hikes at high altitudes (6,000–9,000 feet).

Rituals honoring the water element, however need to be done
in, on, or near the lake itself. We found the most potent spot to be the
crater atop Wizard Island even though one can only be there for a
limited time, and rarely alone. Since the Underworld, like the
womb, is the place from which things grow, this is a good place to
plant your prayers, dreams, and visions. Deep in the crater, you can
plant a metaphorical seed for something you hope to give birth to in
your life.

The early morning walk down Cleetwood Trail can be your ritual procession. Here you can focus on your visions or your spiritual purpose. Think of the boatride as your spiritual passage, much as in Greek myth, the ferryman, Charon, took passengers across the River Styx to the Underworld.

When you arrive at Wizard Island, take the low trail to the swimming arc. If it is early morning, chances are you will be relatively undisturbed. This is your opportunity to take your invigorating ritual bath! After bathing and dressing, ask the lake for a bit of "holy water," imagining that it has special cleansing and growth producing powers. Put the water in a vessel that you can carry to the top, to water the psychic seeds you wish to plant.

While walking up the trail, you may wish to observe silence, so as to best be able to tune into the potent energies of Wizard Island. Upon reaching the top (a goodly climb) we recommend catching your breath and acclimatizing to your new location before beginning anything else. Walk the rim a few times to get the feel of it—get your bearings of North, East, South, and West.

When you are ready, you may wish to begin by walking the rim clockwise or counterclockwise, depending on purpose. Clockwise (deosil) for manifesting, counterclockwise (widdershins) for letting go of something. Stop at the four directions and call them to you. This may be done by calling to the land that lies in that direction (e.g. California to the South, Washington and Canada to the North) or by calling to the elements commonly associated with that direction. In Western magical systems, East is associated with air, thoughts and communication; South with fire, power and will; West with water, feelings, psychic realms; and North with earth, form, and function.

At the central lava-rock altar down in the crater, you can set up your ritual items, and invoke whatever spirits, Gods or Goddesses you wish to invite to enhance your purpose. You may wish to invoke your higher self, your ancestors (the land of the dead is especially good for that) or your patron saint or deity.

Then, with this magical circle about you, filled with the elements and spirits of your choice, you may wish to walk down to the deepest part of the crater, carrying your water and a symbol of the seed you wish to plant. It may be a small rock or crystal you have found, an actual seed, or (most appropriately) a thoughtform. Please do not bring anything large or unnatural. The site should look exactly the same after you have left. Here you may place your seed in the crevices between the rocks and water it while charging it with whatever prayers or chants feel appropriate to you. A brief period of meditation is recommended to follow, as you may find yourself especially receptive to bits of wisdom or insight about your task.

When you feel complete, give thanks to the spirits and elements you have called in reverse order of their invocation, dismiss your circle and release whatever energies are still lingering. You may wish to stay in or around the crater for some time to rest or have lunch, but as other people will be moving in and out it is best to make your ritual short and sweet and to take down your circle before wandering around.

FOR MORE INFORMATION

Where to Stay

Crater Lake has two public campgrounds, Mazama and Lost Creek, and backcountry camping is possible by permit. Mazama campground is exceptionally nice with 198 wooded sites (many of them are quite private), restrooms and dump station, located seven miles south of Rim Village. Summer campfire programs include geology talks and other topics at the Mazama amphitheater. Lost Creek is a smaller and more primitive campground, with twelve rather exposed sites, located 3 miles down a branch of the southeastern portion of Rim Drive. Motel-type cabins are available near Mazama Campground from mid-May to mid-October; write to Crater Lake Lodge Company P.O. Box 128, Crater Lake, OR 97604, or telephone (503) 594-2511 for reservations. Historic Crater Lake Lodge is closed for renovations and will not reopen until sometime in the mid-1990s.

By car one can get to Crater Lake from the south by taking Interstate 5 as far as Medford, then taking Oregon Route 62 to the park. From the north leave Interstate 5 at Roseberg and take Oregon Route 138 to the park US Highway 97 passes close to the east side of the park and is joined by Routes 62 and 138, which may be taken from this direction. In winter, however, check with Highway Patrol for weather conditions, as heavy snow may sometimes close the roads.

PENNSYLVANIA

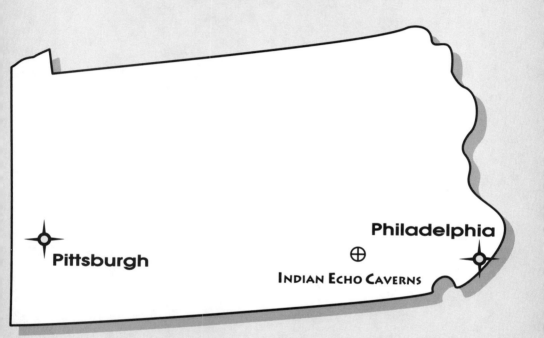

Philadelphia

Pittsburgh

⊕

INDIAN ECHO CAVERNS

Indian Echo Caverns

Jenine E. Trayer

Along the banks of the meandering Swatera Creek, 10 miles from the Susquehanna River, lie the Indian Echo Caverns. Here, the internal beauty of Earth Mother is estimated to be three to five million years old.

The magnificent entrance to the Caverns can be seen only from the creek. One must either traverse dozens of steps from the high ground directly over the caverns, or reach the clearing in front of the caves by canoe. As you reach the last of the stone steps the profound beauty of the area immediately encompasses you. Voice tone down to a low murmur as your inner self becomes aware that "something sacred" resides here.

The first inhabitants of the Indian Echo Caverns were the Susquehannock Indians. From this peaceful people came a great deal of ancient healing wisdom that they shared with William Penn's settlers in the New World. Later their healing practices, mixed with Gypsy charms and spells, came to be known as "Pow-Wow." The name for the Shaman of the tribe was Powaw, meaning "he who dreams." Not long after the settlers reached the Swatera area of Pennsylvania, the Indians were on the move. They quit the region, and some tribes eventually joined with larger groups in New York state.

Indian tradition claims that the caverns are full of evil spirits; however, Native Americans were known to have dwelt in the foreroom of the caverns and they used parts of the caves for refrigeration of food.

There are three main attractions inside the caverns: The Indian Ballroom, The Rainbow Room and Crystal Lake. The Indian Ballroom is 110 feet wide and was formed by two rivers that merged into a whirlpool, carving out the huge room. The area, and indeed the entire cavern system, is filled with stalactites, stalagmites, columns and flowstones. Some of the formations are over one million

347

years old. The Rainbow Room is 79 feet high and its ceiling is the highest in the cavern. This room holds a mystery that will be discussed in the next section.

The third attraction, and by far the most beautiful site in the caverns, is Crystal Lake, which can be viewed from two vantage points. These mystical waters will touch your soul with deep tranquility. The lake itself is 6 feet deep at your first vantage point and the water contains a high mineral content. A path winds around the small lake and ends on a wooden bridge. The water level at this point is over 10 feet deep. At this juncture, you are 125 feet underground.

Indian Echo Caverns.
Photo by John C. Baker.

MYSTICAL SIGNIFICANCE

The caves that comprise Indian Echo Caverns represent a holy trio of related precincts joining in a single sacred center. The initiatory nature of this sacred center is clear from the very distinct emotional vibrations which resonate from each chamber. The Indian Ballroom, carved out by the swirling torrents of two confluent

Underworld rivers, is a place of beginnings, where the receptive visitor first touches on the subterranean *genius loci*, an invaluable experience for the newcomer in need of personal experience to convince himself of spiritual realities. It is also significant for the adept, who gathers renewed strength from such immediate contact with the Divine.

Inner strength is occasionally needed to confront the powerful visions that sometimes appear in the lofty Rainbow Room. Here, the mood shifts dramatically from one of revitalizing empowerment to cold evil. It is this room which was undoubtedly responsible for the Cavern's not wholly undeserved reputation as a haunt for devils. While the Rainbow Room may not be an annex to Hell, its ambiance is decidedly negative, and spectral appearances in its chilly chamber have been sometimes on the grisly side. One of the better known apparitions, which has been witnessed by at least a dozen visitors over a two-year period beginning in 1987, involves an immobile, glaring Indian warrior holding the severed, bearded head of a corpse lying at his feet. The dead man's attire appears to be medieval European dress—which interestingly corresponds to some Turkish coins dated to the 13th century found in the Rainbow Room in 1919. Other visions observed here have been less graphic, although no less malefic. In any case, bring your camera (and some high speed film), and you may get a shot of something more memorable than a stalagmite.

The mood shifts radically once more when visitors adjourn to the Crystal Lake. The water glistens with the resolution of past conflicts, cleansing all energies of negativity, while the spirit rises on mists ascending from the translucent lake. It is the higher focus of Indian Echo Caverns as a sacred sight, a center of inner joy and transcendence, reassuring in its tranquility and a tonic for troubled souls. Crystal Lake is a bright antidote to the dark-sited Rainbow Room; in a sense, the three caves might be seen as combining to form an under-earth macrocosm of the human condition, with our inherent capacities for evil and for redemption. Indian Echo Caverns is a place where we may touch the eternal springs of nature and our own divinity.

SUGGESTED RITUAL

If you stand at the mouth of the Caverns and face the creek, the afternoon sun of the West shines victoriously. In the lore of the Indian Medicine Wheel, West stands for the journey of inner vision. After you have toured the Caverns, find a peaceful spot on the grounds above where you will not be disturbed.

An appropriate form of meditation employs archetype Power Animals. The Native Americans believed that each animal had specific medicine that It would share with human beings, if approached properly. Examples would be:

The Raven – Dreams and Prophecy
The Brown Bear – For Inner Healing
The Jaguar – For Shamanic Travels
The Mountain Lion – For Strength, Cunning and Secrets

The first three animals are direct representations of the West. The Mountain Lion was native to this area of the country.

You may wish to hold a piece of fluorite (which I have found to be an excellent bridge to past lives) or a piece of amethyst or crystal to assist you in forging a link between yourself and the spirit world.

Sit on the ground, so you will be close to Earth Mother, facing West. Mentally project a magic circle around yourself. Breathe deeply several times and open the chakra centers until you have a rainbow pattern of light swirling about you.

Visualize the sacred animal of your choice and ask it to assist you on your astral journey. Explain what you most need to enhance your spiritual fulfillment. The Power Animal may lead you into the caverns themselves or beside the serenity of the creek. You may travel to another time period. Do not be afraid to ask questions along the way. You may even wish to cleanse your astral self in the energetic waters of Crystal Lake.

When you are near the completion of your journey, ask the Power Animal for a gift. Thank the animal then count from ten back to one. Open your eyes, take several deep breathes and tell yourself three times that you are wide awake. Close the chakra centers and ground any excess energy.

If you keep a journal or tape your experiences, record them now for future study. You may wish to leave a small stone or gem or even a pinch of tobacco to honor the good medicine you have received from the animal.

The Caverns are open as follows:
Memorial Day to Labor Day 9:00 a.m.–6:00 p.m.
April, May, September, October 10:00 a.m.–4:00 p.m.
March and November (weekends only) 10:00 a.m.–4:00 p.m.

Because of potential dangers within the Caverns, visitors are not permitted to wander about unescorted. You are, however, permitted to walk along the creek a short way after the tour is over and there is plenty of room above the caverns to explore.

The grounds over the Caverns provide a very large picnic pavilion, children's playground with equipment, a replica of a waterwheel where you can pan for gems and stones, and, of course, the ever present gift shop full of interesting items. During the summer months horse and buggy rides are available.

Tickets to see the Caverns for adults are $6.00 and $2.00 for children under twelve years of age. The tour lasts approximately 45 minutes. Although some snack foods are available in the summer, it is suggested that you pack a picnic lunch.

In October portions of the Caverns are decorated for the "Haunted Caverns" attraction.

FOR MORE INFORMATION

Directions

From U.S. Route 322 take the Middletown/Hummelstown exit and follow signs 1/2 mile to the Caverns. From I-283 take the Vine Street Middletown/Hummelstown exit and follow the road to Hummelstown approximately 2 miles. From the Pennsylvania Turnpike take exit 19, follow I-283 east and exit at the Vine Street Middletown/Hummelstown exit and follow the road to Hummelstown approximately 2 miles. The Caverns are located 1 mile south of Hummelstown.

Lodging

Campgrounds: RT 39 Hershey High Meadows, 1/2 mile from junction of 322 and 422 or 6-1/2 miles from 81 on 39E. 3 miles from the Caverns. Telephone (717) 566-0902. Rt. 743, Hershey Conewago KOA Campground 1590 Hershey Road, Elizabethtown, PA 17022. Telephone (717) 367-1179. Closed during winter months.

Other Accommodations

Because the Caverns are only 3 miles away from the internationally famous Hershey Park, there are over 100 motels, hotels, and travel inns to choose from, with fees and accommodations to fit your needs.

To obtain assistance in finding accommodations you can call the Harrisburg-Hershey Area Tourist Promotion Agency (717) 232-1377.

For Further Information on the Caverns

Indian Echo Caverns P.O. Box 745, Hershey, PA 17033. Telephone: (717) 566-8131.

TENNESSEE

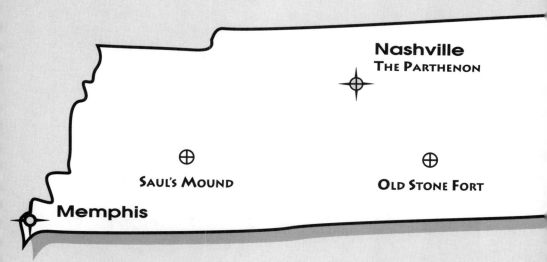

Nashville
THE PARTHENON

SAUL'S MOUND

OLD STONE FORT

Memphis

Parthenon

Frank Joseph

It is not necessary to travel to Greece to see the foremost monument of the Classical World, or, at any rate, its faithful recreation. The architects, Ictinus and Callicrates, who built the Parthenon in 439 B.C., never dreamed it would come to be regarded as the most beautiful structure ever raised by man. The white marble temple is an epitome of the so-called Doric Order, the simplest and most refined of the Hellenic systems of proportion and decoration. Its 25 fluted columns support a low triangular pediment of relief sculpture at the east and west ends depicting the Olympian gods. The interior comprised a walled, rectangular chamber, the cella, which contained one of Western Civilization's greatest treasures, the Athena Parthenos, a 38-foot statue of "Athena the Virgin," after whom the building was named (literally, "Hall of the Virgin"). Made of gold and ivory, the colossus portrayed her standing erect in battle gear holding the diminutive goddess, Nike, in her hand.

Light admitted through an eastern doorway and reflected off the gold ceiling was the single source of illumination for the 101-foot wide by 228-foot long structure. The Parthenon remained intact for 800 years, until Christianity transformed the pagan temple into a 5th century church. The new owners tore down the huge chryselephantine statue of Athena and sold off the pieces of ivory and gold. Later, Islamic Turks trashed its installed Christian paraphernalia, replacing it with their own, including a minaret in the southwest corner. In their battles for Greece with the Venetians, the besieged Moslems used the cella as a powder magazine. During the course of a bombardment, it received a direct hit, destroying the center of the building. Further degradations occurred when an English nobleman bought most of the surviving sculpture from the obliging Turks. Other sales went to French and Danish connoisseurs. Today, the battered, raped Parthenon still stands essentially intact, or, at any rate, its basic structure exists.

The Parthenon.
Photo by Frank Joseph.

Its Nashville counterpart is a recreation of the Parthenon in its original condition, complete with all its restored statuary. One of the few concessions to modernity is the use of concrete; the use of marble on so grand a scale would have been impossibly expensive. The Tennessee replica was completed for the 1897 Centennial Exposition, celebrating Nashville's reputation as "the Athens of the South." The brick, wooden lathe and plaster structure survived the Exposition because of popular demand. By the 1920s, however, it was crumbling badly, so a ten-year restoration project was proposed by the city park board. Reopened to the public in 1931, it attracted more than 10 thousand visitors from 46 states and a dozen foreign countries during its first month. Fifty-six years later, a 20-month renovation up-graded the site to its present level of excellence. But the restorers' crowning achievement was unveiled in May, 1990, with sculptor Alan LeQuire's plaster statue of Athena. At nearly 42 feet tall, it is the largest piece of indoor sculpture in the Western World. The spear she supports with her left arm is 36 feet long. She stands on a 5-foot high marble pedestal decorated with golden panels depicting the immortal Olympians present at Athena's birth. Surrounding her, beyond the cella columns, are casts made of the original Parthenon sculptures of gods and goddesses.

Portals at either end of the temple frame the largest set of matching bronze doors in the world. The Greek originals were so heavy, teams of mules were needed to open and close them. The Nashville Parthenon's doors weigh 721 tons each and are decorated identically as those found in the Athenian naos. Visitors enter at the east side and should not miss the gift shop and three galleries of American art on the lower level. Outstanding is the Parthenon's permanent Cowan Collection, featuring the works of Albert Bierstadt, William Merrit Chase and Winslow Homer.

The Tennessee Parthenon is not a substitute for the original. It is, rather, the other, missing half of the Parthenon experience. Those fortunate enough to visit the Greek Acropolis will feel their perception of this sacred site completed after having seen the temple in a close approximation of its pristine condition.

The Goddess of Self-Mastery, Athena.
Illustration by William Wild.

MYSTICAL SIGNIFICANCE

Although the Nashville Parthenon is a modern replica consciously unconsecrated to any supernal concept, it is nonetheless a
rapidly developing sacred center through the influences of sympathetic magic; this term refers to the transference of spirit power from
its first source to another location resonating with the same, or very
similar, theurgic vibrations as the original. Perhaps the most apparent instance of sympathetic magic generally encountered in the Parthenon is a "kindred presence" experienced here as at the Greek
original. Some ascribe this uncanny respectful feeling to our human
responses to "the gods," and site as an example the hushed tones
into which most tourists fall when they are confronted by the
Athena colossus. Others believe our genetic memory is partially re-
activated in the presence of the Nashville simulacrum, as the image
of the great temple that has epitomized our spiritual instincts for
centuries. Whatever the cause, America's Parthenon is unquestionably a magical place.

It is also interesting that the hill in Nashville's Centennial Park
on which the modern Parthenon stands was a sacred center long before it was constructed. The Tennessee replica occupies a unique position on the 475 mile long series of inter-connected trails and waterways linking the Cumberland and Mississippi Rivers. Known as the
Natchez Trace, it was traveled by Spanish explorers, tribal Indians,
Mound Builders and even more enigmatic culture-bearers over
3,000 years ago. Numerous ancient structures line the Trace, at the
northern terminus of which is located the Parthenon. Synchronous
with Athena's war-like protection of civilization, it was at the hill
which later became the site of her recreated temple that Andrew
Jackson rallied his army for one of the most strategic victories in
American history, at the Battle of New Orleans.

Forty years later, the same hill was the focal point of the Northern Armies in their War for the Preservation of the Union. In 1897, it
was named part of Centennial Park, commemorating the 100th anniversary of Tennessee's constitution. So it would appear that the
Parthenon and its colossus of Athena are but the latest additions in
an ever upwelling sacred center consecrated to the eternal human-
izing forces of civilization.

SUGGESTED RITUAL

Before actually going inside the temple, climb the broad stairs to the upper level and stand in front of the towering bronze portals decorated with mythic themes. There is a feeling of expectation here, as through the 15 tons of doors were about to slowly swing open at the touch of a divine hand.

A walk down the peristyle face across the west entrance and back up the south side completes a ritual circuit of the sacred center and sublimely prepares visitors for the greater inner experience of the Parthenon. Enter at the east end, ascending a short flight of stairs to the cella. Behold the great representation of Athena Parthenos standing magnificently under soft natural light from the 50-foot high ceiling. Even persons not spiritually inclined feel compelled to speak softly, as though in the presence of a great living power. Behind her shield at her left side coils a huge serpent, a multi-symbolic device signifying the Pelasgian, or "Sea People," origins of the Greeks, together with the spirit of regeneration, as implied in the serpent's ability to cast off its old skin for a new one.

In her right hand is Nike, the little goddess of winged victory. The white marble base is surrounded by gold-gilt panels depicting Greeks and Amazons in combat. Other relief sculpture reproduced and surrounding the cella represent battles between men and centaurs and the Titanomachy, a primeval war in which the Olympian gods overthrew the old world rule of the giants. All these portrayed conflicts demonstrate the victory of order and creative intelligence over chaos. The Amazons characterized unbalanced female energy, just as the centaurs stood for baser masculine passions, while the giants were perceived as the forces of brutality. Athena personified the civilized triumph of harmony, self-mastery and reason. Standing before her much larger-than-life image, we realize she is the potential for triumph within ourselves. With her own hand she literally offers us victory over all our imperfections which cause us unhappiness.

Walking around the Athena Parthenos to the western section behind the cella, visitors will find casts of original sculpted reliefs from the Greek Parthenon representing the birth of Athena in the company of all the Olympian gods, and her contest with Poseidon, the sea-god, for possession of Athens. This contest signifies the triumph of the conscious mind over subconscious chaos. Authentic Hellenic vases, executed in all the colorful grace, adroit liveliness and skill for which they are prized, are also on display. Re-enter the cella to pay final homage to Athena, then descend to the lower level and enjoy the art galleries. Before leaving the site, complete another circuit around the outside of the temple beginning once again in the east, walking west along the south face, across the western entrance, then along the north end to the east.

FOR MORE INFORMATION

Directions

Centennial Park is located 5 minutes from downtown Nashville, at Charlotte Avenue and 440. For further information, contact The Parthenon (Curator), Centennial Park Office, Nashville, TN 37201. Telephone (615) 259-6358.

Accommodations

Motel-6, 311 West Trinity Lane, Nashville, TN 37207. Telephone, (615) 227-9696. Fifteen minute drive south to the Parthenon. $25.95 for single. From I-24 West and I-65 North, take Exit 87B, Trinity Lane. From I-24 East and I-65 South, take Exit 87B to stop sign, turn left, go to traffic signal, turn right at top of hill.

Red Roof Inn, 110 Northgate Drive, Goodlettsville, TN 37072. Telephone (615) 859-2537. I-65 at Long Hollow Pike Exit 97. Twenty-five minute drive south to the Parthenon. $35.95 per single.

Camping at KOA, 2626 Music Valley Drive, Nashville, TN 37214. Telephone (800) 8336995. Briley Parkway Exit 12 or 2B. Go 1-1/2 miles to Music Valley Drive. Thirty-five minute drive south to the Parthenon. $16.95 per single tent site, two adults.

Bibliography

Bowra, C. M. *Classical Greece*. New York: Time-Life Books, 1969.

Daniel, Glyn and Thomas, Y. *Encyclopaedia of Archaeology*. New York: Crowell Company, 1977.

MacKendrick, Paul. *The Greek Stones*. New York: St. Martin's Press, 1962.

Old Stone Fort

Frank Joseph

High on a remote and deeply wooded bluff, overlooking two swiftly flowing rivers, an unknown people arrived to create a sacred center that would last for the next 2000 years. While Rome ruled the other side of the world, they erected an enclosure more than a mile long, skillfully raising a line of stone walls along the edge of the steepest slopes. The lofty ramparts which surrounded 40 acres of hallowed ground had been set aside strictly for ceremonial purposes. During the next 4 centuries, the walls were built, repaired and reconstructed, as unguessed thousands of celebrants conducted their lost rites of empowerment within the holy clearing. Then, just as suddenly as they appeared, the inhabitants abandoned their ritual precinct in the early years of the 5th century A.D. and vanished into North America's pre-Columbian past. The reason for their abrupt departure remains as mysterious as their identity.

When early white settlers stumbled upon the overgrown site in the late 18th century, they presumed it originally constituted a military complex; hence its erroneous name, Old Stone Fort. One archaeologist assigned the Fort's construction to the Middle Woodland Tradition, a period in which highly organized societies flourished throughout the Ohio Valley and down through Tennessee. They discovered its true function as a religious center.

The enclosure is approached through a complex arrangement of walls, mounds, ditches and embankments. A pair of conical mounds adjoining the walls stands on either side of the entrance. Just beyond lay an eight foot deep ditch, giving the site a roughly rectangular outline. Little of the original configuration remains. The prodigious ditch, once as much as 3/4 of a mile long, is now a 4-foot dip, but its position on the site's high ground affords the best panorama of the sacred clearing. It was formerly entirely surrounded by water, a condition afforded by the ditch connecting the Big and Little Duck Rivers.

Old Stone Fort, aerial view of the Sacred Precinct.
Photo courtesy of Ward Weems, Old Stone Fort Museum, TN

The average height of Old Stone Fort's walls is 4 feet. They were constructed in an unusual manner. Stones were piled in parallel rows forming a trench floored in between with small shale slabs, then filled in with rubble. The ramparts were finally covered with earth to make a smooth cap. They begin where the cliff ridges end, presenting the appearance of having grown from the bluff itself.

The Big and Little Duck Rivers run on either side of the sacred site, dropping one hundred feet to create a dramatic waterfall with numerous deep pools at the northwest over-look. A small but important and informative museum, imaginatively constructed in a building style of the ancient architects who built Old Stone Fort, stands a few paces before the original entrance to the enclosure. Wonderful views of the Big Duck River are available from the museum roof.

MYSTICAL SIGNIFICANCE

The official guidebook to Old Stone Fort says, "the site was probably a special and mystical place even before the enclosure was built. Its location in the forks of a river may have given it special significance. The cliffs and the waterfalls were certainly as remarkable as they are now." The eastern walls of the site run above the banks of the Little Duck River, stopping parallel just before a small island, at which the rampart suddenly turns due west. Here the sacred center demonstrates its response to the hallowed landscape. The little island in the stream was a consecrated spot which compelled the construction of the walls to execute the turn. At this point, as perhaps no other part of the enclosure, the site reveals mystical interdependence on the special environment.

The park guidebook also mentions the "processions which may have passed through the entrance alley-way and the ritual significance the entrance-way may have had as you passed from the outside world to the sacred ground enclosed beyond." Rites associated with the Sun were probably carried out at Old Stone Fort, because "the ritual significance of the entrance way" was determined by archaeo-astromomers in 1989, when they discovered that it was oriented to sunrise of the winter solstice. Examination of the walls showed that their ridges had been "worn down from traffic on top," where massed processions took place over hundreds of years.

Although raised by the same peoples who built a similar structure at Ohio's Fort Ancient, the two sites differ markedly, in that the Tennessee enclosure is an open clearing of land, and, in effect, an island. Another telling comparison lies in the apparent beginning of the ramparts just above Big Duck Falls, continuing upstream to the entrance complex, a feature paralleling the wall's relationship to the island in the Little Duck River discussed above. The falls may have represented the voice of the natural *genius loci*. The place is certainly overflowing with prehistoric mystery. Aside from the implications of the winter solstice sunrise commemorated by the ancient people, nothing of their mysticism, practiced for 16 generations at the Old Stone Fort, is known.

Meditation area, the modern museum roof.
Photo by Frank Joseph.

SUGGESTED RITUAL

The proper introduction to Old Stone Fort begins at the museum and visitor center, which features dioramas of the site during its florescence and artifacts recovered through excavations in the area. The roof of the museum is an unusually ideal spot for effective meditation. Overlooking the Big Duck River, the vibrant natural environment is wonderfully conducive to conjuring the proper frame of mind.

Following the plainly marked trails, visitors skirt the entire enclosure with ease, beginning at the northeast and walking along the walls through the surrounding woods. Climbing on the fragile earth-works themselves is forbidden. Sometimes the walls seem to disappear and reemerge from the overgrown cliff face, softly blurring the uncertain boundaries between man and nature. The visitor with a pure heart and a free mind should listen for the energy-echoes of the Ancient Ones, where the naturally magic ground has been additionally charged by four centuries of ritual activity.

Where the walls running parallel to the Little Duck River turn away to the west, a break in the enclosure may be taken into the far end of the ritual precinct.

Resuming the trail, follow the hallowed walls along to the Big Duck River. Soon the voice of the falls is heard. The power of their perpetual call through the woods increases with every footstep. Past a large old tree, the visitor walks to a slight rise for a commanding panorama of the whole enclosure. The location is a power point, scene of the original, complex entrance oriented to the winter solstice sunrise. Twin mounds, like the positive and negative terminals of a psychic battery, stand nearby to the northwest, where the site gives itself up to the worthy visitor—not so much in words or even visual imagery, as in its sensation of connectedness to the higher truth of spiritual reality.

FOR MORE INFORMATION

Directions

From Nashville, south on I-24. Exit 55 west. Follow signs to Old Stone Fort. For further information, contact Old Stone Fort Archaeological Park, Route 7, Box 7400, Manchester, TN 37355. Telephone, (615) 728-0751.

Accommodations

Motel-6, 114 Chaffin Place, Murfreesboro, TN 37129. Telephone, (615) 890-8524. From eastbound I-24, take Exit 78B, Tennessee 96 East to first right. From I-24 westbound, take Exit 78, Tennessee 96. Turn right one block, then right again to motel. Thirty-five minute drive south to Old Stone Fort. $24.95 per single.

Best Western Old Fort Motor Inn, US 41 & I-24, Exit 114, Manchester, TN 37355. Telephone, (615) 728-9720. Five minutes drive to Old Stone Fort. $28 to $38 per single.

Ideal camping in the state park adjacent to Old Stone Fort itself. All facilities. Signs at entrance to Old Stone Fort Archaeological Park. Telephone, (615) 728-0751. $11 per tent site, two adults.

Bibliography

Old Stone Fort State Archaeological Park interpretive Path Guide, Manchester, Tennessee, 1983.

Kopper, Philip. *North American Indians*. Washington, D.C.: Smithsonian Books, 1986.

Saul's Mound

Frank Joseph

Among the largest, most unusual and dramatic of North America's ancient cities, Tennessee's Pinson Mounds complex is also part of the continent's great, human mystery. The grandest ceremonial center of the Middle Woodland Period, it was constructed by an unknown race around 1 A.D. Thirty mounds, some of enormous dimensions, dominated 1,162 square acres of consecrated ground that drew pilgrims from as far away as Florida and Louisiana.

The area was first surveyed in 1820 by Joel Pinson, after whom the site was named, but no one knows what the site was called in the days of its glory. A religious capital without a resident population, it featured only a few burials. Careful excavations revealed no signs of war or pestilence, social unrest or natural disasters. Yet, after 400 years of construction and ceremonial life, Pinson Mounds was suddenly abandoned, its people lost to the land's unknown past. But they left behind abundant evidence of their genius for large-scale ritualized building.

A single, long path leads past a low, egg-shaped mound, across a broad expanse of green park to the colossus of Ancient Tennessee. Saul's Mound is not only the tallest earth-work in eastern North America, it is one of the most singularly impressive structures from native antiquity. At 72 feet in height, it is second only to Illinois' Cahokia. The perfectly proportioned dome of clay and soil required an estimated 37,200,000 basket-loads of earth heaped up by about a thousand workers pulling 10-hour shifts for nearly three years. The impact for the modern observer beholding it for the first time is generated not only by its massive bulk, but by the monstrously tall oak trees growing up from its sides, which magnify the mound's height and massiveness. They tower like gargantuan pillars, lending Saul's Mound the aspect of a titan's crown.

The path leads up to and around the south end, where a wooden flight of stairs ascends to a viewing platform at the Summit.

From there, visitors may best appreciate the greatness of the Mound Builders' achievement. Trails spread in several directions from the broad base of the structure, but the preferable pathway includes a fifteen minute walk across lovely countryside to the Eastern Citadel. It comprises a squarish, truncated, flat-topped pyramid, about thirty feet across and twelve feet high, encircled by a ruined embankment. Nature trails lead through a magical, dark forest to a boardwalk and an over-look where one may rest while watching the Forked Deer River glide by. It was undoubtedly along this very water-way that the Ancient Ones came to their sacred complex. The boardwalk ends at a path with a sign pointing to the "Duck's Nest," an unusual depression in a secluded part of the woods atop a slight rise. About fifteen feet in diameter and perhaps four feet deep, it was used for bonfires of great heat.

Saul's Mound.
Illustration by William Wild.

The trail returning in the direction of Saul's Mound passes another ovoid structure, then back toward the visitor's center. One may either drive or walk to the Western Mound Group, which differs markedly from the other features at Pinson. The path just off the road approaches a beautiful, small lake through a pleasantly wooded area to yet one more egg-shaped structure containing a single burial, that of a middle aged man, probably one of the site's most prominent personages in life. Surrounding his privileged grave lies a horseshoe shape formed of clay and the cremated remains of at least several human beings. A few paces away are the unique twin mounds—two earth-works joined at one end, another burial complex of multiple graves and ritually constructed of different-colored layers of clay: red, yellow and black. Not far from this little necropolis stands Ozier Mound, a 32-foot tall, truncated pyramid with a sloping entrance ramp leading up its east side, which is oriented to the spring solstice sunrise. Dated to around 100 A.D., it is the oldest known structure of its kind in North America and makes a suitably memorable climax to any visit.

MYSTICAL SIGNIFICANCE

Although the structures at Pinson Mounds offer a great deal of variety in shape, size and configuration, emphasis throughout the site is most likely one of regeneration, rebirth, as suggested by the several egg-configured earth-works and the Ozier pyramid's alignment to the vernal solstice sunrise. Even the dominating Saul's Mound is more ovoid than perfectly circular, and is, moreover, bounded on four sides by a quartet of much smaller structures equidistant from its center. These positions might signify the Four Cardinal Directions, thereby defining the larger structure as an axis mundi, or Navel of the World, the midpoint of Creation, the Womb of the Cosmos, from which all life is eternally reborn.

SUGGESTED RITUAL

Visitors to the site are immediately put into the proper frame of mind by the large mound replica. Walking through it is a marvelous introduction to the ancient Otherworld and serves as a passable barrier to the sacred center beyond. One's first view of the immense Saul's Mound framed by the short tunnel-like south exit makes a dramatic beginning for the inner journey here. Although the huge oak trees growing up from its flanks were not intended by its builders, they make the structure even more impressive, perhaps weirdly so, as though a sacred work of man had been blessed with an oaken crown by the God of Nature. The special atmosphere of Saul's

Mound intensifies the closer one draws near it. Walking up to its foot and around to the south stairway, visitors climb to the top, where the over-look platform affords abundant space for ritual activity.

Facing north, throw a small pinch of either tobacco or sage in that direction and thank the *genius loci* for allowing you to visit this sacred center. Repeat the process three times more, facing east, south and north. Then stand at the center of the platform and imagine the focused earth-energy of Saul's Mound rising from underneath its base, accumulating in the massive dome of sculpted soil beneath you, finally streaming through the soles of your feet, up your backbone, enlivening the spine's seven points of light, out the top of your skull and into the vastness of the sky overhead. An experience atop the mound can purge spiritual and psychological impurities. At the very least, it re-establishes our own personal link between the cosmic forces of earth and sky ("As Above, so Below"), a connection required by anyone seeking the higher levels of existence.

From Saul's Mound, follow the park signs to the Eastern Citadel. Its segmented, encircling embankment surrounds another sacred site peacefully ideal for short meditation. Proceed to walk around the flat-topped pyramid once, starting from the south east corner, going from west to north, back to east, in a ritual reenactment of departure from the physical world. Proceed to Mound 30, the bird effigy earth-work symbolizing the soul in flight.

Follow the nature trail through the woods to the boardwalk leading to the Forked Deer River over-look. This forest passage to the prehistoric waterway represents the soul's journey through death to the River of Oblivion in the Otherworld each of us has taken and shall take again. Hardly the ultimately dreadful experience we anticipated, it is nothing more than a dark, comforting, pleasant journey into a gently altered state of consciousness.

The boardwalk leads out of the forest of death to the so-called Duck's Nest, the fire-pit, from which the spark of physical existence was re-lit and the soul purged of its past in another opportunity for a more enlightened life. Offer a single pinch of sage or tobacco, meanwhile thanking the fire-spirit for allowing you to visit. Step into the pit and envision its pure flame enveloping you in its Phoenix-fire to scourge away all those accumulated imperfections that drag at one's being.

From the Duck's Nest, walk north past an egg-shaped structure (Number 17) to the east. Circumambulate Saul's Mound once more in an easterly direction, signifying the purified soul's return to the material world. The Western Mound Group forms a separate experience. Follow the designated path passed the small lake to the burial mounds, beyond to the impressive Ozier pyramid. Walk its perimeter once in a westward direction before climbing the sunrise-oriented ramp to the summit. Offer a pinch of sage or tobacco or a small water libation toward the east, thanking the *genus loci* for allowing the visit. Meditation at the top may result in past-life flashbacks or even glimpses of the elusive Akashic Records, most often seen as rapidly changed color slide photographs projected on a large screen. More usually, wordless emotions of peace and reassurance may be had from the accommodating spirit of the Ozier pyramid. Descend the ramp and follow the trail passed the burial mounds to the lake and the road out of the park.

FOR MORE INFORMATION

Directions
From I-40, exit 45 south to Pinson Mounds. For further information, contact Pinson Mounds State Archaeological Area; Ozier Road, Route 1, Box 316, Pinson, TN 38366. Telephone, (901) 988-5614. Open year-round, 8:30 a.m. to 5:00 p.m.; Sundays, 1:00 p.m. to 5:00 p.m.

Accommodations
Best Western Executive Inn, 2295 North Highland Avenue, Jackson, TN 38305. Telephone, (901) 668-1145. Exit 82A south off I-40 one block. Twenty minute drive south to Pinson Mounds. $33 to $43 for single.

Camping at Parkers Crossroads KOA, Route 1, Box 62, Yuma, TN 38390. Telephone, (901) 968-9551. I-40 exit 108 (Parkers Crossroads). North 1 mile on TN 22. One tent site, two adults, $12.

Bibliography
Harner, M. *The Way of the Shaman*. New York: Harper and Row, 1980.

Lankford, George E. *Native American Legends*, Milwaukee: Hughes-Brailey Publications, 1989.

Mitchell, John. *The Earth Spirit*, London: Thames and Hudson, 1975.

TEXAS

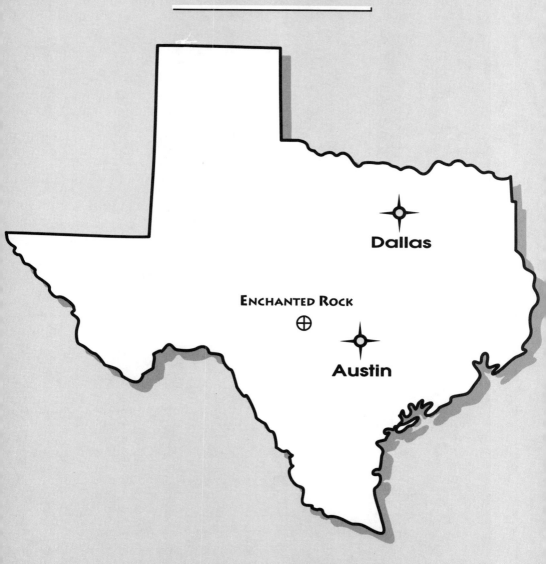

Dallas

Enchanted Rock

Austin

Enchanted Rock

Kathleen L. Boehme

There is deep in the heart chakra of Texas a living, breathing, pink granite entity called Enchanted Rock. This magical 500-foot granite dome batholith is millions of years old and covers 640 acres. A batholith is a large body of fire-produced rock which crystallized at a considerable depth below the earth's surface and is bounded by irregular cross-cutting surfaces or fault planes. Enchanted Rock is among the oldest exposed rock in North America. In the Native American language the name given to Enchanted Rock means holy mountain or "island mountain." For over 10,000 years Native Americans drew their spiritual and physical life from this island mountain. The Kiowa, Apache and Comanche spoke of the presence of the holy mountain spirits who protected and imbued the Rock with life.

It was created by molten fire and energy millions of years ago and was catapulted from the depth of the inner earth by a force too powerful for most men to comprehend. It carried the sacred energies of the inner earth which, as it surfaced, exploded into every cell of its being.

Enchanted Rock State Natural Area is located 18 miles north of Fredericksburg on RM 965, in the heart of Texas hill country. The park's landscape is dominated by Enchanted Rock, but four other massive, dome-shaped hills of pink granite adjoin it: Little Rock, Freshman Mountain, Turkey Peak and Buzzard's Roost. The park includes 1,640 acres and rests in a geological region known as the Llano Uplift.

Hiking and rock climbing are the most popular recreational activities. Rappeling and free climbing are the only climbing methods allowed in the park. Both skilled climber and novice find the satisfaction of a challenge and the accomplishment of the climb. The rock has been friendly to its climbers; no accidents have been reported.

Enchanted Rock State Natural Area.
Illustration courtesy of Ira Kennedy,
Enchanted Rock State Natural Area, Fredericksburg, TX.

Although Captain Henry S. Brown, on a military expedition in 1829, was attributed as the discoverer of Enchanted Rock, there were many previous inhabitants. Archaeologists have found evidence of prehistoric Indian inhabitants, bands of hunters and gatherers, as early as 9,000 B.C. in what is termed the Paleo-Indian Period. The most intensively occupied archaeological sites occur either near Sandy or Walnut Springs Creeks. These springs flow continuously even during dry seasons of the year. Findings of arrowheads, dart points, spearheads, knives, pottery and grinding stones indicate their occupation of Enchanted Rock from prehistoric times through the 1700s. Until the mid-1800s the area was inhabited mostly by Comanche, Apaches and Tonkawa. The Tonkawa most likely were the descendants of the hunter-gatherers of Enchanted Rock since the Comanche and Apaches had moved into the region in the 1600-1700s and were not native to the area. In the 1700s the area around the Rock experienced the coming of the Spanish Explorers and missionaries and later in 1846 the colonization by German immigrants. Although most of the native Americans are gone from Texas, a few remain to tell the tale of the gathering of the tribes of the Comanche, the Kiowa, the Apache, the Delaware, the Shawnee and others and how they spoke to one another in sign language of the Holy Mountain and how they held it in awe and reverence.

Legend says that the spirit guardians of the Rock move about freely at night. Legend also says that the Indians feared the rock because of its groans in the night and that when the moon was full, it sparkled and glistened. (Scientists have explained that it glistens because of the many small rock pools that have caught water and that the strange noises come from the rock contracting in the cool night air having expanded on a hot day.) Artifacts found there indicate that fear of the Rock was not true in all instances, and that many of these were stories passed down to modern Native Americans of the region. Many Indians used the height of the Rock for a rallying point and for ritual. Vision Quest was at the heart of the Comanches' culture. From the summit of the holy mountain they sought the guidance of the Great Spirit. To this day, modern man, perhaps unconsciously, pursues this same quest upon Enchanted Rock.

People through the centuries have experienced the sacredness of the rock. Indians, missionaries, explorers and miners found it a place of refuge and peace. In more recent times, various church services have been held on the summit of the rock. In the early 1900s, the Reverend Dan More was noted for his services there. More recently, on Sunday, August 16, 1987, the Day of the Harmonic Convergence, Native Americans of the region returned to the Holy Mountain for prayer and ritual as well as thousands of other pilgrims who had been directed there by their own inner prompting. The Harmonic Convergence was a day for all men of all races to "come together" in spirit to pray for and demonstrate world harmony. An approximate 550 million people all over the world joined together in a day of global spiritual unity to focus upon peace. Ancient and modern cultures blended in harmony in their plea for peace. Those who speak of lay lines, specific lines of energy that join places on the planet, have said that Enchanted Rock is joined to Ayers Rock in Australia and Tor Hill in England. The Native Americans on Enchanted Rock were joining in spirit with the Aborigines of Ayers Rock as well as with all other cultures on the planet. Native Americans in Arizona, New Mexico, Montana and other states partcipated in peace ceremonies on August 16. A magnificent medicine wheel made of stones from Enchanted Rock was left on the summit for all who ventured upon the Rock that day, reminding modern man of its ancient heritage and uniting all in the peace and harmony of Enchanted Rock itself.

Enchanted Rock.
Photo by Kathleen L. Boehme.

The way up to the summit is rocky and challenging but filled with interesting plant and animal life as well as unusual formations of rocks and boulders. Squirrels, armadillos, rabbits, raccoons, lizards and white-tailed deer are often spotted on the trail. From the top of the Rock the climber experiences a panoramic view of the hill country, the valleys and the plains. The peace, fulfillment, fresh air, and breathtaking view at the top make the effort of the climb well worthwhile and one experiences a harmony with all nature. You can contemplate the peace of the green hills below or the beauty of the sky above. Sunrises and sunsets are particularly uplifting and inspirational from the top of the mountain.

Enchanted Rock Cave, one of the largest known granite caves, presents you with a different perspective of this rock entity in that you move within it. Smaller structures called A-tent caves are found in one area near the top of the rock and add a beauty and mystery of their own. There is a legend that massive caverns are hidden beneath the rock and such a legend entices us to pursue in our imaginations the many mysteries the rock holds.

The plant life of the Rock proclaims its uniqueness and its sacredness. Over 500 different species grow here, from colorful lichens on the rock surface to tall trees such as elms, pecans, hickories and oaks along the creeks. Typical plants include Texas persimmons, prickly pear, agarita and mesquite. Both desert and wetland species abound because there is both shade and southern exposure. Water that's caught in the boulders and cracks supports species you will not find a mile from the park. A tropical fern, *Blechnum Occidentale*, is found only at Enchanted Rock and isolated areas in tropical Florida in the United States. Two other plants make their home only in the granite region of Central Texas. These are the basin bellflower and the rock quillwort produced in the vernal pools. The vernal pools, depressions that gather rainwater and soil, produce the bellflower, lichens and rare fairy shrimp. The early Native Americans, in tune with nature as they gathered the plants of the Rock for their food and medicine, recognized this yield to be a gift of the Great Spirit through the Rock.

Now, in addition to the legendary spirit guardians of Enchanted Rock, park rangers take the role of protectors of the Holy Mountain. The Parks Department purchased Enchanted Rock from the Nature Conservancy group in 1978. The Park Superintendent in 1985, Warren Watson, stated, "Now Enchanted Rock is a living museum with both historical and natural attractions. One of my goals is to educate the public into an attitude about Enchanted Rock State Natural Area that's different from any other state park—to develop a special reverence for this place." All who visit Enchanted Rock and the park will affirm that this area still abounds with the reverence of the native American for this gift of the Great Spirit and that reverence and appreciation for nature and all life flows into every fiber of their beings and is carried with them back into their homes.

The enhancement and expansion of the energies of the individual can be accelerated by communion (both physical and mental) with such an entity as Enchanted Rock. The ancients knew this; that is why they called it "sacred." This communion can take place, through awareness, at any time, and is encouraged for the benefit of all. To actually come in physical contact with the rock—touching, embracing, climbing—puts one in touch with the powerful spiritual energies the rock emits and these energies can be transmuted through awareness to the healing of self and of the earth.

FOR MORE INFORMATION

Enchanted Rock State Nature Area is open year round. Accommodations include tent sites and facilities for overnight camping such as tent pads, picnic tables, nearby water faucets and restrooms with showers. There are three remote separate areas of primitive campsites for adventuresome backpackers along the trail. For day visitors there are picnic tables, a playground and rest rooms. A pavilion is available for large group functions or picnics. A 4-mile hiking trail winds around the granite formations and a short, steep trail leads to the top of the Rock. Only foot traffic is allowed. Rock Climbers and rappelers must check in at headquarters for climbing rules and route maps. The park hours are from 8:00 a.m. to 10:00 p.m; park office hours are from 8:00 a.m. to 5:00 p.m. Admission is $2 per car. There is an additional $6 for overnight camping and an additional $4 for primitive campsites. Pavilion use (by reservation only) is $12 for 1 to 26 people and $24 for 27 to 175 people. Call (915) 247-3903 for camping reservations no more than three months in advance. Visitors should make reservations at least one month in advance at any time of the year. For information write Park Superintendent, Enchanted Rock State Natural Area, Route 4, Box 170, Fredericksburg, TX 78624.

Bibliography

Allen, Nelson. *San Antonio Express-News.* "Enchanted Rock: Hill Country Area Captures Imagination." July 15, 1989.

Fredericksburg Standard Newspaper. "Natural Wonder Draws Eager Climbers," August 18, 1982.

Kennedy, Ira. "Enchanted Rock: Holy Ground to the First Americans." *Texas Highways,* January 1985, pp. 22-33.

Texas Parks and Wildlife Department (Texas Parks and Wildlife Maqazine). *Enchanted Rock, State Natural Area.* PWD-BR-4506-1 19-6190.

UTAH

Salt Lake City

Canyonlands

Zion National Park

Hovenweep

Zion National Park

L. Christine Hayes

From the book, *Zion National Park: Towers of Stone*, by J. L. Crawford, the naming of the park was bestowed in an enlightened moment by a Mormon settler named Isaac Behunin: "One evening while sitting on his front porch in the lingering twilight, he gazed across the vast expanse of he canyon. He was so moved by its gradeur that it inspired him to remember a passage in the Bible (Isaiah 2:2), which mentions a place called Zion, found 'in the top of the mountains,' where 'the Lord's house shall be established.' Isaac felt that he had discovered such a place, and from that moment on, he called it Zion."

This National Park in southwestern Utah contains high cliffs, mesas, and deep canyons of extraordinary beauty. The major portion of the park was established in 1919, with an additional inclusion in 1956. In all, it occupies an area of 229 square miles.

Since Utah is largely a Mormon (Church of Latter Day Saints) state, the unique geological features of the park are named after the historical-religious beliefs of the Latter Day Saints. Some of these sites include: The East Temple, Towers of the Virgin, Temple of Sinawava, Mount Moroni, Angels Landing, Mountain of the Sun, The Beehives, The Three Patriarchs, and The Great White Throne (an awe-inspiring visage of stone rising 2,394 feet above the canyon floor). Winding through the impressive vistas of the park is the Virgin River.

Zion is abundant in wildlife, harboring and nurturing such animals as mountain lions, mule deer, and more than 150 species of birds including hawks and eagles. Although a semi-arid region, there are broad-leaved trees and wild flowers growing near the river.

The Anasazi (a Navaho word meaning "old people") Indians once inhabited this land, living in small villages containing large circular, semisubterranean "pit houses." It would seem that they aban-

doned the Zion region by 1200 A.D., somewhat earlier than did their
brethren in other areas of the Southwest. It is believed that they
eventually became part of the ancestors of the Hopi Indians.

Zion National Park.
Courtesy of the National Park Service.

MYSTICAL SIGNIFICANCE

The area of Zion National Park was and continues to be held sacred by Native Americans. When visiting Zion years ago, I was told of the distress Native Americans of the region feel in seeing so many people camping in the park. To them, it is a sacred temple, a place to pray, meditate, and talk to the gods and ancestors. But it is not, in their estimation, a place in which to play, eat and sleep, anymore than we would wish to see people camping in the Cathedral of St. John the Divine.

But the park is sacred not only to Native Americans. I have seen cities of inter-dimensional forms residing within the natural crystalline towers of the park. Reverence is the key of entry to the Temple Zion. Enter it as you would a church. You are most definitely not only on sacred ground, but *within* a Holy House.

A message was channeled by this author on May 30th, 1990. In this message, the following information on the park was given:

"From the summits of Earth's majesty, sacred places on high, doth the energy of the Light Tower's (holy entities of planetary consciousness once incarnate as leaders on Earth) bonding to this orb abide. As these mounts of matter shed their hulls, they become Knights ridding the steeliness of their armor for the robes of quest. They shine forth the rays of the Light Towers, calling them to the bosom once again, being caught upon the winds, like birds of flight. Numbering among these dwelling places of SHEKHINAH are Mt. Sinai (Sinai), Mt. Tabor (Israel), Ayers Rock (Australia), the man-made, star-designed Pyramid of Giza (Egypt), and also Tor Hill (Glastonbury, England), whose etheric body dwarfs the 'hill' of matter in which the greater form resides."

"As these energies are released . . . so they penetrate the *Door of Zion*, which is the Perfected Nation, the Absolute Realm that suffers no bondage to those who behold its golden chains, links to the Kingdom within."

"In the world of matter, this Door is to be found most prominently in the sacred land of Zion National Park, in Utah. This place between land and (etheric) sea contains the greatest aggregation of consciousness for the New World matrix."

"She is a silent angel, whose trumpet gleams in the moonlight, awaiting a rising sun. She walks unshod among men, her face hidden from them. No pilgrimages are made to her granite tresses, no sepulchers of anointing are raised within her folded wings. Yet her

horn will surely issue a clarion call with the dawning of a Day soon
to rise above the shoulders of the world. Only those who Guardian
her breaches know the kindling flame within. It is within her body
that the Light Towers survive their antiquity to become vigorous
servants whispering through the cacophony of endless dream,
those seed-thoughts of new visions for the Children of Zion."

The meaning of this message is that there is that there is a con-
ductive energy which is contained in certain sacred high places,
such as Mt. Sinai, and even the man-made Pyramid of Giza. This
special energy penetrates the "Door of Zion," which is both a spiritual state and a physical place. The place is that of Zion National
Park, which is called a "silent angel," for it is not a well-known spiritual center as is Mt. Shasta (California) or Sedona (Arizona).

Zion National Park is a collection of spiritual energy containing holy tones or signals for future spirit-matter creation. Upon the
threshold of the "New World," we will need to be brought into unison with other dimensions of reality that bridge our own, connecting us to Spirit. The crystalline structure in Zion contains the
engrams or programs for this evolution of our realm into a greater
absorption of Spirit Being. Divine commands were imprinted in nature's hand long before we descended as god-men/women into the
Eden consciousness to begin our plight as star-born beggars at the
Temple gates. Zion is the Last and the First of these Temple gates. It
is the last of the Old World and the first of the New.

SUGGESTED RITUAL

Zion National Park is a dimension all its own. Once entering
this Temple-World, the voyager is enveloped in the etheric might of
its ramparts, shining like sails of granite through a sea of sun and
color. The contrasting of height and depth, of dark and light is per-
sonalized more in Zion than it is in most canyons. There is a quality
of Shang-ri-la in its sheath of warmth that is not only peaceful but
enduring. Much like a cathedral, the walls of the canyon both shelter
and inspire. They are close and abiding, like stone angels reverent in
the presence of the indwelling spirit. It has been said by those who
live near the park and often pray within, that doors are seen to open
and close high upon these summit walls. In the wake of the Latter
Day Saint's angel Moroni, tablets of gold have been viewed within
suddenly appearing caches. Both angels and demons have material-

ized to believers within this Temple, yet the divine images always prevail.

Allow yourself time alone in a location or locations of your choosing within the canyon. All energy in Zion is raised up, spiraling into the sky-world. Lift your mind and heart in this direction and see yourself soaring as an eagle, your wings spread in plumes of perfect balance. Experience the joy of rising into the winds above the land and then slowly descending into the clear waters of the Virgin River. You are every place and no place. You have become the still point within that is pure Light.

If you are in a climbing mood, ascend some of the more reachable precipices. There is an ancient kiva (built for sacred rituals of the Anasazi) on the edge of one of the walls. Position yourself above the floor of the canyons and feel the massive power of crystal-stone beneath you. Summon the angelic beings to grace you with their presence and remain humble in their sight, for they are the anchors of our souls in the waters of the divine. The angels of Zion National Park are hosts for the coming Age—preparators for the creations of the New Elohim, which is the Human Race. This torch has been passed to us by the Elohim of Old. Now we are to begin the construction of the New Earth Temples. In communion with the Angels of Zion, you may ask for your personal charge as a "New Elohim."

FOR MORE INFORMATION

Directions
Take Interstate 15 from St. George, Utah to Hwy 9, which will take you through the small towns of Hurricane and Virgin, on into Zion National Park.

Lodging
Zion Lodge contains motel units, cabins, a restaurant, snack bar, and gift shop. for information on accommodations, write: Utah Parks Division, TW Recreational Services, Inc., 451 North Main Street, Cedar City, UT 84720; or call (801) 586-7696. Advance reservations are recommended. There are also campgrounds open on a first come, first served basis, one of which is open all year round. A fee is charged. Both have fire grates, picnic tables, water, restrooms, and a sanitary disposal station for trailers. There are no utility hookups or showers. Some sites are set aside for the handicapped. Group

campsites are available by reservation for organized groups of 8 to 40 people.

Other suggested accommodations: Springdale, Mt. Carmel, and the larger towns of Hurricane, St. George, Cedar City, and Kanab have motels, restaurants, service stations, and grocery stores. A private campground in Springdale has full utility hook-ups and hot showers.

Bibliography

Crawford, J. L. *Zion National Park—Towers of Stone*, p. 46, published by Sequoia Communications. This book can be purchased from the Zion Natural History Association, Zion National park, Springdale, UT 84767. To order by phone: 1-800-635-3959 (credit cards only), price $6.95. Add $3.00 for shipping and handling.

"Zion National Park," *Encyclopedia Britannica*, Ready Reference, Vol. 112, p. 922.

New Work Cycles of Celebration Almanac & Calendar Journal—1990, published by New World Celebrations, P.O. Box 6054, Charlotte, NC 28207.

Temple Doors, issue #2–90, published by the Star of Isis Foundation, P.O. Box 4872, San Antonio, TX 78285. Send $3.30 for introductory material and back issues listing, payable to L. Christine Hayes.

Zion National Park map, published by the National Park Service in Utah.

Hovenweep

Florence L. McClain

Hovenweep (Deserted Valley) is a Ute name given to six groups of ruins in southeastern Utah and southwestern Colorado. Square Tower, Horseshoe, Holly, Hackberry, Cutthroat Castle, and Cajon are unique in this land of the unusual.

Long, lonely canyons cut through almost barren mesas, offer little promise of an environment compatible with human life. But, each canyon guards a Secret—a life supporting spring of water. Surrounding the approaches to these springs, majestic stone towers cling to the canyon rims, or rise from the tops of solitary boulders, over mounds of brush-covered rubble which were once pueblos, giving silent testimony that human beings once lived and thrived in this harsh land.

The builders of Hovenweep were bold and innovative, adapting their designs to the peculiarities of the terrain. That they were intelligent and observant is evidenced by reservoirs and check dams built on the mesas above the springs, which caught the runoff from the sparse rainfall and allowed it to percolate through the strata, enhancing the flow of the springs. They terraced the lower areas of the canyons and raised crops of beans, squash, and corn.

The Monument headquarters is located at Square Tower Group. Here, as at the other ruin groups, self-guided trails meander up and down the canyons to allow one to examine these architectural wonders. Whether it is Hovenweep Castle or Stronghold House at the Square Tower Group, or Tilted Tower at Holly, or Cutthroat Castle, or any of the other strange and beautiful ruins, one can only respect and marvel at the ingenuity and skill of the craftsmen. (Actually, many archeologists and anthropologists say that women were the builders of the Southwest.)

As harsh and stark as the land appears at first sight, there is great beauty in the settings. A blue, blue sky serves as a fitting background for the golden-red sandstone. Patches of bright green pinpoint springs and seeps. And, on the eastern horizon, seeming an appropriate memorial to the ancient peoples who once labored here, is the reclining figure of a man: Ute Mountain, commonly called "The Sleeping Ute."

Hovenweep Boulder House.
Photo by Florence L. McClain.

MYSTICAL SIGNIFICANCE

Whether for mystical or purely practical reasons, or a combination of the two, the people of Hovenweep were observers of the skies.

At Square Tower Group, Hovenweep Castle and Unit-Type House give evidence of this. The doorway and small windows of the large D-shaped tower of Hovenweep Castle appear to mark the summer and winter solstices and the spring and autumnal equinoxes at sunset on those days. At Unit-Type House, four small openings mark the solstices and equinoxes and possibly the 19-year cycle of the moon.

At Holly Group, under a rock ledge just south of the Great House ruin, is an astronomical device reminiscent of the Sun Dagger at Fajada Butte in Chaco Canyon, New Mexico. Three figures are pecked on the wall of a narrow sandstone passage. On the left are two spirals. One appears to have been partly obliterated by either water seepage or erosion. A short distance to the right, the classic Pueblo sun symbol is represented by three concentric circles with a dot in the center. Faintly visible just to the left and below the sun symbol are two small circles joined by a line—a twin figure which may represent the Morning Star and Evening Star, twins of Pueblo mythology. To the right of the twin figure is the figure of a snake.

On the morning of the summer solstice, approximately an hour after sunrise, an arrow of light appears to the left of the spirals. As it crosses the second spiral, a second arrow of light appears to the right of the sun symbol and begins to move across it until the tips of the arrows join into one band of light. This process occurs over a period of about 7 minutes. The band of light then moves down the sandstone wall until the twin figure and the bottom section of the snake are illuminated.

This device also notes the spring and fall equinoxes but the winter sun at the time of the solstice does not reach the spirals on the sandstone wall.

Possibly and probably there are other solar observatories at Hovenweep which have disappeared as buildings fell into ruin.

Perhaps the most mystical aspect of Hovenweep is that human beings came into what appears to us to be a hostile environment and were able to live in harmony with the environment and flourish. They did not come with the attitude of conquer and subdue. This is seen in the fact that they did not attempt to change the terrain to accommodate their buildings, but accommodated their buildings to the existant terrain. They were not content to simply use the life-giving springs. They did what they had learned through observation to aid nature in conserving water and giving life to the springs which made their lives there possible.

SUGGESTED ACTIVITY

In our modern world so oriented toward material possessions and progress, it is easy to think of ourselves as something separate and apart from nature. We alienate ourselves from the roots of life when we see ourselves as anything less than as an integral part of a living planet.

Almost anywhere at Hovenweep is an ideal place to contemplate and meditate upon the character of the people who lived there and contrast their style of life with our own. They were completely self-reliant and self-sufficient. They took from the land only what was necessary to sustain life. They used their minds inventively to adapt what was at hand for tools for whatever needed to be done. They appeared to be aware that nature's resources are finite and used those resources with care and respect.

FOR MORE INFORMATION

Directions
From Cortez, Colorado, take US 666 northwest to Pleasant view, then at sign, take unnumbered county road 20 miles west. Or, from Blanding, Utah, take Highway 191 south to Highway 262. Turn east to Hatch Trading Post. From there follow dirt road 16 miles to Square Tower Monument Headquarters. Maps to other ruins groups are available there. The roads leading into Hovenweep are graded dirt and can quickly become muddy and impassable during and following rainstorm. At best, the roads are rough and a high clearance 4WD vehicle is preferable.

Food, Lodging and Gas
Water and toilet facilities are available at the campground near the ranger station at Square Tower Group. Food, firewood, and gasoline are not available. The nearest supplies are at Hatch Trading Post, 16 miles west, or Ismay Trading Post, 14 miles southeast.

The nearest motels are in Blanding, Utah and Cortez, Colorado.

It is off the beaten path, but well worth the effort and can be done in a long day.

Additional Information
Superintendent, Mesa Verde National Park, CO 01330. Telephone (303) 529-4465.

Canyonlands, the Needles District

Florence L. McClain

Canyonlands. Unique lands. Mysterious, grotesque, beautiful beyond reality—the leavings of heaving earth, surging waters, erod-
ing winds and rain, and time—vast eons of time.

Each mile unfolds a changing vista; mountains still snow-stip-
pled in early summer, wildflower meadows which bloom in the
spring and again after late summer rains, undulating waves of slickrock which look as if sandy beaches and ocean waves have been frozen into stone, deep and lonely canyons which bombard the senses
with feral beauty around each turn, eerie mazes of sandstone spires
eroded into fantastic shapes which fire the imagination, and soaring
arches which frame skies of incredible blue.

The the Anasazi have left equally intriguing traces of their long
ago presence here. Sharp eyes can see tiny granaries or cliff dwellings tucked into seemingly inaccessible niches high on sheer cliffs.
Ruins of stone houses dot the perimeters of meadows where crops
once grew. Exotic, spectral figures painted or pecked on canyon
walls evoke a profusion of emotions as one wonders what inspired
the artists. One red, white, and blue figure, remarkably prescient of
the United States flag, is aptly named "The All-American Man."

Other rock art portrays familiar creatures—deer, rabbits, bighorn sheep. One particularly touching record is almost lost among a
host of figures pecked on a rock wall. Large footprints are accompanied by much smaller footprints ending at the body of a deer pierced
by an arrow. One can almost see the proud father making a record of
the first hunting trip with his young son. And, there are handprints,
rows of red handprints with strange lines etched in the palms.

In the heart of this fantasy land, a trail begins on the bank of a
usually dry wash. The primitive path crosses Chesler wash and
leads up among the strangely eroded columns of sandstone. It
twists and turns, not heavily traveled, not always easily discerned

393

Chesler Park.
Photo by Florence L. McClain.

as it crosses rocky outcrops. Occasional wild-flowers are in bloom, seeming exceptionally beautiful because of their scarcity. A few cacti have found pockets of soil to sustain life. Stunted junipers and pinon pines provide infrequent bits of welcome shade. Off the trail, areas of sandy soil are covered by a black crust called cryptogamic soil. (It is vital to plant life that this crust remain undisturbed and intact. It protects the soil from erosion and helps to hold what little moisture this area receives. A careless footstep can destroy it for many years, perhaps permanently.)

One tree, long dead and turned to silvery grey by sun, rain and time, stands twisted and coiled into a work of art lovely enough to grace any museum.

After almost a mile, the path leads to a narrow stair of stacked rocks. Climbing up, one enters a passageway rich is dark and cool. This is the entrance to "The Joints." A short distance ahead, a large boulder and a smaller, flat slab of rock are flooded with light in the center of a junction which is open to the sky. A few yards to the right, an opening leads outside. To the left, around the boulder, the path enters a narrow crack, or joint, between high, sheer walls of stone. The pathway is covered with several inches of white sand. For almost a mile you are in a strange world of stone and sand roofed by a narrow band of indescribable blue. Occasional side joints branch off, most leading to dead ends or narrowing to impassable cracks. At times the walls narrow so that both can be touched simultaneously. It is quiet and tranquil and has a strange, intense beauty.

At one point, a tumble of boulders seems to choke the narrow passage. These can be climbed easily to the path which continues at a slightly higher level.

At the end, a stone stairway leads up and out into the broad basin of Chesler Park. Rolling waves of rock, creased by narrow seemingly bottomless fissures, are bordered by soaring cathedrals and spires of red sandstone banded with white. In every direction, either nearby or on the far horizon, there are feasts for the eye.

MYSTICAL SIGNIFICANCE

This red land holds danger for the imprudent, i.e. the careless or inexperienced off-road driver, the ill-prepared backpacker, the foolhardy and over-confident, those who ignore or choose to be ignorant of the perils of the terrain. A sudden rainstorm upstream can turn a dry creek bed into a raging torrent within minutes. A canyon floor may seem to offer a firm crossing when the reality is a trap of quicksand just beneath the surface.

Paradoxically, this is a benign land, a quiet land, a place of rare tranquility. There are no power lines, no telephones, no highways crowded with vehicles, no sky filled with airplanes. The sounds are songs of nature: a gentle breeze, a buzzing insect, an ebullient bird-call, the distant, lonely cry of a coyote, or there is profound silence.

Somehow, this area of the Canyonlands seems to shed human vibrations as easily as it sheds the sparse rainfall. Events which have occurred throughout the countless centuries have left only physical evidence in the ruins and rock art. The psyche has the rare opportunity for autonomous exploration of self in relationship to the challenges of the surroundings uninfluenced and unhampered by old psychic records of other times and peoples or interference from modern technology. It is seldom, if ever, in our busy world that one has the opportunity to be so completely alone with self. This place is indifferent to human presence. It remains whether one goes or stays, lives or dies. Each individual has the choice of how profound or superficial the experience will be.

The only experience which is unavoidable is the self-knowledge which is gained when one is forced to meet and handle emotional and physical challenges presented by the environment. The challenges of simply getting there and returning can be formidable.

SUGGESTED ACTIVITIES

At least one night spent in the open, preferably in a warm sleeping bag, is a never-to-be-forgotten experience. On top of the rocks at Bobby Jo Camp is an ideal place. The night is never quite dark, even without a moon. Millions upon millions of stars not visible from inhabited areas form a glistening dome of light.

There is indescribable beauty and tranquility. You may freely open yourself to the night without fear on any level. The very least which you may experience is a night of sleep so festful and full of peace that it will be wistfully remembered for the remainder of your life. Or, it just might be that you will soar among the stars.

"The Joints" offers a variety of opportunities. After climbing the stairway into the entrance, stop and rest in the dim coolness for a moment. Perhaps have a sip of water. Give yourself a few minutes to adjust to the changed surroundings.

From this point on, much symbology comes to mind, but it is for each of you to find your own significance in the experience.

Walk to the boulder and the flat rock which are spotlighted at the crossroads. Sit on the edge of the flat rock and lie back until you can look through the opening overhead. Empty your mind and relax. Allow yourself to flow with the time and the place.

There seems to be a gentle force or energy at this place which "centers" one's being—as if all which is out of phase between the body and spirit and nature gently shifts to bring one into harmony.

When you choose to continue left along the narrow path between the sheer rock walls, pick a place and take a moment to be alone, out of sight and hearing of anyone. Look and listen and feel. Contemplate the forces of nature and the time which has been necessary to form that particular place. Rather than being awed or fearful, allow yourself to integrate into that powerful flow of energy and time.

When you climb the stairway into the broad expanse of Chesler Park, take a moment to appreciate the contrast of open space with the narrow confines from which you have just emerged. You might find it pleasant to spend a few minutes in meditation. Then, explore and enjoy. Even from a purely pragmatic viewpoint, it is a grand adventure.

You can return by the same route. Or, for those who feel particularly energetic and adventurous and are skilled at map reading, a poorly marked path circles Chesler Park and leads onto the jeep trail where you have parked your vehicles at the trailhead, approximately 3.5–4 miles.

FOR MORE INFORMATION

Preparations

Getting into the Needles District of the Canyonlands requires a great deal more than just knowing which road to follow. The roads are minimally maintained and can quickly become impassable for several days during rain storms. The road surface varies from deep, sandy ruts to washboard to rock ledges and steep slickrock grades. A high clearance FWD vehicle with an experienced driver is a necessity. It is preferable that at least two vehicles travel together. Carry emergency equipment and tools for emergency repairs. A pair of handheld CB radios is a good investment. Over some of the steep areas of rock ledges, the driver has poor visibility of the roadbed. Someone walking ahead to direct the driver can prevent serious damage to the vehicles. Chances are that you may not see another vehicle or person while you are in the interior of the Canyonlands. Assume that you are essentially on your own and plan for it.

Water is of primary importance. Water is limited, usually non-existent. The dry desert can cause rapid dehydration. Drink frequently enough to satisfy your thirst and then a little more. Carry at least one gallon per person per day for drinking and extra for other needs. Carry extra food and water for emergencies.

Campgrounds are primitive. Be prepared to sleep in your vehicle, in the open, or in a tent. There are no sanitation facilities. All trash, including toilet paper, must be carried out. Burnable trash may be burned if you have a campfire in a designated site. All firewood must be brought in from outside the Park and all ashes must be carried out.

Good maps of the area and the ability to use them are essential. The roads and trails may not always be exactly as shown on the maps. In some instances, roads and trails outside the Park boundaries may no longer exist. Do not judge travel time by the mileage involved. If no side trails other than The Joints and Chesler Park are explored, allow one day travel time to get into the area of Bobby Jo Camp from Dugout Ranch (approx. 40-45 miles), one day for exploration of The Joints and Chesler Park, and one day for exiting by way of the SOB Hill—Elephant Hill Route (approx. 12 miles).

Directions
Take Highway 191-163 north from Montcello, Utah, fourteen miles to Highway 211 across from Church Rock. Turn west on 211. At approximately 10 miles, stop for a look at Newspaper Rock State Park, then continue for approximately eight miles to the Dugout Ranch turnoff on the left. Here you will be leaving the paved road and turning onto a dirt road which is very rough and needs high clearance in some areas. It will climb out of Cottonwood Creek onto Bridger Jack Mesa, then cross Salt Creek Mesa. Continue to follow the road into the Beef Basin area through House Park, Middle Park, and Ruin Park into Pappy's Pasture. Somewhere in this area you may see a sign: "County Maintenance Ends." You are allowed to laugh, cry, or make whatever remarks seem appropriate. At this point the road becomes a primitive jeep trail and descends a steep

grade of sand, loose rock, and rock ledges into Bobby's Hole. Stop at the top of the grade and explore the condition of the road before committing yourself to it. Many people consider this segment of road as one way—down only. When it is dry, others do choose to come out this way rather than going out by Elephant Hill. Do use extreme caution in either direction.

At the trailhead to Joints—Chesler Park.
Photo by Florence L. McClain.

At the bottom of this grade, ignore the sign (if it is still there) which says: "Abandon hope, all ye who have entered here," and continue on for approximately 6–7 miles until you see a sign on the left for Bobby Jo Camp and Horsehoof Arch Camp. You will probably be more than ready to make camp.

From Bobby Jo Camp, it is approximately one mile to the spur on the right which leads to The Joints-Chesler Parit trailhead. This mile is rough in places and at least one area has very tight clearance for tall vehicles and campertops. It is 1/2 mile on the spur to the trailhead where you may park. There is one picnic table and an outdoor toilet. No water.

You may choose to return by the same route if the condition of the climb out of Bobby's Hole permits. Otherwise, return to the main trail from The Joints-Chesler Park spur and turn right (north) into Devil's Lane. This is one of many "grabens"—long, narrow, rock-walled valleys. The first obstacle to be tackled is called SOB Hill. The name is well earned. Rock ledges, loose sand and rocks, tight turns and generally rough road make it memorable. At one point a very tight turn ascending a rocky ledge is impossible to make with a frontal assault. You will note an area you can head into which then makes it possible to back up this segment. A large vehicle will have a great deal of difficulty with this maneuver.

Approximately three miles from the Joint-Chesler Park spur, on the far-side of SOB Hill, a trail turns to the right toward the Devil's Kitchen Camp. DO NOT make this turn. It is part of a one way loop to Elephant Hill. Shortly past this spur you will encounter a half-mile segment known as the Silver Stairs. These are relatively smooth rock steps with drops of from three to four feet, so named from the color of the metal left from the undercarriages of passing vehicles. Proceed with caution.

Approximately a mile beyond the Silver Stairs the trail junctions. Take the junction to the right toward Elephant Hill. You will note the Devil's Kitchen segment of this one way loop joining the Elephant Hill trail after a little more than two miles. Another mile or so brings you to the base of Elephant Hill. This is the most difficult part of any of the roads you have encountered so far. It is most wise to walk the road and look at the problems involved. It consist of steep rock ledges and narrow switchbacks. Take note that it is necessary to back up one switchback segment and plan accordingly. You will also note that it is necessary to back onto a rock ledge overhanging the canyon to get in position to make the approach to the final brutal segment to the top. Slow and steady in Low-Low 4WD guided by an observer with a handheld CB should bring you safely to the relatively flat mesa, possibly to the cheers of less daring folk who have parked their cars on the far side and climbed up to watch the fun.

Here you can stop and take a break before attempting the descent from Elephant Hill. The descent is over steep grades of rough, loose rubble and then down a very steep slickrock slope to a graded dirt road. At this point it looks like a super highway. Closely observe the rock wall on the left side of the road between Elephant Hill and the Squaw Flat Campground where the pavement begins for interesting Anasazi rock art.

The pavement is Highway 211 on which you can return to Monticello. Do not attempt this exit route without at least 4-5 hours or more of daylight.

Alternate Routes

You may, if you choose, enter the Needles District of the Canyonlands over the Elephant Hill route. Should you choose to backpack, you can park either at the Squaw flat Campground (usually full in good weather) or at the base of Elephant Hill. There are backpacking trails from both points which enter the north side of Chesler Park. They are minimally maintained, not always well marked, and not for the neophyte.

You should carry water and food for a minimum of two days.

Another possible approach is from Blanding, Utah. Take Highway 191-163 south to Highway 95: "The Trail of the Ancients." Turn west on 95 for approximately 7 miles to the first paved road turning north between Brushy Basin Wash and Cottonwood Wash. Approximately six miles north at the junction, go left. The pavement will end shortly after crossing Cottonwood Wash. Twelve miles will bring you to Kigalia Ranger Station and the junction to the right which is variously known as Elk Ridge Road, the Big Notch Road, etc. Go approximately fifteen miles north where you will join the road coming in from Dugout Ranch a few miles south of the Beef Basin area.

Inquire about road conditions in Blanding. This road over the Abajo Mountains is very narrow and is covered with snow or deep mud into late spring. Once committed, there is little, if any, opportunity to turn around. It is beautiful country but makes the approach from Dugout Ranch seem tame.

It is difficult to be exact about mileage. Signs are sparse to nonexistent. Details may vary from map to map but maps and a compass are your best tools for a successful trip.

Suggested Maps And Sources

Trails Illustrated Topo Map of Needles District, Canyonlands National Park, Utah. (Highly recommended).

USGS 15 minute series topo maps for The Needles, Fable Valley, Harts Point, and Mt. Linnaeus quadrangle.

Quick and excellent service on phone or mail orders from Holman's Inc. 401 Wyoming Blvd, N. E., Albuquerque, NM 07123-1096; phone (505) 265-7901.

Southeastern Utah road map (highly recommended). Published by Utah Travel Council, Council Hall, Capitol Hill, Salt Lake City, UT 04114.

These maps and others are available at area visitor centers.

Lodging, Gasoline, and Food

Lodging, gasoline, and food are available ONLY at Monticello or Blandings. Campgrounds in the Canyonlands are on a first come-first served basis.

Additional Information

Superintendent, National Park Service. 125 West 200 South, Moab, UT 044532; phone (801) 259-7164.

Many resources and addresses are listed on the Southeastern Utah road map.

Suggested Reading

Barnes, F.A. *Utah Canyon Country* (No. 1) (Utah Geographic. Series, Box 0325, Salt Lake City, UT 04108).

—————. *Canyon County Off-Road Vehicle Trail: Canyon Rims and Needles Area*. (No.8) Canyon Country Publications, P.O. Box 963, Moab, UT 04532.

—————. *Canyon Country Prehistoric Rock Art*. (No. 14) Wasatch Publishers, Inc. 4647 Idlewild Road, Salt Lake City, UT 04124.

WASHINGTON

Seattle

Spokane

BEACON ROCK   STONEHENGE
⊕   ⊕

Beacon Rock

D. J. Conway

Beacon Rock, the core of an ancient volcano, is a gigantic monolith that juts 850 feet above the edge of the Columbia River and is the second largest in the world after Gibraltar. It stands a few miles downstream from Bonneville Dam on the Washington State side of the Columbia River. The conical peak itself rises 848 feet on a base of only 17 acres. It was named by Lewis and Clark in 1805; its name comes from the fact that it alerted travelers of a clear river journey to the Pacific Ocean 150 miles away.

Beacon Rock.
Courtesy of the U.S.D.A. Forest Service.

It is possible to hike to the top of Beacon Rock along the one-mile of chiseled path lined with a maze of metal railings. Be sure you are in good condition physically and have a head for heights and sheer drops as there is a 15 percent grade to the path. A plaque partway up the trail commemorates the work of Henry J. Biddle and his aide, Charles Johnson, who preserved the pinnacle from rock quarries and constructed the path to the top. Henry Biddle bought the rock in 1915 and spent two years blazing the trail. His heirs donated Beacon Rock to the state of Washington in 1935.

Once on top of Beacon Rock, the view of the Columbia River and the Gorge is breathtaking. It is a quiet, yet exhilarating experience to stand atop the monolith with the ever-present Columbia winds sweeping around you.

MYSTICAL SIGNIFICANCE

As far as is known, there is no Indian legend connected with Beacon Rock. However, it is quite likely that the legends have simply been forgotten, as the local Indian tribes had legends connected with almost every natural feature in the region. Local tribes called Beacon Rock by the name of "Che-che-op-tin."

SUGGESTED RITUAL

Energy from Air elementals is extremely powerful on top of Beacon Rock. Face into the wind, which is almost constant in the Columbia Gorge, and raise your arms in greeting and acknowledgement. Feel the cleansing power sweeping all negative feelings and conditions out of your life. To end the ritual, ground yourself by placing your hands against the rock and absorbing a burst of Earth force.

FOR MORE INFORMATION

Directions

Beacon Rock State Park can be reached by crossing the toll bridge at Cascade Locks. Turn left on State Route Hwy 14 and follow the road for about 4 miles west. If traveling east from Vancouver, Washington, follow Hwy 14 for approximately 35 miles; the State Park is about 18 miles east of Washougal, Washington. The Rock is clearly visible from both sides of the Columbia River.

Lodging

On the Oregon side of the Columbia River lodging is available at: Bridge of the Gods Motel & RV Park, 630 Wa-Na-Pa, Cascade Locks, OR 97014; (503) 374-8628. KOA Cascade Locks, Forest Lane, Cascade Locks, OR 97014; (503) 374-8668.

There is an excellent facility at Beacon Rock State Park, complete with an overnight camping area. A picnic area across the highway from the Rock has sinks, electric stoves, and a huge covered picnic hall. The closest motels (other than the ones listed in Cascade Locks) are in the Portland area. Additional Information: Chamber of Commerce of Skamania County, Hwy 14, Stevenson, WA 98648; (509) 427-8911.

Bibliography

Drawson, Maynard C. *Treasures of the Oregon Country*. Salem, OR: Dee Publishing Co., 1973.

Lyons, Dianne J. Boulerice. *Washington Handbook*. Chico, CA: Moon Publications, 1989.

Sunset Travel Guide to Washington. Menlo Park, CA: Lane Publishing Co., 1978.

Stonehenge

D. J. Conway

The full-sized replica of Stonehenge was built in 1920 by Samuel Hill, who also built the Maryhill Museum nearby. This concrete model of England's Stonehenge commemorates the regional Klickitat County veterans who died in World War I. Since Sam Hill was four decades ahead of the decoding of the original Stonehenge's positions, this model unfortunately is not aligned to any particular direction.

The Washington Stonehenge, as a full-sized, authentic replica of England's ancient site, gives one a feeling of awe, standing within the circle of monoliths. Stonehenge is situated near the edge of the massive cliffs of the Columbia Gorge. It is a barren, lonely spot, but full of peace and beautiful views. If you cannot visit the original structure in England, this is an excellent place to experience some of the grandeur and awesomeness of a monolithic circle.

MYSTICAL SIGNIFICANCE

Since this is a fairly modern site, there is no mystical or legendary attachment to the place. However, modern Druids have celebrated many rituals at Stonehenge, thus building up a certain amount of energy within it. There appear to be strong currents of both Earth and Air energies within the circle.

SUGGESTED RITUAL

Except during the middle of tourist season, it is possible to have this monolithic circle to yourself, especially if it is raining.

Pace the inner circle of stones three times, beginning in the east and moving clockwise. Imagine yourself walking backward through time and across the great distance to walk within the ancient circle on Salisbury Plain. Visualize this Stonehenge as being directly connected with the original one in England.

Artist's rendition of the full-sized replica of Stonehenge.
Illustration by William Wild.

After the third circling, go to stand by the altar stone in the center. Listen for ancient Druidic voices, sometimes heard in the Columbia winds whispering through the great monoliths. Place the palms of your hands on the altar stone. Feel the ancient energies coursing upward through the stone. Feel yourself becoming physically, mentally, emotionally and spiritually alert and renewed.

Finish the ritual by walking three times counter-clockwise, while visualizing yourself returning to your present time and place.

FOR MORE INFORMATION

Directions

Located 2 miles east of the Maryhill Museum. If you cross the bridge at The Dalles, Oregon, follow US 97 until it crosses Hwy 14 about 2 miles east of Maryhill Museum. You will see the signs directing you to a right-hand turn onto a narrow paved road. Another right-hand turn takes you onto a dirt road which meanders across open fields to the site.

Lodging

The nearest convenient motels are in The Dalles on the Oregon side of the Columbia River. Hallmark Motel, 2500 W. 6th St., The

Dalles, OR 97058; (503) 296-1191; $28–45. Tillicum Motor Inn, 1481 W. 6th St., The Dalles, OR 97058; (503) 298-5161; $33–47. Williams House Inn Bed & Breakfast, 608 W. 6th St., The Dalles, OR 97058; (503) 296-2889; $45–60. Best Western Tapadera Motor Inn, 112 W. 2nd St., The Dalles, OR 97058; (503) 296-9107. Hamilton Motel, 1301 W. 2nd St., The Dalles, OR 97058; (503) 296-9234. Columbia Windrider Inn, 200 W. 4th St., The Dalles, OR 97058; (503) 296-2607.

Overnight campgrounds are few in the area. Deschutes River, off I-84, 17 miles east of The Dalles; 34 primitive, no electric; tents; maximum 30 foot RV. Memaloose, I-84 (westbound access only), 11 miles west of The Dalles; 43 full hook-ups; 67 tents; maximum 60 foot RV; showers, handicapped access to restrooms. On the Washington side of the Columbia, 18 miles west of Maryhill Museum, is Horse thief Lake State Park with 30 camp sites and picnic facilities. Also just above the bridge over the Columbia is 98-acre Maryhill State Park with SC trailer hook-ups. Additional Information: The Dalles Chamber of Commerce, 404 W. 2nd St., The Dalles, OR 97058; (503) 296-2231.

Other Points of Interest

Other points of interest in the immediate area are the Maryhill Museum (on the Washington side of the Columbia River). The Dalles Dam Visitor Center, and the Fort Dalles Museum.

The Fort Dalles Museum, 16th & Garrison, The Dalles, OR 97058, (503) 296-4547 has the remnants of Fort Dalles which was built in 1856; it is on the National Register listing; pioneer history and transportation vehicles. Open May 1–Sept. 30, Tue.–Fri. 10:30 a.m.–5 p.m., Sat.–Sun. 10 a.m.–5 p.m.; Oct. 1–Apr. 30, Wed.–Fri. 12–4 p.m., Sat.–Sun. l0 a.m.–4 p.m.

The Dalles Dam Visitor Center at Seufert Park, The Dalles, OR, (503) 296-1181, is open June–Aug. every day 10 a.m.-4:30 p.m.; a free tour train leaves from the museum to the dam every 30 minutes. This center has displays of the history of the Corps of Engineers, natural environment, history of The Dalles area and cultures and languages of the earlier Indian inhabitants.

The Maryhill Museum, just across the bridge on the Washington side of the Columbia River on Hwy 14, was originally built by Samuel Hill in 1926 for his daughter Mary. Samuel Hill, born in North Carolina in 1857, made his fortune in the railroad boom and married the daughter of James J. Hill, the railroad tycoon. His close friend, the dancer Loie Fuller of the Folies Bergere talked Sam Hill into turning his unlived-in mansion into a museum. Queen Marie of Romania dedicated the Museum in November of 1926 but it did not open until 14 years later. *Time* magazine called it the loneliest museum in the world when it finally opened in 1940. The Queen donated several valuable exhibits which are still housed in the Museum. There are also large collections of Rodin sculptures, impressionist art (Manet, Cezanne, and others), Indian artifacts, Galle glass, dolls, icons, antique chess sets, Romanian royal furniture and much, much more.

For more information, contact the Maryhill Museum of Art, Goldendale, WA 98620; (509) 773-3733. The museum is open 9 a.m.– 5 p.m. daily, mid-March to mid-November. There is a small admission fee.

Maryhill Museum is 18 miles east and above Horse Thief Lake State Park; this 338-acre site has an Indian petroglyph incised into basalt.

Bibliography

Hagen, Robert D., comp. *Totally Oregon*. Salem, OR: Oregon Pride Productions, 1989.

Lyons, Dianne J. Boulerice. *Washington Handbook*. Chico, CA: Moon Publications, 1989.

Sunset Travel Guide to Washington. Menlo Park, CA: Lane Publishing Co., 1979.

Williams, Chuck. *Bridge of the Gods, Mountains of Fire*, New York: Friends of the Earth, 1980.

WASHINGTON D.C.

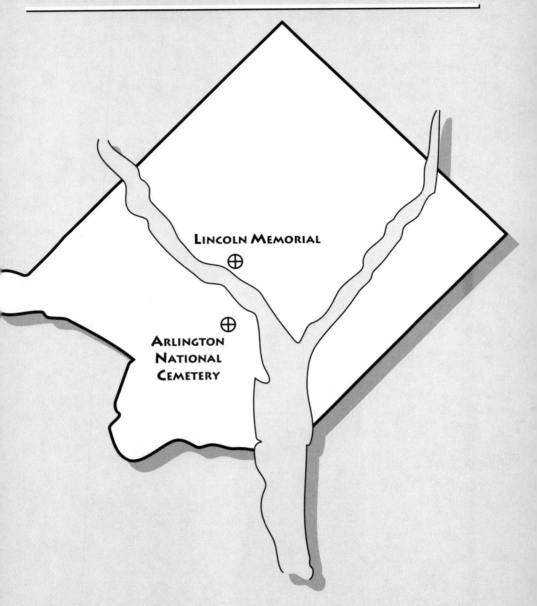

LINCOLN MEMORIAL
⊕

⊕
ARLINGTON
NATIONAL
CEMETERY

Washington D.C.

Diccon Frankborn

For all its importance as our nation's capital, Washington D.C. has seldom been so much as mentioned as a place of power in a spiritual sense, and so it may never have occurred to anyone to search out its sacred spaces. However, Washington does have a few small areas of sacred space, some naturally occurring and some which resonate from human Workings. The surprising thing is that there aren't more of them, as Washington is exceptional among national capitals in having been built deliberately for its purpose, i.e., for illumination, and for efficiently executing the will of its leaders. They took pains to preserve wooded land and grassy parks inside the city limits and to connect the centers of human activity with avenues as straight as a surveyor could make them. The architect of the city was a French Deist, and at least half of the people who approved his plans were Masons.

Most of the easily detectable sacred spaces, however, seem to be the result of psychic residue left from human activities intense enough, or high-minded enough, to leave an imprint on otherwise ordinary locations. And some of those described here are not localities that stand alone, but only the high spots in areas full of sacred energy. It would have been easy to list a score or more of places in Washington where the sensitive could find sacred space—and I don't doubt there are twice as many which would be apparent to someone abler than I am—but room is lacking for such a detailed list.

THE LINCOLN MEMORIAL

On a low rise of ground beside the Potomac River, at the end of the Mall—a rectilinear area of parkland and water stretching just over two miles to the complex of buildings on Capitol Hill—stands this familiar building, facing the rising sun. It is an excellent example of Classic Revival architecture, deliberately built to the model of a Greek temple, and like such temples it is a house for its image rather than a gathering-place for the congregation: for them there is a broad plaza outside, of wide shallow steps dropping down to a long pool which catches the reflection of the Washington Monument nearly a mile away.

Lincoln Memorial.
Photo by Diccon Frankborn.

When built, the Memorial finished off the line of governmental and scholarly buildings which have now been constructed all the length of the Mall. The Memorial itself counterbalances the Capitol, which rises on a hill at the other end of the Mall, although it is too small to resonate with the other building. It was constructed with many symbolic properties—for instance, the architrave is upheld by 36 pillars (the number of states in the Union which Lincoln preserved)—and faced with 48 individual slabs of marble (the number of states at the time the Memorial was completed) the statue, if it were standing, would be 28 feet high (the number of days in Lincoln's birth-month). However, this symbolism (there are many more features which can be picked out by the knowing) is not the source of the sacred space which can be perceived here. Far stronger is the power generated by those who in the past have gathered here "peaceably to assemble, and petition the government for redress of grievances."

MYSTICAL SIGNIFICANCE

For several generations Americans have used this as a place of assembly to work for many causes, most of them drawing strength from some motive that was idealistic at bottom. It is their psychic networking, I believe, which has charged this site with spiritual power. The area where this energy feels strongest (though this is a personal impression) is the plaza, and especially the flight of steps which leads down to the Reflecting Pool—a broad (170 feet wide) flight, a place for crowds to gather. The energy is present night and day, whether the marble Memorial itself is dazzling in the sun or glowing under cloudy skies or shining with its internal illumination by night.

But take a warning too. Those who built up Power here were no serene philosophers, but people who felt they had the right to make others yield to their Righteous Cause and had come here for that purpose. Use wisely the sacred space they have created, but keep clear of the traps in it: the pleasure of being impatient with differences, the pleasure of condemning an opponent as morally loathsome, and—the most delicious temptation of all—the joy of compelling others to obey your stronger will. By that sin fell the angels, whatever you may have heard about Pride being to blame.

SUGGESTED MEDITATION AND RITUAL

The site is not only public but an important tourist attraction. Any ritual you carry out will have to be internal or, at least, inconspicuous enough not to draw attention. But it is not at all unusual for people to pause in meditation anywhere around the Memorial, which has some splendid vistas to enjoy. There are grassy park areas with well-grown trees along the Reflecting Pool for anyone who feels uncomfortable meditating on bare earth or stone.

This is one meditation that can be done effectively here. Bring with you a problem of conflict with another which you have not been able to resolve. As you stand on the steps—or wherever you feel most comfortable—raise your energies to the highest level you can sustain. (There is far more high-level good energy here than there is of the dangerous sort just mentioned.)

As you reach and hold your maximum, feel a strong, confident, calm Power flowing through you and sense your throat Chakra resonating with a Voice, not overwhelming but clear, well fitted to set forth lucid thoughts. The Horned Lord has manifested here, perhaps more than once, but not in His masterful Kingly aspect. This is His wise Sage aspect that you are in harmony with. Bring your other Chakras to life and feel them responding to this power. Absorb as much of this energy as you feel you can—or dare to.

Now bring into your mind the conflict you seek to resolve. Hold the issue in the center of your thought-field and let the energy of this site wash over it. Keep letting it flow through you at the same time. Think of the opposition of your astute and temperate views and your opponents' crackpot notions. Think of them in whatever opprobrious terms you please, but consider them while the power you are tapping scours away the foolish exaggerations and leaves only the residue that is worthy of consideration. And watch while your own ideas are scoured and polished too. There is, you see with a little satisfaction, a good deal of sound thinking there, but now you look at both of the positions at once you can see that the truth goes beyond either. Can you grasp the larger vision that encompasses both? Reach as far as you can...reach, grasp, and hold if you are able.

Become aware of your surroundings again and see the light that glows from Memorial and plaza, a light you now can feel as a sharp internal illumination. Gradually bring your energy level down to normal. Did the Power here let you know a Name? Use it when you give thanks for what you have gained. And before you close down your Chakras, send a blessing to those who will hereafter use this site, and who will—perhaps not consciously—be raised above themselves by a Power to which you have added. Ground and center. Go on from here, and use what you have been able to hold.

FOR MORE INFORMATION

Directions

From in town, or north, follow Constitution Avenue (US 50) west to 23rd Street NW. Walk south through the park for a block. From the south, follow I-95 to the Washington Beltway and take I-395 toward town; follow signs for Memorial Bridge. As you cross the bridge you will see the Memorial ahead of you; turn left and find a parking space. If you are using the subway, take the Orange or Blue Line to Foggy Bottom/GWU station and walk south 8 blocks.

Lodging

Plenty of accommodations for most budgets in the Washington area or in Arlington, across the river.

ARLINGTON NATIONAL CEMETERY

Across the Potomac River opposite the Lincoln Memorial, on a height overlooking the city from the west, lies Arlington National Cemetery, a burial place dating from the Civil War. Those sensitive to such things will find many Sacred Spaces here, even if they have no kinfolk in the Cemetery.

One of the strongest sites for outsiders lies on the high ground beyond the Tomb of the Unknowns, though nearer to the small Nurses' Memorial than to the better-known site. The Cemetery itself is as nearly natural as such a place can be: not flat fields with serried rows of markers, but grassy hills among which footpaths wind. (Driving is not allowed inside except for funeral parties and next-of-kin visiting grave sites.) Significantly, though all the individual grave markers are stones, many of the other memorials within are living trees. If this seems strange to you, you may not be ready to visit this site.

The Tomb of the Unknowns is overlooked by an amphitheater (dignified, but uninspired) overlooked in turn by a short ridge which is almost the highest natural point in the Cemetery. (The roof of the amphitheater is a little higher.) At the end of the ridge, southwest of the Tomb of the Unknowns, is a burst of evergreens, and on the slope below this is the powerful sacred space I told you of. If the Nurses' Memorial were standing alone, I suspect the space would be right there; my impression is that it is a short distance away because of the influence of the numerous but less powerful spaces which are nearby. On the ridge itself, and right above the energy center, is a small plaza on which I was astonished to find what I would never have expected to see near sacred space: a battery of cannon. I went over them carefully, but found them almost inert and certainly not carrying any residual negative energies. Now I think of it, maybe that should tell us something about this site.

MYSTICAL SIGNIFICANCE

This site was not constructed with intent to make it a shrine— the last time it was in private hands it was Robert E. Lee's family home. That just goes to show that if someone feels Sacred Space is called for, we don't have to worry over whether our human plans are entirely right.

*Arlington National Cemetery—facing west, energy space
is the slope in front of the hedge and trees at the center.*
Photo by Diccon Frankborn.

The Cemetery lies west and a little south of the Line of Power which stretches from Capitol Hill to the Lincoln Memorial—not due west (although there is an outlying monument, the Iwo Jima Memorial, exactly on that line) but in such a position that in this latitude the sun sets behind it most of the year. Here we have a clear association with the traditional direction of Passage. The Cemetery and the Mall are unfortunately too large to have a more precise orientation, and there are so many possible alignment points in both areas that deducing some would be mere guesswork.

The curved lines of the roadways—a map will show that even the few which at first seem straight lie in gentle arcs are such as a geomancer would prescribe to facilitate and retain energy flows, and the hills have the gentle rolling contours which serve the same purpose in a landscape. (The ridge just above the energy location I have described is one of the few sharp edges not clearly part of a building.) A healing cover of grass lies everywhere—it is carefully taken up and replaced when a burial occurs, so that the green blanket is never broken for more than a few hours. I have already mentioned the degree to which memorials consist of living trees and not artificial constructions. The Nurses' Memorial which feels as if it were a key to the Sacred Space here is, however, a statue—an austere figure which is a mature woman but could be of any race.

Both the Nurses' Memorial and the amphitheater were erected years after the anomalous battery of guns was set up, so the latter is not an intrusion but was part of their original environment. Were the negative energies of the guns neutralized by the energy of this space, or had they been neutralized before? Certainly, doing a meditation here gained me a hint that it was the whole environment and not the localized high-energy space that cleared them out.

SUGGESTED MEDITATION AND RITUAL

Again, this is not only a public space but meant to attract visitors. You cannot wear ritual garb here or use incense or candles (and you should probably not wear unusual amulets outside your clothing). This is recognized sacred space, and even mundane types who normally have no feeling for such things sense that it should be honored and are willing to protect it. It's just our bad luck that they don't know enough to distinguish the profane from the merely unfamiliar. On the other hand, there should be no difficulty in doing silent meditation, prayer, or other Workings that are recognizable as actions of reverence.

The center of the power spot is not convenient to any of the footpaths around it. If you find it difficult to work from the ridge just above, you must approach it through the nearby grave sites. (If you are reading a book like this, you already know enough to treat such sites with respect.)

Come here, if you will, when you are weary or distressed. This place has great power over pain of spirit or body.

Ground and center yourself. Greet the spirits of this place with respect and ask their leave to do a Working here; use your subtle senses to be sure they consent before you invoke the Quarter Guardians or otherwise begin to make your personal space ready.

Arlington Cemetery, facing north, northwest—energy space is the slope between the evergreens and tombstones, at the center of the picture.
Photo by Diccon Frankborn.

Now become conscious of your subtle body and attune yourself. It will not be necessary to raise your energies once they are attuned; you have only to quiet your mind and, in a fully relaxed state, let your energies be raised. It is hard to distinguish single Beings in the flow of Power you will contact in this meditation (or at least I have found it so) but there are tantalizing whisperings at the edge of perception that may have a message for you. Even if there are not, you can maintain contact with and benefit from the healing energy here for a meditation of long duration. Perhaps I was given what it was good for me to receive; however that may be, the Power I sensed here was not that of either the Lord or the Lady. It was the calm, benevolent but almost irresistible strength of an Entity (or entities; as I said, I couldn't be sure) which is rested and balanced and ready to undertake something new.

When you have received as much as you feel you should, break the attunement and close down your energy centers. Ground and center; thank and release the Quarter Guardians, if you invoked them; and then thank the spirits of this place. Listen once more before you go, in case there is a message you have not yet heard.

FOR MORE INFORMATION

Directions
From in town or north, follow Constitution Avenue (US 50) to 22nd Street NW and turn left, crossing Memorial Bridge. From the south, follow I-95 to the Washington Beltway and take I-395 toward town, following the signs for Memorial Bridge/Arlington National Cemetery. You'll have to park in the Visitor's Center lot (only funeral processions and next-of-kin can drive inside the Cemetery) If you are using the subway, take the Blue Line to Arlington Cemetery and follow signs for Visitor's Center. From there take Roosevelt Drive uphill, following signs for the Tomb of the Unknowns, about a 10-minute walk. Go around to the southwest side of the Amphitheater; you will see two pillars, the right one obviously a ship's mast. The other, on the left, is just above the power site described.

Lodging
Lots of accommodations in Rosslyn, Virginia, north of the Cemetery. The most economical are along US 50 about a mile away, just beyond the Iwo Jima monument.

WISCONSIN

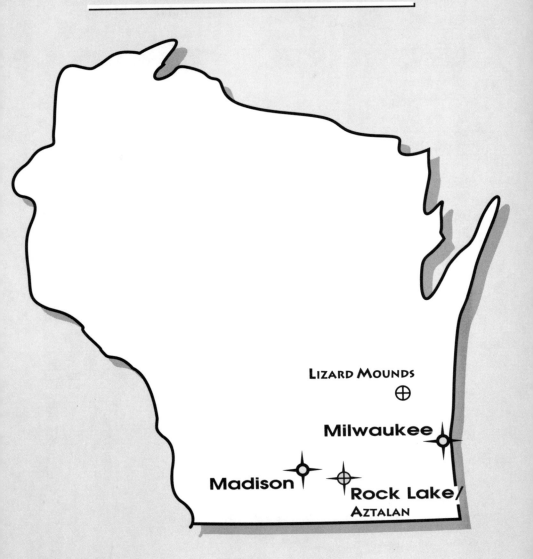

LIZARD MOUNDS
⊕

Milwaukee

Madison

Rock Lake/
AZTALAN

Aztalan

Frank Joseph

Unsuspected by most Midwesterners, and by many Wisconsin residents, are the remains of the capital of an ancient, spiritually potent civilization that once stretched from the Upper Great Lakes to northern Illinois, westward to the Dakotas. Aztalan, between Milwaukee and Madison, housed an aristocratic population of priests, architects, astronomers and engineers behind three enormous walls. Within the triple enclosure reared three earthen pyramids, flat-topped structures surmounted by temple buildings with steeply arched gables. Just outside the walls a line of conical mounds were oriented to the positions of certain stars. In a solitary mounds archaeologists found the so-called "Beaded Princess," the remains of a young woman wrapped in a fabulous garment composed of 1,200 polished shells. Another grave held the skeleton of a headless giant. Colossal earth-sculpture in the forms of birds, snakes, rabbits, oars and crosses adorned the vicinity. The city itself was connected at its north end by a stone aqueduct three miles long to nearby Rock Lake. There the earliest civilizers entombed their leaders under stone pyramids shaped like cones and tents.

In life, the 3000 inhabitants of Aztalan crafted superior pottery, traded for fresh meat with the local Indians and cooked in convection earth-ovens. The area underwent several phases of occupation and abandonment, the last beginning around 1100 A.D. and lasting for the next 200 years. The precise origins and identity of the Wisconsin civilizers are unknown. Resident Winnebago Indians described them as "foreigners." But stylistic similarities to the Monk's Mound complex and the comparative opening and closing dates of Aztalan and Cahokia, respectively, strongly suggest that the former, at least in its final phase, was settled by culture-bearers from the collapse of Cahokia (See "Cahokia," in the Illinois section) As such, Aztalan was the most northerly outpost of the Mississippian Culture that flourished to the Gulf of Mexico.

Aztalan itself ended suddenly, when the entire 21-acre site was consumed by a catastrophic fire ignited by its own inhabitants, who then vanished. Today all that remains of this powerful, mysterious city are the Pyramids of the Sun and Moon, the nearby line of conical mounds and recreated sections of the stockaded skeleton of the original wattle and daub covered walls. The small, adjacent museum making do in an old chapel contains interesting if unspectacular artifacts, side by side with much later pioneer items. The best finds from Aztalan were hidden away from public view in the basement of the Milwaukee Public Museum.

Scuba diving for the sunken pyramids of Rock Lake.
Photo by Frank Joseph.

Despite the ravages of centuries, Aztalan Archaeological Park offers a beautiful, impressive vista sloping gently down to the banks of the Crawfish River, upon which the ancient people first arrived, nearly a thousand years ago. The two large pyramids and partially standing walls lend Aztalan an air of sublime mystery, particularly at sunset, when long shadows cast from these weird features sharply delineate the entire site.

MYSTICAL SIGNIFICANCE

Aztalan is among the most powerfully charged sacred centers in the world. The reasons are several and contradictory in a very dramatic sense. The ancient city, as mentioned above, was torched by its own people, perhaps because of a fundamental split in their society. While one section of the population honored their moon-goddess, an elite priesthood arose, whose human sacrifices to the sun-god became so bloody they ended in ritual cannibalism. It is presumed the former group eventually prevailed, burned the profaned sacred center to purify the ground and deconsecrate the site. Thus, the resident energies are spectacularly strong in Aztalan. Good and evil wrestled each other in a real-life arena behind the triple walls for 200 years, impregnating the very soil with dynamically opposed energies still much in evidence, despite, or perhaps even because of the 14th century purification.

Disparate forces are still apparent in the contradictory human responses to Aztalan. In the daytime conventional Christian wedding ceremonies are sometimes performed atop the Pyramid of the Sun, while at night local devotees of Satanism occasionally leave small, sacrificed animals in painted pentagrams at the same structure. It is clear that contrary powers still resonate mightily in the sacred precinct, and continue to attract personalities suited to their particular form of energy.

Three miles to the west of the archaeological park, Lake Mills is the charming town surrounding Rock Lake, with its drowned city of the dead, a necropolis of sunken burial structures, covered by seven centuries of rising spring waters. Visitors may rent boats at Bartels Landing, on the east side of the lake, and motor out over the submerged pyramids. They lie about 1/4 of a mile off shore, toward the middle of Rock Lake. They are extremely difficult for scuba-divers to locate, because of the water's generally turbid condition. Their presence is more often felt by receptive persons in an open boat. But the energies here are decidedly unfriendly. Numerous paranormal experiences, some of them unpleasant, have occurred in the lake.

Despite ghastly associations with human sacrifice at Aztalan, the Pyramid of the Sun is neither a virtuous nor a sinful place. It is a *powerful* place for good *or* evil, depending on the practitioner. Its ascent is made most dramatically from the east, where a broad flight of stairs climbs to the top. A large, wooden temple, a tall pole protruding through its grass roof, stood there in the days of ancient occupation. The pole was aligned with another across the Crawfish River, at the summit of Christmas Hill, to sight in perfectly each sunrise of the winter solstice. It was this life affirming orientation on the shortest day of the year that underscored the positive principle of the solar cult faith in the eternal return of light and life. The view over Aztalan is best from the commanding height of this pyramid, where the visitor feels telluric vitality rise up through the structure like a fountain of power.

The smaller Pyramid of the Moon at the other end of the precinct was named after its suspected fix with the most northerly rising of the moon. Seven shamans, their bodies oriented to the southeast, were entombed deep in its heart about seven hundred years ago. The resident mightiness of this structure, to put it bluntly, is erotic. A descriptive catalog of the carnal encounters that continue to take place in the vicinity of the Pyramid of the Moon would be long and, unfortunately perhaps, beyond the scope of this Guidebook. It is no wonder people are drawn to Aztalan for weddings and other love-oriented activities. In truth both pyramids are overtly sexual; i.e., the Pyramid of the Sun, always a virile male conception, particularly with its phallic solar pole erected at the center.

The moon-goddess additionally lives up to her reputation in Wisconsin, in that successful telepathy and pastlife experiments have taken place atop her pyramid. The fact that American spiritualism got its start in the Aztalan area during the 19th century was no accident. Accordingly, the energy-level at Aztalan is so high, all things are possible within its living sacred center, both good and evil.

SUGGESTED RITUAL

Since Aztalan is the sacred site par excellence, with unlimited spiritual potential, a simple, introductory rite may serve both the casual visitor and the serious practitioner.

Go to Aztalan at twilight on a clear evening, with the moon visible. Walk from the parking lot toward the site. The whole area is uncommonly safe and the first impression of the place at sundown seems to conjure its innate magic most effectively. Crossing a field of mown grass in an easterly direction, the visitor very shortly comes to the Pyramid of the Moon, a trapezoidal structure about 12 feet high. Immediately off to the north stands the partially recreated wall. Ascend the northern slope of the pyramid. At the top, place a favorite crystal in the very center of the summit, then stand just before it facing north. Pour a few drops of water to the pyramid and say, "I honor the spirits of this place, and signify the pure out-pouring of my heart!" Repeat the libation and declaration facing each of the cardinal directions, turning to the east, then the south and west, returning to the north. Sit down in front of your crystal and mediate for at least ten minutes. Any form of meditation will do (see Introduction), but there are several key images worth visualizing that are of special significance for Aztalan. These are the Spiral, the Moon, the Triangle, the Serpent, the Rabbit or the Cross-Hairs (a cross within a circle). These symbols plug directly into the ancient energies of the *genius loci*.

After meditation, get to your feet, raise your crystal to the moon and thank all the resident powers for allowing you to visit their sacred center. Descend the southern slope of the pyramid. During daylight hours, the identical ritual may be conducted at the Pyramid of the Sun, at the south end of the precinct, with the following differences. Ascend the eastern slope. Begin in the easterly direction, then, in order of offering and declaration, face west, south, north, back again to the east. And use pinches of tobacco instead of water. When completed, descend the same eastern slope.

FOR MORE INFORMATION

Directions

Take I-94 between Milwaukee and Madison. Get off at the Lake Mills exit, south. Turn right at the first stop sign. The road will go directly to Rock Lake. To reach Aztalan from Lake Mills, take Water Street out of town for 3 miles following the signs to the park. The site is open year round, hours generally from 8:00 a.m. to 9:00 p.m. The museum is closed from Labor Day to April 15.

Hours: Daily 10:00 a.m. to 4:00 p.m., $3 admission charge.

Accommodations

Ideally, the place to stay when in Lake Mills is the Fargo Mansion, a splendidly restored Victorian home and one of Wisconsin's great living landmarks. Reservations absolutely necessary. Call (414) 648-3654. Almost as nice is the Bayberry Hotel (same telephone number), near Rock Lake, on Main Street. Rates for the Fargo

Mansion begin at $55 for a single per night. The Bayberry offers sin-
gle-nighters at $40 per person. Cheaper accommodations may be
had at the pleasant Colonial Inn, in Johnson Creek, off I-94 at 26, for
$30 per person; (414) 699-3518. In Lake Mills, pleasant rooms at
moderate prices are available at the Pyramid Motel, right turn off
Hwy V. Rates: double, $35; single, $31. Telephone (414) 648-5909.

Camping is available at a KOA site from April 15th to November 1, about 35 minutes from Lake Mills. Exit 126 off I-90-94 (Dane/
Deforest Exit), at the southeast corner of the interchange, six miles
north of Madison. 81 pullthrus with full hook-ups, $18 per night;
(608) 846-4528. Write KOA, 4859 CTH V, DeForest, WI 53532.

Lizard Mounds

Frank Joseph

The rarest and best sacred centers are those in which all the spirits of Nature—plant, animal, earth and sky—meet to create a very special place. At Lizard Mounds, these forces not only meet, they merge. The visitor approaches the site by car, driving over peaceful Wisconsin farm country. But the moment one turns off Route A on the 1/8th mile long road leading into the park, the sanctity of the center creates the effect of a powerful flash. It stands out with a discernible boldness—a small forest of tall trees alone among the lovely fields spreading for miles around. The feeling of impending numinosity increases the closer one comes, but the impression is never overwhelming. Rather, the visitor with an open heart knows with his or her inner being that they have arrived at a true sacred center.

From the parking lot, a marked trail winds through the woods to each of the 31 large effigy mounds masterfully sculpted from the earth itself into the vibrant images of birds, reptiles, panthers, buffalo and unidentifiable mythical creatures. There are also elegant linear structures, ritual embankments and conical pyramids. About 10,000 such effigies once spread over Wisconsin. Only a small handful survive, and Lizard Mounds is the greatest remaining collection in North America. No other group is so well preserved, diversified in form or exhibits such outstanding examples of the prehistoric art of working on so colossal a scale. The figures are expressionistic, though stylized. Nothing about them speaks of the crude, the savage or the primitive. They are proportional, refined and graceful, reflecting the ordered minds that conceived, molded and appreciated them, to say nothing of the skillfully organized system of labor and level of surveying technology responsible for their creation. Who their creators and worshipers were, not even the resident Menomonie Indians can tell. The place is, therefore, an historic enigma. All that seems certain is that it was suddenly abandoned by its creators about 1310 A.D. for unknown reasons. Even the dates of its construction and occupation are doubtful. It would appear, however, to have been part of the Aztalan Civilization flourishing about 75 miles to the southwest, because identically styled earth-works once surrounded the ancient capital. If so, the structures date to the 12th or 13th centuries, although their provenance could be earlier by a thousand years.

Lizard Mounds.
Illustration by William Wild.

A few of the effigies served as tombs. The deceased were placed in pits beneath the mounds with decorated clay pots, bone harpoons, pipes, copper implements and religious crystals. The precinct was used exclusively for spiritual purposes. No one ever resided within the sacred area, with settlement in surrounding villages. The largest effigy of the group is 300 feet in length, but the site derives its modern name from a 238-foot long figure thought to represent a lizard. Even so, the figures are not so large that they cannot be identified and discerned at ground level. Seen at altidude, however, they assume a startling perspective that implies they may only be fully appreciated from the sky.

More than 90 percent of North America's earth effigies existed in the Wisconsin area. Exceptions such as Ohio's Great Serpent Mound are cultural anomalies. Colossal geoglyphs were rare in the

Ancient World, the only other groups appearing in Britain and among pre-Inca peoples—the Nazca—along the Peruvian and Chilean coasts. The very existence of these widely separated effigies invites comparison, and, in fact, they do share some important points in common. As just mentioned, the Lizard Mound collection is best seen from the air, and so are the British and South American examples. The celestial orientation of many of the figures has been established: the Nazca Spider's alignment with Orion, the Moon and Pleiades, Lizard Mound's own winter solstice configuration, the Cerne-Abbas Giant's relationship with the Constellation of Hercules, etc. Whether these and other parallels suggest the magic of synchronicity or some forgotten cultural contact in the pre-Columbian past, who may say?

Lizard Mounds.
Photo by Frank Joseph.

MYSTICAL SIGNIFICANCE

Lizard Mounds is a most significant sacred center because it re-affirms one's feeling of place in the fabric of Creation. We sense a reverence for all life in and around us. The plants and animals, as exemplified in the grass-covered effigies, are our brothers and sisters, children all of Father Sky and Mother Earth. It is a place of family reunion, and, consequently, of extreme significance in these days of environmental abuse. It is to spiritual sanctuaries of Nature such as these that we must bring our children, so that they may early in life develop a personal empathy and deep reverence for all living things.

SUGGESTED RITUAL

The trail laid out by the park authorities would appear to follow closely the original ritual path used by the ancient worshipers, as their processions wound from one effigy to the next.

The modern pilgrim walks for about 250 feet through the woods as a preparation before coming to the first structure, the longest of the slender linear mounds (some 200 feet). It marks the real beginning of the sacred precinct and might represent the essential uniformity of all spirit—human and non-human. Beyond the linear mound stands a small conical pyramid, followed by a tear-drop figure pointing at another cone of the same size. All the mounds are only 3–4 feet high.

As the visitor walks along the winding path, it may be helpful to envision the colorful, musical procession of hundreds, perhaps thousands of people, who walked this same trail seven centuries ago. Effective visualization in so atmospheric a setting can easily conjure dramatic imagery necessary to the deepest fulfillment of this sacred center. Appropriate music via a portable player may enhance this process. Past-life recollections can occur anywhere along the path, if one is in the properly receptive frame of mind.

The first animal effigy encountered is the so-called "Panther Mound." One comes upon it gradually, imperceptibly, from the point of its tail. The tail thickens by degrees, the animal takes form, and, as it does so, its power gathers momentum, increasing along the back and reaching its highest level at the massive head. The telluric potency at this point is positively tangible. It continues and is focused at a still higher frequency between the last pair of conical mounds. They are 2-1/2 times larger than the last couple. The trail forces each visitor to walk precisely between the twin cone pyramids, where he or she receives a refined boost to the original energy generated by the Panther Mound.

A smaller linear structure immediately following the cones seems to actually step-down the level of earth-power, as though the supercharged geoglyphs were specifically arranged to create an undulating, serpentine effect, raising the emotion of the pilgrim on swelling, ever-heightening strata of experience. A few steps more brings the fore-part of the most massive of the Panther mounds into view. Telluric-animal energies at this point are so high some people feel tendencies toward levitation. Indeed, the power is almost too manifest, nearly frightening, as though a living beast were lying just beneath the turf, ready at any moment to burst from the ground. As before, this power diminishes as one walks along the narrowing tail, then increases again, although not to the formally high level. We confront, head-on, a smaller effigy, energy rippling down its neck and shoulders, traveling along its tail.

There are three more elegant linear mounds before the visitor reaches the chief focal point of the whole site, the *axis mundi* of the sacred center, a pair of very elongated figures facing each other in a combined length of 425 feet. The trail leads directly between their heads, narrowing the sacred site's full spiritual force into a narrow gap. It is important to know here that the sole surviving Indian tradition of Lizard Mounds involves this very spot. The Menomonie remember that each winter solstice, their ancestors gathered behind the bodies of these two zoomorphs to observe sunset before the longest night of the year, marking the world's transition from darkness back into light and the human soul's reemergence from death to life. The leaders of the tribe stood before the twin-headed focal point. At that critical juncture, as the sun shed its last ray of light precisely between the two animal heads, occurred the great merging and unleashing of universal forces.

Just beyond the super vortex lies the effigy mound after which the whole set has been named. The lizard represents the underlying motive force in all living creatures, the vital spirit of action. Over the back of this animal-image the sun still sets on the shortest day of each year, as it has for centuries. The big mound is the only one of its shape in the group and was obviously intended as its chief feature. Visitors who meditate steadily at the creature's brawny shoulders have seen them ripple or twitch with ill concealed power, a startling effect and a little frightening.

The trail leads away from the Lizard Mound in a denouement to other, smaller effigies, including a pair of linear embankments pointing to the only oval mound in the set. Although not as spectacular as the rest, it is the symbolic key to this sacred center, representing as it does the Cosmic Egg, the Navel of the World, the Womb of Life from which we came and to which we shall return for rebirth. More than any other figure, the oval mound identifies the site as a sacred center.

The trail passes between the heads and along the outstretched wings of two great birds. Perhaps they signify the feeling of spiritual liberation each visitor experiences at the close of the Lizard Mound pilgrimage.

FOR MORE INFORMATION

Directions

Take Route 144 four miles northeast out of West Bend to County Trunk Highway A, following the directional marker. The site is closed from November 15 to April 15.

Accommodations

Motel-6, 5037 South Howell Avenue. Go north 1/2 mile to motel. $24 per person, single.

Best Western Harborside Motor Inn, 20 miles north of Milwaukee, on Lake Michigan, three miles east of Highway I-43. Telephone: (414) 284-9461. $55 to $59 per person, $61 to $65, doubles. About 35 minutes drive to Lizard Mounds.

Suitable camping sites are available April 15 through October 15 at KOA's Fond du Lac grounds, a half hour drive to Lizard Mounds. The camp lies 5 miles south of Fond du Lac on CTH "B," 1-1/2 miles east of US 41. Address information, KOA, West 5099 Highway 8, Fond du Lac, WI 54935. Telephone: (414) 477-2300. Visa, Master Card acceptable. $12 for tent site with two adults.

STAY IN TOUCH

On the following pages you will find listed, with their current prices, some of the books and tapes now available on related subjects. Your book dealer stocks most of these, and will stock new titles in the Llewellyn series as they become available. We urge your patronage.

However, to obtain our full catalog, to keep informed of new titles as they are released and to benefit from informative articles and helpful news, you are invited to write for our bi-monthly news magazine/catalog. A sample copy is free, and it will continue coming to you at no cost as long as you are an active mail customer. Or you may keep it coming for a full year with a donation of just $5.00 in U.S.A. and Canada ($20.00 overseas, first class mail). Many bookstores also have *The Llewellyn New Times* available to their customers. Ask for it.

Stay in touch! In *The Llewellyn New Times'* pages you will find news and reviews of new books, tapes and services, announcements of meetings and seminars, articles helpful to our readers, news of authors, advertising of products and services, special money-making opportunities, and much more.

The Llewellyn New Times
P.O. Box 64383-Dept. 348, St. Paul, MN 55164-0383, U.S.A.

• • •

TO ORDER BOOKS AND TAPES

If your book dealer does not have the books and tapes described on the following pages readily available, you may order them directly from the publisher by sending full price in U.S. funds, plus $1.50 for postage and handling for orders *under* $10.00; $3.00 for orders *over* $10.00. There are no postage and handling charges for orders over $50.00. UPS Delivery: We ship UPS whenever possible. Delivery guaranteed. Provide your street address as UPS does not deliver to P.O. Boxes. UPS to Canada requires a $50.00 minimum order. Allow 4-6 weeks for delivery. Orders outside the U.S.A. and Canada: Airmail—add retail price of book; add $5.00 for each non-book item (tapes, etc.); add $1.00 per item for surface mail.

FOR GROUP STUDY AND PURCHASE

Because there is a great deal of interest in group discussion and study of the subject matter of this book, we feel that we should encourage the adoption and use of this particular book by such groups by offering a special "quantity" price to group leaders or "agents."

Our Special Quantity Price for a minimum order of five copies of *Sacred Sites* is $44.85 cash-with-order. This price includes postage and handling within the United States. Minnesota residents must add 6.5% sales tax. For additional quantities, please order in multiples of five. For Canadian and foreign orders, add postage and handling charges as above. Credit card (VISA, Master Card, American Express) orders are accepted. Charge card orders only may be phoned free ($15.00 minimum order) within the U.S.A. or Canada by dialing 1-800-THE-MOON. Customer service calls dial 1-612-291-1970. Mail Orders to:

LLEWELLYN PUBLICATIONS
P.O. Box 64383-Dept. 348, St. Paul, MN 55164-0383, U.S.A.

Prices subject to change without notice.

EARTH POWER:
TECHNIQUES OF NATURAL MAGIC
by Scott Cunningham

Magick is the art of working with the forces of Nature to bring about necessary, and desired, changes. The forces of Nature—expressed through Earth, Air, Fire and Water—are our "spiritual ancestors" who paved the way for our emergence from the pre-historic seas of creation. Attuning to, and working with these energies in magick not only lends you the power to affect changes in your life, it also allows you to sense your own place in the larger scheme of Nature. Using the "Old Ways" enables you to live a better life, and to deepen your understanding of the world about you. The tools and powers of magick are around you, waiting to be grasped and utilized. This book gives you the means to put Magick into your life, shows you how to make and use the tools, and gives you spells for every purpose.

0-87542-121-0, 176 pgs., 5-1/4 x 8, illus., softcover
$6.95

IN THE SHADOW OF THE SHAMAN
by Amber Wolfe

Presented in what the author calls a "cookbook shamanism" style, this book shares recipes, ingredients, and methods of preparation for experiencing some very ancient wisdoms—wisdoms of Native American and Wiccan traditions, as well as contributions from other philosophies of Nature, as they are used in the shamanic way. Wolfe encourages us to feel confident and free to use her methods to cook up something new, completely on our own. This blending of ancient formulas and personal methods represents what Ms. Wolfe calls *Aquarian Shamanism.*

In the Shadow of the Shaman is designed to communicate in the most practical, direct ways possible, so that the wisdom and the energy may be shared for the benefits of all. Whatever your system or tradition, you will find this to be a valuable book, a resource, a friend, a gentle guide and support on your journey. Dancing in the shadow of the shaman, you will find new dimensions of Spirit.

0-87542-888-6, 384 pgs., 6 x 9, illus., softcover $12.95

THE MESSAGE OF THE CRYSTAL SKULL
by Alice Bryant & Phyllis Galde

The most fascinating, mysterious artifact ever discovered by mankind. Thousands of years old, yet it is beyond the capabilities of today's technology to duplicate it. Those who have touched the skull or seen photographs of it claim increased psychic abilities and purification. Read this book and discover how this mystical quartz crystal skull can benefit you and all of humankind. Famed biocrystallographer Frank Dorland shares his research of the skull.

0-87542-092-3, 224 pgs., mass market, illus. $3.95

Prices subject to change without notice.

THE NEW GOLDEN DAWN RITUAL TAROT DECK
by Sandra Tabatha Cicero

The original Tarot deck of the Hermetic Order of the Golden Dawn has been copied and interpreted many times. While each deck has its own special flair, *The New Golden Dawn Ritual Tarot Deck* may well be the most important new Tarot deck for the 1990s and beyond.

From its inception 100 years ago, the Golden Dawn continues to be the authority on the initiatory and meditative teachings of the Tarot. The Golden Dawn used certain cards in their initiation rituals. Now, for the first time ever, a deck incorporates not only the traditional Tarot images but also all of the temple symbolism needed for use in the Golden Dawn rituals. This is the first deck that is perfect both for divination and for ritual work.

Meditation on the Major Arcana cards can lead to a lightning flash of enlightenment and spiritual understanding in the Western magickal tradition. *The New Golden Dawn Ritual Tarot Deck* was encouraged by the late Israel Regardie, and it is for anyone who wants a reliable Tarot deck that follows the Western magickal tradition.

0-87542-138-5, boxed set: 79-card deck and booklet   **$24.95**

BIRTH OF A MODERN SHAMAN
by Cynthia Bend and Tayja Wiger

This is the amazing true story of Tayja Wiger. As a child she had been beaten and sexually abused. As an adult she was beaten and became a prostitute. To further her difficulties she was a member of a minority, a Native American Sioux, and was also legally blind.

Tayja's courage and will determined that she needed to make changes in her life. This book follows her physical and emotional healing through the use of Transactional Analysis and Re-Birthing, culminating in the healing of her blindness by the Spiritualistic Minister Marilyn Rossner, through the laying on-of-hands.

Astrology and graphology are used to show the changes in Tayja as her multiple personalities, another problem from which she suffered, were finally integrated into one. Tayja has become both a shaman and a healer.

In *Birth of a Modern Shaman* there are powerful skills anyone can develop by becoming a shaman, the least of which is becoming balanced, at peace with the world around you, productive and happy. By using the techniques in this book you will move toward a magickal understanding of the universe that can help you achieve whatever you desire, and can help you to become a modern shaman.

0-87542-034-6, 272 pgs., 6 x 9, illus., softcover   **$9.95**

THE AZTEC CIRCLE OF DESTINY
by Bruce Scofield and Angela Cordova
The ancient Mesoamerican calendar and divination system known as the Tonalpouhalli has been revived for the third Llewellyn New Worlds Kit by authors Bruce Scofield and Angela Cordova, using both historical research and a fascinating variety of psychic techniques. The 260-day calendar of the Aztec and Maya civilizations had been buried for centuries due to neglect and repression by conquistadors and missionaries. A reading of the incomplete manuscripts left by two 16th-century Spanish friars, Fray Diego Duran and Fray Bernardino de Sahagun, offers a glimpse into aspects of the calendar known to its ancient practitioners. Now this accurate and ancient Mesoamerican calendar and divination system has been revived by the authors using both historical research and psychic techniques.

The result of the author's careful research has resulted in a complete and entertaining system of divination. Enclosed is a fascinating book with many unique images of the gods, sample card layouts, readings, and a complete list of associations for card layouts, readings, and a complete list of associations for the calendar days. Here is an easy-to-use and helpful system of datekeeping and divination for your increased well-being.

The beautiful images created by Bruce Scofield for the 20-card set are done in the bold colors and elegant lines of ancient Mesoamerican art. Images of the gods and decorative glyphs adorn the book's pages, which also contain sample card layouts, readings and a complete list of associations for the calendar days. *The Aztec Circle of Destiny* invites the reader to discover anew a nearly lost system of daykeeping and divination.

0-87542-715-4, 256-pg. book, 13 wooden chips, 20 cards, cloth bag $24.95

WHEELS OF LIFE: A User's Guide to the Chakra System
by Anodea Judith
An instruction manual for owning and operating the inner gears that run the machinery of our lives. Written in a practical, down-to-earth style, this fully-illustrated book will take the reader on a journey through aspects of consciousness, from the bodily instincts of survival to the processing of deep thoughts.

Discover this ancient metaphysical system under the new light of popular Western metaphors—quantum physics, elemental magick, Kabbalah, physical exercises, poetic meditations, and visionary art. Learn how to open these centers in yourself, and see how the chakras shed light on the present world crises we face today. And learn what you can do about it!

This book will be a vital resource for: Magicians, Witches, Pagans, Mystics, Yoga Practitioners, Martial Arts people, Psychologists, Medical people, and all those who are concerned with holistic growth techniques.

0-87542-320-5, 544 pgs., 6 x 9, illus., softcover   **$12.95**

TRANSITS IN REVERSE
by Edna Copeland Ryneveld

Have you wondered about whether you should take that trip or ask for that raise? Do you want to know when the best time is for a wedding? How about knowing in advance the times when you will be the most creative and dazzling?

This book is different from all others published on transits (those planets that are actually moving around in the heavens making aspects to our natal planets). It gives the subject area first—such as creativity, relationships, health, etc.—and then tells you what transits to look for. The introductory chapters are so thorough that you will be able to use this book with only an ephemeris or astrological calendar to tell you where the planets are. The author explains what transits are, how they affect your daily life, how to track them, how to make decisions based on transits and much more.

With the information in each section, you can combine as many factors as you like to get positive results. If you are going on a business trip you can look at the accidents section to avoid any trouble, the travel section to find out the best date, the relationship section to see how you will get along with the other person, the business section to see if it is a good time to do business, the communication section to see if things will flow smoothly, and more. In this way, you can choose the absolute best date for just about anything! Electional astrology as been used for centuries, but now it is being given in the most easily understood and practical format yet.

0-87542-674-3, 320 pgs., 6 x 9, softcover   **$12.95**

READING BETWEEN THE LINES: The Basics of Handwriting Analysis
by P. Scott Hollander

Anyone who reads and follows the procedures in *Reading Between the Lines* will come away with the ability to take any sample of handwriting and do a complete analysis of character and personality. He or she may even go forward to use the skill as a professional tool, or as the basis for a profession.

This self-teaching textbook demonstrates how to analyze handwriting, how to counsel others, and how best to use the subject once learned. Unlike the many "cookbook" graphology books on the market, this book gives a very thorough and considered approach to the subject.

Handwriting analysis can help you gain insight into your own strengths and weaknesses and can provide a means to make wiser decisions in your personal and professional life. You will have a quick, sure means of discovering what someone else is really like, and you can use graphotherapy to effect character and personality changes.

Reading Between the Lines also contains an excellent section on the writing of children, and an Index of Traits which summarizes and reiterates points made in the book for quick reference.

0-87542-309-4, 272 pgs., 7 x 10, illus., softcover   **$14.95**

Prices subject to change without notice.

A PRACTICAL GUIDE TO PAST LIFE REGRESSION
by Florence Wagner McClain

Have you ever felt that there had to be more to life than this? Have you ever met someone and felt an immediate kinship? Have you ever visited a strange place and felt that you had been there before? Have you struggled with frustrations and fears which seem to have no basis in your present life? Are you afraid of death? Have you ever been curious about reincarnation or maybe just interested enough to be skeptical?

This book presents a simple technique which you can use to obtain past life information TODAY. There are no mysterious preparations, no groups to join, no philosophy to which you must adhere. You don't even have to believe in reincarnation. The tools are provided for you to make your own investigations, find your own answers and make your own judgments as to the validity of the information and its usefulness to you.

Whether or not you believe in reincarnation, past life regression remains a powerful and valid tool for self-exploration. Information procured through this procedure can be invaluable for personal growth and inner healing, no matter what its source. Florence McClain's guidebook is an eminently sane and capable guide for those who wish to explore their possible past lives or conduct regressions themselves.

0-87542-510-0, 160 pgs., 5-1/4 x 8, softcover $7.95

CELTIC MAGIC
by D. J. Conway

Many people, not all of Irish descent, have a great interest in the ancient Celts and the Celtic pantheon, and *Celtic Magic* is the map they need for exploring this ancient and fascinating magical culture.

Celtic Magic is for the reader who is either a beginner or intermediate in the field of magic, providing an extensive "how-to" of practical spell-working. There are many books on the market dealing with the Celts and their beliefs, but none guide the reader to a practical application of magical knowledge for use in everyday life. There is also an in-depth discussion of Celtic deities and the Celtic way of life and worship, so that an intermediate practitioner can expand upon the spellwork to build a series of magical rituals.Presented in an easy-to-understand format.

Celtic Magic is for anyone searching for new spells that can be worked immediately, without elaborate or rare materials, and with minimal time and preparation.

0-87542-136-9, 240 pgs., mass market, illus. $3.95